LEMMY:
MEMORIES OF A ROCK 'N' ROLL LEGEND

By Ian Carroll Author

© 2016

Dedicated once again to my ever loving & extremely understanding, wife the lovely **Raine** and my three sons, **Nathan, Joshua** & **Rex**

Also thanks to my other supporters including
Laura McCartney and **Gary Martin** for listening to me going on about how the book was progressing.
Also, thanks to the Herald newspaper in Plymouth for their continued support.

Thank you also for all your support and help friends on Facebook and Twitter

This Book is licenced for your personal enjoyment only. If you would like to give this book to another person, please purchase an additional copy for each recipient.
Thank you for supporting the hard work of this author

Introduction

My initial encounters with Motörhead and their gruff and gravelly voiced lead singer and icon, Lemmy, began when I was still a 'fresh faced' 15yr old boy, still at school.

I bought the 'Golden Years' Live EP on 7" vinyl in 1980. It was on the Bronze record label, that was home also to the Damned, Girlschool and Hawkwind – bands that in the future – and in the past – were all connected with Motörhead, having toured, played or recorded with them.

Myself and my best friend at the time (who I haven't seen now for over 20yrs), Michael Watkins, played the EP to death, never having heard anything as fast and raucous before – at the same time Lars Ulrich of Metallica was probably thinking exactly the same.

The sound of Motörhead fused punk and metal and good old rock 'n' roll and was like nothing else around at the time; metalheads loved them, punks loved them, rockers and even Teds loved them, they crossed all the boundaries and appealed to anyone who loved fast and crazy rock music, played with a passion, played from the heart.

At the time, all we listened to was 'Rock and Metal' and we usually went down the park ('The Marsh'), near to our homes, with a large 'ghetto blaster' playing the albums - Judas Priest 'British Steel', Black Sabbath 'Heaven & Hell' and Saxon 'Wheels of Steel' as well as compilations such as 'Metal For Muthas', whilst we messed around or even on occasion went and did a bit of train spotting!!

I used to wear a camouflage jacket which my mother had bought for me at a local army surplus store in Plymouth – I was only 15 years old – and she then stitched on all the patches that I had bought in our local indoor market, including a Motörhead one that *went straight across my shoulders on the back; I still remember it today, it was a black patch 12" by 3" with silver glittering stitch work/embroidery on it, I looked the 'bees knees' – or so I thought...*

It wasn't until three years later that I actually got my first chance to catch them live and went to the Cornwall Coliseum, it was well worth waiting for.

This was the first time for me to watch Motörhead *and the last tour that featured Phil 'Philthy Animal' Taylor and the very short lived* Motörhead *career of Brian 'Robbo' Robertson (ex-Thin Lizzy) as they both exited after the tour.*

But the show was of course amazing, but my memories of it were very poor, being very, very drunk. I wrote a short 'piece' in my book 'Welcome to Cornwall Coliseum' which said:

"The day that we went to see Motörhead on the 'Another Perfect Day' tour, it was a perfect day.
It was July 3rd and a very sunny day, so we went first up onto Plymouth Hoe (we lived in Plymouth) and got very drunk on 'Blue Curaçao' – not sure who else went with us apart from my friend Theo Christian and I think Rob Lintern, but by the time we arrived at the Coliseum we were all wasted.
This was the first time for me to watch Motörhead and the last tour that featured Phil 'Philthy Animal' Taylor and the short lived Motörhead career of Brian 'Robbo' Robertson (ex Thin Lizzy) as they both left shortly after.
But the show was amazing, what I remember of it and the crowd were up for it."
Ian Carroll (Author)

Fast forward to now and I have seen Motörhead *many times since that initial show, at the now sadly demolished Coliseum. Although I must confess to not buying many of their albums (though I have some in my collection), seeing them live for me was always one of the things I enjoyed experiencing from them the most.*

One of my favourite memories of Lemmy was when he casually strolled on stage – unannounced – cigarette in hand, dark shades on, to play with DKT/MC5 at Download Festival in 2005. We were on the DKT/MC5 guest list and we knew nothing about it either!
He played 'Back in the U.S.A' also featuring another guest, ex-

Guns 'n' Roses member Gilby Clarke.

I went to my one and only Motörhead Press Conference at Download Festival at Donington Park in June 2008.

Lemmy, Phil and Mikkey all attended and I got some awesome photos of them against the obligatory Download Festival logo strewn backdrop They were friendly and funny as always and fielded many questions from the worlds press over a period of fifteen minutes and the tent in the press area was absolutely packed to the rafters, if the tent indeed had any...

Then jump forward a few years and I was alone in the dressing room with Mikkey Dee, backstage at the Pavilions in Plymouth. Such a nice and very friendly guy.

I was interviewing him for my book 'From Donington To Download: The History of Rock at Donington Park' – his entry in the book was sandwiched between Duff McKagan of Velvet Revolver and Joey Belladonna of Anthrax and was as follows:

"I watched Mastodon, they were great and System Of A Down, Slayer and Slipknot.
UK festivals are great, just as long as they are not pissing down with rain; it seems to be that in the summertime, the weather in England is worse than Scandinavia. We walk around in London and it's a great day and then we head out for the festival a day later and here comes the rain!
It is still a great festival, with a lot of good bands always."
Mikkey Dee (Motörhead – Drums)

And that, unfortunately was my one and only meeting with any of the recent members of Mötorhead. I did actually interview Fast Eddie Clarke for the Donington book at Butlins, Minehead, on one of the 'rock weekends', but he was talking about his recent appearance at Download Festival with Fastway, as by the time Motörhead had been booked to play the hallowed ground of Donington Park in 1986 he was long gone.

I was actually booked in to interview Lemmy in Bristol the following year, but sadly missed the opportunity as my wife, at the time, was very unwell having been diagnosed with cancer and as we all know, family are very important to us all, so I missed my one and only chance to meet the great man himself.

Sadly, a few years later my wife passed away from the Big 'C' and for her, Lemmy and all the other cancer survivors, relatives, widows, orphans and people whose lives have been touched by this most awful and destructive of diseases, I had the idea of donating 75% of the royalties from this book to Cancer Research UK.

Every donation helps towards finally discovering a cure and I feel that we as fans of Motörhead are doing our little bit in helping save the lives of people all the world over.

So, here we are at the beginning of the book. I will always regret that I failed to go and see them at the the 'Eden Sessions' at the Eden Project in St Austell on June 27th 2015, the day after they made their debut and final appearance on the mainstage at Glastonbury. The Eden show ended up being their final UK show. Supported by the Stranglers and on a nice and sunny evening in Cornwall, this would have been a fitting end to an amazing UK touring career and a way to say goodbye.

My wife Raine was looking forward to seeing them at Download this year, Motörhead being a band that she hadn't seen that she wanted to tick off her 'musical bucket list', but it just wasn't meant to be.

This book will have to suffice, to remind everyone of the great times, the amazing gigs, the vast back catalogue of music that has been left as Motörhead's legacy to the music fans of the world.

And this book contains just that – 'music fans of the world'. So many people – and artists - have been in contact from all over the planet, wishing to be included in the book, sharing their thoughts on **Motörhead and Lemmy, a legend, a rock 'n' roll icon and an all round 'great chap'**…

Hammersmith Odeon (Eventim Apollo) January 2016

Argentina

Capital City: Buenos Aires
Population: 43,417,000
Currency: Peso
Bands: Los Abuelos de la Nada, Asinesia

Nestled in the farthest end of South America, Argentina is a stronghold for 'metal' music. Fans are in abundance for Motörhead and

"The first time I listened to Motörhead *I was 12 years old, I am now 47, Lemmy is my idol."*
Angel Pappo (Buenos Aires, Argentina)

"I am fan of Motörhead *since 1985, 31 years ago!*
I am have attended 20 gigs of Motörhead *in my country Argentina since first gig in 1990. The ultimate gig was 'Monsters of Rock'* Motörhead, *Judas Priest and Ozzy May 2015."*
Ssebastian Fernandezz Lanos (Buenos Aires, Argentina)

Monsters Of Rock
Buenos Aires
2nd May 2015

Shoot You in the Back
Damage Case
Stay Clean
Metropolis
Over the Top

**The Chase is Better Than the Catch
Rock It
Do You Believe
Lost Woman Blues
Doctor Rock
Just 'Cos You Got The Power
Going to Brazil
Ace of Spades
Overkill**

"I was born in Argentina and Motörhead were one of the pioneer bands of rock and heavy metal.
I personally had such fun seeing them here.
Motörhead is part of my life, I listen from 14 years old and I am now 48 years old.
I love Lemmy and Motörhead."
Daniel Roca (Buenos Aires, Argentina)

"Viva el Heavy Metal!"
Victor Kiss (Rafael Castillo, Buenos Aires)

"When I hear the news I DONT BELIEVE A WORD, later feel LIKE A NIGHTMARE And think in the moments that he And his ROCK AND ROLL save me from the dark from my darkest times, you LEAVING HERE this fucking METROPOLIS, we are BROKEN but will STAND together ON THE ROAD, maybe this was TOO GOOD TO BE TRUE, just wish see a TERMINAL SHOW just ONE MORE FUCKING TIME, see you IN ANOTHER TIME Lem, I will remember you TILL THE END even know I'm BORN TO LOSE I try to LIVE TO WIN ALL FOR YOU..."
Cristian Galas (Buenos Aires, Argentina)

Australia

Capital City: Canberra
Population: 24,300,100
Currency: Australian Dollar
Bands: AC/DC, Airbourne, Rose Tattoo

"Seems so many great memories in my life, were set to the sound of Motörhead roaring in the background. There will never be another Lemmy, may his legend live on, long and loud."
Catherine Higgins (Newcastle, New South Wales, Australia)

"Probably saw him with Hawkwind at the Wintergardens, Possibly Motörhead at Carlyon Bay?"
Clive Rodell (Manly, New South Wales, Australia)

WHAT WOULD LEMMY DO?

"Ok, I'd been out drinkin' all night & kinda hooked up with these two girls, a blonde & a brunette, neither of which I was interested in but hey, better to drink in company.
Come 3am, the Pub's closing & we're all getting kicked out.
"What you doing now?" the blonde asks.
"Goin' home."
"Why don't you come with us to my place. We've got beer."
Fairly drunk by this stage and not having any beer back at my place, I reply, "Yeah, ok."
Drinking at the blondes house, the brunette eventually passes out, on the toilet. Upon checking she's still alive, we leave her there.
The sun starts to rise & I say "ok, time for me to go."
"It's been a long night, why don't you stay here?" the blonde replies.
Drunk, uninterested, & thinking practically I go "Yeah, I guess it has. Ok then."
Thinking nothing of it, I'm settling down to sleep at one end of her

bed, when 'the Poke' comes. She pokes me in the back with her finger.
"What? I'm trying to sleep."
Another poke.
Then the penny drops.
"Oh my god!" I think to my drunken self as I realise she wants a shag.
Now, at this stage I know, a decision must be made.
I think to myself, "What would Lemmy do?"
"He'd shag her" was the reply.
"Sorry Lem, can't do it."
I got up, grabbed my clothes, grabbed a beer from the fridge, & hightailed it outta there quick smart.
And that's how the WWLD tattoo idea came about."
Craig Lee McGuinness (Sydney, Australia)

"When I first heard of Motörhead as a kid I never ever thought I'd get so caught up in it.
I first went too see Motörhead in Sydney back in 2007, I didn't have any of their albums or anything associated with them at all, I hadn't even heard the song 'Ace of Spades' or 'Overkill'.........I'd heard of those songs but that was it, so I didn't know what was about to hit me.
Fuck man when they came out it was a fuckin' earthquake!
There was the scorching sound of Phil's guitar playing, I felt every beat of Mikkey Dee's drumming and the thunder of Lemmy's bass, the show was nothing short of fuckin' awesome.
I got to meet Lemmy after the show, I walked up to him and shook his hand and said how much of a great show it was and he was very gentleman like saying thank you and all and then I got to get a photo with him aswell.
I saw Motörhead again in Sydney in 2011, the show was 1000 times better, considering I now knew a lot more of their music.
There's just something about Lemmy and Motörhead that really does it for me. Their music has been my inspiration and motivation and helped me through some hard times and it's given me some really great times too. Nothing beats just sitting back chilling out with a few beers and listening to FUCKIN MOTÖRHEAD really loud and I just love that loud grovelling voice that Lemmy had. He was the coolest mother fucker ever to walk the planet and I don't think there'll ever be anyone you'll ever be able to compare to him.
It's been nearly a month now since he passed away I still think of him everyday and I really wish I had gotten into Motörhead when I

was younger co's it kinda feels very short lived with Motörhead in my life.
I think it was meant to happen for me when I took my very first ever overseas trip from Australia to Miami to get onboard Motörheads Motörboat, I really had the time of my life on that thing from the moment of getting on there and meeting Mikkey Dee just after I checked in and then later on meeting Phil Cambell and then Lemmy the great man himself again and watching them play the 2 nights. They played and we just hung out, drinking with so many great people and taking part in the Motörboating competition and then actually winning it and then having so many people to stop me and congratulate me and get photos with me, the Aussie guy!
That was all thanks to Lemmy and Motörhead who I couldn't thank enough for it, Motörhead's Motörboat where else would ya wanna be, There's times where I really do think I'm the luckiest guy in the world for having being able to have experienced that (apart from the great life I already live with all the great people in it) all I can say is I really miss the guy and it's a real struggle to come to terms with the fact that Motörhead is no longer.
I just wanna thank Ian Carroll for asking me to be part of this book it's a real privilege to be able to speak on behalf of the greatest man to ever walk the planet who had such an impact on my life and I also thank you for that too Ian.

And finally as a closing statement I just wanna say MOTÖRHEAD!!!!!!!!!!!!!!

MOTÖRHEAD FOR LIFE!!!!!!!!!!!

LEMMY!!! LEMMY!!!!!!! LEMMY!!!!!! LEMMY!!!!! LEMMY!!!!! LEMMY!!!
(Feel free to chant along)

MOTÖRHEEEEEEEEEEEAAAAD!!!!!!!!!!!!!"
Patrick Lamerton (Perth, Australia)

"When I was 15 my life went to shit.
Someone I knew committed suicide, I had depression and tried killing myself every chance I could.
But then I saw a video of Motörhead playing live and then I just got lost in the music. The depression and suicide just left me when I listened to 'Overkill' for the first time.
Lemmy inspired me to become a musician so I could make people

feel how I felt when I listened to music.
Motörhead also made me more self-confident and now, at 17, I'm the happiest I've ever been.
If I had met Lemmy, I would thank him for everything his art did for me.
Rock in peace Lemmy you deserve it."
Kaleb Lee Thorp (Newcastle, New South Wales)

"What more can be said about THE Greatest Rocker that ever lived, that hasn't already been said?
He was my hero. I live my life the way I want because of the example Lemmy has set.
He's inspired past, present and future generations. If that's not a legacy to be proud of, then I don't know what else to say.
Words fail me in summing up what Lemmy and Motörhead mean to me.
Born To Lose.
Lived To Win
Thanks Lemmy ♠ "
Tim Jones (Adelaide, Australia)

"As a 10 or 11 year old kid, obsessed with horror movies... I got my first allowance $10!!! Wanted to buy my first album/cassette, went straight to the record store and searched all the album covers to find the scariest one there was.
With no previous knowledge of heavy metal or bands, I selected this album on the cover alone... That album was Motörhead's 'Rock 'n' Roll'. I couldn't turn it off!!! That started me on my rock n roll journey.
Now 40 years old, I'm still obsessed with the heavier style of music. Motörhead were always there, when other bands were breaking up or disintegrating, Lemmy and co were trustworthy and reliable, a band u could always rely on.
Saw Motörhead a couple of times in my hometown of Melbourne, but never met Lem. If I had I would have thanked him for doing what he did. In a world of one hit wonders and fame obsessed wannabes... He kept the real spirit of rock n roll alive.
I am and always will be...MOTÖRHEAD FOR LIFE."
Blake Reid (Melbourne, Australia)

"I first heard of Motörhead and Lemmy as a young lad, at a time when I was into AC/DC and KISS obsessively.
I was big into rock, but they were my two. I know a lot of Led

Zeppelin, Aerosmith, Bon Jovi, Iron Maiden and later Motörhead. I was around nine during that time.

When I was probably twelve, I had an assortment of Motörhead songs on my iPod. Later on, when I really got into metal, Motörhead and Lemmy always stood out.

They didn't care what you thought. They were tough. They had an attitude.

They wrote great songs and the album artwork was amazing.

They intrigued me, at a time when I was first discovering Saxon, Judas Priest, Motörhead, Megadeth, Metallica (I knew these bands, but I mean fully).

Lemmy was the 'King of Metal' it seemed to be.

His voice can sing a lot, and most people really don't tend to realise that. Go listen to him cover Iron Maiden's 'The Trooper' or Ben E. King's standard 'Stand by Me'.

He was a genius songwriter, as evident listening to the albums. He was an excellent bassist. His tone makes it easy for some fools to think it's rhythm guitar.

I unfortunately never got the chance to see Motörhead live, which is a regret, I was eleven last time they toured Australia.

Lemmy will be missed by musicians from every genre and his music and character is timeless."

Jakam Kourasanis (Australia)

"Lemmy is God, although I never got to see him, I always wanted to."

Dom Villiers (Newcastle, New South Wales)

"My Motörhead story began way back in 1977.

My grandmother, upon seeing my reaction to hearing them and instinctively headbanging at the ripe age of four, decided to buy me my very first Motörhead t-shirt. I still have that shirt, and I know that Lemmy is rocking away with my nan in Rock 'n' Roll Heaven!

I met him very briefly in Sydney, told him the story and he seemed genuinely touched. Such a massive influence on me not just as a consumate musician, but also on how one should tread their path throughout life.

Rest In Peace Lemmy, you helped myself and many others more than you ever knew."

Skott Phillip Williamson (Australia)

"The first Motörhead song I heard was on a BMX video when I was 11 or 12 and that was it, love! Can't stop listening!!

ROCK OUT, WE WILL NEVER FORGET!!"
Ralph Byles (Kingscote, Australia)

"RIP there – 'Rock In Peace' Lemmy as you will always in us, who will always live for Motörhead and metal!!!
Rock 'N' Roll!!"
Danny Chaos (Melbourne)

"I first heard of Motörhead when I was 10 years old.
I heard them through WWE, through Triple H's entrance theme song 'The Game' from the album 'Hammered' released in 2002 you're a legend Lemmy even when dead you're still the ultimate legend.
His music style was unique I mean who the fuck plays bass like a guitar and fucks around with the sound to make it sound like a distorted guitar? LEMMY is who his music style was, 'legendary'.
He may have been a rough looking character, but was really a gentleman.
Lemmy was one of a kind nuff said.
R.I.P Ian "Lemmy" Fraser Kilmister 1945-2015"
Mason Dean Metcalf (Molesworth, Tasmania, Australia)

"This is an edited version of the post I made in the official Motörheadbangers fan club group. For any of you guys who haven't joined, do it. It's the closest family (unrelated by blood) that I've been a part of.
Many of you whom I now have on my Facebook friends list may recall that I posted a status in response to the news of Lemmy's death, in which I said that 'knowing death is inevitable does not mean one knows how to deal with it.' an unusually profound statement from a man who usually posts statuses about Portsmouth FC or rants at his internet service provider/the TV/anything.
For those of you who are reading this for the first time and you're wondering who the fuck I am, it's because I rarely post in Motörhead related groups. If I do, it's usually limited to a comment or an attempted-witticism here and there, or the occasional like on a photo I haven't come across or a post that articulates thoughts on Motörhead/Lemmy. Introductions aside, I will now attempt to articulate my thoughts about Motörhead as best I can. I sincerely thank Ian Carroll for allowing us to all have a platform to share what we all hold so dear, and that of which we have in common:

Motörhead. Articulating my feelings via the written medium is one thing I can count amongst my skills.
I was at work when I found out about Lemmy's death. text messages started flooding in before I knew what was going on - friends of mine outside of our Motörhead family know how much I love Motörhead: Motörhead memorabilia, several tattoos, CDs and vinyl, action figures, photos, posters, a blown-up photo of the time I met them, the love of a well-made Jack and Coke (a Lemmy)... you name it. If it's Motörhead, I will try and collect it (dependent on limited finances, of course). After the sixth text message coming through saying "chief, are you alright?" I figured I'd find out what the fuck was going on.
Brothers and sisters, family and friends, I had to leave work. I couldn't fulfil my duties having found out the greatest influence on who I am (aside from my mum and dad) had suddenly passed away. So I decided to ask permission to leave work... it was denied, but fuck it. I was distraught, so and I left. And I cried. And I cried, and I cried, and I cried. I'm only 25; it's not considered a sign of masculinity to burst in to tears at this age, but I fucking cried. I mean what the hell? Two days prior I had been saying how my greatest dream was to see Motörhead play again in another country. And now? "An aggressive form of cancer"? Motherfucker, he had TWO days between diagnosis and death! That's more aggressive than the adjective 'aggressive' describes. 'Barbaric' would suit better. 'Militant' perhaps. Or, 'a fucking sudden cunt of a thing' would probably be best. All that being said, my method of grieving was to take solace in the idea that he had enough time to inform those whom he was close to. We see from his memorial that this was the case (health concerns and visa issues affecting Messrs. Philip 'Augustus' Campbell III and 'Fast' Eddie Clarke respectively, of course).
I remember I was 14 or 15 when I first heard them, but 17 when I first really discovered how much they meant to me. I first saw them headline a concert in Melbourne in October 2007, as they played the Australian leg of the 'Kiss of Death' tour. My father and I had been stressing the week leading up as it was an 18+ only gig, however I think we managed to hide me with a bunch of bikies and I put on my dirtiest, meanest look and spent the week growing my pathetic attempt at facial hair (I'm still trying, too). I managed to get in undetected! Rose Tattoo and Airbourne opened, and that was almost enough for me. I couldn't believe the power and sound coming through the wall of amplifiers... and then!
The lights went down and the Rickenbastard thundered. Thunder

in your guts. I was as blown away, almost literally by this fucking wall of sound. I remember specific points of the concert: I can remember 'One Night Stand' (I love the opening moment where Phil's guitar wails into the air). I can remember Mikkey Dee's drum solo and as a drummer, that absolutely stunned me. The speed! The coordination! The power! I was floored! I also distinctly remember someone in the crowd throwing a drink at Lemmy and Lemmy pointing to him and calling him a "fucking worm" and then launching in to another song. I nearly fucking exploded at that point. You see these "pop stars" refuse to take the stage when someone gives them Pepsi instead of Coke, and then you've got this grizzled, old school rock and roll star cop a drink to the face, call the cunt a worm and then start playing another song? What a fucking hero. I was hooked!

It wasn't until I had to face my own mortality that I realised just how important Motörhead was in my own life. They saved me not only from death, but from my own mind. Lemmy's unique brand of music articulated thoughts and feelings in my head better than I ever could. The thing I am most grateful for, though, is that I could share that with Lemmy and the guys. I looked Lem in the eye at the gig in Melbourne in 2011 and thanked him for his music. And instead of brushing me off, he shook my hand, looked me in the eye and thanked me. Me, a nobody from Melbourne! Some cunt who, in early 2011, had only a denim jacket with a couple of Motörhead patches and a tattoo to display his allegiance. Never once did I consider Lemmy Kilmister would have the grace and humility to treat me like a human being. I'd have licked his boots clean yet this idol of mine looked me in the eye and thanked me? Those of you who have met him would know the sincerity with which he answers people with. I couldn't believe it, but I felt it.

In closing (if you've read this far through the mindless drivel then I'll buy you a beer one day), there's a part in the Lemmy documentary (I have played it at least once a week since he died) that deals with how people will react when he dies. I'd like to think that we are all grieving in our own, unique way. On December 28 2015 I, for one, came home to organize all my Motörhead t-shirts, have a strong jack and coke and play all the Motörhead albums I have on my shelf. Before that, of course, a tear was shed for a man whose influence on my life was only behind my mum and dad's.

And what my plans are for the future with Motörhead, I hear you ask? I'll turn it up loud. Louder than I've ever played it before.

RIP Lemmy, and thank you. Born to lose, lived to win."

James Bunker, MHB3267 (Melbourne, Australia)

Forum Theatre, Melbourne
9th October 2007

Doctor Rock
Stay Clean
Be My Baby
Killers
Metropolis
Over the Top
One Night Stand
I Got Mine
In the Name of Tragedy
Sword of Glory
Rosalie
Sacrifice
Just'Cos You Got the Power
Going to Brazil
Killed by Death
Iron Fist
Whorehouse Blues
Ace of Spades
Overkill

"I was 16 when Countdown (Australian pop music TV show) showed a 2 minute collage of clips called 'The New Wave of British Heavy Metal' ...the two bands that caught my eye (and ear) were Iron Maiden and a live clip of Motörhead with the huge 'Iron Fist'

*stage prop.
I was into Kiss and a few other rock bands but the harder sound and Lemmy being a badass with the mic above his head sparked my curiosity.
That week I bought the 'Iron Fist' and 'Number of the Beast' albums and was converted to Metal.
Perth Australia is a pretty remote city so I was stoked when Motörhead toured in 1984 on the back of 'No Remorse', now a 4 piece with Phil and Wurzel.
The roof of the small venue almost collapsed and to this day it is still one of the loudest gigs I have been to.
Fast forward 30 years and having seen the band a few more times in between, I was privileged to be on the inaugural 'Motörboat Cruise' in 2014, flying some 18000km with a friend to have one of the best experiences of my life. Alas this would be the last time I had the pleasure of seeing Motörhead and Lemmy.
Lemmy you were a unique man and the music you created will be played louder than everything else for eternity.
Motörhead for Life \m/ "*
Mike Higgs (Perth, Australia)

"I first heard Motörhead in year 5 and I was instantly hooked. Lemmy to me was like a second father and now the music world will never be the same again."
Darren Lucas (Newcastle, New South Wales)

Austria

Capital City: Vienna
Population: 8,662,588
Currency: Euro
Bands: Speedy Weekend Band, No Bros

*"I am an Austrian Motörhead fan.
I became a fan in their last 6 moths. It started with 'Ace of Spades', later I downloaded 'Enter Sandman'.
'Bad Magic' is the only album that appeared when I had already been a Fan. Later I got around 20 older songs and I often thought: "Wow, they are doing this for 40 years, which is a fucking long time".
So, it was a shock to hear that Lemmy had died and I was sad that I had never seen him on stage."*
AJ Reindt (Austria)

"My favourite song is 'Overkill', because it was one of my first albums I bought by myself and nobody played Double Bass drum like that."
Gerhard Strasnik (Graz, Austria)

"RIP lemmy Best musica."
Josef Sparber (Rum, Tirol, Austria)

Capital City: Brussels
Population: 11,190,845
Currency: Euro
Bands: Aborted, Ostrogoth, Enthroned

"Since '78 I am fan of Motörhead. I saw them 286 times. It's my life. I am sad, sad, sad... for Philthy and Lemmy."
Ubaldo Desimone (Seraing, Belgium)

"R. I. P."
Geert Debboudt (Oudenaarde, Belgium)

"A true legend for metal rock 'n roll!
Many come and go....Motörhead stays!!!"
Johnny Stecchino (Kortenberg, Belgium)

"This is my personal story: Lemmy his music picked me up always, the time when I grieved for the loss of my son I always played his music very loud to help me in my difficult times and I still do.
Last Friday I put on the same place as my son, his tattoo that I have on my arm 'LEMMY IS GOD' so now he is very close."
Saskia (Antwerp, Belgium)

"I saw Lemmy about 30 times and it was always a blast.
He was a God for me and he played more than rock and roll, he played with passion every time."
Schrayen Gigi (Kwaadmechelen, Limburg, Belgium)

"I can't express with words how much Motörhead means to me but I will try.
This band helped me through a lot of shit in life. Lemmy was an idol to me in a way that it changed my views on a lot of things.
He was the epitome and the godfather of heavy music which I started get into at the age of 5 and it helped get me to what I am today, it made me strong and by strong I mean mentally and physically.
*Lemmy was the role model who showed me to not give a f*ck what others think and always live your life your way, no matter what others think, but on the other side always be respectful and kind to*

*the people who got your back.
There is no bigger rock star than Lemmy. Lemmy is Rock, Lemmy is the baddest dude that walked the planet and I say this because he always will be.
Lemmy didn't die, he just went to another place but he will always live on in the fans, the friends and the people he touched and I'm sure there are many of them!"*
Mehdi Assadi (Roeselare, Belgium)

*"I follow Motörhead for over 25 years and each time I got back to rock vibe just as Motörhead can.
I still cannot believe that Lemmy is gone from us.
I have seen him many times in the AB Brussels, Graspop, Dessel 2015 was the last time I saw Motörhead and it was top!!!!
Every day I put Motörhead vinyl on.
I will miss him very hard. Fucking rock!"*
Joris Binon (Oud-Heverlee, Belgium)

*"I've seen Motörhead live 4 times.
The first time was in 2008 @ Rock Zottegem.
Lemmy called us "the best audience of the tour yet" after asking us "is it loud enough?" and you could hear that he really meant it.
The third time was 4 years later @ The Brabanthallen in Deinze.
Afterwards, I had slight tinnitus for almost the whole week and I was nearly deaf until the next morning.
Yes, that was the loudest concert I've ever been to lol.
Kudos to Lem, Phil & Mikkey.
Long Live Rock & Roll.*
Filip Mertens (Dendermonde, Belgium)

Brazil

Capital City: Brasilia
Population: 205,338,000

Currency: **Real**
Bands: **Sepultura, Shaaman Violator, Angra**

"I never forgot the first time I heard Motörhead!
At my age the most obvious thing happened and I was listening to 'Ace of Spades' on VHS borrowed from a friend around 1999.
That sound was strange to me and I did not quite understand, I was used to hearing more fast and technical things like Kreator, Nuclear Assault, Metallica, Megadeth and I still had no idea who was the father of all these bands... so I didn't digest the sound immediately, but the band has always given me a respect that was fermented even with fictitious stories they told here about Lemmy being a truck driver who kept the band as a hobby.
This is a story that all metal/rock fans wanted to hear and watch the band performed the sound with that visual which left me no doubt: totally ridiculous - Lemmy wild, with your Rickenbacker, "Fast" Eddie Clarke 70's guitarist, accurate on the trigger and Philthy Animal, grinding drums and unpretentiously chewing gum. Damn, that's it... this bunch of drunks who do the dirtiest rock 'n' roll you can hear.
Living in a small town was still difficult at the time to have access to material of certain bands and Motörhead was included.
Since was founded, despite a consensus among lovers of all musical genres related to the Rock and Roll was not a very popular band here. Unlike today when 'the long-awaited recognition' happened, the difficulty of obtaining material from a band was a determining factor. If that store had no materials and any friend that would ask to share with you in some way, I could only settle for that story that hopefully you've read in some magazine / zine. So without these benefits provided in our post-modernity, in a small town you could only rely on luck and even inheriting a collection of vinyls from my brother - I believe, I have not had.
Anyway, time passed and another great friend introduced me to the band with huge excitement and then yes I could feel the true Motörhead essence and was totally connected with that most primitive idea I had of how and to what music should be done. No wonder, because Lemmy above all a man who admired and had grown along with the style, he really always knew what he was doing and clearly translated it to anyone seeing it. Thereafter, from

2007 until this present and fateful moment, there is not a single day I spent without hearing at least one Motörhead song without pressure ... just for the sheer pleasure of listening to a song done honestly and it often helps improve your day!

Music for me was, is and will always be an important issue and this guy more than anyone was, is and will always a great influence on me, either with words or with the shrill notes sounding of your Rickbenbacker, or just drinking a well bitter booze and smoking a cigarette.

Talk all you want about Lemmy, the thing is, he lived with a legitimate class of a marginal rock star and many today who take advantage of his image were those who spat on it before. But Motörhead is about Lemmy, and Lemmy came to live in a fast paced rhythm, well in your way and kickin' the ass of all imbeciles! Fortunately I saw Motörhead in 2011 and I feel blessed for the rest of my life!!

Even the captain abandoned the crew, we'll be there with gratitude for all that was left for us!

Eternal Lemmy, everlasting Motörhead!!!!"

João Marcos Rodrigues da Silva - MHB 3750
(São João Nepomuceno – MG, Brazil)

"I am 51 years old and my life was dedicated to Motörhead...
Got a job as a bank teller trainee when I was 17 years old in 1981 and to get back home a friend gave me a ride in his car and inserted a cassette in his radio player and than started a furious, raw and fast song ... a live one...
That was like a punch in my stomach... what was that???   He answered "Motörhead... No Sleep till Hammersmith"...
Geez...
Few days after I rushed to the record shop to buy that LP."
Marco Claudio Loiacono (Sao Paulo, Brazil)

"One thing that struck me was a time when Lemmy was without a front tooth."
AlbertoQuinette Rickenbacker (Sumaré, Brazil)

"My song - 'God Was Never On Your Side'
Artur Barboso De Oliveira (Rio De Janeiro, Brazil)

"Lemmy was without doubt one of the most influential musicians of the 70's and today, beginning his career to success with

Hawkwind, Lemmy only did well starting from the moment he was fired from the band, and thus founded the Motörhead.
Lemmy has always been the same person, charismatic, happy and enjoyed life, living it intensely.
Undoubtedly he has a legion of fans because of his wonderful work with Motörhead, and several songs that marked a generation, like, 'Ace Of Spades', 'Orgasmatron', 'In The Name Or Tragedy', 'Killed By Death', 'Iron Fist', 'Life's A Bitch' and 'Metropolis' among many other songs.
Unfortunately I have not had the opportunity to meet Sir Ian Fraser Kilmister, but personally I am a longtime fan and when I learned of the death of Lemmy, others cried, it seemed I had lost some relative of mine.
Lemmy was and always will be an influence for a generation of crazy and passionate fans of Rock 'N' Roll. The only thing left to say is that Lemmy will never be forgotten and his work will always remain alive in our minds and in our day with your music."
Richard Machado (Timbó, Brazil)

"The date of 04/18/2009, at Via Funchal in São Paulo was my first Motörhead gig.
I stayed too close to the stage, right on the front of Lemmy and he was still healthy, strong and powerful.
The sound was too fucking loud and I got deaf for a whole week. They played 'You Better Run', amazing rock´n ´blues from the album 'March or Die'; they also played 'Whorehouse Blues' and others classic songs from the extensive Motörhead discography.
A fan threw a flag on stage, Lemmy took it and gently hung it on the Marshal amps and over there it remained the entire gig! What a night! Everthing, absolutely everything that came to me from Motörhead always was too good and unforgettable.
Sometimes its so sad to think that they won´t be around anymore, specially Lemmy..."
Franklin Dourado (Brazil)

Via Funchal, São Paulo
April 18th 2009

Iron Fist
Stay Clean
Be My Baby
Rock Out
Metropolis
Another Perfect Day
Over the Top
One Night Stand
You Better Run
I Got Mine
The Thousand Names of God
In the Name of Tragedy
Just 'Cos You Got the Power
Going to Brazil
Killed by Death
Bomber
Whorehouse Blues
Ace of Spades
Overkill

"I'm from Brazil and in 1989 I was living and working in Germany because I won a world contest in 'Computer Graphic Design' and so I was invited to do some work and I stayed there for 5 short years, the best years of my life. I made the best friends ever like, Anuschka, Tanya, Karl, Dirk, Franco, Sven, Schmier (Destruction), Chrystal, Cibily, Ramit and the list goes on...
I was living in a small village called Kleinkems and before I met all these friends I was all by myself living in a Hotel called The Gashouse Zoom Blumenn Hotel, just beside the Autobahn. In a magazine I saw the add about a Motörhead concert in Manheim Germany, 250km away from where I was, I got crazy about it, it was a dream cause those concerts were never possible in Brazil and I had just bought the '1916' cd, it was perfect.
So I went to the concert, first row, right in front of Wurzel (RIP), it was fantastic, a dream come true, the girls joined the band at the end, just amazing.
So I was the last one to leave the place and I went to my Land Hover, 8cc in to the autobahn, Motörhead cassette tape playing loud and 200km/h full throttle!!!!!!!!
Well, alcohol, Motörhead, all the excitement and I went out of the

autobahn near to Kleikems and I just spot the turning beside the road and went there with my car doing 120km/h and suddenly I spotted the blue lights in my view mirror...UPS...POLICE!!! Then I thought to myself...if I stop I will lose my driving license for 1 year and 1500 Marcs, if I run I may have I little chance and I'm driving a V8 and... Motörhead out loud and FULL THROTTLE......

Right in front of the Hotel, the parking was full and some snow left in the road and a car was just leaving a spot, just right on time I park like crazy, I have no idea how fast I was, it was just insane. I just parked and lay down inside the car turning the mirror so I could see what was going on outside and I saw the Police passing by 5 times, that was crazy...

In the next morning I just walk up and went to the car to go somewhere to get some food and guess what happens? Just started the car and a fuckin' loud noise in the engine like the engine has broken apart... so I called the mechanics and... the main shaft just split apart right in the middle!!! How is that possible? HA HA

So I went back to my room, put on the Video Tape I bought in the Motörhead concert 'Everything Louder...' and I lost myself in my thoughts...something like:

"Why do I make fuckin' plans and create so high expectations before the fuckin' things actually happens?"

And the music just stops in the fucking video, I turn back my attention to it and there was the fuckin' Lemmy saying exactly the same fuckin' thing?!?!?! That he doesn't make plans or create expectations for anything cause whatever happens it will be always something new, you will always be learning something, good or worse it will always turn good cause you've just learn something new!! Fuckin' bastard, how I admire that bloody dude!!! And so my life has been like it, learning in the daily bases!!! Thanks dude, I love you Lem!!!

A friend of mine called "Celso Fuiú" who introduced Motörhead to me back in 1981. He is a great and very simple man, he is a truck driver and don't speak a world in English, not a single word...but he can sing every single Motörhead song while driving his truck around the whole country out loud!!! Amazing!!!

I do some charity work on my own and with my own resources (30 years now doing this) to try to help kids to get off drugs and craziness. I put out some free concerts calling all the new kids rock bands to play on it along with my Motörhead Tribute band "MotörVäder", so they don't waste time on shit and keep playing music.

Bands: Anvil, Rush, Billy Talent, Alexisonfire

"As far as shows we did with Motörhead we played an entire UK tour in 1983 called 'Another Perfect Tour'. It was months before that I refused the guitar playing offer from Motörhead when Eddie left the band.
I was in the midst of writing and recording 'Forged in Fire' which meant it was impossible to help out Lemmy. I saw him at the Reading festival just afterwards and he was furious with me...I tried to explain but he was not interested so I just said sorry hope you get it all sorted.
The next time I saw him was months later at a gig in Brugge Belgium called 'Heavy Sounds Festival' 83'. Although Motörhead were not playing Lemmy was there and his gig for the day was throwing commemorative collectors towels on the crowd flying above them in a hot air balloon. I still have mine!! I was walking by his backstage container change room when I was grabbed by the fringes of my leather jacket from behind me. I turned around and there we were face to face!! He began by saying we'll be touring the UK together have a listen to the new album, 'Another Perfect Day'. He was really hyped and positive and was anxious to hear what I thought. He told me that Brian Robertson the Thin Lizzy guitarist had brought a really cool melodic flavor, new to the Motörhead sound. I listened and of course loved it!! I still think it was one of their all time best. He asked me why I didn't at least do the tour that Eddie left, I explained why and he totally understood but also added, "it could have done wonders for your career." Lemmy always said exactly the honest truth. The tour that came after was a lifetime experience. On that tour I got to know Lemmy and learned a hell of a lot!!!
On one particular occasion Lemmy invited me to his hotel room to have a drink or two, yeah right!!!! A 40 ounce bottle of Vodka!! He pulled out these massive tall glasses and poured at least 6 shots and orange juice...to say the least after the first drink I was well buzzed.
It didn't stop there!!! He looks at me with this look of 'you silly kid' and proceeds to pull out a small leather pouch with white powder. It was amphetamines or powdered speed. He dipped a pocketknife into the powder and stuck it under my nose, he goes "sniff!!!" It seemed like nothing happened!!! I suddenly realized I'm no longer drunk!!! He pours yet another wack of Vodka and orange

juice and we continue this for what seemed only a couple of hours. Suddenly there's a knock at the door, it was the tour manager. He says "ok boys pack up your shit, time to get to the gig!!!" I was shocked. We had been drinking for a full 24 hours!! It was a day off and we had spent the entire time talking and it was indeed time to go play!!!
I made my way back to my hotel room grabbed my belongings and headed for the concert hall. I felt like a dead man walking!! I entered the backstage area when Lemmy caught sight of me. He walks up to me with a 6 pack of Foster's beer hanging off of his bullet belt and pulls out a plastic bag filled with little black capsules. He says "You look too knackered take two of these, they're called black bombers."
I took one!!! Within ten minutes I could run a marathon and do the gig in one breath!!! Holy shit!!!!!
Although the crazy antics seem to have the most impact when you tell stories but the real person and the conversations had much more significance to me. I was in awe and expressed my feelings to Lemmy. I told him how unique his voice and bass sound were and how he's influenced the entire genre.
He was humble to a fault and told me that in ten years or less there will be someone sitting and saying the same things to you!!! The interesting part is I went to see Motörhead in Ft. Lauderdale Florida in the 90's. I got to the tour bus in mid afternoon and knocked at the door. Lemmy looked out the window and immediately opened the door of the bus and came out holding an attaché case and a can of beer. He said he just woke up and took a long swig of beer...As we walked toward the entry of the hall he turns to me and asks "did it happen like I said? Have you had the experience of someone telling you the things you told me?"
I was shocked he remembered our conversation from over ten years previous, the answer was yes!!!
When we got to the change room Lemmy opened the attaché case and pulled out a bottle of Jack Daniels and poured it into his half finished beer and says "the rest of my breakfast!!"
Lemmy was like an older brother, somehow I felt like he was me in the future, experiencing everything first!
My last conversations with Lemmy were about diabetes. His body was being ravaged by this horrid disease. It just so happens my late older brother was a research scientist working on diabetes. This was of major interest to Lemmy and we talked quite extensively on the subject. If you know about this disease it always kills. Eventually major organs lose their ability to function due to

circulation problems resulting from the disease. Slow death...I felt devastated hearing what he told me. I knew I'd probably never see him again in person and I didn't.
On my newest album coming out in a week or two, I sang a line in one of the songs purposely like Lemmy...In hopes he would hear it, sadly he won't.
I will miss him and never forget a moment!!!
Lips (Anvil – Vocals/Guitar)

"Lemmy is a huge part of my musical makeup.
I own a Rickenbacker bass because of him, and hope to do him proud.
I've worn out many Motörhead *England shirts over the years, every time I just go get a new one.*
I even named one of my ferrets after him!"
Adam Bell (Ottowa, Canada)

"Finally met the great man the day after a concert in Calgary, Canada, but first seen the band Nov' 1980 'Ace Up Your Sleeve' tour as 14 year old. Fast forward 30 years a shitty venue in Calgary Alberta, Canada met Phil Campell after the gig Lem had gone to the only smoking allowed venue in town, which just happened to be a casino.
Then Tim Butcher and Campbell told us their hotel, but not to show up before 12noon, next day bumps into Phil in the lobby and we have a few Strongbows in the bar, which he says is shit – didn't even have a piano (top Ramada in town), then gets a call to get Lem up to get on the bus.
Campbell was one of two people allowed to wake him. Lem is suffering from a major hang over, so when we finally meet on the bus he's a little weak, but still has time for pics (me, the misses and girlfriend) and signs my 'Overkill' tatty, then very politely he says "got go sorry, I am still a bit rough."
Many thanks to the great man and also his brother in arms Phillip Campbell and all the rest of the crew I have met over the years as they all seemed to be good muckers, no bullshit 'us and them'.
I'll never forget my last two shows on the first Motorboat, where I also got the privilege of meeting some great people and new friends."
John Evans (Calgary, Canada)

"I've always wanted to meet Lemmy.
To be at a Motörhead show is a dream that'll never come true for

me now. But in one way I did get to meet Lemmy.
I had a dream the day he died.
I dreamt that I was at a Motörhead concert and afterwards I tried to get backstage without a pass. Security refused but Lemmy saw me and let me in.
We talked for a while and discussed other bands. After a while he said "you know, we should get together for a drink some time."
I was ecstatic. To be asked to share a drink with Lemmy was like my biggest dream come true. He said he'd pick me up the next day.
I went home and couldn't sit still all night, I was that excited. The next morning I found out that Lemmy passed away. I was crushed.
Later at night, a black car pulled up outside my apartment building and Lemmy walked out. He called me down from the window and I ran down. I was stunned, I asked him how he was still there.
"I heard that you died!" he replied "I made you a promise didn't I? Not gonna miss a drink with one of my biggest fans now am I?"
We drove to a bar and it was like people couldn't see us.
Then people started shouting "We Love You Lemmy!" he looked around and smiled. The bartender asked us what we'd like to drink. We both said at the same time "Jack and Coke". He looked at me and said "wow you really do follow me a lot don't you" and smiled.
I got a call from my dad asking me to come home as it was getting late.
I asked Lemmy if he could drop me off at the bus stop. He dropped me off and said "Alright son, we had that drink, I gotta go now" he got out of the car and started walking.
I called after him and followed him. He turned a corner and walked into an old building with a big yard out front. I entered but there was no one there. There was a lady at the front door. I asked her where Lemmy went. She told me that I wasn't allowed in the building yet. I went back to the bus stop and his car was gone.
I woke up In the dream then and was bummed because It wasn't real, I got out of bed and walked into the kitchen, there was something on the counter. His hat and a note saying "Thanks for a Great night, keep the hat and rock on –Lemmy."
When I actually woke up, I couldn't stop thinking about the dream. I never got to meet him in real life, but he never let me down.
He gave his fan what he wanted even though he wasn't alive anymore. You might call me crazy, but this is one dream that I treasure greatly.
RIP Lemmy, thanks for everything!"

Hassan Rizwan (Calgary, Canada)

"I got turned on to Motörhead in 1981.
They have always been there when I needed a high volume break from the monotony of everyday life, even if just for 1 side of a vinyl LP.
Lemmy inspired me to pick up the bass in 1984 and find my groove and sometimes escape though music.
I'm gonna miss everyone that was involved in bringing that wonderful music to all of our eager ears from the first album to the last and every concert that rang our ears in between those albums."
Clifford Capezzuto (Kitimat, British Columbia)

"Well I am glad that my hubby asked me if I heard of Motörhead and got me to listen to 'Ace of Spades'.
Need less to say I fell in love with Lemmy.
Lemmy moved my world to a whole new level. When he passed away it broke my heart.
So to all Motörhead Fans keep on rocking for Lemmy like there is no tomorrow."
Holly Jodoin (Athabasca, Alberta, Canada)

"What can be said that hasn't already been said?
Lemmy and Motörhead were, and will continue to be, a massive part of my life.
True definition of gentlemen and Rock 'n' Roll.
He may be gone, but never forgotten!"
Adam Thornton (Fort Saskatchewan, Canada)

"Born to lose in 1973.
First heard Motörhead through a music video channel here in Canada in 1984-85. I saw Motörhead live for the first time in 1997.
I started collecting and cherishing everything related in the early 2000's. I became a member of the fan club in 2015. Through that I believe I'm part of a growing family that will remember Lemmy as legendary and that Motörhead's music will live on forever.
I've seen 'em live maybe 10 times and the memories will remain. It helped me through hard times in my life.
I'm part of the Motörheadbangers family.
It is now 2016 - Lemmy has passed and through his music and everything he stood for I LIVE TO WIN. Thank you Lemmy."
Martin Gadbois MHB 3997 (Hull, Québec, Canada)

"Motörhezbollah from Edmonton did a tribute show for the man on February 6th R.I.P."
Billy Hersche (Edmonton, Alberta, Canada)

*"Went to Germany and saw the November 25th, show which was my best mates birthday who I met at the 'Orgasmatron' tour in Toronto and they played 'Orgasmatron' in Ludwicksberg. God bless you both Dennis and Lemmy!!
Motörhead for life."*
Dean Adams (Mississauga, Ontario)

*"Long live Motörhead, best band ever!
"I was born in '71 and Motörhead came out in '75 started to listen to them when I was ten.
Best metal band ever man, long live Motörhead.
RIP Lemmy the 'God of Metal.'"*
Brad Mills (Winnipeg, Manitoba)

"True hard grit rocker, hard act to follow."
Bob Lovelace (Orangeville, Ontario)

*"I would not write the music I write today if it was not for Lemmy! I swear his blood runs through all of us!!!!
RIP brother!!! We lost a great man!!!"*
Chuck Swire (Orillia, Ontario)

*"I was born 3 days before Motörhead came to be...the soundtrack of my life...
Lemmy inspired me to play guitar on my bass! And I've been doing it for 30 years!!!"*
Francois Lamy (Vancouver, British Columbia)

*"Lemmy told it like it is.
There was no bullshit from him.
Rest In Peace Mr Kilmister."*
Raymond Gary Dodman (Ottowa, Ontario)

*"I met Lemmy shortly after Robbo had joined the band.
Confused as to why Eddie Clarke wasn't with them I asked Lemmy.
"Why did Eddie Leave?" Lemmy's reply
"Because he's a fucking arsehole!"*

You have to respect his honesty.
It was so cool to have met him and fortunately I did see Motörhead on the previous tour with the original three, opening for Ozzy with Randy Rhoads no less.
Best memories ever \m/"
Keith Manning (Vancouver, BC)

"*The first time I met Lemmy was in Montréal in 2003.*
I met him outside the venue, spoke with him a little, and took a picture with him. I was more than happy to meet this man in person and I was surprised how nice and patient he was.
I met him a second time at Heavy Mtl in 2011.
I was working at the outside festival that day and I had access to the backstage (a huge parking lot transformed into the artist area) During the day, before he arrived, I had time to walk onstage and take pictures with his bass and amps and speak with Tim his bass tech, a really cool guy.
Lemmy arrived in a white van and we were maybe 5 or 6 staff people there. He was alone walking on stage when I followed him. Hours later when it was time to go on stage, I was still there, 6 feet to him.
He was sitting with his bass on his lap, relaxed, with his hands shaking, maybe due to Parkinson's(?), ready to walk on stage. Girlschool was playing that day, and I watched the show from the side of the stage with the girls. It was an emotive moment seeing this man walking up the stage at this age and rocking like that. This man is an inspiration for me and will be truly be missed."
Eric Marsan (Montréal, Québec)

"*When I lived in Toronto for about 10 years, I saw Motörhead 4 times, in Montreal. My ears rang for days after and my work mates always knew when I had gone due to a lack of hearing for those few days haha. Some of my favourite gigs I ever saw.*"
Meghann Leclair (Vittoria, Ontario)

"*Saw Motörhead once, Toronto Metal Fest 2010. Great show! Lemmy's rusty pipes were in full effect, his stage presence was amazing. Consider myself lucky to have seen Motörhead in all their splendor.*
A memory I will cherish always."
Edmund Joseph Lehn (Vernon, British Columbia)

"*When I was five years old my first cassette tape my mother gave

to me was 'No Remorse.'
Ever since then Motörhead and Lemmy have never left my side.
He was an inspiration. A gentleman.
And if there EVER was an incarnation of Rock'n'Roll it was Lemmy.
Over the years I've collected whatever I could get my hands on. CD's, Vinyls, shirts, everything.
Lemmy died on my birthday, which was a bittersweet thing.
But I feel like I can learn something from his life. Which is to never be afraid, never let go and never bend for anyone.
He was more than an influence for me, more than a role model.
For me Lemmy was something like a father, I truly loved that old man."
Felix 'Jack' Lentge (Hamilton, Ontario)

"My Lemmy memory was, the few times I got to see Motörhead in my life they were so loud, rattle your ears loud, louder then the headliners even. I thought that was the most rock n' roll kickass thing ever!!
Cheers Lemmy!"
Michael Belyan (High Prairie, Alberta)

"My first Motörhead show was Toronto in 1980. I was a depressed teenager until I heard 'Stay Clean' live and it instantly changed my attitude toward life.
After seeing Motörhead over 100 times since, Lemmy had become more of a big brother to me than a musician his honesty, staying true to his beliefs was a inspiration to me and I believe there will never be a rock icon like him again.
THANK YOU MOTORHEAD FOR EVERYTHING!!!!!!"
Patrick Lane (Calgary, Alberta)

"I first saw Motörhead live in 2006 at the Newcastle City Hall on tour with Clutch, it was my first ever concert that I went to and I was hooked.
Since then I went to every show they put on in Newcastle, be it City Hall, Carling Academy or Metro Radio Arena, including such shows as with Alice Cooper, etc.
My all time favourite moment would have to be when they played the Academy with Saxon and Biff Byfford came out on stage to perform 'Born To Raise Hell' with Lemmy and the crew.
He will forever be "The Man Who Put The Hassle Into Newcastle".
Rock On, and more importantly, Rock Out.

Adam Kadmon Bradley (Moncton, New Brunswick)

"I met Lemmy quite a few times.
We used to hang out with Motörhead + Girlschool. The bouncers at the Marquee tried to get us to pay to get in, we were with Lemmy just arriving from another boozer. He just said
"Hey they are with me let 'em in ha ha."
Great bloke he was."
Mickey Beharry (Toronto, Ontario)

Chile

Capital City: Santiago
Population: 18,006,407
Currency: Peso
Bands: Los Jaivas, Los Prisioneros, La Ley

"Motörhead is part of the legacy that my brother left me, it was he who introduced me to the world of rock and all the passion involved.
Lemmy's character stands out for me for being an icon of that carefree attitude, that no moss rock board, that energy to keep moving.
But besides the great admiration I feel, I can not avoid mentioning the recurring joke about Lemmy, is that my brother had invented the myth that before each concert, his voice is prepared by gargling with steel wool, because there no other way to get the voice of a motorcycle, except for that rustic hahaha method."
Elias Figueroa Cifuentes (Santiago, Chile)

"My story goes back to 2007 – 'Kiss of Death' gig!
I was 15 years old and my mother (single mom) and I lived in a village a bit away from the capital of Chile, Santiago.
1st day of May Testament played, and the next day Motörhead too.
My mother gave me the horrible task of having to choose just one of the concerts. The rest is history!
I spend 1st May with my stomach pressed for the big event, which I would part the next day.
15 -year-old Carolina arrived at Estadio Victor Jara, all alone and I chose to make conversation with a man in the line who was speaking - in a very enthusiastic way - about vomiting, that became one of the best human beings I've met in my life (still my friend).

We entered the stadium and Motörhead came on promptly at 21:00hrs playing!
Never am I going to forget Lemmy's shoulders moving and playing 'Be My Baby' (I wanna put a big and sweet smile in here).
I don't have to explain what I felt with Motörhead that first time, most of you know there is no way to put it in the right words!"
Carolina Barrios MHB3609 (Santiago, Chile)

Estadio Victor Jara
Santiago
2nd May 2007

Doctor Rock
Stay Clean
Be My Baby
Killers
Metropolis
Over the Top
One Night Stand
I Got Mine
In the Name of Tragedy
Sword of Glory
The Chase is Better Than the Catch
Rosalie
Sacrifice
Just 'Cos You Got the Power
Going to Brazil
Killed by Death
Iron Fist

**Whorehouse Blues
Ace of Spades
Overkill**

Czech Republic

Capital City: Prague
Population: 10,541,466
Currency: Czech Koruna
Bands: Brutal Death, Goregrind, Black

"Lemmy was my role model."
Lád'a Kolář (Jilovice, Jihočeský Kraj, Czech Republic)

Denmark

Capital City: Copenhagen
Population: 5,707,251
Currency: Danish Krone
Bands: Lars Ulrich, Volbeat, Mercyful Fate

"1996-1997 'ish, my friend and I are sitting at our table in the small rock club 'TEX' in Copenhagen DK on a thursday night...
In walks this cool cat in a white suit and proceeds onto the small stage with his two mates - Phil & Mikki - in tow - where they blast out 'Ace of Spades' and walk off stage again and right past us with a comment on my friends green Bay packers Cap - nobody knew what'd just hit us!!
P.S my friends name was Kim Paulsen"
Stefan Kozuch (Copenhagen, Denmark)

Finland

Capital City:	Helsinki
Population:	5,486,125
Currency:	Euro
Bands:	Hanoi Rocks, Turisas, Nightwish, COB

"Motörhead has been my life for 36 years. And it still means to me a lot!! I love the music that Motörhead made, travelled to England, Sweden, Germany and last summer we rode from Finland to Hungary on motorcycles to see Motörhead gigs!!
I have met through Motörhead people who became my best friends!!
I also have Motörhead tribute band called Mötherhead. Only tribute band in the world which has it's own 'BOMBER'!!
Most precious thing to me is my self handmade bass Rockenbacker. Yeah, it looks like a Rickenbacker but I named it ROCKENBACKER!! :)
I got Lemmy's signature on it 16.12.2008 in Helsinki Finland. Not for SALE!!!!"
Pete Kalmari (Finland)

"I found Motörhead when I met my husband in 2006...then we went to a Manchester gig in 2012, it was something that I never believed to be true!
It was the first gig for me and my husband ever!
Then we waited and waited for them in Finland, but they cancelled 3 times, because Lemmy's health problems.... then on 6/12/2015 they come in Finland and we were nervous if it really would happen...hell yeah it happened. The boys got on stage...then I started to cry.... something tells me that this is last time when I see Motörhead...
They played well, but I saw that Lemmy was not doing well...I cried when the gig was over!! And it was the last time, but I will always be Motörhead fan and love, love them all of my heart."

Marjatta Liimatainen (Palokka, Finland)

Hartwall Areena
Helsinki
6th December 2015

Bomber
Stay Clean
Metropolis
When the Sky Comes Looking For You
Over the Top
The Chase is Better Than the Catch
Lost Woman Blues
Rock It
Orgasmatron
Doctor Rock
Just 'Cos You Got the Power
No Class
Ace of Spades
Whorehouse Blues
Overkill Ft Michael Monroe of Hanoi Rocks

"I've never met Lemmy, but he always had a special place in my heart.
I first started listening to Motörhead when I was in 7th grade, but it wasn't until last year when I started to really get into their music. I started buying their CDs and Vinyls; I put up a Lemmy poster in my room and a Motörhead flag on its walls.
I finally saw Motörhead live on 6th of December, 2015. It was the best thing I've ever seen. Energy filled the room, and I could not believe that it was the Lemmy himself up on that stage.

*Then, before the month could even end, he died.
I couldn't realise what had happened. I don't think I fully realise it even now. But I do think that Lemmy predicted his death.
I bought a shirt at the gig that said "Victory or Death: Motörhead 1975-2015". And I know that Lemmy gave it his all.
RIP, Legend."*
Anton Rostislavovich Shakhtakhtinskiy (Vantaa, Finland)

*"I do have memories related to Motörhead / Lemmy but the thing that pops up the most is this which is not really a memory but a source of inspiration:
Years ago when I read 'White Line Fever' for the first time. I didn't know then that Lemmy had done some roadie work with Jimi Hendrix.
I had been dreaming for years of getting into the music business, well of course as a musician. I should rehearse as often as I can but I'm too lazy haha!
I thought "Hell, if I don't learn to play something. Why not to be a roadie? Lemmy was also roadie so why not me also?"
Soon after that I was drinking Jack & Coke in my home and sent an email to a band that I'd been following for few years. They replied soon and after that I was a merchandiseman.
After that I've gotten more responsibilities such as a roadie, driver and so on.
I started with nothing and no way into the music business.
Nowadays I'm proud road crew member for bands such as: Rytmihäiriö, Moonsorrow, Barren Earth and occasionaly Swallow The Sun.
And getting more and more jobs here and there with this and that band.
For the huge inspiration from Lemmy. I have now made something out of myself and made my dream happen.
This literally changed my life and I'm forever in debt for Lemmy.
We are born to lose, but we live to win."*
Tero Doukas MHB 4136 (Lahti, Finland)

France

Capital City: Paris
Population: 66,627,602
Currency: Euro
Bands: Gojira, Anorexia Nervosa, Kronos

"My friend was a fan from 1979 and of course I followed since I met him!
We have met Lemmy several times during these 15 past years, I was so shy at the beginning, I've been trembling each time I've met him but I was the only one who spoke English so I was the first in line!!!
I was happy when the meeting was short cos for most of the time I was paralyzed, losing my English and I went back home so proud for having meet him, being so close, I was so impressed, whoa!!!
And one day, it was in 2007, in Dijon (France), Dan came to me one or too songs before the end of the show and stuck something on my t-shirt!!! I didn't expect that, it was an after show pass, my God, I was completely under stress, it was unbelievable!
Then it was an incredible night, one hour talking and drinking Jack with Lemmy, he was so nice, so cool and very happy and we were on a cloud in paradise!
I think of that night very often and I want to keep this scene in my head, it was perfect and it was the real first time! We have never missed a tour, trying to save enough money to follow them for several shows in Europe until the last one in Dusseldorf last November!"

Carole Ostrowicz (Saint-Bonnet-le-Château, France)

"If we take the time to put all the words of Motorhead discography we can enjoy in a strange poetry that smell old number 7 and the speedfreak poetry -

In 1975 they told us that we are On Parole 'cause we took too many Motörhead that give us the pleasure of Overkill Bomber.
Later I found the Ace of Spades in a Iron Fist just like Another Perfect Day ... All we needed was an Orgasmatron on Rock 'n' Roll. 1916 was the birthday of the March ör Die Bastards, like a Sacrifice Overnight Sensation. But sex was so unclean and the Snake Bite Love drived as a state of mind where We Are Motörhead and Hammered. Living in Inferno and the Kiss of Death Motörizer me... Finely The Wörld is Yours only in an Aftershock because Bad Magic in 2015
Motorhead was our way of life, like On Parole when Vibrator on a Iron Horse teached us that we were Born to Lose in the City Kids where Fools are The Watcher because they Lost Johnny
An Overkill makes you Stay Clean but (I Won't) Pay Your Price it was just like if I'll Be Your Sister under the Capricorn porn mark. There is No Class in a Damage Case. You can Tear Ya Down in Metropolis it will always stay Limb from Limb
Dead Men Tell No Tales to the Lawman, that is a Sweet Revenge for the Sharpshooter. There is no Poison that makes you Stone Dead Forever even All the Aces Step Down and Talking Head like Bomber on the ring
Having the Ace of Spades have sense when you Love Me Like a Reptile. I will Shoot You in the Back cause Live to Win is Fast and Loose. But (We Are) The Road Crew and we Fire, Fire the Jailbait Dance. Try to Bite the Bullet and you will understand The Chase Is Better Than the Catch. When The Hammer is back at the Funny Farm it will Shine and we will Dancing on Your Grave. Just Rock it like One Track Mind to Another Perfect Day.
Marching off to War, I Got Mine Tales of Glory. Die You Bastard! Understand that Rock 'n' Roll is built to Eat the Rich cause they have a Blackheart Stone Deaf in the U.S.A.
Blessing The Wolf! The Traitor is like Dogs, and they came All for You told the Boogeyman Deaf Forever ... I said Nothing Up My Sleeve, that Ain't My Crime but your Claw ... You! Mean Machine are Built for Speed ready for Ridin' with the Driver with Doctor Rock in an Orgasmatron

I am The One to Sing the Blues cause I'm So Bad (Baby I Don't Care). There is No Voices in the Sky, when you re Going to Brazil just Nightmare/The Dreamtime. Don't forget to Love Me Forever in the Angel City. That Make My Day – or I will R.A.M.O.N.E.S. you and Shut You Down until 1916

If enjoying watching the cat scratch fever is like a bad religion, you will see me like Jack the Ripper... I know that I ain't no nice guy

1. I am to going to be the hellraiser with the asylum choir. It is True and if You Better Run never Name In Vain the speedfreak
2. So ... March or Die
3. Stay On Your Feet or on Your Knees ...Burner is the way to Death or Glory. I Am the Sword I am Born to Raise Hell
4. Don't Let Daddy Kiss Me, Bad Woman! He is the Liar Lost in the Ozone
5. Come, I'm Your Man, We Bring the Shake to the Devils
6.
1. Your Sacrifice over Sex & Death will always be Over Your Shoulder. We do War for War in Order/Fade to Black in a Dog-Face Boy.
2. At the end All Gone to Hell and Make 'em Blind
3. Don't Waste Your Time In Another Time Out of the Sun
1. Be ready for Civil War... They said I am Crazy Like a Fox
2. If I Don't Believe a World, you will Eat the Gun
3. The Overnight Sensation is when Love Can't Buy You Money and stay Broken
4. Them Not Me! The Murder Show Shake the World
5. You just have to Listen to Your Heart
6.
1. If Love for Sale, the Dogs of War practice Snake Bite Love
2. Enter the Assassin and Take the Blame
3. I will be Dead and Gone in a Night Side
4. So Don't Lie to Me and make Joy of Labour ... If I Desperate for You I am Better off Dead
5.
1. See Me Burning in the Slow Dance when I Stay Out of Jail
2. Don't worry God Save the Queen but Out to Lunch
3. Wake the Dead One More Fucking Time that will be Stagefright/Crash & Burn
4. (Wearing Your) Heart on Your Sleeve cause We Are Motörhead

5.
1. If you Walk a Crooked Mile and Down the Line to the Brave New World. You will heard Voices from the War, they are Mine All Mine
2. So Shut Your Mouth and Kill the World with Dr. Love and No Remorse in a Red Raw dawn I am the Serial Killer

3.
1. At the Terminal Show, the Killers In The Name Of Tragedy play Suicide over a Life's A Bitch hymn
2. Down On Me In The Black, we will Fight in the Year Of The Wolf
3. Looking for the Keys To The Kingdom and Smiling Like A Killer in the Whorehouse Blues -

4.
1. Your Sucker and his One Night Stand life style like the Devil I Know...
2. Trigger Under the Gun because God Was Never on Your Side
3. Stop Living in the Past, slay Christine with my Sword of Glory – 3:57
4. Be My Baby in the Kingdom of the Worm – where we Going Down with

The Thousand Names of God
A Runaround Man Teach You How To
Sing The Blues When the Eagles Screams
Rock Out in One Short Life or you will be Buried
Alive like a English Rose
Back On The Chain to the Heroes, Time Is Right
Ok I am Born To Lose and I Know How To Die,
but I will always
Get Back In Line with Devils In My Head in
the name of Rock'n'Roll Music
I am Waiting For The Snake Brotherhood Of
Man, this Outlaw I Know
What You Need
Bye Bye Bitch Bye Bye
Heartbreaker is a Coup de Grace in the
Lost Woman Blues
Is it the End of Time for her, Do You Believe?
She is a Death Machine with Dust and Glass
ready for Going to Mexico

Silence When You Speak To Me or you will
Crying Shame dirty *Queen of the Damned*
Take my Knife and *Keep Your Powder Dry*.
You will stay *Paralyzed*
The last words but not the least are Victory or Die in
Thunder & Lightning and that Fire *Storm Hotel*
Time to Shoot Out All of Your Lights, feed
The Devil
and enjoy
Electricity to grow up *Evil Eye*
Teach Them How to Bleed Till the End
and *Tell Me Who to Kill* - 2:57
If that can stop *Choking on Your Screams* - 3:33
When the Sky Comes Looking for You it is time for
Sympathy for the Devil."
Dimitri Bulan (Étretat, France)

'LAST FOR MOTO-RAID LEMMY' – A short story

The blows struck violently on the low release the first notes of the monumental 'Ace of Spades.'
But even before Phil starts pounding his drums, the third went!
The powerful machine responds instantly to the throttle I operate.
On my bike, a US 1300, I quickly reach a speed of one hundred and seventy km/h!
Now the curves and corners are connected, while echoing heavy riffs of my faithful friend Fast Eddie.
For years, I know, that one, and the sound of his guitar is still as good!
Right, left, back right, and left again.
My mechanical horse rears at the discretion of the pressures that I exercise on the handlebars.
Do forming one with my body; my little powerhouse swallows the miles in a real orgy of decibels.
My knees brush against asphalt, a few centimeters away from the breaking point.
At each of my manoeuvers, it is still at the last moment I straightened the bar, to not end up in the buildings.
With a simple flick of the wrist, I avoid obstacles, these cars out of nowhere who cross my path.

Right, left, again!
The landscape runs at a dizzying speed, so fast that I cannot distinguish any details.
Above all, I dare not cast any look, even stealthily, at the speedometer needle, afraid to finish my run off the road.
Tonight, in a large concert hall in Lyon.
The great Lemmy is back, Motörhead is more alive than ever.
After all these years, all these albums and many tours around the world, her heavy rock 'n' roll anthems, have the same power.
The public will be there; faithful fifties, the first timers and young teens taking up the torch, they sing in chorus all these titles as powerful as each other. A career of over thirty years and always the same energy, the same rage, the same madness.
I have a few kilometers and very little time to go.

"♫ ♪ Built For Speed".

All eyes on the white line in the middle of the road, I do not care about what may come across. I rush straight ahead, thoroughly.
I'm not especially suicidal, it might even be the opposite.
It's just that I love having thrills.
Near-death experience something pleasurable.
The adrenaline rush is a need, almost a drug.
And the speed is exhilarating.
Life fully.
Always.
Far, anywhere, anytime, but thoroughly.
No limit for the excesses, of course.
Anyone else would have died ten times, but not Lemmy.
Not me.

"♫ ♪ Stone dead ... forever!".

How long will I be on my machine?
How many kilometers remains for me to go, before the end of my career?
I feel eyes will shine on me.
I know everyone expects me to turn.
I am even sure some would rejoice to see me fall.
But Lemmy will not fall.
Lemmy is immortal.
The roar of my machine demonstrates the strengths that I still have.

I guess the needle of the rev counter is panicking in the red. I know my time is limited.
I open up the throttle, at the risk of not being able to control anything in the second coming.
This long straight fatal risk to myself, my arms are about to give way.
I feel I let go!

"One short life 🎵 🎵".

I close my eyes and I look shocked.
NOW !!!

Everything stopped.

More music, more light, more speed, more vibration.
I open my eyes.
I am alive !
Lemmy does not die!
Lemmy is immortal!

But the verdict is clear:
"GAME OVER ... INSERT COIN".

Which foot, this simulator! !

For the fan of rock and roll and motorcycles that I am, two minutes forty-eight seconds that the game lasts is a real appetizer, before the concert tonight promises to be always apocalyptic.
Lemmy time to become a mad dash to the rhythm of the hymn what Motörhead 'Ace Of Spades' is a moment of jubilation.

"🎵 🎵 One More Fucking Time!" ....

I appeal bartender: "Una cerveza, por favor! "
Meanwhile he betrays me my ration hop, I slip a coin in the slot of the simulator and this left me for another crazy race...

"We are Motörhead 🎵 ... 🎵 ... born to kick your ass ... !!!".

Jean-Christophe Kieffer (Colmar, France)

"Motörhead, that could be the original sound of my adult life...

I am born in '73 in Le Havre (France), around my 14 years old I was looking for some new stuff in music. In a youth hostel I discover a metal tape of Judas Priest. At school I make new friends, hard rockers and a metalhead.
In 1989 I had a summer job and I bought LP's – 'No Sleep Till Hammersmith' is my very first Motörhead album.
The sound was kick ass... A revelation...There were all the famous glory of Motörhead on !!!

1992-1999
After my time in military service I find '1916', a very deep album. I am not full addict... I do not listen them a lot, I turn to 'black metal.' After listening to 'Bastards', with metalheads at work I stayed on Motörhead. A lot of titles talked to me here, 'Bastards' (yes ! that is what we are) ; born to raise hell (that was my job... Police); devils (good fellows). We are Motörhead came and we sing it all time. Not a lot of money at this time, I bought 'Hellraiser' best of, to continue to get some Motörhead

2006-2008
In 2006 I bought 'Kiss of Death'... That is a very good LP ...
I go to tattoo studio and get a heart on my arm and the artist that did it was in a picture with Lemmy at a tattoo convention. So we listened to 'Kiss of Death' during his work on me.
I divorced this year, just some Motörhead songs sounded better to me...
It was like listening an Uncle talking about the meaning of men's life..
I went to Belgium and bought my first Motörhead tee shirt "England" in black and white (today, my 17 years old daughter wear it proudly (size S...)
Waiting new songs, I turn back to past and eat 'Hammered', 'Another Perfect Day', 'Snake Bite Love', 'Sacrifice'...
'Motorizer' arrived ! Whaaa!!! Good Motorhead and it sound very good

2010
'The World Is Yours' arrived, just like another perfect rock 'n' roll opus
I told to myself this year; there is few bands that can rock after 20 years on the road...
I left down all the bands I listened to during my early life... And more the time goes by and more Motörhead I listen to in a week...

I rediscovered the very old LP's 'Bomber', 'Overkill', 'Iron Fist', 'Rock 'n' roll, 'Ace of Spades' and 'Orgamastron'...

2013
'Aftershock' arrived.
I said ok! This year I want to see them live in Paris. I bought ticket but they cancelled due to Lemmy's health...
I thought ok next year he will be stronger than hell.

2014
They came to Paris, but this time it was me that was sick and could not go. That was a fucking day. I watched later the show on the web...

2015
I cover up my tattoo by something like pirate (remember captain Davy Jones) and we listened to 'Aftershock' and others during 3 hours sessions. Henri B made very good job.
I was excited new album forthcoming and pre ordered it. I followed daily all the news about the band to listen first.
And 'Bad Magic' is the album that turned around and around on the sound system without pause...
I was impressed by it
I entered at all the Motörhead competitions around 'Bad Magic'...I finally had my face on their web site on the fan wall paper... Great moment in my life...
I wanted to go to see them live... But I didn't buy a ticket... And here came trouble with terrorists attacks in Paris.
The Prefet de Police cancelled the Motörhead show that should be done, I said ok 2016 will be the year for me.
My Christmas Eve was Motörhead for me... Tee shirts, books, cd's... It was good.
But a morning in December, I was in my bed reading my mails before waking up and I thought it was a bad joke about him passing away, it was not.
This day I cancelled my sessions and cried all the day...
I was those ten last days Motörhead addict, I listened to them once a day (a single or an album). Shared regulary on social network clips from them and only wore my Motörhead tee shirt the weekend.
With my girlfriend we followed the last goodbye in streaming
we spend this night like Motörhead inspired us. Jack to drink, good things well cocked to head and have sex also.

And now? What happens?

*We are Motörhead... That is what we use to sing all the time
My HYMN IS "Rock N' Roll"*
Dimitri Bulan (Étretat, France)

*"The only thing I can say about him is the fact that I began to smoke and drink because of Lemmy.
I saw the last reportage and I said to myself "That's cool let's do this too."*
Nico Laleque (Saussines, France)

*"I met him once and it was magical. I saw them 5 or 6 times on stage sound - orgasm every time. A god.
Bye Lemmy."*
Serge Lafitan (Tarbes, France)

"Lemmy forever."
Stephanie Barrier (Lyon, France)

*"Meeting Delphine Wespiser (Miss France 2012), a few minutes before Motörhead's show in Colmar (France), August 2014.
...the last time I saw Lemmy & Co."*
J-Chistophe Keifer (France)

*"Lemmy was God for us, not a god, just God.
A fucking inspiration to me.
Respect for him and for Motörhead."*
Isis Debono (Apt, France)

*"Lemmy for me was the only true rock 'n' roll star. Because even if he had money he lived in a small apartment, toured with the crew in the bus and didn't change his ideas or his way of living.
I only had the chance to see him once last summer at the Hellfest it was a pure rock moment.
Lemmy is a true inspiration to me he is not playing rock 'n' roll, he IS rock 'n' roll.
RIP Saint Lemmy."*
Guillaume Delecroix (Paris, France)

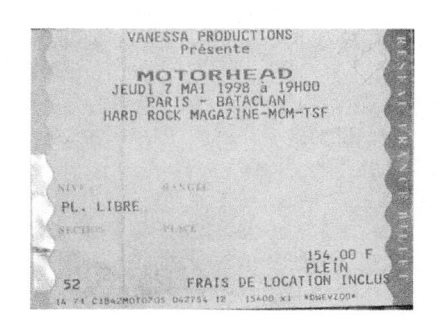

"We are Motörhead, and We play Rock'n Roll ♠♠"
Kłęmeńś Ćiasnoçha (Outines, France)

"Lemmy is my reference.
When someone asks me to make them discover rock or metal I immediately think of Motörhead.
When I listen to Motörhead I know I'm listening to a legendary band and it's even better when you know that this awesome music comes from someone that you can proudly admire, not just musically but also humanly.
Darren Fabreguettes (Toulouse, France)

"I've always been a huge Motörhead fan.
I listen to Motörhead with my daddy since I was a child and so does my brother!
We've been to three Motörhead's gig here in France with my family: Beer for the grown ups, earplugs for the young ones.
We were all singing with Lemmy, because we are 'hellraisers'!
It has always been a wonderful time sharing our common passion for rock 'n' roll.
It's heartbreaking but every good moment comes to an end. Now we'll play louder than ever, paying tribute to Lemmy.
I will never forget him."
Cassiopée (nr Paris, France)

"I've seen Motörhead only one time.
It was at the biggest French festival, the 'Hellfest', last year. I wanted to see Motörhead for years and years, the 'Hellfest' was a great oportunity. I knew that I would see a lot of bands at the festival, but I went for Motörhead. More precisely, I went for Lemmy.
It was one of the best gigs of my life. Lemmy looked tired but was still there. It was his last French show. I bought my ticket for

another show in France, he died 2 months before. How sad I am..
I have never met Lemmy, but a few months ago, I lost my rock'n'roll father. See you in another world my friend."
Lucas Chopin (Amiens, France)

Hellfest
Val de Moine, Clisson
19th June 2015

Shoot You in the Back
Damage Case
Stay Clean
Metropolis
Over the Top
The Chase is Better Than the Catch
Rock It
Lost Woman Blues
Doctor Rock
Orgasmatron
Going to Brazil
Ace of Spades
Overkill

"Lemmy for ever!"
Cyril Cochard (Paris, France)

"I will try to translate one of my favourite memories with Motörhead,
I saw Motörhead 14 or 15 times in my life, and I'm only 28.

And I never met Lemmy...
I'm so sad about this...
But, the funniest memories I have with Motörhead happened on the song 'Hellraiser.'
Every unusual event in my (short) life happened with this song.
Everytime I go to festivals in Europe or famous concerts, the last song in my car is 'Hellraiser'. I promise, it's not my fault, I just put the CD 'March or Die' on and everytime, the last song is this one!
When I bought my Harleyn, the last song in the car was 'Hellraiser'... It's really funny!
Love you Lemmy!
See you in the over side."
Pierre Miglierina (Parroy nr. Nancy)

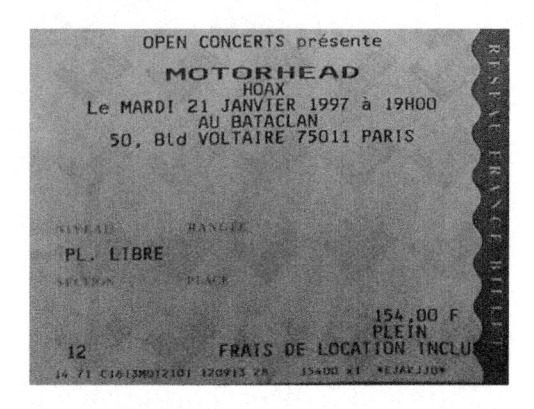

"Lemmy is the basis for everything!!!
Motörhead will remain forever in my heart!!!
My son's name is Lemmy."
Prein John (France)

"For me LEMMY was like a symbol of rébellion and of course the Godfather of Rock 'n' roll.
His MUSIC was a mix between heavy rock punk and rebel MUSIC...."
Edouard Jaques (Paris, France)

"I saw Motörhead for the first and the last time in 2007, this was in a little place in the southern France.
It was a great, great show. Motörhead rock and roll sound is forever in my head since a long, long time ago.
I want to thank them for this great pleasure..."

Jaques Menard (La Ciotat, nr Marseille)

"Lemmy forever."
Stephanie Barrier (Lyon, France)

*"I'm 22 and I'm listening Lemmy and Motörhead since I'm 11 years old.
My first concert was in 2007, one of a greatest Day in my life.
Motörhead was all my life.
I'm wake up, eating, fucking with Motörhead.
The first time I fuck was on 'No Class'.
Lemmy was my spiritual father and the last man who lived without rules.
Thanks for all, thanks Lemmy and Motörhead.
My teenage years were fucking cool with you.
♣♣♣ "*
Thomas Civieri (France)

*"Well, I think the whole thing began when I was 15 years old....
I was in my bedroom and I was bored to death listening to the radio. I was looking for a new radio station when I heard something completely different, crazy, brutal. The radio host was talking about this band called Motörhead...
The day after I went to the music shop and I was desperately looking for a Motörhead CD.
The only one I found was that compilation called 'Welcome To The Bear Trap' (released in 1990), bought it and listened to it over and over...
I saw my first MH concert in 1995 in Paris, I was 19 years old and my ears were certainly not prepared for this show!!
I couldn't hear anything for 3 days lol!
I'm a lucky girl who works backstage at Hellfest Festival (France).
I met Mikkey and Phil in 2010 and finally Lemmy in 2015 just after the show and he was tired, however he did not refuse to take a picture and I can't stop smiling as long as he was holding me in his arms, I was so happy.
25 years after, concerts after concerts, festivals after festivals, album after album my love for Motörhead is never-ending."*
Melanie Bunel MHB4186 (France)

RONNIE PRODUCTIONS
PRÉSENTE

motörhead

+
GRIP INC
+
PHOBIMANIACS
EN CONCERT
PARIS
ZENITH
SAMEDI 27 MAI 1995 A 19H

HARD N HEAVY

145 FRANCS   N° 0311

Germany

Capital City: Berlin
Population: 81,459,000
Currency: Euro
Bands: Rammstein, Scorpions, Accept, Helloween

"I think I was about 8 or 9 Years old, when I First heard the 'Rock 'n' Roll' Album on tape from the big brother of a friend of mine. I heard some harder music before, like Maiden, Priest, Anthrax or German thrash metal. But this Album was different.   It was not as mythic, like Maiden or clean like Priest or brutal like Kreator. But it was Rock 'n' roll music in its purest form.
From this day on, Motörhead became a straight line in my life. Motörhead   forever   -   Forever   Motörhead!
Andi Stark MHB 3981 (Igensdorf, Germany)

"My favourite is 'We Are the Road Crew'.
It reminds me of what my singer in my band told me, when Lemmy came out to watch the Crew at work after Motörheads Gig.
Lemmy told him that he rather watching honest people at work instead of listening to the bitches at the aftershow Party. That means Lemmy to me. Always honest to his bones and a gentleman.
Oh, btw, everytime I play 'Ace of Spades' I greet the great man in my mind and I thank him for becoming a bass player myself.
Strange but true."
Bass Sistah (Rockscars)

"Over the years I saw Motörhead on stage for 71 times. The last time in Düsseldorf Germany in November 2015.
We all knew that the end of Motörhead was near. Several cancelled shows, the pictures of Lemmy thin and those eye bags.
Anyway, we booked the two shows in London because I and my

friends wanted to see the band live at the mighty Hammersmith Odeon…but it never will happen.

Over the years I met him two times in person, when I worked for a metal magazine in '84 during the Easter 'Metal Blast' concerts in Dortmund and in '98 in Cologne where the band was on a promoting tour for the album 'Snake Bite Love'.

Both times I remember him as a really honored calm man. But why is Lemmy always in my life? In 1979 I heard them for the first time in my life on a German radio show. No one knew the band at that time. The reporter says be careful of your ears this song is fast and loud. What did I hear? Double bass mayhem of the mighty 'Overkill'. I went to my local record store and the new album called 'Bomber' was out, my first Motörhead record in '79.

Another story of Motörhead is in our ears, more precisely in the ears of my lovely wife Monika. We are out to see Motörhead on the 29th November in the year '87, it was the 'Eat The Rich' tour. Opening act was no one else than King Diamond and Destruction. Dude this gig was loud, louder than hell and during the Motörhead gig my girlfriends gets a hearing disorder. She spent up to one week in hospital until she could hear up to nearly a 100%, so until today, Motörhead is in our heart but also we can say 'killed by deaf' it is also in our ears.

If you take a look at the last 25 years or so Motörhead played in my area before the Christmas time in Düsseldorf, Oberhausen or Cologne. It was my ritual to wait during the summer for the latest tour updates, book my ticket and wait for the Motörhead day at around Christmas time.

What will I do in 2016?

I think I will meet some friends, have a drink or two and then we will watch a DVD of their classics concerts.

This is my story with Lemmy for over 37 years of loving and supporting the band…the wörld is yours….

Of course my wife's birthday is on the 10th January. We celebrate into it. But at around midnight as we raise our glasses the funeral has begun and we sit in front of the computer and watched it live from Los Angeles to hear the last tune of Lem's Bass feedback coming out of his Marshall stack…we've come full circle."

Siggi Hahn (Herne, Germany)

"I wish, I could write a personal 'Motörmemory' but my English is not good enough."
Max Power MHB 3412 (Flensburg, Germany)

"Lemmy was a man with a fine sense of humor and a feeling, when he has to be loud or not.
His points of view on many things going on around the world deeply impressed me.
He was our idol, mentor and hero for over 37 years and of course, a cool guy!
I remember 2 funny stories about him and the band: before a gig in Hemmerleinhalle Neunkirchen near Nuremberg Phil was sitting in the dressing room. There was a small window going outside to the hallway and he starts drumming against it. But a few hits later the glass broke and he just laughed. After the gig we and the whole band drove to Nuremberg city. We entered a hard rock club called 'Metal Mania' and Lem said to the owners "Ok, here is some money, all guests have to go now, we will make a private party."
I cannot remember all details of this party, but to mess with the hangover, it must have been great! What year was it? 'Iron Fist' or 'Bomber' tour? I dunno, cos I am getting old brö!"
Fred Burger (Erlangen, Germany)

"LEMMY = Rock 'N' Roll"
Karl Heinze (Hasbergen, Germany)

"I hear Motörhead since 1989 - before this I heard other music. My first song I've heard was 'Ace of Spades' ♠ in a Bar that was called "American House" (in Germany).
I loved this song and have been often in this Bar. I had lovesickness and the music helped me very much.
I heard Motörhead over all these years and Lemmy was always a Person and man, I liked very much because he lived Rock 'n' Roll to the bone.
He lived his life like he wants to live and didn't care, what other people think about him, his lifestyle or his words. He said, what he thought and did what he said. He was a very nice person, a sexy and great man, a reader, a man who wrote great texts in his music, a helpful person, a friend, a great musician who played with passion, a deep thinker and he is a legend for me.
I feel so sad that I have never been to a concert of Motörhead or met Lemmy. I loved the music from Motörhead in good times and in sad/ bad times because it helps in all situations... it and Lemmy gave and give me so much power and energy with this wonderful, great Rock 'n' Roll.

My favourite song is "Rock 'n' Roll" because this song always gives me the energy & power of Lemmy & Motörhead.
Tell's me that if there's only Rock 'n' Roll you have it's not so bad. His music gives you strength and power to carry on, never give up, do your best, "till the end " "when the sky comes looking for you".
I admire that he stood on stage so often and till the end (even if he was so ill since the last two years), gave interviews although talking was very exhausting for him, produced the last album 'Bad Magic'.
On his 70th birthday he could look at all who were there on his day, so sorry that his body and him were so weak that he couldn't party like he did earlier.
I always thought 'Oh, Lemmy, give yourself a time to relax!' - but he would not do this - because he did it like always before. Giving all. He was 40 years the best!
His band members shared so much time with him and we all couldn't imagine, how sad they feel. And his son would have a very difficult time with the loss of Lemmy.   All people and friends which knew Lemmy sure feel very sad.   My condolences to all of them.   I am sad, shocked and will go on hearing his music and show all the concerts and interviews with Lemmy/ Motörhead.   The wörld (!ö) is sooo sad because he died.   We couldn' t imagine, how many people are in his favourite bar or on livestream with the Rainbow Bar & Grill' at 9.1.16 to think of him and give him a worldwide memorial evening / day / hours. Do it like it's written on the Motörhead page: hear Motörhead louuuud, with people & friends who love him and his fabulous music, always remember him and his words...and drink a "Lemmy's drink"- Jack Daniels & Coke on him!
He will be our hero, a true legend and forever in our hearts."
Märy Röse - My new name changed 28.12.15 from a "Rose" to "Röse" (Friedrichshafen, Germany)

"It was my first contact. The beginning of a lifestyle. It's 1987 in Donauwörth. I have been here a many times. Now he's gone but the lifestyle is still alive. Rock on Lemmy."
Sven Maier MHB 3229 (Erding, Germany)

"Lemmy is a legend! I Love him. He is my greatest inspiration He is like a father I never had. His music took me out of crises. I can't find words to explain how much I love this man.

He has a great sense of humor and every time I saw an interview I had to laugh a lot!
It's difficult to realize that this wonderful man is no longer there. Especially because my brother died of cancer too. #fuckcancer
I hope my thoughts could take you, I haven't written a lot but I hope you feel how much I love him. This is a very emotional thing for me."
Iris Diehl (Bayreuth, Germany)

"His music always cheers me up no matter how I feel.
He will be missed."
Claudia Wilms (Bielefeld, Germany)

"I got into Motörhead when I was 12 years old. My best friends gave me the 'Bastards' album. One year later, in 2006, my parents took me to my first Motörhead gig.
When I saw Lemmy stepping on stage for the first time in my life… I was caught. The band and their music accompanied me through all the ups and downs of my teenage years. So it was only logical that as soon as I became a major, I made an appointment at my local tattoo shop to decorate my arm with a beautiful picture of 'snaggletooth'. Three years later, the first Motörboat set sail. I couldn´t make it, because it was too expensive for me that year. But as soon as I saw all the pictures and read the reviews of it, I knew I had to be part of it in the coming year.
So, I scraped all my money together and booked my flights as well as my cabin for Motörheads Motörboat 2015. It was my first time across the big pond and also my first time abroad all on my own. Therefore I was pretty anxious when I got onto the plane that took me to Miami. I was afraid, that my expectations were way too high and that I wouldn´t manage to get along in the USA. My trip consisted of some days in Miami, two road trips to the last concerts of Motörheads current tour in Florida and the cruise itself. What could I say? Every penny I spent on it was worth it, since it was the best vacation of my life. I managed to meet some of my idols face to face (including Mikkey and Phil), I met many great people and saw some great shows in the middle of the ocean. It was great to watch Lemmy gambling every night at the casino. It was great to see all the bands in such a private sphere and it was great to be among people that feel just the same about it.
Back in Germany I was able to see a couple more shows of the current tour, including Motörheads last gig in Berlin on the 11th of December.

With 2015 coming to an end, I thought to myself, that I had a perfect year. Especially the Motörboat cruise crowned it and I was sure nothing could mess it up. That was until my girlfriend woke me up on the 29th of December with the words:
"Tom, Lemmy is dead!"
I was shocked, I felt gutted and I still can't quiet grasp what it means.
From time to time, when I hear some particular songs I still can´t manage to stop the tears, but when that happens I also have a slight smile on my face. I know that my hero lived his life to the fullest and that there is actually nothing to be sad about. Motörhead and especially Lemmy influenced me in many ways. They taught me to take responsibility for my actions, to show respect to everyone who deserves it and to stand up for myself and the things I believe in. I am grateful, that I was able to experience their music and their attitude firsthand.
I will keep their music and all the memories in my mind for the rest of my life. Lemmy was right when he wrote the song "Till the End" from "Bad Magic": There is one thing I will never lose and that is his singing in my head that will still be with me till the end."
Tom Albrecht MHB 3673 (Dresden, Germany)

Max-Schmeling-Halle Berlin 11th December 2015

Bomber
Stay Clean
Metropolis
When the Sky Comes Looking for You
Over the Top
The Chase is Better Than the Catch

Lost Woman Blues
Rock It
Orgasmatron
Doctor Rock
Just 'Cos You Got the Power
No Class
Ace of Spades
Whorehouse Blues
Overkill

*"I really do appreciate your idea of a book about Lemmy.
I myself have written a song the day after Lemmy passed away.
It is called "The Servant And The God Of The Metal Nation". I have also recorded and performed it a few days later. You may watch it on YouTube:*

https://youtu.be/N6RmKj9Ulf4"

The Servant And The God Of The Metal Nation

I give a goddamn shit 'bout conformity!
Just free your soul from uniformity!
Speak out your mind in veracity!
Just raise your glas - Cherio! - and lay back in serenity!

You live! You fly!
You laugh and you die!

A joker and a gentleman!
A truly inspiration!
A gangster and a gambling man!
The servant and the god
Of the Metal Nation!

The son of a preacher man
The leader of the pack
The Godfather of Rock'n Roll
The knife in your back

You live! You Fly! ...

Falo Faltu (Wuppertal, Germany)

"Back in May 1998, I went to my first Motörhead Gig.
It was in a small Location in my Hometown Völklingen in Germany. It was the first time that I saw Motörhead, they destroyed my Ears and infected my Soul.
Me, at 16 years old had never ever seen something like this. For me it was a revelation and it shaped my life.
After that I attended all the concerts that were possible for me. It was more than 40 Concerts in which I participated. At the best times I saw 3 concerts a week throughout the country.
One of my greatest memories was after a gig in Saarbruecken, when I first met Lemmy personally.
The saddest memory was the last concert I attended, which was also one of the last concerts of Motörhead at all in November 2015. I know this would be the very last time I saw them.
He already looked bad, and his voice was no longer as powerful as it once was. But anyway the show kicked ass. Respect Mister K.
I knew the day would come, but that it went so fast I did not expect. I am proud to see that piece of Rock and Roll History over years. At least one day my children would ask:
"Dad, what is that Motörhead?" and the only right answer is "Everything louder than everything else"
R.I.P."

Christian Shrönk (Völklingen, Germany)

"It must have been around late '96 early '97 when I was first introduced to the sound of Motörhead via the end credits of 'Hellraiser III'. At first I was irritated about the fact that other than in part I and II there was not the classical score playing over the film yet a heavy sounding metal song lead by a very unique sounding voice but with repeat viewing I liked it more and more.
So my introduction to Motörhead and Lemmy Kilmister was through my love for horror and even though I remained a casual fan, it happened that we kept crossing paths.
A former friend of mine was and still is a big metalhead and he introduced me to a lot of bands and it is because of this that I grew fond of the sound of Motörhead and especially one song became sort of our hymn whenever preparing for partying, it was 'Ace of Spades' and I kept this tradition up with other friends and it remained a staple in their playlists as well as in mine.
Lemmy was someone you sadly, not in real life but in media, kept bumping into, so even if I hadn't listened to his music, I saw him in

movies like 'Hardware' and as well as in his appearances in a bunch of Troma productions and it was a welcome and funny moment to see him as the president in 'Return to Class of Nuke 'Em High'.
Through interviews and behind the scenes material I learned that he was quite a character, he was truly metal through and through and he had a unique voice.
I am thankful that I discovered the sounds of Motörhead and this incredible voice of Lemmy and their love for metal, it is mostly thanks to them that I became at least a part time metalhead.
It is incredible how people you never have met can influence your life with what they do, giving you joy and shaping your memories with their lyrics, their movies, their art."
Morten Rolfson (Hamburg, Germany)

"In November 1999 I sat listening to the 'Snake Bite Love' album and then the blame came on. I smoked a lot of hashish when I was 16 and instantly when listening to this song and those lyrics, I went and threw everything hash related into the garbage. I never touched the shit since then. Thanks to Motörhead.
Was fortunate and was granted an audience at the White Trash Bar in Berlin, the night before the cancelled Berlin gig in 2015.
I had a brief chat with Lemm, got to show him the last 'Snaggletooth' that Joe Petagno drew with the Motörhead logo above it, he was really interested and stared at my arm and said "oh really", when I told him about it.
I told him I had the original framed with me, and that I was gonna give it to him tomorrow, but that did sadly not happen.
Chatted with Paul after the tour and was supposed to send it, but it never happened.
Will always treasure that meet and chat."
Kent Julnes (Hellborn, Thuringen, Germany)

WHERE IS THE REST OF THE BAND?

"A friend of mine was working in production for different rock bands that were on tour about twenty years ago. He used to call me and asked me to come by and see him when he was coming to Hamburg/Germany. I usually went there in the afternoon to meet him backstage at Docks and hang out for a while.
Most of the bands he was touring with, I'd never seen before. And I had never heard of them either. When the shows started I used to go see the first couple of songs, see if they were any good, but

mostly they were not. At least not for me. In fact, a lot of bands were just making some terrible noise. So usually after about three songs I went straight back to my friend backstage to hang out with him again. I thought spending time with him was more important than ruining my ears by listening to bands with a front man yelling and screaming as high as if someone permanently kept stepping on the tail of a cat.

Today I can't even remember who any of those bands were. But as bad as they sounded to me at that time, it didn't prevent me from going to see my friend again in the future. Lucky me!

Because the next time my friend called things turned out to be a bit different.

Same procedure as always. The band starts playing and only this time I was instantly hooked. What's this? What the fuck! After the third song I stepped closer and closer to the wall of speakers piled up left to the stage. If it had been possible, I would have climbed in! The power and the tunes that came out went straight through my body and shook me like a thunderstorm!

When the show was over, I went backstage right away. "That was unbelievable!" I said, the moment some of the band members got off stage passing me by. "Where is the rest of the band?"

"We're only three!"

That was in 1995. My personal kick-off moment with Motörhead. Twenty years ago.

Being a professional photographer, the band soon let me take their photos a couple of times over the years. Some of the photos, mostly black and white, were published on the "25 & Alive - Boneshaker" CD/DVD booklet and on the cover of the "Lemmy - White Line Fever" Autobiography. What an honour!

Thank you Lemmy! Thank you Phil! Thank you Mikkey!
What an incredible ride!
Thank you Motörhead!"

Nicola Rübenberg – Photography (Hamburg, Germany)

"Lemmy was like I father to me.
When everything got too much and I needed someone, I could just play a Motörhead song and feel home and safe. I never got the chance to see them live but it felt like they were there for me."

Celina Meyer (Saterland)

"LEMMY MEANT SO MUCH TO ME.
HE TAUGHT ME TO LIVE AS I SEE FIT, AND IF PEOPLE DON'T ACCEPT U AS U ARE, FUCK EM- U DONT NEED THEM!!

ROCK OUT FOREVER!!!
War Wolf (Niederndorf, Germany)

"Thank you so much Lemmy for being such an inspiration in my life. You had always inspired me in my musical influence and the way you played your bass guitar was great influence for me, as well.
I always wanted to play a Rickenbacker bass like you did and believe me, one day, I will have one.
There is no other band from which I bought more CD's and no other band I spent more seconds to listen.
Lemmy, thank you for Motörhead which has given me support during a really hard time at school where I have been bullied and disgraced for many years. In this time you gave me the strength to survive every single day, knowing that I will be better than anyone of them could ever be.
I am afraid that I could see you guys only one time in Stuttgart. But this was my first concert I went and I will never forget it.
Lemmy with every Jack & Coke I will drink, I will remember you. Rest in Piece, Lemmy!"
Felix Ege (Dettingen an der Erms, Germany)

"Great Idea... a "Book of Memories"
I saw Lem with Motörhead 5 times live here in Germany but unfortunately I never met him personally.
32 years I was a loyal fan of a great man and his Band. This man gave me a lot on all these years and I wanted to give him a little bit back.
So I started, in beginning of 2015, and worked like a crazy at my "Tribute" for Lemmy. It should be finished at the 70th birthday, but... that don't get reality.
And now... the work goes on and I hope to end this project in December, as a homage to Lemmy.
Okay, thats my story about Mr. Ian Fraser "Lemmy" Kilmister.
P.S. for details please have a look on my side:
https://m.facebook.com/NUT-S-LOS-Entertainment-1218287404854658/?ref=bookmarks
Stefan Schubert (Germany)

"Well...I love Motörhead but I have no big story, just seen them several times."
Werner Oehme (Dortmund)

"I have never met Lemmy face to face but I saw Motörhead live once. Unfortunately the concert fell on the same day like an op I had. So I had the op in the morning and around midday I was already on my way to Hamburg. I saw that concert!
The decision was a bit crazy, but that's what metal fans do, isn't it? It was the 9th of December 2015, the penultimate concert Motörhead has ever given. That's something I can tell my grandchildren! So I saw the legend and my father his hero for at least once in our lives.
Lemmy taught me always to be myself and to do things my way. He must have been a great guy!"
Gina Heitmann (Greifswald, Germany)

Alsterdorfer Sporthalle Hamburg
9th December 2015

Bomber
Stay Clean
Metropolis
When the Sky Comes Looking for You
Over the Top
The Chase is Better Than the Catch
Lost Woman Blues
Rock It
Orgasmatron
Doctor Rock
Just 'Cos You Got the Power
No Class

Ace of Spades
Whorehouse Blues
Overkill

"I met Lemmy once after a concert in Bremen/Germany at a Rock 'n' Roll Bar.
After finishing my beer I wanted to go, opened the door and Lemmy stood in front of me. Me:
"Wow, Lemm, fucking great concert, thanks a lot" and shook his hand. He with his rusty voice:
"Alright!"
I had a drink with Phil Campbell and him and had a good talk with Phil and was impressed that these guys don't get pissed at the hotel lobby, no, they go to the darkest bars in town. That was a night I will never forget.
RIP Lemmy"
Roman Urbanietz (Bremen, Germany)

"Motörhead was the band with whom I grew up. I remember that I got to listen to harder music earlier as a small child, especially Motörhead, since my father listened every morning in the shower, usually at full volume level.
He also ran a shop with Metal Shirts, where I for example often got 'Snaggletooth'. Although I was never averse to this music and this "monster" in the Motörhead shirt was really cool, it did not interest me particularly as a small child.
One day the annoying pop and children's songs became a pain in the neck, and I was just very thirsty for something hard (perhaps was because my father since my parents' wedding heard less and less metal, and for example, his long hair was cut off, much to my dislike?)
What is cooler than a long haired Daddy? But on this day he was wearing a Motörhead shirt, and when I saw it (it was the motive for 30th Anniversary) I knew I what I should look for.
I went to the huge CD rack, and at some point I saw something by Motörhead, pulled it out and then I looked at the image, the exact monster was shown fighting in a battle, the same as my fathers t-shirt.
I took the CD, put it in my discman, put my headphones on and pressed 'play'. Since that moment I was an absolute Motörheadbanger in the first hour.
I built little by little my small collection consisting of all that

Motörhead released and began to let my hair grow.
A short time later I discovered other bands, such as Metallica, Sepultura, Black Sabbath, Iron Maiden and co. And so I came to the Metal. Despite being so influenced, no band inspired and excited me like Motörhead, then as now.
Finally, I got to see Motörhead live in Berlin in 2012 (it was genuinely my first Metal concert).
Let's say, I expect that it is noisy, but when I came and Anthrax played I thought I would be shot, so popped purely the double bass. Then Motörhead - absolutely gorgeous!
After this concert I myself with the thought "Okay, I've seen at least once live my favorite band before it no longer exists", but then I invited my buddy in November 2015 to come along to Motörhead Hamburg.
I think I have all year in anticipation nothing but Motörhead part (except for the new Maiden album).
After a wait until December it was time - I was allowed to see my favorite band from the second row live!
As the intro began to 'Bomber', I thought, I get an orgasm. I'm happy like a little kid! And although Lemmy no longer looked as well, he played down the concert with dignity. A good buddy of mine was then still in Berlin at the concert. We both had no idea that we had just experienced the last Motörhead concerts live. Forever the last. But we knew how lucky we were to have seen it again.
One month later I went at 1:00am to bed, totally exhausted I threw a quick look on my mobile phone ... a message from an American Facebook friend 'Lemmy died.' Only these 2 words.
I searched for a while and found that it was true. The tallest man in the world was gone. I was just shaking and crying in bed.
This year, 3 family members died, but no death has me so much taken as Lemmy. I finally got up and heard all Motörhead discs until the late hours of the morning. I owe this man so much ... that I have become as I am.
Great moments that I have experienced with this music, as well as 2 magnificent concerts that I will never forget and of which I will tell my grandchildren. I could write a book about my feelings about Motörhead and Lemmy, but I will not indeed be the only one here.
This man and this band was an extreme asset to my life, I will miss him very much! Fortunately we have his music forever, and I will carry to the heart and play 'Bastards' purely!"
Arthur 'Metalking' (Rostock, Germany)

"A story our Prof at University told us during class:
He's been on a festival in Germany as a lawyer and there had been some trouble backstage so he got involved and met Lemmy.
After the trouble was gone, he spoke to Lemmy and Lemmy had been on tour for months and of course, drunk a lot and during the conversation Lemmy asks where he is right now and didn't even have a clue on which continent (!) he was.
Might be in the 90's. That's rock 'n' roll, I will never forget this story and I'm not able to tell this how my Prof did!"
David Schäfer (Cologne, Germany)

"My wife bought me a Motörhead ticket for the Feb 26th show at Offenbach's Stadthalle as Christmas gift.
Became fully sad after hearing of Lemmy's passing shortly after.
The place where I saw Motörhead various times in their early years. I remember a concert in '83 or '84 with Twisted Sister (fucking posers). But different to other heavy rockers he would not ever put himself above others, although he really was much more iconic than the rest. R.I.P. Lemmy one of a kind Rock and Roller.
Us Hard & Heavy guys lost our Godfather - how he was called by Metallica and they are completely right."
Marcus Tiede (Offenbach, Germany)

"Saw Motörhead many times live. It was always impressive.
Some of the finest moments of my life are tied to Lemmy and his music. Especially a hard and exhausting stay in Amsterdam with near friends, listening mostly to Motörhead's 'No Sleep 'till Hammersmith'..."
Booriser Romanus (Nuremberg)

"RIP Lemmy the greatest rocker all time!"
Andreas Spörer (Thanhausen, Bayern, Germany)

"I have never had the chance to see them, but my son Roman and my daughter Dana and I are great fans.
R.I.P. Lemmy, we hear your music, you will always be with us."
Anja Leyhr (Müsingen, Germany)

"My first contact with Motörhead was, when I bought a record player from a neighbour. I had no records yet, so he gave me one. "Well, if you like it, I got another one from that band".
So the first was 'No Sleep 'til Hammersmith', the second (which I bought 45 minutes later) was the 'Beerdrinkers and Hellraisers'. I

*was completely in love. That was 1985.
I was raised by a single mom on social security in a middle-class area. Sometimes I even had to wear the clothes of neighbours-kids, because we just couldn't afford new stuff. So I was kind of an outsider, bum, you name it. Very few friends, if any...
And then there was Lemmy, who told me, that it was ok, that I was perfectly fine, going my own way, not to be member of the well off society. BUT: stay clean mate, that does not necessarily mean to wash your legs...they can't get you then.
And show some integrity, that's most important.
Wise words I tried to live by for the last 30 years. My most important role model so far, not just an idol...
Now I play bass in 2 punk rock and 1 blues band and run my own little shop for organics. I don't think my life would be the same if I never listened to Lem's words, oh and I only met him twice, in '88 for autographs after a show at the tour bus and in '89 when my buddy and me somehow made it behind the stage.
Lem didn't want to share my bottle of vodka...
"Thanks mate, I got my own" and off he went...
I saw them 17 times, the greatest moment was always 'Overkill', first row, completely exhausted and these 3 shadows in front of the strobe-lights, and then the song starts again and again...."*
Olli Röseler (Osnabrück, Germany)

*"In 2011 I took my eldest daughter Lily to her first ever Motörhead show here in Stuttgart.
Unfortunately, a couple of days prior to the gig, she broke her arm while inline skating and had it in a plaster cast.
I emailed the band's manager Todd Singerman and asked if we could get the cast signed by Lemmy and the boys. He liked the idea and generously provided us with two backstage passes.
The day came and we were both getting more and more nervous and excited. We were allowed backstage and were led into Lemmy's dressing room by Lemmy's then PA Alan Hungerford. And there he was. The big man himself.
He looked up, saw my daughter, said "oh, hello" and immediately put out his cigarette (which shows once again what a very considerate man he was). We shook hands and chatted for a bit. Lemmy wanted to know exactly how my daughter broke her arm. We had the plaster cast and various other things signed and a picture taken of the three of us.
Lemmy even gave my daughter two kiddies Motörhead shirts for her and her little sister, which, along with the plaster cast, are*

prized possessions in this house. After a bit more 'chit chat' it was time to say goodbye.
"I hope you will enjoy the show," Lemmy snarled.
"We sure will. Hope you enjoy it too" I replied.
"Oh, I certainly will" he laughed.
A final shake of hands and best wishes were exchanged and we went back into the audience area for a kick ass performance by the mighty Motörhead.
Unfortunately Phil and Mikkey were asleep at the time, so we didn't get to meet them. However, after the show we came across Duff McKagan, who was support act that year, who also signed the plaster cast.
After Lemmy's unfortunate passing, Lily and I even made it onto the BBC news website, when my wife submitted the story of our wee adventure.
Carsten Hahn MHB 2967(Gechingen)

"My husband took our daughter to her first Motörhead concert a few years ago.
Unfortunately she broke her arm a few days before, but this did get her and her dad - a Motörhead devotee of many years - backstage to have her cast signed by the man himself.
He also gave her a couple of girly Motörhead t-shirts for her and her sister.
Duff McKagan signed that cast too, and it's a treasured thing."
Jacquie Hahn (Gechingen)

"I'm Felix, a promoter from Berlin, Germany and I saw Motörhead two times here in Berlin.
I never met Lemmy personally but I saw him live on stage and it was a blast everytime. - This man is a legend! The way he lived his life was unbelievable. He really lived his life and showed and teached us how to live a life right - until the end!
I still remember the day of the last show forever of Motörhead in Berlin. I stood backstage in front of the Motörhead dressing rooms and watched the local crew people bringing cigarettes and alcoholic drinks into the dressing room. It was funny but in this moment you could feel the spirit of Lemmy a little bit. This and the concerts of Motörhead were one of the greatest experiences in my life.
Lemmy was and is a piece of every metal heart. He left us his life's work, his music. 'Ace of Spades', 'Overkill' or my favourite song "In the Name of Tragedy' - every single one of them changed this

world (and also my life) a little bit.
It really was a pleasure to see and feel him live on stage. He was the greatest motherfucker I've ever known.
Thank you Lemmy for that! - You shall never be forgotten.
BORN TO LOSE - LIVED TO WIN!"
Felix Pirk (Berlin, Germany)

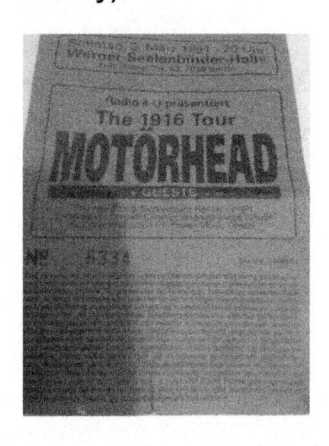

"I made an art project for art class in grade 11 two years ago.
We did stencil prints in the style of street artist Banksy and I chose a picture of Lemmy with a quote because it resembled his lifestyle, reminds you to live the life you want to have and it shows Lemmy's sense of humour pretty well.
Luckily, I had the chance to see Motörhead last year at the 'Rock am Ring' festival in Mendig and I was absolutely amazed how he kept being so powerful on stage after all these years.
I live near Siegen in Germany, which is the birthplace of the famous baroque painter Peter Paul Rubens and the hometown of German thrash metal pioneers Accu§er. By the way, "siegen" is the German word for "to win". "Born to lose, live to win". Or in the German version "Geboren um zu verlieren, leben um zu gewinnen."
Karlheinz Georg (Germany)

"A crappy day now is coming, so slow to end. Sometime during the morning I had to overcome my state of shock and was fully determined to once again take the edge to say farewell.
Now that I could see a few moments ago the bottom of the second bottle of beer, I felt somehow that it made me feel more depressed.

*When you're mentally pretty tired, alcohol is not a good counselor.
For me today the world has collapsed and at the moment I feel pretty shit and alone. I always thought you were immortal and this gave me the faith to never give up.
You were on a good day my companion, but also in the hard times and whenever the void tried to get wider you were there and you kicked me in the butt and said –
"Arise wimp and fight."
And now? Yes, I know death comes to us all and yet I feel now, at this moment, a bit down.
Okay maybe that's unfair, but you're gone and I'm still here.
Scheiss situation!
Many will read these sentences, shake their heads and think "what a full post", but just imagine there is one thing on which you absolutely depend and which you hold dear and suddenly it's taken away from you, irrevocably.
When who know this feeling, perhaps you can understand?
Motörhead for Life!!"*
Karsten Haeberle (Friesack, Germany)

Greece

Capital City: Athens
Population: 10,955,000
Currency: Euro
Bands: Firewind, Nightfall, Septic Flesh,

*"I've never met Lemmy in person :(
But as a high school student, I was hearing all the time stories, about Motörhead's 1st appearance in Greece (12-13-14/March/1988), many troubles happened in these 3 days... Skirmishes with the police & with the fans among them...
So the 3rd time (1998), it was IMPOSSIBLE to lose Motörhead again, so I bought tickets for both days. Finally the moment has arrived, Lemmy appeared shaved for first time & the band kicked some ass. I'd like to mention, that I was partially deaf, after the second day... :)
I watched Motörhead many times (5-6 in total)
But the live appearance, that I will NEVER forget, It was in summer of 2005, in a very big festival in Holland (23 bands!), the 'Fields of Rock', some of the bands among others were: Papa Roach, Slayer, Velvet Revolver, Audioslave, Black Sabbath, Rammstein.
Motörhead's time was 15:00-16:00 (after Papa Roach & before Slayer).
They ended with 'Overkill'!!! (I have heard 'Overkill' live, many times before, but in small clubs, never in such a huge place!!!)
The sound was SO LOUD & SO MASSIVE!!! So I stayed frozen, motionless and shuddered...
The feeling was like a HUGE armored vehicle, is about to, DEMOLISH EVERYTHING AND RUIN THE PLACE!!!
As you understand, the festival for me was over, Motörhead were the best band of the day, by far. The only reason that I didn't leave so early, was only for Black Sabbath.
R.I.P. Lemmy, thanks for the memories, thanks for everything."*
Dimitrios (Jimi) Anestopoulos (Zografou, Athens, Greece)

Fields of Rock
Goffertpark, Nijmegen
Netherlands
June 18th 2005

Doctor Rock
Stay Clean
Love Me Like a Reptile
Killers
Over the Top
No Class
I Got Mine
In the Name of Tragedy
Dancing on Your Grave
Just 'Cos You Got the Power
Going to Brazil
Killed by Death

Ace of Spades
Overkill

Hungary

Capital City: Budapest
Population: 9,855,571
Currency: Forint
Bands: Five Finger Death Punch, Superbutt, AMD

*"The first rock that defines my musical taste.
God bless Lemmy!!!!!"*
Mangliár Ervin (Zalaszentgrót, Hungary)

Indonesia

Capital City: Jakarta
Population: 255,461,700
Currency: Indonesian Rupiah
Bands: Koil, Kekal, Slank, Superman Is Dead

"I'm a great fan of Lemmy Kilmister!"
Paul Rait (Medan, Indonesia)

Ireland

Capital City: Dublin
Population: 4,635,400
Currency: Euro
Bands: Thin Lizzy, The Answer, Primordial

"I wanted to share my memory of meeting Motorhead. Unfortunately the exact date has eluded both my memory and the research I could do online, but I know it was 1980 during the 'Bomber' tour that I saw Motörhead when they played in the Students Union, in UCD Belfield, Dublin.
I arrived at the gig to find all the external windows criss-crossed with masking tape like Blitz-era London and sandbags at the entrance. Wandering around the venue before the gig I spotted a casual acquaintance from other gigs including AC/DC during the same year, whom we only knew by the name Judas, talking with some people and I went over to say hi.
There was so much smoke, mostly hash in the air that I didn't realise until I was standing beside him, that he was talking to Lemmy, Phil Taylor and Eddie Clarke. I stood there completely overwhelmed and starstruck with my mouth half open like an idiot when Lemmy looked at me and said these immortal words –
"Alright?.......Are you going to pass that joint around or are you going to stand there staring till it burns yer fucking nose off".
What a night, what a gig, never experienced anything so loud and completely exhilerating ever since. I managed to get their signatures on the back of a cigarette box but lost during a chaotic period of my life.
Can't wait for the book, brilliant idea and such a fitting tribute to one of the very few people who actually deserve to be called legendary."

A Poem For Lemmy

I believe in Lemmy
I believe in Rock n Roll
I believe that only Motorhead
Can ease my wounded soul
How can the loss be counted
A hurt too great to mend
He'll live forever in my heart
Always....Till The End

Derek Carroll (Celbridge, Ireland)

"I've been a massive Motörhead fan since '95 when a friend of mine gave me a lend of Motörhead's 'Another Perfect Day' CD, when I heard the song one track mind I was converted there and then.
Sadly I never had the pleasure of meeting Lemmy but I saw them live for the first time in Brixton in '95 and have seen them in total 22 times, 18 of them headliners and had tickets for both Hammersmith gigs at the end of January.
I have truly no words to describe the impact Lemmy and Motörhead have had on my life for the last 21 years, Motörhead for me is not just a band but a take no bullshit, never let the bastards grind ya down way of life.
Motörhead's fast paced, everything louder than everything else, sleazy, filthy, heavy brand of Rock 'n' Roll is an institution in itself and will live on forever.
As a Motörhead fan, Lemmy's sudden death hit me hard but I'm beyond grateful for the 22 albums they left us with and the same number of times I've seen them live and I wish nothing but the best for Mickey and Phil for their future musical endeavors.
Peter Morrissey (Rathdrum, Wicklow, Ireland)

Israel

Capital City: Jerusalem
Population: 8,462,000
Currency: Israeli New Shekel
Bands: Orphaned Land, Salem, Melechesh

"I love Lemmy for ever, I'm his biggest fan in Israel!"
Dana Joseff (Israel)

Italy

Capital City: Rome
Population: 60,795,612
Currency: Euro
Bands: Lacuna Coil, Fleshgod Apocalypse, Zu

"So this is MY Story, the Day I met Lemmy.
July 2009, 3 shows in Italy: Rome, Firenze and Padova.
I'm from Parma, and Rome is not too far away for me, and I go to Firenze and Padova (the last was a gift from a friends for MY birthday).
I was in the morning in Firenze, and we spend a lot of time in the subterranean parking because is the hottest day in Italy (46 degrees), we eat salami; drink wine and beer till the show starts.
During the show, a friend take me apart, and give me the pass for the backstage aftershow (is the first time in MY life) and MY mind blow up..
The show is amazing like always, and at the end I pass the line between the stage and the audience.
Unbelievable! I'm inside, Mikkey was on my side, Phil talked to me like we know from a lot of time, Photo, smile, joke... But Lemmy don't come out and nobody enter in the dressing room... At the end, we leave, I'm very happy, but... No Lemmy...
Surfing the night I drive to Padova, stop for a sleep, and the morning after I was in the place of the show! Meet the others, go crazy with the show, but I don't have the pass this time.
When I'm ready to go back to home, I have a phone call, and my friend tell me wait to leave there is police on the road... So, I have some beer in my body, and I wait, in front of the entrance of the backstage to see who is coming. At 3 o'clock, came the tour manager and tell us (there is me and five or six people) two at a time and don't make trouble!
Somebody ask, What happened? And I tell, our dream come true!
I get a boy with a good camera, and I enter in the dressing room ...

I am in the same room with Lemmy... He ask if I need an autograph, I say, no, I need a photo with you, it's been 30 years I want a Photo with you!
We made the Photo, and what he say made the difference between Lemmy and other rockstar:
On the way back to home I cry, because yes, he was really a special man!"
Damiano Gioppa Giovanelli (Fontanellato, Italy)

Rock In Roma
Rome
July 15th 2009

Iron Fist
Stay Clean
Be My Baby
Rock Out
Metropolis
Over the Top
One Night Stand
I Got Mine
The Thousand Names of God
Another Perfect Day
In the Name of Tragedy
Just 'Cos You Got the Power
Going to Brazil
Killed by Death
Bomber

Whorehouse Blues
Ace of Spades
Overkill

"To be honest I cant really remember when exactly it was when Motörhead stepped into my life and changed it more and more during I grew up. I just know it was very, very early and all starts with an old LP of "No sleep till Hammersmith" which my dad played sometimes at home.
My dad said always I liked it straight away and I was asking very often for it. So I think it's becoming the LP we were playing the most at home quite quickly. We have still got an old family video which I saw for the first time a few years ago which shows me running through the living room, playing the air guitar and 'No Class' in the background was turned up at least till 10.
So I really need to say thanks to him and my mum because they brought me into all that and took me also to my first Motörhead gig when I was 8 in 1999.
They played in Biesenthal near Berlin on their 'Snake Bite Love' Tour at a Harley Davidson Biker Festival which was hosted from the Club Born To Be Wild. After that I couldn't wait till I can see them again. But that would take a while.
During the years I bought most of the albums and plenty of different stuff. My second gig was then in 2006 in Berlin and afterwards was no way back.
I went then every year to the gigs in Berlin and I had the pleasure to see the guys 12 times in total and one time Lemmy with his side-project the Head Cat.
In 2013 I moved to England and booked straight away a ticket for the Wolverhampton show. It was one of the first actions when I arrived at my new home. Unfortunately the tour was canceled because of the health problems of Lemmy.
In the years 2014 and 2015 my dream comes finally true and I saw them the first time in their home country. It was the show in Birmingham and the next day I made my way down to Wembley in London. Both gigs were amazing and I met so many great people. The last time I saw them live was at the Eden Project in Cornwall.
My favorite moment was in 2010 at the Arena Treptow in Berlin. My best mate and me were on the way to the gig and as always we started early to manage it to see the gig on the barrier. As we arrived at the venue a big tour bus came around the corner and we thought it's one of the support bands but we needed to find this

out.
As the bus rolled to the parking position Lemmy was next to the driver and we can't believe our eyes. As the door opened we said, "Welcome to Berlin Lemmy, how are you doing?" He just answered, "it's fucking cold in Berlin." We asked him if we could take some pictures with him and he said, "Yes of course."
After Lemmy Mikkey walks out of the bus and he had some time for a small talk and some pictures as well. We were the happiest boys in town.
These great moments and all the great concert nights I will never forget in my live. I am very proud to be a small part of the Motörhead family and I like to say thank you to all the great people I met. R.I.P. Lemmy!!! Your music will be with me... till the end."
Christoph Gollnick, MHB 3678 (Tavullia, Italy)

"I got autographs in Milan during 'Orgasmatron' tour.
I remember all of them (Philthy, Lem, Wurzel and Phil) were very nice.
I also saw Motörhead live at Hammersmith London in '90, great feeling being there."
Marco Pezzo (Milan, Italy)

"Lemmy is the 'essence of Rock'n roll.
He has never compromised with anything.
Miss you friend, you are in heaven watching over what remains of rock 'n' roll.
R.I.P. Lemmy Kilmister."
Italo Fulgenzi (Rome, Italy)

"For 13 years I have compiled the 'Past Tour Dates' page on the official Motörhead website. I began to be interested Motörhead in 1985 and I met Lemmy for the first time in 1995.
I met him about 35 times, except when Motörhead were playing in Sardinia for the only time in their careers, so having the chance to go with him four days of his stay on my island. I have attended a total of fifty two Motörhead shows in eleven different countries.
Lemmy at first glance would seem to be a person not easy to handle, everything is picked up confidence and then you discover the very unusual person that he is.
A very shrewd man and an outstanding knowledge of culture, while our car rides he even talked about Sardinian history ("an Englishman who came to speak to me of Sardinian history, sheer

madness" I told myself). Also a very jovial, very rarely I saw him in bad mood.
Nevertheless, despite his inner strength and his humanity, sometimes shows its weaknesses and vices, mixed with the hunger of those who still want to be there and get there, despite all the rock world knew his name. And I am sure this was the secret of his ongoing success.

Tuesday, August 16, 2005

The calm before the storm, I would say. I was quiet in my house when a call (that had the power to make me shake like a leaf) warns me - Lemmy decided to leave Venice and depart immediately for Cagliari. The arrival is scheduled for 19:35 at the airport. The promoter sends a Mercedes minivan with seven seats and I go there with my car.

Lemmy arrives. He shakes my hand and immediately goes outside to smoke, he is recognized and someone asks him for a photo. Phil Campbell is with him.

They ask me for stripper clubs (see), bowling (all closed those days) and casinos (there are none in Sardinia).

"What do you have then?" - asks Phil – "just sun and beaches?". Lemmy: "bitches everywhere!" and he points out two nuns walking not far from us.

After a while we meet again at the hotel, time to settle in and see each other at the bar, poolside.

We begin to talk about every kind of stuff, I ask him how he is, if he has recovered well (he had suffered from dehydration in early July). He replies that he feels fine and as for the dehydration, it was not as bad as some newspapers reported.

Then I start tapping on his shoulder: "I cannot believe that you are here!", he quickly replies: "And I can not believe I am in fucking Sardinia! Ha! Ha!"

Then he asked me if I liked 'Stagefright'. Me: "no, I did not buy because it is not yet in the stores here in Cagliari."

Actually 'Stagefright' was already available at least as online order, but then I didn't have much money, so I wanted to everything to hang around with him.

We stay a bit in the sun, Lemmy is inspired to sing a part of "O Sole Mio", an old and famous Italian song. He stopped after a couple of verses because he didn't know all the lyrics, so I sang another part of the song. More talk and an appointment to see each other later.

I went to see him at 11:00 p.m... A brief chat, then he asked me to play the fruit machines. I replied OK and ask him to get in my car. I often used to listen to Motörhead in my car but I never thought to have him on board! I ask him to fasten his belt and we went to a pool club where there were several machines. A good place for him I though, because he asked to stay away from Motörhead fans.

I stayed there all the time in another room, watching TV while Lemmy, literally crazy for those machines, changes coins all the time to feed the machine. Immediately I have ordered for him bourbon and coke with lots of ice (he always drinks whiskey and coke). Sometimes I look through a small window to be sure his glass is always refilled in time. Until about 2:00 am in the room there were also two young boys, mumbling about "that strange English gentleman with moustache", as they call him. As soon as they go Lemmy stays alone and I tell him he can light a cigarette. In Italy it is forbidden to smoke in closed spaces open to public.

The hall is owned by two of my cousins, they know Lemmy is playing the fruit machines and they don't mind to stay open as long as he wants to stay.

At one point, one of my cousins comes toward me, laughing and says, "Look what he's doing!" I look out the room and see Lemmy standing in front of the machines, putting coins into two machines at the same time and pushing buttons, like he was playing a piano.

At 4:30am, Lemmy looks at his watch and asked me to return to the hotel. I keep the radio turned off; I just want to enjoy the talk with him. As we arrive at the hotel he asks me to call him again in the morning around 11am.

When I drove with him in the car usually he spoke of 'life on the road', stories of glory and dust, which are part the world of rock and roll.

I told him about some difficult travel I did to Germany to see Motörhead and he tells me about touring with the Michael Schenker Group. The singer was strongly stuttering (I think he was Gary Barden), except when he sang, then to talk with Lemmy he was forced to sing all the time!

Then he talked about poor Dee Dee Ramone, dragged to the grave because of heroin (Dee Dee was his real friend in the Ramones).

He tells me about a concert on the beach in Greece, part of the stage collapsed in the sand and they had to play "uphill". He told me stories of girls, inevitable. At least for one story I would have to plug my ears!

Wednesday August 17th, 2005

I call Lemmy at 11am and he tells me to show up at 1p.m, if I remember. Lemmy is used to sleep in the morning, but I can't do that. I stay in the pool with him, with us there are some roadies and a friend of mine. The day before I asked what he wanted to see, so I plan to go the archaeological museum, where there are also relics of 8,000 years ago. Among other things there is also a marble statue of Julius Caesar.

I ask him if he wants to take a picture with him, "No, because then people will think I am two thousand years old! ", he says. I believe that Caesar would have wanted a photo with Lemmy! :-)

The highlights of the museum are the ancient small bronze statues and we spent some time talking about the bronze age. "The Bronze age!" he says, with a smile. :-)

We leave the museum, which is located inside the Castle, in the heart of Cagliari. The first settlements of the city date back to 3500 years ago and were in the lagoon area. Then the city was moved onto a rocky hill for security reasons. The geological structure enabled the construction of colossal walls, interrupted only by four huge towers for surveillance that regulated access.

Let's take a short walking tour of the castle, admiring the view from the walls of the city and talking with Lemmy of what has been the history of our capital, the World War II bombings and so on.

He shows much interest in the story, as usual, and I explain the origins of the Sardinia flag. He is always reading history books, I have never met in my life a more avid reader than him.

The walk ends at the Bastion of St. Remy, where begins a monumental staircase that leads down to the less ancient part of Cagliari. We stay there to talk in a cafe and inevitably, it starts flowing with whiskey and cola. (When I translate this into English, I learn that the most authoritative American magazine "Food and Beverage magazine said they wanted to give the name 'Lemmy' to the classic blend of Jack Daniels and Coca Cola).

After a while 'Lemmy decided it was time to go home and asked me to come and take him down in the big lift that goes down the Bastion.

While in that I reached the point agreed with the car, I take 'Another Perfect Day' and shove it into the player. Whatever you think of Brian Robertson, it is one of my favorite albums. We get in the car and after a few minutes, I turn on the car stereo, putting the title track on. I was wondering about to see his reaction. First seconds with low volume. After ten seconds Lemmy turns up the volume. After another few seconds: Lemmy again puts the volume so high. He keeps the pace beating his hand on the door. The song comes in the middle: "Ha! We put the fucking gong at this point."

Lemmy is "captured" by the riffs, playing the song with his air bass! 'APD' and 'Inferno' were the only CD's that those days I left in the car. Deliberately did not add more CD's, because I have learned over the years that with Lemmy it's best to be as spontaneous as possible.

Before getting out of the car he asked for the CD, "I want to download it on my PC, I want to listen to it tonight."

After the break we met again at the hotel around 21:30. I show him a business card about a strip club, it is one of those cafes where it is better to go with al least 100 Euros in your pocket. Lemmy asks me to go, I do not pay attention to the time and actually we get there too early, just 22:00. We have to wait but Lemmy is not the kind of guy that waits

He says "let's go to the pool tables." OK. Let's go back to that pool tables and the fruit machines. As we were driving to the pool tables, Lemmy tries to sing "Buonasera Signorina" by Fred Buscaglione and also begins to sing "Volare" by Domenico Modugno: "Volaaaree, oh-oh, cantaaaree, oh-oh-oh-oh... I'm singing in italian too!".

I must admit I liked that short cover version by Lemmy :-) "Can you replace 'Going to Brazil' with Volare?" LOL!

At 1:30 (a bit early), due to a misunderstanding with Stefan (the lighting technician who was with us), Lemmy leaves the club and I take him to the hotel. Actually me and Stefan wanted to go in the small bars along the beach and come back to pick him up later.

Anyway, I didn't complain too much because I had the chance to go back home to sleep properly, because staying awake most of the nights, drinking jack and coke from time to time, it was getting me tired. I had the feeling that I wouldn't survive to that kind of life.

We agree to meet in the afternoon tomorrow but he can't tell me the time because that afternoon has to come with his girlfriend, he tells me to call him around 17:00 to update.

Thursday August 18th, 2005

Before calling Lemmy I go anyway in the afternoon to the hotel to talk to Motörhead tour manager, I look to the pool, where he told

me he was waiting. By chance I see Lemmy in a swimming costume, diving!
Later I go back to the hotel and had the chance to meet his girlfriend. She was Moua, Swedish singer from Meldrum. Who was with us at the thirtieth anniversary in London, I saw her on stage for 'Killed By Death'.
We get in the car, with us my friend Piero Bonetti (owner of Fabrik, club where the aftershow party will take place), in the backseats Lemmy and Moua. I notice Lemmy put on the same boots he used in 2003 on stage for some shows, white ones with the star in the centre. He had them made in Texas but the design was inspired by an Italian medal of the last war. Ugly or beautiful?
Depending on your point of view. No doubt they fitted his style.
A stop at a pizzeria and then off to the Poetto, Cagliari's main beach. The Poetto is eight kilometers long and is full of bars where concentrates the summer movida. Often they host live music.
We go in the first little bar and I realize that Lem doesn't feel comfortable, he agreed to go to that beach club upon Moa's request (but now I do not remember why). He asked me twice not to move too much, even five minutes in car for him was too much, unless we go to places he likes :-) This is because he spent much of his life on the bus and he tended to be nervous when we drove too much.
However it is impossible to get bored with Lemmy, we enjoyed anyway that moment. I thought there was a rock band that night but we saw this strange band, kind of reggae lullaby. Boring. So boring that at some point Lemmy says: "What is that shit?!". Lemmy watched them for a few seconds and started to laugh. We didn't have tomatoes to throw them, unfortunately.
Then we finish the whiskey and cola and we go to another little bar.
This beach bar is very crowded and Lemmy asked to go around to get to the tables, he does not want to go into the crowd.
We stayed there some time, Lemmy was asked for some photos by fans. We chat and listen to another band, which was definitely better than the previous one. Lemmy at one point says: "Stefano, what time is it?"
"2:20am".
And he looks at me smugly, also because he sees Moua is a bit 'tired and DEFINITELY wants to go back to the hotel.

As soon as we finish our whiskey and cola Lemmy says: "Let's go to play fruit machines!". Moua, "You go to play fruit machines, after you take me to the hotel! ". How Lemmy had expected.

I go to the car with a Finnish girl, she came here to write about Motörhead and she was staying in the same hotel (then also told me that it was her first Motörhead concert!).

So we get in the car and I got Lemmy in the backseat again. He was excited to have girls around. I put on the 'Inferno' CD and Lemmy started to sing 'In The Name Of Tragedy', I think his favorite song of the album (Lemmy singing in my car, it was a dream come true!). At some point he pushed my right leg, to make me to push the hammer down.

In a brief time we overtake 120 Km/h. Slalom among other cars, Lemmy telling me to speed up and make the bends on two wheels and the girls pleading to slow down.

"What Lemmy says is an order", I replied.

Another infringement by immediate withdrawal of the license and then I slow down, too many cars sounded their horns in protest.

There is an epilogue to this story: the day after the Finnish girl says me: "You're terrible Stefano, Lemmy told me also that you use to text with your phone, while driving."

"Oh no - I said - it is not true, he is kidding you!"

As we leave the girls at the hotel we go to the pool hall. Same story of the previous evenings, except this time I waited with Lemmy for a while, he was completely blissed at the game.

He stayed seven hours standing on the machines, without even going to the toilet. At 7am I was so tired, I went inside the room and asked him to go back to the hotel,

"before I sleep on the pool tables" . He replies: "sorry, I forgot my wristwatch at the hotel and I didn't know what time is it."

At 7:30 we arrived at the hotel about: goodnight or good morning? We agree to an interview for the Italian Motörhead fan site – 'Motörhead Italia', even though he doesn't like interviews. He replies, "It's not that I do not like interviews, I don't like the stupid questions!"

Friday 19th August 2005

I already knew that Lemmy would stay in the hotel all day with Moua, before going to the venue after the interview.

In the afternoon I phoned and he told me to join him in the room at 17:30 for the interview. He lets me in the room while he is in his underpants.
Lemmy before leaving asked me to get him two packs of cigarettes, red Marlboro soft pack. Of course you cannot call a taxi for such a thing. I go, I come back and they tell me Mikkey MacDee arrived, so called because the drummer is crazy for burgers.
The event is scheduled for the evening at the Stadium of Sarroch, 25 km from Cagliari.

19:30 h

I walk with some friends and we start to give some invitation cards for the aftershow.
At 10:30 p.m. is show time, Lemmy gets on stage with his daily clothes (he is Lemmy 24h a day), the microphone and screams: "Sardinia, AjÚ! We are Motörhead and we play rock 'n' roll!" AjÚ is a typical Sardinian word that means "let's go", but has a wider meaning indeed.
The crowd says MO-TOR-HEAD! MO-TOR-HEAD! They start with 'Doctor Rock', then the setlist is the same as the 'Inferno' tour, except for 'Whorehouse Blues'.
I witnessed the concert downstage, over the barricades, when it was time for 'I Got Mine', Lemmy has found words to tell the crowd my name: "This song is taken from an album that in Sardinia nobody has, except that guy, Stefano!" I have experienced Motörhead quite a lot in the previous years but this was really exciting for me.

After 'Iron Fist' they did a pause and came back for the encore: 'Ace Of Spades'. Lemmy then introduces Phil and Mikkey, as usual. Phil introduces Lemmy when a Sardinian flag is thrown on stage, he picks it up and opens it, triggering an inevitable LEM-MY! LEM-MY! From all the crowd.
Then they played 'Overkill', bass on feedback and final bow, the legendary Motörhead have played Sardinia, at least for once.

Set list:

**Doctor Rock
Stay Clean
Shoot You In The Back
Love Me Like A Reptile
Killers
Metropolis
Over The Top
No Class
I Got Mine
In The Name Of Tragedy
Dancing On Your Grave
Ramones
Sacrifice (with drum solo)
Just 'cos You Got The Power
Going To Brazil
Killed By Death (with Moua)
Iron Fist
Ace Of Spades
Overkill**

The show, for those unfamiliar with Motörhead on stage, was beyond all expectations. Reflecting on the concerts that I saw after Sardinia and that in 2008 began the decline of Motörhead, the Sarroch one was one of the last and best Motörhead shows I have attended.

Half an hour after the show, while I manage something for the aftershow, the tour manager calls me on the phone:
"Lemmy wants you in the dressing room."
I was a bit worried, wondering about what Lemmy wanted from me and hoping to have no problems for the aftershow, I hope there are no problems. I knock the door and see him sitting on the sofa with Moua. Much to my surprise he lends me a copy of 'Stagefright'.

Needless to say that since then, it has become the most valuable piece in my collection.
Then Lemmy tells everybody to get ready to leave in the next few minutes, to go to the club for the aftershow party.
Before leaving Mikkey Dee tells me that in Bilbao, Venice and Sarroch, the latter was the best gig.
I want to thank my friend Piero Bonetti for opening his club's door for the party; the club is usually closed at summer time. Piero is a long time Motörhead fan and was extremely happy for the proposal.
The moment that I liked the most was when the band arrived at the club. Everyone was silent inside and then it was a standing ovation.
The celebration began before 1:30 a.m., needless to say we started drinking as much as possible, well, not me indeed, because I had to drive the band back to the hotel. After about two hours I was again summoned by Lemmy:
"Stefano, let's get out fast, now."
He wanted to go away without taking pictures and signing autographs, and so we did (but someone has been successful when Lemmy entered the club). Indeed, it was a reasonable request as there were almost 200 people inside. We get up suddenly, we leave the room and we ran into the car. I turn my car under a hail of flashes and after a while we are back to the hotel.
I had come the next morning to say goodbye to the band before they would leave Sardinia."
Stefano Loi (Cagliari, Italy)

"My first and (sadly) sole opportunity to see one of my favorite bands ever onstage was back in 1986.
They were touring with Twisted Sister and Girlschool, but when they hit Bologna (Italy) Girlschool were missing, luckily there were three Italian bands onstage to complete quite an interesting bill.
By the way, I was there mostly for Motörhead and it was a big surprise to see they were opening for Twisted Sister and not closing the event. I guess that's because the New Yorkers were receiving a lot of attention and great feedbacks also from outside the metal scene and were often on the pages of generic magazines, by the way not a big deal, Motörhead were there onstage and that was the deal for me (not that Twisted Sister released a lesser or lamer set, to speak the truth).
It was a special night for me, I had the opportunity to see Lemmy and his pards delivering some of my all time favorites and - since

then on - they always had a special place in my life.
I can't remember the set list, the details of the show or other specific things, but for sure they hit me so hard I never left my taste for their music. I kept buying every single album, reading books and magazines covering them and always had them on my radar even when I moved to the hardcore punk scene, started to listen different stuff like black metal, industrial, doom, noise, drone, post metal or whatever as I wrote (and still write) on zines and were always able to dive into different styles and curious to check new languages.
But Lemmy and Motörhead were always by my side, I bought their albums when I did my final exams at school, when I was running a crossover label with some friends, when I got a job, when I started to promote stuff or organizing shows in a local squat, when I got married, when my daughter was born and so on... till the last one, that I loved so much.
It's hard to stress why they were always able to fit into my tastes beside every kind of stuff I was listening to, but for sure I never regret or lost my interest or true dedication.
They were welcome when I hit the noise scene, the HC, the doom, whichever music fans I met I always met someone into Motörhead and able to appreciate their music. That's the magic of this band and that's why I love them so much.
Sadly, I never had the opportunity to see them onstage since that night. I had some disaffection for big festivals and metal gatherings in early '90's, some economic crisis later, I was involved in organizing shows or supporting the local scene, then my daughter was born and I had to go back to the family.
Then it was like: next time, this is too far, there are too many bands, I have no money, Motörhead will last forever so that's enough time to postpone it... and now it's too late and this regret will back me forever.
Well, that's how life goes... But, believe me, Lemmy was always in my home, like a safe harbor, a reference, the essence of r'n'r itself and not just the early stuff, because I don't like people referring just to the first line up.
I quite love every album they did, with some preferences of course, but without disliking a single one or being like: they disappointed me! No Way, they're Motörhead and they play rock'n'roll!
So, thanks for everything Lemmy!"
Michele Giorgi (Ancona, Italy)

Palazzo dello Sport
Bologna, Italy
June 23rd 1986

Iron Fist
Stay Clean
Nothing Up My Sleeve
Metropolis
Doctor Rock
Killed by Death
Ace of Spades
Steal Your Face
No Class
Motörhead
Overkill

"I saw him and Motörhead in Italy for the first time on June 25th 2011. It was a Sonisphere festival and they raised the bar!
Everyone, and I mean EVERYONE, was raising hell! Youngs and olds!
It was mind-blasting to see Lemmy on the top of the stage, so much charisma. He was like a king!
Amazing time. R.I.P. Lemmy."
Samuel Silver Silvegni (Italy)

Japan

Capital City: Tokyo
Population: 126,919,659
Currency: Yen
Bands: Dir En Grey, Crossfaith, Baby Metal

*"I heard Motörhead for the first time in the late '70s when I was boy.
They had just released 'Overkill' and 'Bomber' in Japan. I was so excited and became a Motörhead fan immediately, it was just before NWOBHM movement...
My first Motorhead gig was 1991 in Japan (really missing 3 motor-guys of all members...) and after that I was trip to Europe and US for 'Motör-gigs' many times.
Motörhead for life is normal for me. I proudly became a Motörheadbanger (member of the Official Motörhead Fan Club) and also did promotion about movie "Lemmy" with film-distributing agency in Japan.
My last Motör-gig was their special cruise festival "Motörboat".
...And I would like to say should have been the 40th anniversary gig in Hammersmith (Jan/2016). Yes, that was a cancelled concert but we (Motörheadbangers world) did "Special tribute funeral gig" by ourselves.
Hammersmith is one of very important places/venues for Motörhead and also our promised land.
Motörhead played at Hammersmith since 1975 and they did special gigs several times there (I was there for 30th anniversary gig).
And don't forget, Motörhead born in London which "Motörhead - England" show us their popular trademark T-shirt.
♠ Lemmy, Motörhead and Motörheadbangers world Forever!!
Motör-cheers*
Taka MHB2310 (Japan)

Luxembourg

Capital City: Luxembourg City
Population: 562,958
Currency: Euro
Bands: Pagan Lorn, Le Grand Guignol

"I first saw Motörhead in Rodange (Luxembourg), in a small club called "Blue Note". There were about a hundred of fans there, I think it was in 1979, I was 13 years old.
I was a hundred of meters away, when I first heard that "noise" it was very loud!
When I arrived there, I opened the door and I saw him, Lemmy, with this incredible voice he had. Since that day, Motörhead was in my life.
Thank's for all you gave me."
Raoul Fassi (Rodange, Luxembourg)

Mexico

Capital City: Mexico City
Population: 119,530,753
Currency: Peso
Bands: Santana, Rodrigo Y Gabriella, The Chasm

"I first heard Motörhead when I was 8 years old. By that time I studied at elementary school and didn't know tons of things about life. Time passed by and a certain day of 2005, I decided to buy the album 'Deaf Forever: The Best of Motörhead'. Didn't imagine that it would change my life. I knew bands like Black Sabbath or AC/DC, but Motörhead was different; you could feel electricity flowing through your veins song after song.

My most cherished memory is when I saw Motörhead live for the first and last time. It was on May 17th 2013. You can't compare a Motörhead show with anything else, it's pure energy from the begging until the end. Weeks before the show, I suffered a car accident which got me really shocked, I didn't feel good at all. The best medicine I could get were Lemmy's chords. Unforgettable.

I remember the moment when I heard carefully the lyrics of 'Built for Speed'. I was 14 and as a teenager many things didn't make sense, I wasn't compromised with anything and everything looked like a joke to me. After paying attention to those words, suddenly I started to cry not because of sadness, but of joy. Lemmy's words were exactly what I needed to listen to.

From that day until now, every single time that I feel down, confused or lost, I just put play to that very song and believe me or not, I found the strength to keep on going. I'll be forever grateful with his music for giving me words of encouragement when no one else did it.

¡Gracias por todo Lemmy!"
Frida Martinez (Mexico City, Mexico

Force Fest
Palacio de los Deportes
Mexico City
17th May 2013

I Know How to Die
Damage Case
Stay Clean
Metropolis
Over the Top
Doctor Rock
The Chase is Better Than the Catch
Rock It
You Better Run
The One to Sing the Blues
Going to Brazil
Killed by Death
Ace of Spades
Overkill

"For me is an honor knowing that our Uncle Lemmy was one of the largest by the great God of metal, Ronnie James gave despite our condolences for all of us fans clubs friends fans and especially the family we will have it in our hearts forever.
Lemmy Kilmister big greetings from Monterrey, Mexico "
Isra Lan (Monterrey, Mexico)

"Everything begins when one night when I was about 18 or 19

years.

That day I have went out with my cousin and in that moment one of my best friends Erik, we were going deeper into the Metal World, so we were looking for a place to go to listen good music and drink beer, so that day we try a place named 'La Bodega del Metal' (The Metal Warehouse).

It was a nice place and as the name said it was a warehouse, metal any moment, beer and metal heads wherever you looked, so in that place there was a little stand with 2 guys selling Metal bands t-shirts. We went to go to see the shirts and suddenly I see a Motörhead one and it was like if something told me to buy it and I did.

But as I said it was just the beginning, before I get back home I start to download Motörhead Songs, at that point I was never hear a Theme of Them, so I listen to the songs and something didn't match at all and for me was cool but I was looking for something different.

Time passed and I became a Dad. We went through a hard time; I even cut myself in some kind of desperation act. I felt like a piece of shit, nothing was going the way I had to be, problems everywhere. I was unemployed and had 2 babies to look after.... really tough times.

But one day when everything looked to be falling to pieces, I was thinking about what to do and started to listen to metal.

Song by song was going on and I just felt awful, but then like a message from heaven, like if god had said 'It's enough', I start to listen to one of the most Greatest Motörhead's songs and as the track was playing I felt like someone was talking to me and saying "Cmon Boy!!! You are no a Crap...get up from your knees and move your ass from the wall."

It was like a friend, like a brother...like someone who cared for you...and wanted you up.

The song I was listening to was 'Ace of Spades'!!!!

Then it comes 'Iron Fist', 'Orgasmatron', 'The King Of Kings', 'The Game', 'Jack The Reaper' and as the songs were playing and shaking my mind everything started to match in my head, in my heart.

Lemmy's bass felt strong and full of power and strength and it put me on my feet.

Since then I listen to Motörhead as long as I can. I don't get bored of it, I love to listen to Motörhead because they saved me from doing stupid things. They took me back to real life and gave me strength to go and ride over the life troubles.

Life it's a Bitch, I was Born To Lose, Now I Live To Win, Dr. Rock Heals my Wounds one More Fucking Time... I Ain't No Nice Guy.... I'm The Ace Of Spades!!!!"
Abraham Rodríguez (Mexico City)

Netherlands

Capital City: Amsterdam
Population: 16,971,452
Currency: Euro
Bands: Within Temptation, Cirith Gorgor, Altar

"*My* Motörhead *history is not as long as most fans, but short and sweet.*
The 1st time I saw Lemmy, I could not take my eyes off of him and what happened to me, during the concert was indescribable, I stood transfixed. I was on a balcony and saw him standing on a Persian carpet with all of those great fans. The music, his strength, it became so intense with me inside. So all of a sudden I was intrigued by this man.
Soon I went collecting, CD's DVD's T'shirts, patches, books etc. and it is through this collection that I have learned more of that man, I became more and more fascinated by him.
This man was not just a singer of a rock band, but in life is a true icon. His wisdom about how he looks to daily stuff is almost overwhelming. Such awareness of things, which not many people dare to say.
Unconsciously someone went under your skin, not in an annoying way, but the feeling of a kind of commitment. The lyrics that Motörhead *make, are not about the ordinary things in life, but went deeper, feel what's in it, the rage, the disappointment, the passion, it describes exactly and with the right musical setting, the way as I also experience.*
Listening to Lemmy and Motörhead *feels like coming home! I have never had the change to meet him unfortunately, but do have experience of beautiful things, I'm was there at the Walhalla, or Hammersmith in London.*
I saw him play with Würzel, and the girls from Girlschool.
Of course, I became a member of the Motorheadbangers fan club, and I am still very proud!
Not the most comprehensive story of years of admiration, again, short and sweet. And now... Now he's dead!
Thank God I saw him last summer, and I enjoyed his enthusiasm

and warmth that the 3 Motörhead members felt to each other.
The news was nevertheless a hard blow, my world collapsed very briefly in. ... But my love for Lemmy and his music will always exist. But there is also a piece that died in me!"
Diana Bouwmeester -Motorheadbanger no. 304 **(The Netherlands)**

```
                    ARENA
            O    motörhead    A
            p       DIO       i
            e     SAXON       r
            n   PRIMAL FEAR
              KAMIKAZE FREAK SHOW
                WICKED MYSTIC
            Including Metal - Market - nr 130
              Zondag 13 juni a.s. vanaf 14.00 uur
                Anholtseweg 49, Dinxperlo
                  Achterhoek Arena
            DISCODOMEIN DER NEDERLANDEN
```

"I first saw Motörhead on a German TV show called Rockpalast.
I immediately fell in love with the music, this was 1984/1985 I was eleven or twelve years old, it was after midnight so I watched the whole show alone... back then there was no internet I had no knowledge of what was going on in the world or even about HeavyMetal. Back then tape trading was the thing to do, to get the latest on heavy music, between all thrash metal I never found any Motörhead.
Then one day my dad came home with the Led Zeppelin LP 'Coda', Van Halen's 'Women and Children First' and on top of all that a tape by Motörhead, that was the beginning of the end.
I was into Motörhead, Slayer and Metallica in that order.
The first song I learned to play on guitar was 'KILLED BY DEATH'.
After that it went downhill and I went on to play the bass, trying to play Lemmy style; didn't get it for quite a few years.
All around me I gathered people whom were wearing Motörhead patches, Martin, Danielle, Andries, Roland and Andre Paul, Rick quite a rowdy bunch.....
Finally the year 1991 Motörhead was touring '1916' and I was in Amsterdam for the first time see Motörhead and meet them also. NO, they didn't play that night some trouble with the stage extension or other crap.
Well there I was buying t-shirts, patches and all the merchandise I could afford, with my bags stuffed, Eddie the Bald Eagle and Tim

Butcher who we actually had fun with in the first place, suddenly closed shop and buggered off. Somebody yelled at us to leave the venue, Motörhead wasn't gonna play that night.... WHAAAT!!!!!!!!!!
I'd been waiting for 6 years, spent all my money and now no show? Man I was really pissed off!
We were thrown out of the venue, while I was venting my displeasure, suddenly Lemmy, Phil, Philthy and Wurzel were standing in front of me. I explained to them my displeasure and disappointment in The band I most loved, Motörhead!!
I was 17 years young. Man, where do I start?
Lemmy man, Lemmy – 'My Hero'.
Lemmy mumbled a few apologies, so did Campbell, and Taylor on Philthy looked angry and ready to go, Wurzel left first.
Then came a huge skinhead and an even larger Punkrocker they took over conversation, and Lemmy started running with the rest of the band following him.
That was the first and the last I did see of Lemmy and Motörhead for years. In 2002 (I believe) I went to see them again in Amsterdam, and they were good it was on the 'Hammered' tour, I forgave Lem and the band and decided I'd be a full blown Motörhead fan again.
The last time I got to see Lemmy, Phil and Mikkey was in Nijmegen Holland 'Fields of Rock' 2005.
It was a great show and the last I've ever been able to attend unfortunately. I caught up on buying all the albums I didn't listen to in my hiatus of being a Motörhead fan. I became a Hawkwind fan a Headcat fan and ever since Lemmy was with me on my mp3 player, my vinyl, my DVD's. Lemmy's voice and the music of Motörhead pulled me through a HELL of a time.
'Killed By Death' the first song I learned to play, 'All For You' my divorce anthem, 'One Nightstand' well... ok I performed with several bands 'Ace of Spades' as a singer or a bass player.
Through Motörhead I met the Dutch Motörhead, Hammerhawk
that's how lemmy became my biggest musical influence.
Thnx lem, thanx all friends past, present and future whom I've met through Motörhead.
My new friends In Motörheadbangers fanclub worldwide
You are the fanclub!! and we listened to ROCK 'N' ROLL!!
Töm Puch MHB 4109 (Ljmond, Holland)

"Lemmy Gave me a t-shirt in a drunk t-shirt exchange after the show, Saturday October 24th 1998 at Zaal Schaaf Leeuwarden. A Motörhead shirt for a Hammerhawk shirt, good deal!

Rio Thys Brujins and me were talking to Lemmy in a bar in Leeuwarden, Thys ran out to the Hammerhawk van to get some CD's and in the mean time I gave Lemmy my sweaty Hammerhawk shirt that I was wearing at the Motörhead show.
I was deaf and drunk from the Motörhead show and Lemmy said, "Look man I really appreciate it, but please don't shout in my ear." So actually I was in the bar without a shirt. Lemmy went away and later came back with his 'Snake Bite Love' tour shirt.
We talked about Brian Robertson and the 'Another Perfect Day' album (love it!)
A few years later, at the Rainbow surprisingly, he still remembered me and we had a Jack 'n' Coke together with Dr Heathen Scum of the Mentors. Later we met again at a Testament show in L.A. Lemmy was always surrounded by hot chicks and he was always a real gentleman rocker."
Paul Van Rijswijk (Hammerhawk)

"When I was 13 (1981) and started listening to rock, I asked my dad to bring me a UK Subs t-shirt when he had to go to London for a business trip. I got a Motörhead shirt instead and it was then when I seriously started to listen to Motörhead and discovered the best band ever. Since that day Motörhead is a constant factor in my life.
When I was 30 (1998) my son was born and so I became a dad. He started listening to my music when he was still really young and was picking up a guitar at the age of 7.
So, it was 27 years after I started to listen to Motörhead when I decided to take my then 8 year old to see them for his first time. He really liked Kiss then and both bands were playing at a Dutch festival. I told him that Kiss was nice but that his life would never be the same again after his first Motörhead show. Of course I was right and since then he is also a Motörhead fan.
(People asked him during the last tour if he remembers his first show at age 8 and he does!)."
Jos and Cas Plenter (Motörheadbangers Holland)

Arrow Rock Festival
Nijmegen, Netherlands

June 15th 2008

Doctor Rock
Stay Clean
Be My Baby
Killers
Metropolis
Over the Top
One Night Stand
Rosalie
In the Name of Tragedy
Just 'Cos You Got the Power
Going to Brazil
Killed By Death Feat. Dee Snider – Twisted Sister
Ace of Spades
Overkill

"In 2010 I took him to his first international show (London and Brighton in the UK).
We were allowed backstage and at the age of 12 my son met his idols. How cool is that! Lemmy was of course really friendly only he couldn't pronounce Cas (his name).
He tried it "Gus? Guz? Gaz? ...... What? Cas? Well that's a strange name, he said"
Anyway, after that I decided to do as many shows together as possible, as a special father and son thing.
Together we have done now many Motörhead shows and I am convinced that I have given my son something that he will treasure for the rest of his life. The love for the best rock n roll band in the world and a lot of pleasant memories.
We have travelled all over the continent to see our band perform, went to many summer festivals and venue shows, driven thousands of kilometers, stayed in luxury hotels and saw a lot of beautiful places.
We have met the band on several occasions. We've also met a lot of other Motörhead fans. Some of them became good and close

friends over the years.
Motörhead, Lemmy, you have given me pleasure, strength and joy and you were there for me in good and bad times! I (we) want to thank you for bringing joy and pleasure into our life!
Right now I am still heartbroken about your passing away.
You were my Hero and you will never be forgotten
Cheers my friend! Rest in piece, master of rock n roll!

Goodbye my hero.

Unfortunately an important part of my life is gone. My hero has left this world.

I will never feel the power of that show again.
I will never hear him shout again.
And I will never be standing with that big satisfied smile on my face again when their show is over.

The show is really over now and that hurts.
No more Motörhead...and even though I know that this day would come I didn't expect it to come this soon.
For sure I wasn't ready for it and I also didn't expect that it would hurt as much as it does.

Goodbye my hero!
Motörhead till the end!
Motörhead for life."
Jos and Cas Plenter (Motörheadbangers Holland)

"From the time I first heard 'Overkill' in "77 at 13 I was hooked.
I never realised at the time how lucky I was to attend a gig on the 'Bomber' tour at Hammersmith Odeon I was 14 or 15. To me the original lineup were magical, 'No Sleep' is testimony to that.
I moved abroad to Amsterdam in '86 and apart from the music did not follow the new line up. In subsequent years I'm glad I did however, I saw them, all over the Netherlands from Tilburg to Zwolle, Heerhugowaard to Amsterdam.
Especially in the last 10yrs I was at every gig and twice I took my son in 2011 first time he was 11.
Motörhead is more than music it's an attitude, a way of life. I'm 51 years of age but I still wear the shirts and patches with pride. Motörhead is my religion and Lemmy was a bit like the father I'd dreamed of. Never met him unfortunately but we came close.

In '93 on the 'Bastards' tour my mate and me went to see them in Utrecht. Now we were up in the balcony overlooking the band. We had also been up all night drinking and using large qtys of coke. I was literally flying as a board as Lemmy puts it.
We arrived, the building was already shaking and I got right into it dancing in the aisles like a madman. My eyes were out on stalks 'Motörhead' was my tune. I was easily the most wasted kid there. Lemmy could not take his eyes off me. He played, looked and stared, played, looked and stared; it went on for what seemed like ages. I can only assume he wanted some of what I was on. Over the years I have always wondered about that night we were really connected. Would have loved to have been backstage that night partying with him. RIP Lemmy and thanks for everything we will keep things going now you're gone."
Marko Nonnac (Amsterdam, Netherlands)

"I saw Motörhead live in 2015 at 'Graspop' and it was fucking amazing man.
I went with my best friend and to him, Lemmy is like a god. I just really like his music and his style, it's legendary. His voice, his talent, his way of living his life and his way of writing music is a true inspiration to people all around the world including myself and my friends.
To see him on stage at my favorite festival, 'Graspop', with the band that he loved to play with the most, that is truly amazing.
He changed the whole music scene and never changed himself, and you know what a man like that is called? A LEGEND.
I will never forget him and the way he changed me and my way of writing music.
Thank you lemmy, cheerz!"
Bram Pelgrim (Goes, Zeeland, The Netherlands)

"Lemmy was an inspiration to stay true to myself.
Motörhead still is a great and loud soundtrack to my life."
Martijn Schaink (Tubbergen, The Netherlands)

"I was grew up with his music, my dad is a really big fan of Motörhead so everyday we play a song of Motörhead.
When this great man died we played all of his CD's from Motörhead.
In every song is a great memory.
Thanks lemmy for all your great Music!!! You're a legend!"
Roos Hendricks (Asperen, Netherlands)

"I have never seen Motörhead live.
In 2015 I had made the plan to see them play this year, but that was never gonna happen.
I have seen many bands play and the one band on my list to see was Motörhead.
Lemmy's death hit me hard. He lived his life the way he wanted to live it. Born to lose, live to win."
Dennis Van Eeuwijk (Zwolle, Netherlands)

"He was and will be my greatest hero in rock 'n' roll music.
Seen Motörhead many times and I will be missing that.
R.I.P. Lemmy"
Wilfred Kruigenza (Winschoten, Netherlands)

"Hey a story from Graspop:
I can remember when I saw you...
Standing somewhere up front...
Thousands of people....
You said: "we are Motörhead and we play rock and roll"
The ground started shaking....
Dust was blown high in the sky...
The crowd started moving...
The pit opened.....
A big smile appeared on all faces...
All was forgotten, the crowd became one!
A brothership...
A brothership of rock'n'roll...

\m/

Mark Johanns 'Mettal Mark' (Haarlem)

"I never got to meet him, I just discovered his music a few years ago, and it quickly grew on me.
It didn't take long for me to listen to it regularly.
His passing hit me pretty hard as well - but hey, he gave it all he had until the very end. At least he passed away still doing what he loved, and doing it well!
Rest in peace, man."
Mick Van Geldorp (Heiloo, Netherlands)

"It must have been somewhere back in '97 or '98 when I saw my

first Motörhead concert. I instantly loved it.
After the first show I had the privilege to see them 20 more times.
Because of Motörhead I started listening to the louder kind of music, which I still listen today.
Lemmy inspired me to start practicing the bass guitar, hope I can play it like he did one time lol.
I had the honor to have a chat with him one time after a Motörhead gig they played in Tilburg the Netherlands. It was great, he was really kind, and it gave me a great feeling.
When Lemmy died, it really hurt and it still does today.
Knowing there will be no more Motörhead ever again, gonna miss them on the festivals I always go to.
Or never hear any more new Motörhead albums...
May he rest in peace and rock on in heaven."
Sean van Asten (Eindhoven, The Netherlands)

"My friends and I went to a festival in Bolsward in the Netherlands.
Motörhead was filling in for another band how didn't show and it was a horrible show not because of the band but the sound was awful.
Lemmy was complaining all through the show and cursing at the sound guy on stage.
He ended the show apologising for the horrible sound and promised to make up for it next time (which they did even doing a duet with Twisted Sister) this could have ended just being a bad Motörhead show but.....
As we walked back to buy some beer we walked passed the sound stage where the sound guy was being escorted away by security with a bloody nose and his hand over his (probably) black eye.
Now I don't know if it was the Motörhead road crew or the fans that did this but the message was clear:
Nobody fucks with the sound of the loudest band in the world!"
Bas van den Bor (Amsteleveen, Netherlands)

"9-10-2011 was the date that Motörhead would play the IJsselhallen in Zwolle. It would be my 10th, or so, time seeing Motörhead in concert.
My oldest son, William, would turn 9 years on October 27th and he wanted to come along that night.
Motörhead are always known to be a band for the fans, so I went to Zwolle early to see if they were already in town.
When I got there, with some albums, camera and a marker, the tour bus was already there. It was very easy to walk around the

IJsselhallen and to watch the crew unload all the stage and equipment.
When watching and waiting there, Tim walked by. I got to ask him if the band was still in the tour bus or if they were in the IJsselhal allready. He said that they were in the bus and did not know when they would show up. We had a little chat about the gig and being the bass-tech for Lemmy. He really took the time for a talk, and a photo was no problem at all.
After a while I saw Phil walking around on the parking lot, relaxing and smoking a cigarette.
He had no problem to take a picture with me and to sign my 'Orgasmatron' record. He asked me if I was going to the show that night. I said that my oldest son, 9 years old, would come tonight with me, a kind of birthday present for him. When he asked when my son's birthday was, and I told him it was October 27th he told me that his son also was born that date. Phil told me to wait and walked back in the tour bus. When Phil came out again, he had a hand full of Motörhead plectrums "for your son" he said. That was a great gift!
Phil then went off to the dressing room inside for lunch and later rehearsals.
Not much later Lemmy walked by. I greeted him and shook his hand. When I asked if he wanted to do a photo, Lemmy apologised and said that he just woke up (it was 3 o'clock in the afternoon) and did not look awake yet...For me he just look like Lemmy always did, with his boots and his hat. Lemmy then said that he would come back a little later to do a photo. Sadly he did not come back. Still that tiny little chat we had that day (also to meet Phil) was one of the coolest things that I remember.
That evening with my son watching Motörhead was an evening he still remembers and for me, that day was the proof that Motörhead was indeed a band for the fans.
My first Motörhead show was Waldrock 2000 and the last was Düsseldorf 2015...
Deaf forever! Motörhead for life!"
Raymond and William Pronk (Raalte, Holland)

"Seen Motörhead 14 times in 7 years, all in the front of stage right for Lemmy. Lemmy saw me every time and smiles to me!
I never forget that!
Love you forever Lemmy."
Marjorie Buijinck (Apledorn)

New Zealand

Capital City: Wellington
Population: 4,596,700
Currency: New Zealand Dollar
Bands: Ulcerate, Dawn of Azazel, Blacklistt

"In March 2014, after perhaps one too many JD's I booked my cabin on the Motorboat. Then started to worry, how was I going to make this happen? But as you all know... it did.
The countdown was made even more eventful by Kevin Boren. This awesome guy on Motorboaters page on Facebook did a video countdown that was priceless. I managed to hook up with two fantastic like minded ladies as cabin mates.
After all the long waits in airports and even longer flights I arrived in LA. I had booked a great B&B in West Hollywood just walking distance to the Rainbow and so many great places. One of these was just two blocks from my apartment, The Great Frog jeweller where I purchased my Motörhead ring. FANTASTIC!
Now after a great three day stay in LA it was off to Miami and the MOTORBOAT to meet my cabin mates. I really had no idea what I was getting into and what was in store for all those headbangers.
The bands on the cruise were Motörhead who as my husbands states are my obsession, they're not, I just love them and have been a fan of Lemmy and the boys for too many years to tell you.
Some of the other bands were Megadeth, Anthrax, Down, Testament, Zakk Wylde, Jim Breuer, Fireball Ministry, Wilson, Danko Jones and more. Dave Mustaine pulled out at the last minute due to health reasons but The All Star Metal Allegiance band more than filled the gap.

Well hundreds and hundreds of headbangers lined up for the ship, quite a few worse for wear after party nights in numerous hotels in Miami, the look on the staff's faces was hilarious. Tattoos and black t-shirts for miles, I really don't think I have seen such a diverse bunch of people. Apparently, like with all cruises, there is a *lot of waiting around.*

All aboard the magic is about to happen and magic is what this cruise was. It was the best thing I have ever done in my life and to use the words of Kevin "Let's Do This Shit"

Motörhead did two shows, they were fantastic, it was a shock to see Lemmy on the first night but it was just the fourth concert he has done since his recovery. But then came those immortal words "We Are Motörhead and We Play Rock and Roll"; they gave it everything and the next show was even better.

I was lucky enough to get a photo with Phil and then one with Mikkey and best of all I got to talk to Lemmy. He really is the most awesome guy I have ever met, it made the trip perfect!

Bands played on both the deck and in the theatre inside. Down was great and Phil Anselmo was funny. Testament rocked, Anthrax was fantastic and Scott Ian did "The spoken word" about his beginings with Anthrax and drinking session with Lemmy, he really is an entertaining guy.

Yet another fantastic show was Metal Allegiance, the best of the rest of "Megadeath" (No I didn't miss spell it the PR guys did. So all the merchandise on board had Megadeath on it, funny, we had a good laugh. In fact four crazy girls got off on our port of call in Cozumel, Mexico and got a temporary tattoos of Megadeath with an X over the A. Dave and Chris thought it was hilarious.

Phil Campbell and Mikkey Dee got up on stage with Metal Allegiance. Really guys just picture it... your'e on a beautiful cruise ship in the middle of the ocean and the best musicians in the world are playing just metres away. Joey Belladonna sang Dio songs and Scott Ian was up there with the guys from Down, Testament ...magic.

All the bands had 'Meet & Greets' so we all had a chance for a photo. Got Dave Ellefson's signature on his book and a photo with him and Chris. It was amazing to see all the band members walking around the ship. Pepper Keenan was at our table in one of the restaurants, great guy.

It is really hard to put into words what it was like and the feeling you still have after the cruise is over. It felt a little like a private club you were in.

All those like minded headbangers, just a nod and a smile and you knew how they were feeling, not to mention a nod and a wink from the boys in the bands. I got to know some fantastic people. Dawn and Randi my cabin mates I hope will always remain my friends. Met some fantastic MHB's from all over the world, but we were already family. We really rocked this boat!

You always get the not so great things as not everything is perfect and doesn't go as planned but it really didn't matter. One thing I must add after talking to a couple of the staff and security guys when leaving was they all said, 'they were apprehensive about a metal cruise but we were the best crowd they had ever dealt with, no problems at all.'
Even though I am from New Zealand I have been lucky enough to see Motörhead *quite a few times, this cruise really was four days of PURE MAGIC.*

*"**2016:** How strange it is to mourn someone you hardly knew, but thought of as a friend.*
That was what Lemmy and Motörhead *was to me and I know to so many of you.*
I am having trouble coming to terms that Motörhead *will never play live again but we all know it will be played "Louder Than Everything Else" forever.*
I was privileged to get to talk to Lemmy privately for about half an hour just over a year ago. He looked unwell but wouldn't dwell on it; the giant of a man was still there.
He asked me questions, telling a joke or two, what an amazing man he was and it was truly one of the highlights of my life. We drank a couple of Jack & Cokes and had a cigarette or two, it only took me a few minutes to feel totally at ease in his company. We talked about Motörhead, *music, the earthquake in my home town Christchurch NZ and how the repairs were going. He then introduced me to his girlfriend. I really felt privileged.*
When I left my head was in the clouds and I couldn't wipe the smile off my face.
I have followed Lemmy's career via his music from The Rocking Vickers when I was young, through Hawkwind and crashing into Motörhead *and not forgetting all the covers and work he did with so many other bands.*
Even though I live way down here, I have had the privilege of seeing Motörhead *in San Francisco with Dio and Iron Maiden, Auckland, Sydney, Gold Coast, both concerts in New Plymouth and last but no means least THE MOTORBOAT 2014 !!!*
I know I will shed a tear or two more as the loss feels so real, he always seemed larger that life, but my heart felt thoughts and love go to Phil, Mikkey Dee, Paul, Cheryl, the "Road Crew" and so many of his close friends that must be finding this so hard.
Lemmy will be remembered by so many as an honest man with a talent that was as big as the universe, for the amazing one liners

that gave us a glimpse into his wonderful sense of humour, the fantastic lyrics and that booming bass.
He lived his life on his terms and I think he left this world on his terms as well.
I will watch the "Lemmy" movie, "Live Fast Die Old" documentary, read his book, listen to the music, watch my many DVD's again and again. They will make me laugh and they will make me cry because now I know the ending.
Thank you to Alan for all the hard work you have put in for so many years and I hope the fanzine will continue for a while yet.
Thank you to all MHB's and fans on Facebook that have posted so many pictures and shared so many of their experiences with Lemmy and the band, for making us all laugh, cry and become even closer.
Thank you to Lemmy, Philthy, Wurzel, Fast Eddie, Phil and the best drummer in the world Mikkey Dee for giving us Motörhead.
Thank you to all those MHB's out there that helped them be what they were and will always be "The best Rock n Roll band in the world"
And last but not least thank you to my husband Grant for putting up with my passion that is "Motörhead "
Lemmy is gone from us but will never ever be forgotten.
Love to you all X"
Eira Wylie MHB3010 (Christchurch, New Zealand)

Motorboat
Carnival Ecstasy From Miami
25th September 2014

Damage Case
Stay Clean
No Class
Metropolis
Over the Top
The Chase is Better Than the Catch
Rock It
Lost Woman Blues
Doctor Rock
Rosalie
Just 'Cos You Got the Power
Going to Brazil

**Killed by Death
Ace of Spades
Overkill**

*"I remember meeting Lemmy in 1988 at a Metallica concert at Hammersmith Odeon.
I showed Lemmy the cassette 'No Sleep At All' that I just happened to buy the very same day for him to sign. He then took the sleeve out of the plastic box and started to read it. I asked him:
"How come you are reading the sleeve"? He replied that he hadn't seen the finished product yet. How cool and proud was I that I was the first person in the world to show him his finished album, which of course he signed. This happened while Metallica were playing. How awesome is that that Lemmy took time out to do this for a fan.
I then saw Lemmy in a pub after the show where he introduced me to Boom Boom - Zodiac Mindwarp's drummer. Boom Boom asked who my friend was and I told him that it was her birthday.
Lemmy then proceeded to sing "Happy Birthday" which the whole pub joined in with. How cool and what a true gentleman.
I was also at the concert at the Playrooms in Surfers Paradise in Australia in 1991 when Motörhead walked off stage after dickheads threw plastic cups at them.
Love you Lemmy.... RIP fella."*
Mason Smyth MHB795 (New Zealand)

Nicaragua

Capital City: Managua
Population: 6,071,045
Currency: Córdoba
Bands: Grupo Armado, Necrosis, Crisis, Q69K

*"I have 'White Line Fever' book, and 'Live To Win' a photo book from Alan Bridge in my collection, some posters, photos, magazines I collect.
I never met Lemmy in personal."*
Thodoris Damianos (Rivas, Nicaragua)

Norway

Capital City: Oslo
Population: 5,214,900
Currency: Norwegian Krone
Bands: Dimmu Borgir, Mayhem, Leaves Eyes

"The date was December 9th, 1993, and Motörhead played a show in Oslo (Rockefelle music bar).
At that time I worked as a barkeeper at Elm Street Rock Café in Oslo, but I had the night off to see the show. It was a great show, and after the show me and a friend went to Elm Street to drink some more and play some pinball.
My friend wasn't keen on the pinball machine, so he just sat at the bar, pretty drunk.
I hadn't been there a long time when the Man himself, Lemmy, entered the room. He was escorted in a side door right next to the pinball machine I was playing and asked if he could join me.
I didn't need time to give him a positive response, and he said; "If you teach me how it works, I'll provide the drinks".
I tried to talk to my friend to get him to join us, but he was too drunk, and went home without knowing Lemmy was there. Lemmy and I played and drank Heineken for nearly an hour, before he left the joint.
Before he left, I got him to sign a piece of paper for my friend.
The next day, I visited my friend, and gave him Lemmy's autograph. He almost started crying!"
Sigbjørn Haugestøl, MHB 3751 (Høbråten, Norway)

Sentrum Scene
Oslo

9th December 1993

I'll Be Your Sister
Traitor
I'm So Bad (Baby I Don't Care)
Metropolis
Liar
Stay Clean
Lost in the Ozone
The One to Sing the Blues
You Better Run
On Your Feet or on Your Knees
Burner
We Bring the Shake
Going to Brazil
Born to Raise Hell
Killed by Death
Overkill
Cat Scratch Fever
Ace of Spades

"While playing in Villarobledo (Spain) in Metalmania Festival 2003, the Murder One had interferences caused by a Trance music radio station. It only could be heard between songs, Lemmy's roadie tried to eliminate that but he could not.
Meanwhile Lemmy said "Nice music, Phil, isn't it?" Phil answered "Yeah, Lemmy, and I like the radio station."
The interferences finished and they went on playing and closing the fest."
Miquel Orts Guarner (Berg, Norway)

"I have been to Motörhead conserts since 1985, until the last here in Oslo 3. December 2015!"
Tommy Grønlond (Stabekk, Norway)

```
        Live Nation Presents
              MOTÖRHEAD
      Foto & lydopptak forbudt
             OSLO SPEKTRUM
         Dørene åpner 18:30
       Torsdag 03.12.15 kl 19:30
         For info og billettforsalg:
              www.livenation.no

   INNG: 10 / Ståplass              RAD:
   FELT:                             PLASS: 3691
   PRIS KR: 505,00 INKL.AVG.KR: 40,00 Ståplass   11 07 2015
              Stefan Sture                 836498    /3
         62 450 M16330SP03121 07117069 57   50500 x3
```

"The first time I heard Motörhead I was about 14 years old, around the release of 'Aftershock' in 2013.
Right away I was thrilled. That album introduced me to a whole new world of great rock 'n' roll music.
Shortly after, I started reading books and autobiographies about Motörhead. I watched as many live DVDs and listened to as many albums as I could. After reading "White Line Fever" I realised what an intelligent, well read and badass trooper Lemmy was.
Even though I've never talked with him, I believe that I've learned a lot from this crazy speedfreak of a rocker.
Lemmy lived his life how he wanted to every day. Not because somebody asked him to do it, but because he wanted it himself. A down to earth, honest and noble gentleman is what he was. He taught us that it doesn't have to be hard to live an enjoyable life. And that is something that we all can learn from.
Just three weeks before his passing, I saw my favourite band for the first and last time, in Oslo, Norway. During the outro of "Overkill", he looked down at me from the stage as he threw a couple of picks my direction. I caught one, and I'll keep till the end.
For me, I could not have wished for a better memory to have. I won't trade it for a thing.
Thank you for introducing me to rock 'n' roll. Born to lose, live to win."
Kristian Fossland Domås (Oslo, Norway)

Oslo Spektrum,

Norway
3rd December 2015

Bomber
Stay Clean
Metropolis
When the Sky Comes Looking For You
Over the Top
The Chase is Better Than the Catch
Lost Woman Blues
Orgasmatron
Doctor Rock
Just 'Cos You Got the Power
No Class
Ace of Spades
Whorehouse Blues
Overkill

"We went to Sweden Rock on our motörbikes.
Off to Oslo and then the ferry to Denmark, Copenhagen and from there to the festival outside Sölvesborg approx 180 km drive from Copenhagen.
Arrived the day (Thursday) before MH should play and had a great time seeing lots of great bands.
Among them one of Lemmy's old favourites Blue Öyster Cult!
But there was a constant murring in the back of our head.
MH was playing in Bergen, Nörway on Sunday so......
The Bergen show actually was supposed to happen the year before in December but due to Lemmy's voice troubles after the Oslo show the day before that was cancelled.
(Aina and I were put on the guest list by Lemmy for Oslo when we met him in Plymouth Nov 2011).
Unfortunately I couldn't do it 'cos I had to be out at sea on duty at the ship I work on. FUCK!
I almost had to "force" Aina to go to Oslo alone.

Don't think she regret that when after the show ending up at The Hard Rock Cafe in Oslo where Motörhead got their personal Victory motörbikes and there was a press conference and of course a party afterwards where she had a nice chat with Phil and Mikkey. Lemmy wasn't in "talking modus" so left early after just a hello and good bye. No wonder since he got that problem with his voice)
Friday came along and a lot of great bands played before (and after) our guys entered the stage.
Bömber rig (the old one;) and everything! Great show!
I had to leave the fence in the middle of the show due to overheating.
I was wearing a thin fleece jacket under my hoodie, 'cos it was a cold evening. Stayed in tent and yes U know. Scandinavian summer.....Smartass I was.
Aina rescued me from fainting like a girl on a boyband show:-)))
Some air, water and a drink (or two) I was back to life and ended watching the show from in the middle of the crowd.
Afterwards Twisted Sister headlined the festival that night.
When we got tired of those aunties trying to entertain people on the "memory lane" we left to see a band that fetched our interest by reading about them up front. Graveyard!!! WOW! Great! Ok enough of that.
We were now up to 90% sure of leaving the festival on Saturday and heading for Bergen!
Saturday came. We had breakfast. A guy next to us at the breakfast table we had known for one and a half days said "U guys consider leaving for Bergen? Right?"
Eh yeah... "I can see it in your faces" he replied!
Off we went to see Girlschool at 12 O'clock.
That was it!!! No we were in a desperately in need for more Motörhead!!
We fucked off back to the motorcycle camp and sadled up!
Should we buy some gasoline before we leave Aina wondered (They were selling gas and beer.... from a 4WD "bike" in the camp)
No I said. We stop at the first gas station on our way and then we hit the road!
BIG mistake!! Aina ran out of gas almost at once. Ok. I headed on. Found a gas station after some kilometers. A self service one. No kiosk where to buy a bottle of water or a gasoline can to carry the "medicine" in.
What to do? Oh yes. I got a couple of bottles in my saddlebags. With liquer in it. Found a half drank 0.5 liter of "Gammel Dansk" . U

should try it. Delicious;-)!
Almost put it to my mouth to empty it. Bad idea so I poured the liguer to the ground. Oh dear. That's "blasfemic".
Remember I'm Nörwegian and alcohol is more expensive than drugs up here...
Ok. With 0.5 liter of gas I headed back to my lost virgin by the highway.
May seem a bit weird by people passing by see a guy pour his girlfriends bike a drink...
Off to gas station to fill up and then full throttle! Everything's fine and we headed for Oslo. Approx 600 km ride where we should spend the Saturday evening. Leaving behind the festival, as Slade, Lynryd Skynryd etc etc played at Sweden Rock.....
BUT! The good thing was.
The Nörwegian coverband Ovërhead played in Oslo that evening at a small bar called Fiasco. It ended just like that. Not for them but for us!
We were already late and when we thought we should hit the highyway a couple of hours before the Norwegian border. ROADWORKS! So we had to do the small roads and lost more time.
In Oslo we struggled to find the right streets 'cos the capitol of Norway mainly exists of one-way roads!
At last, Hotel Plaza 20 meters from the bar Fiasco (right by the venue Spektrum where Motörhead played several times and also Sentrum scene and Rockefeller where they played even more shows during their time). BTW we brought Ainas three kids 12, 14 and 16 yrs old to MH last show in Spektrum the 3rd of Dec 2015...)
Back to the fiasco. For us...
Show was over an hour ago when we arrived but we had a nice chat with the guys (which we knew from before) and they was partly chocked and amused that we left Sweden Rock at Saturday three O'clock in the afternoon to reach them and MH in Bergen!
Sunday morning we woke up to rain outside and we left Oslo heading for Bergen (I almost cap-seized on the slippery bricks as a group of people waiting for a bus outside hotel wanted to hear me reving the engine when leaving...:-)
Ride went ok and sun was shining.
We started to relax a bit 'cos we could see we had enough time to reach Bergen in good time before the show.
I was a bit ahead of Aina like an eager rabbit or dog and on a roundabout I turned left as I thought I knew the way.
After a while I switched on the GPS navigator and I saw a big red

arrow on the screen that demanded me to turn around!!
WTF??? Can`t be true??? I stopped and rang up Aina. She answered via intercom. "Where the hell are you I asked" (shouted) "Same to you" she answered!
She was going straight ahead on the roundabout and was heading for Bergen.
"Yes I thought I also did and was sure about it" I replied "but now the GPS says I should turn around???"
"Yes 'cos it`s set up to choose a route without ferries" she said.....
"Ok. No time to turn around and go back" I said so I had to trust on that ferry and I hit the road again.
Almost crying:-)
By the way Aina was also in a hurry trying to catch up with me and she told me she had to stop for a while when the brakes boiled in the steep downhill roads...
When I finally reach the ferry harbour and could see the ferry in the middle of the fjord it seemed to me like the slowest ferry on this planet!!
At the ferry I met a bunch of men in their fifties on motorcycles and as normal you have to talk to other bikers and discuss bikes routes etc etc. They must have thought I was drunk. My only focus was to hit the other side and the road again as fast as fuck! But I tried to be polite. Wish I also had a more anonymous bike right there and then.
At once the ferry opened the hatch in front I was on the dock almost before the ferry was and then I disappeared in a big RRROOOOAAARHHHHhhhhh....! (Never saw the guys on bikes again behind me)
After what turned out being a 200 km solo ride, I came to a cross road and I knew that this can end up being a success 'cos I knew the distance we had left before Bergen and Aina should be in front of me.
Right after the city Voss there were some road work traffic signs...!
X"#?Z& then some!!!! If this is an ongoing issue I will kill someone I thought! It wasn't and in front of me by the stop sign I saw an ass I never been so happy to see in my life before.
Even if it was inside leather pants with saddlebags behind it!
So there we were, together again and heading for Bergen and Motörhead. Only 120 km left.....
We reached Bergen two hours before the show started.
WE MADE IT!
We checked in. Parked our bikes in the hotel garage and headed for our room, a shower, drinks, and some potato chips before

going off to show!
By the venue (Grieg Hallen) we met some friends.
Among them, one had that lost his mother the day before after a period of sickness. Respect!!
He made his decision and drove for some hours to get some treatment for his big loss and deep sorrow!
I think many of us can see ourselves in that situation. Motörhead help against EVERYTHING!
Another friend who was supposed to be there couldn't make it and he even got two backstage passes/tickets for him waiting there.
For no reason (or...?) I just did an "awful" thing...
Went up to the ticket office and said I was my friend using his name.
"Do you have any ID" the lady at the desk said.
"No I left my wallet at the hotel" I said "cos I don't want to lose my cards and stuff."
"Happened before at a Motörhead show" I said (which is true and a another story. Ended up with 3.60 Euro in my pocket on a 'gay friendly' (it said in the description I got after booking)... flotell boat not far from the venue where I had booked a cabin, in Berlin, and a show to catch in Wiezbaden the very next day...)
Lady at the ticket desk gaveme the tickets and passes and into the venue we went for another brilliant MH show!!!
No time for using backstage passes anyway and wouldn't do it 'cos just embarrassing if get caught trying to sneak in somewhere with another mans passes.
The feelin' of doing 1200 km on bikes since last afternoon (200+of them separated in big doubt if we ever managed to reach the show or see each other again...:-) was completely gone and the wörld was once again ours while we stood there by the fence!
After the show we went outside and together with others waited by the exit where Lemmy, Phil & Mikkey sooner or later would appear (we hoped)
It was quite fun being there and having a chat with other fans.
Since it was Sunday evening and a 'work day' the next day there was no "dead meat" around, just more or less hardcore fans. Most of them were even sober. Aina and I felt more or less sober even though we weren't but anyway after this travel we needed some "medication" to hang on. Some of the others we never met before. Some we "know" via Facebook.
We watched while the crew filled the trucks with the gear and we had a nice chat with Lemmy's bass tech Tim that told us they also had quite a trip from Sweden Rock up to Bergen when we told him

we left S Rock yesterday afternoon.
They had a flat tyre on one of the trucks and he was really "impressed" over the Norwegians road. But the nature was a great view he said.
After a while we start realize that Motörhead maybe would not show up. Sad but true.
We were only approx 15 to 20 people left there.
Instead a guy from the crew show up and collected items we brought in case of a chance for signatures…
He collected some of the stuff and ran off backstage.
When he returned I and a few others stood ready to get an item signed. My self I got a picture of Aina, Lemmy and me taken before the Plymouth gig in 2011 and the two backstage passes I "stole "at the ticket desk.
There also was a guy with a 'Snaggletooth' tattooed over his entire back.
You have to go inside I said to him before the guy from the crew returned.
When the dude returned with the signed items I said to him "this guy wants to get his tattoo signed so you have to bring him with you and while you're at it can you please get these backstage passes and this photo signed?"
"Sorry pal you're too late" he replied.
"NO I'm fuckin' not too late" I said!
And added "My girlfriend and I left Sweden Rock yesterday on motorcycles to attend tonight's show and we made it so we're not too late;-) These two passes belong to a friend of mine who didn`t manage to show up and I want to give him one of them and the other one I will give to a friend who lost his mother yesterday but still attended tonight's show but has gone home now. Pic you can see is girlfriend, me and Lemmy so would be fun to get that too signed." If he believed all this I don't know but he grabbed the items and got them signed.
After all this it was time for us and Motörhead to leave.
Their exit was not perfect from our point of view.
A minivan was backed into the venues off/on loading area and gate closed before it was opened some minutes later and the minivan left with Motörhead inside.
At least they waved and smiled to us as they drove off to the hotel just a few hundred meters away. Same hotel as we stayed at BTW.
But, we didn't bother to try to stalk them and instead headed for the rock pub 'Garage' and had a good time with friends hoping that

the guys maybe would show up there. They never did.
Of course we could spent time in the hotel lobby hoping to have a few words, maybe get our bikes signed (they were dirty anyway so no).
The thing is that with Motörhead it's as well important and funny to meet new friends and have fun with them and old ones as chasing heroes all night long.
The next day I imagine Lemmy & Co were up and out of the hotel a long time before we opened our eyes...
You can say this was much stress just to attend a MH show (and be sure, lots of our friends do just that!) But all you MHBs will understand.
It was worth the effort!
There's nothing like this common interest and there will not be another...
"My girlfriend and I met Lemmy backstage after Hammersmith show in Nov 2009.
When he started sign our tickets and a couple of CD's it showed up that he didn't have a proper working marker pen. One from the crew fetched him a new one. Afterwards it ended up that I got the marker pen in my hand as we left his wardrobe.
The very next day after the Wolverhampton show it was same story all over again when the band gave some signatures to the few of us waiting outside in the cold for them to come out from the venue and enter the bus. When Lemmy was supposed to sign my ticket his marker was fucked.
"Does anyone have a marker pen," he growled.
"Yes you can have mine," I said, "Got it from you yesterday."
"Yes I know!" he murmured.
Fucking spinal tap (Don't know if he did know but Lemmy was never out of answers!)
In the Lemmy movie you can see scenes from inside/outside the bus that night.
Another time it was in December 2010. I headed for Germany and two Motörhead shows. Berlin and Wiesbaden.
My girlfriend couldn't go due to work. I booked plane tickets and hotels. More exactly in Berlin I ordered a room at a 'flotell' (boat) as it was cheap and not far from the venue in Berlin. Off I go.
I was a bit proud that I managed to take a bus and then find the right station to jump off for the subway. Pretty near the venue it was.
I walked by as a big black limo entered the well-guarded gate to the back entrance of the venue. I can't for sure say it was "our"

guys but who else could it be? The time for sound check was right so I believe it was the boss himself.

No chance for me to enter due to eager guards everywhere so I headed off to that hotel boat and a couple of drinks.

I was a bit anxious due to the fact that when I got the booking confirmation it says it was 'gay friendly'. Never heard about 'gay unfriendly' hotels and myself I have nothing against gay persons, but here I was. Alone a man and about to check into a 'gay friendly' hotel boat. What can happen???

Anyway, The lady in the reception desk was friendly and she get jealous when she heard I was going to a Motörhead show. I offered her a ticket as I had got one extra but she couldn't do it anyway. So after a few drinks and a shower off I went to the venue. I sold the extra ticket in the ticket queue (normal price) and entered the venue.

Doro and Skew Siskin supported. Top notch as always! I remember I put my wallet in my shirt pocket and not in my back pocket to avoid it from being stolen.

But... after buying a drink before Motörhead entered I forgot about that and put it in my back pocket of my jeans.

The MH set was excellent!!! I was by the fence rockin', shouting and had a jolly fuckin' good time! THEN after. Fuck .My wallet was gone!!

Either someone had grabbed it or I just lost it, anyway it was gone! I looked all over the floor and I asked several guards where to ask for missing/found items etc.

I was in the venue till I had to leave it and then went to the security office but nothing there either. Left them my phone number just in case and then headed back to the hotel boat.

What the fuck do I do now??? I was out of money. All my cards gone cos I had the bright idea that I should not leave a card back at the room on the boat or some money cos maybe someone could break in and steal it anyway. Yeah right. What's the odds that could happen? Lost my wallet and my room being robbed???

So there I was. Alone in Berlin with 3 Euros and 40 Cents in my pocket...

I called my girlfriend and explained the situation. Then spent the rest of the night wondering what to do. Sell my ass on that 'gay friendly' boat to get travel money or maybe sell some cigarettes? I got a carton. My Jack D bottle I emptied.

The next day I checked out and headed for the bus stop to reach the bus to the airport. Hoping I had enough money for the trip. I got my plane ticket and hotel in Wiesbaden which was prepaid. But, I

needed food, drinks and bus money to go from airport to hotel and back. Bus was 2 Euros 60 so I managed.
I was on the phone constantly with my girlfriend and insurance company. Drank some water from the tap at the airport hotel. Fuck I was feelin' fucked up.
When I landed in Wiesbaden there was arranged money for me both from Aina and a small amount from the insurance company. I just had to find the office where to get the money and I managed!!! Fuck I was feellin' happy when I had again got money in my pocket!!
The first thing I bought was a fuckin' bottle of water and a salt Kringle (German cake). Oh dear!! I really was far out!
Caught the train and off I went to Wiesbaden to find the hotel. I fucked up and got off at the wrong station and had to walk and then caught a bus. Had no idea where I was but showed up that the bus stopped just 100 metres from my hotel and the venue was 200 from that again.
I had a couple of hours relaxing at the hotel in the tub. Had some drinks and then off to the venue. But I was so tired after constantly worrying about my situation over the last 20 hours that I was totally exhausted.
I was again by the fence during the show but I think if Lemmy noticed he would think I was the calmed down twin brother of that maniac lunatic 'look-a-like' by the fence in Berlin the night before!
Then after the show I went outside and there just outside the back entrance there was a big white limo parked with lights on.
There they were again, I was thinking. The reason for all this shit I going through. I didn't go up to the car but just stood there looking. No one else did either. After a while someone came out and entered the limo. No one from Motörhead as far I could see but they could already be in there.
Just when it turned out into the street the window on the right back side opened and an arm came out and a middle finger was raised to say good bye to us standing there.
I started laughing. It was just so fuckin' perfect! Here I had struggled as fuck to catch up and it had been busy all day trying to "survive" and reach the show and this was their message to me. It started with a black limo passing my nose when arriving in Berlin and ended with a greeting from a white limo in Wiesbaden. This tour had been perfect....
The very next day I had to wait 7 hours at the airport to get back home to Norway due to delays caused by heavy snowing.
It's only Rock 'n' Roll but we like it...

A few days after I got back home I got a packet in the mailbox. It was my wallet with everything in it except from the money and a note saying – 'I found this laying in the snow in strasse so and so... No name. Hope everything's in it!' No name of sender so I could thank him/her
Hope to see each and everyone everywhere!!
RÖCK OUT!"
Aina & Vidar Holm MHB 3403 & 2729 (Trondheim, Norway)

"I have never met him. One thing he never did he never compromised his music. He was true to his music, himself, the fans and the band. He loved his work and met his fans. And he was very funny too."
Tone Marie Antonsen (Sarpsborg, Norway)

"Went to see Motörhead for the first time in Oslo 2015, one of their last gigs.
The moment Lemmy said
"We are Motörhead, and we play rock 'n' fuckin' roll", was definitely one of the most awesome things I've ever experienced.
I was deaf for a week afterwards and still haven't fully recovered, but it was 100% worth it.
Lemmy is the definition of the term "rock-star" and one of my biggest inspirations. The memory of the awesomeness that happened in Oslo that night is something that'll make me smile like an idiot at all times. Cheers to Lemmy!"
Marius Nilsen Kleppe (Baldersheim, Norway)

"Just want to say thank you Lemmy and Motörhead for the music and memories!
Motörhead has been there and will always be there through the good times and the bad times in my life.
Rest in peace Lemmy, Würzel and Little Philthy!
I guess I'll see you all on the ice."
Erik Follestad MHB 3497 (Ørsta, Norway)

"My love affair with Motörhead started when I was 14 years old. 'Go to Hell' was blasting from the speakers at a friends house. Lemmy had me at "Hello" you might say.
His characteristic voice and the 'angriness' of the sound spoke to me like no other music had before. From that day on, I was a MHB, without even knowing that there was a club just for us. Growing up in a small place in Norway, I did feel like the odd girl

out at times, but I couldn't care less. Rock 'n roll was MY music. Motörhead was there through my rebellion as a teen. Blasting (as much as a casette player could "blast") Lemmys music so that my parents could FEEL my rage, was a great feeling.
Motörhead has been with me through all of life's ups and downs. The band I never grew tired of, the band who always had a track fitting any kind of mood, the band I will love 'till the end.
In the early 90's I was in L.A on holiday for a month. Ended up in a tattoo shop not far from The Rainbow, it turned out the artist was a friend of Lemmy. Long story short, I got the opportunity to have a few drinks at the Rainbow with my hero.
I was starstruck for about a minute, until Lemmy included me in the conversation asking about Norway.
That he knew more about Norway's history during WW2 than I, is an understatement. I was in awe, not because I was there chatting with my hero over a drink, but at how friendly and including he was.
Many years later I had the opportunity to sit down backstage with the band as they played in Hamar. I was interviewing Mikkey for the local newspaper as Lemmy walked in, greeted us kindly and invited me in for a chat after my work was done.
I of course blurted out something like
"I've loved you since I was 14!"
To that he grinned, and said
"Thank you, that's nice to hear!"
I felt like an utter fool! I am sure he didn't remember me from the Rainbow, (I mean how many short blonde girls must he have talked to in his life?) He was however, as kind as before, and gave me his full attention for a long time.
Lemmy means the world to me, he will always be a huge part of my life. I can even say, that through Lemmy and MHB, I found true love.
The Motörheadbangers family will forever keep his legacy alive. Hearing the news of his passing was devastating, I was, and still am, crushed by grief.
I will continue to play it loud, cheers Lemmy, I love you!"
Monica Iren Moe Masdal MHB #3423 (Ørstal, Norway)

"I saw the first Motörhead concert in Norway, Jordal Amfi, 1985.
I was 16 years old, and had been a fan since I was ten. After the show I spoke with Phil, Würzel and Lemmy - and got all their autographs. Lemmy signed the ticket and shook my hand to thank me for coming to the concert. He also signed my cigarette pack

after taking a cigarette for himself.
All of this is now lost, except the memories. But the memories are good; he was nice and talked with all of us who had lined up for autographs. Lemmy even told off the tour manager when he came to get them to stop. There were still a few fans in line.
My last Motörhead concert was 3.12.15, Oslo.
So I caught both the very first and very last Motörhead show in Norway, 30 years apart.
This last time I had my son, 16 years old, to the show. In Oslo I took a photo of the stage before Motörhead was about to play 'Whorehouse Blues'. It's an empty stage.
When I got the message that Lemmy was gone, I saw it on Facebook - an update from Stacia of Hawkwind fame, the photo took on a new significance for me.
Motörhead has been my favourite band for 37 years and a constant in my life."
Stefan Andreas Sture (Sarpsborg, Norway)

"Me and a friend of mine got to meet Lemmy and the band backstage in 1995, 'Sacrifice' tour in Oslo.
All thanks to my friends uncle, he was a freelance photographer and knew all the tricks to get in. They were doing an interview with Norwegian radio, so we were guided to the bands backstage and to be honest, heartbeat raised when we saw Lemmy entering the room. I had been a fan since '91 and had just seen the man on telly and on videos. So I was a bit unsure of how he would be. But we got to talk to him, don't remember anything, but we got to take a lot of pix with them.
Remember asking Lemmy if I could have his nazi memorabilia, that he wore on is jacket, he just laughed and said he would give me this, and showed me his fist.
Then it was stagetime and Lemmy disappeared for a moment. Mikkey said Lemmy always needed some minutes alone before a gig, but Phil just laughed and said it was
"white line time." Oh yes!
There was a very beautiful Asian woman there, she interviewed Lemmy and then the photograper said,
"haha I know that Asian woman, I got a lot of pictures of her at home." So I guess Lemmy got entertained during the interview. But what I remember the best, is the hospitality Lemmy and the band showed us. Mikkey came in quite shocked by the way, sometime during the meeting. He had been downstairs and on the way back he saw a woman pulling her pants down and peeing on the

window he passed by on the way to the backstage again. He mentioned that quite a few times afterwards. That was '95.
So in '97 we got to meet them again.
This time around we managed to meet them by ourselves and now we had the pix we got in '95 with us. So we were hoping to get them signed.
This time they recognised us and invited us to the 'holy grail' of backstage. Lemmy was walking around in a military uniform and doing military salutes to us.
We could even put our Motörhead LP's, pictures of them back where they had their riders set up. And my oh my, that rider was quite something.
Well, we got our stuff signed, although Lemmy just wanted to sign 3 items from the each of us. I don't blame him, we had lots with us. So I got my picture with me and Lemmy signed and the 'Overnight Sensation' and 'Sacrifice' LP signed.
After that session was over I thought that they would get rid of us, but no, Mikkey and Lemmy said we could keep our stuff there until the gig was over. So we just walked around and got the whole deal. They offered us drinks, food and snacks. They just let us do anything. I mean, that's hospitality and to trust their fans.
I remember saying to Lemmy –
"You're getting better and better for every record."
He smiled and said –
"Yeah, like wine and horrible cheese, even that gets better with the years."
We got to listen to the sound check, they played 'War For War' and a Rolling Stones number and man, that was loud!!!
After the sound check Lemmy went to play Terminator pinball and he actually asked if we could,
"Lemmy a fiver."
'Cos that was what it costed back then and about an hour before the gig, Lemmy wondered if we had the 'Bomber' CD or cassette with us, cause he would like to listen to the ending of 'Bomber'.
Don't remember, but it might have been on the set list.
I must say it was quite a view to see Lemmy on his knees in front of a CD player listening to the ending of 'Bomber'.
Then Phil came by and he pulled some pranks on us and shortly after, gig time.
It was loud as always, but we enjoyed it, that's for sure.
After the gig, Mikkey came to us with all the things we had backstage, and said it was party time. But we had to go, and to be honest, we couldn't have asked for more anyway. We were treated

as gold. So that's the stories from the 90's.
Met them in Oslo 2011 and a friend of mine should take a picture with me the band. But he had the mobile turned the wrong way, so he photographed himself, not me with the band and we didn't figure it out until it was too late....."
Espen Dellerud (Raufoss, Norway)

Pakistan

Capital City: Islamabad
Population: 199,085,847
Currency: Pakistani Rupee
Bands: Entity Paradigm, Mizraab, Karavan

"I learn to play guitar and sing metal.
Lemmy has an incredible vocal style. I have listened to every single one of their albums. I like their countless songs.
They've been working since 1975 and Lemmy is known to be the great bass guitar legend.
I wish to become a metal singer. Although here in Pakistan metal singing is not very popular and people criticise me a lot over my passion.
I can also sing like growl voice and still learning to play guitar.
It is only me who listens to metal in my family. But all of my family members and I think the people all around the world like their songs that they sung about Triple H, 'The Game' and 'King of Kings'.
My favourite songs by them are 'Ace of Spades', 'Rock Out', 'Overkill', 'Killed by death' and 'Stone Dead Forever'"
Jack Pli (Pakistan)

Poland

Capital City: Warsaw
Population: 38,483,957
Currency: Złoty
Bands: Behemoth, Vader, Artrosis, Graveland

*"Fantastic concert ... Only one sixty minute ...
My GOD Lemmy & I."*
Michał Staniszewski (Łódź, Poland)

Sonisphere Poland
Lotnisko Bemowo, Warsaw
10th June 2011

Iron Fist
Stay Clean
Get Back In Line
Metropolis
Over the Top
One Night Stand
The Chase Is Better Than the Catch
In the Name of Tragedy
I Know How to Die
Going to Brazil
Killed by Death

Ace of Spades
Overkill

*"When it comes to me I got to know Motörhead few years ago. I firstly wanted to know some facts about it, than was music.
After these years I managed to listen to this great band and appreciate their music.
To me Lemmy was a very interesting and outstanding person. I still miss him so much and I try to live with the fact that he's dead.
He had a huge impact on my life, when it comes to music and attitude to bassists.
Now I'm listening to his music and I'm happy to know him and his band."*
Paulina Nogaj (Rzeszów, Poland)

Romania

Capital City: Bucharest
Population: 19,511,000
Currency: Romanian Leu
Bands: Negură Bunget, Trooper, Byron

*"Rest in Peace/Power, Lemmy Kilmister.
What can I say... He was like a father to me, even though we were not relatives. I lived and am still living some of the things he lived. My father was never around, he never gave a shit about me and I was raised by my mother and my grandmother.
I think that's what brought me really close to his music and what he meant. Never been the one to take shit from anybody. His music, to me, was like the advice a father should give to his son when he needs it. It always took me up when I was 6 feet under, figuratively, shaked the dust off me and got me on my feet again, standing tall, proud and mean.
Maybe it sounds stupid, but for me, the feeling brought by his passing is a lot similar to the feeling someone gets when he loses*

a close relative.
He was a great man, indeed. He lived his life doing what he loved, not taking shit from anyone and enjoying every fuckin' moment.
To Ian Fraser 'Lemmy' Kilmister! Born to lose, live to win!
At 'OST Fest', Bucharest, Romania in 2012 I saw Motörhead *for the first and only time. Rest in power."*
Christian Boiangiu (Bucharest, Romania)

Ost Fest
Bucharest
17th June 2012

Bomber
Damage Case
I Know How to Die
Stay Clean
Metropolis
Over the Top
One Night Stand
The Chase Is Better Than the Catch
The One to Sing the Blues
Just 'Cos You Got the Power
Going to Brazil
Killed by Death
Ace of Spades
Overkill

Serbia

Capital City: Belgrade
Population: 7,041,599
Currency: Serbian Dinar
Bands: Pop Mašina, Cactus Jack, Night Shift

"Serbia loves Motörhead."
Mile Gajic (Cacak, Serbia)

"I had the privilege to be born in the same year when Motörhead formed by the legendary Lemmy. So last year we celebrated together our 40th jubilee.
Band is marked my life in the full sense, Lemmy was my spiritual guide. Growing up in the era of communism, the majority of the most important philosophies of life, I received through, Kilmister lyrics and statements in media.
Infected in my early age with raw 'n' furious music, all along I was determined to succeed in my life attitudes.He taught me how to live, smile, be rebelious, see the difference between good and evil, be kind, honest, honorable, helping the weak and be a man.
It was so exciting to hear their music on a record for the first time, raw energy overtakes and never lets you down.
My first Motörhead show happened 26 yrs ago, 1990, March 28th, I was only 15yrs old.I was so excited, when the guys show on stage it was like in some SF movie for me at the time.Like a big wall of sound crashed at me with pure essential energy drives me till the end of the show. During the war in ex-Yugoslavia and economic sanctions, their music was so much of a help and needed.His words of sympathy and messages of hope in interviews, helped us all to overcome, those terrible years.Even when NATO bombed us in 1999 for a 3 months, he never let us down, despite most of musicians he had the warm words of comfort for us. It is proof of his humanity.
Twelve years after the first, comes the second show, this time in a stadium, it was a summer.

Night before the show, a friend of mine, a musician, invited me to a pub gig to hear his band, that night the promoters came with Lemmy, Phil, Mikkey Dee and the road crew.
Kilmister set table near mine, I say hi to him and cheers with a pint of beer, Lemmy says cheers with a Jack 'n' Coke.
He was sitting like an ordinary fan, drinking and chatting.
After the gig he stood outside until the last fan had, had their picture with him. Next day open stadium was full packed with Motörhead fans from all over the Balcan's. Thrills and excitement kept us all waiting.
The band sent us enormous energy, it was mutual, I felt like 12yrs ago, like a 15 yrs old kid I had chills.
Lemmy turned up his bass amp after every 2 songs, the show and the atmosphere was great!
Thirteen years passed in a waiting for a 3rd Motörhead show in Serbia, It happened last summer on a 40th Anniversery tour. Main stage on "Petrovaradinska Fortress" on Exit festival.
I had three Anniversaries - my 40th birthday, Motörhead's 40th birthday and my 33yrs of enjoying their music and message.
I arrived immediately before the show. In front of stage was fully packed with fans from all over the world, a fabulous crowd all together, eagerly waiting to see the guys on a stage.
The show started like before, despite his bad condition, Lemmy's, determination to play was commendable. Despite this, he kept playing and played a full show. That deserved full respect.
I wish him to rest in peace, if he would have perhaps more liked to tell him to rest in eternal party on some higher level.
The 'Last Mohican' of uncompromising rock 'n' roll attitude. Thanks for all the music, contributions and warm words.
His legacy is priceless and it will stay forever for the next generations.
Of Motorhead 'n' Lemmy, I'm an eternal fan."
Milos Milosevic (Novi Banovci, Serbia)

Killed by Death!
In memory of Ian 'Lemmy' Kilmister

"2015 ended with one of the most tragic events for Rock 'n' Roll.

On December the 28th Ian Lemmy Frazer Kilmister died. Pretty sad news to close the year with. I heard about it at 8 am and I refused to believe that the incarnation of Rock 'n' Roll is no longer with us. There was an urban legend that said: "After the post Nuclear War Apocalypse, the only remaining things on earth would be cockroaches, rats and Lemmy!" But sadly, we were not lucky enough to see that. I used to joke with my friends that those big moles were his source of power, and that he would eventually die if one of these moles fell off of his face. A lot of you may think something like: woooahh, this guy is rude!! but man, as far as I know, Lemmy was the guy who appreciated humor of all sorts more than anything in the world.

Anyway, after hearing the bad news I tried to fall asleep again but that was pretty impossible at the moment. As soon as I sat down on my computer, the web was already flooded by this. Then I put One more fucking time in my playlist and started to cry as a baby. I cried till my eyes went dry. Still, I cannot believe he is not with us anymore. His music really means a lot to me. He is the man that taught me to say 'FUCK YOU' to everything I don't like. He was like a father or a mental guru of some sorts that opened my eyes during the teenage years even more than my friends and my family. His lyrics and the way of thinking shaped my mind for good (although I cannot say the same for his lifestyle). Lemmy said that doing acid made him a better person. I am quite sure that millions of people think the same for his music. Everything about him is just exceptional. Not many people can say that they remember a time when there was no Rock 'n' Roll (and who can also claim to had seen his favorite band - The Beatles - before they even recorded their debut album or to had been the roadie for Jimi Hendrix for instance??). He may not be the founder of this genre, but I deem to say that he was definitely one of the most iconic musicians of all time. It's also good to notice that he was born right after the WWII on December the 24th 1945. Pretty cool if you are familiar with Lemmy's interest in history, and collection of his war memorabilia. As I mentioned above, he was THE incarnation of Rock 'n' Roll. And there are plenty of reasons for that! First of all, no one looked as badass as him. His image was truly unique. As far as I know, Lemmy was probably the first guy who introduced bullet belts into classic Rock 'n' Roll /metal image. His way of living was also badass and over the top: sex, drugs, Rock 'n' Roll were part of his everyday life. It's like a line in one of his songs: Everything changes, except for Lemmy!!! He was an axiom or algorythm of some sorts that stayed the same throughout time with no sign of regret in his life. Not many people remained true to themselves like Lemmy.

As far as his music is concerned, he left a HUGE legacy to the world behind him. Motörhead was one of the few bands who could unite metalheads, Rock 'n' Roll fans, punks, hardcore kids, bikers, skinheads etc. under their wing and cast all their differences and hate aside. And that's the ultimate power of music. The impact he had on the genre was tremendous! I mean, his music palette was overflown with subgenres of Rock 'n' Roll: psychedelic stuff (Hawkwind) classic Rock 'n' Roll, blues, rockabilly, punk, hardcore, thrash metal. His harsh vocals may be recognized as a "proto death metal growls" (long before Jeff Becerra or Chuck Schuldiner). Some of his songs, like 'The Hammer', 'Orgasmatron', 'Tear Ya Down', 'Metropolis', or 'BURNER' (the list could go on) can make Slayer or Morbid Angel or any extreme metal bands sound like pussies. And yep, Motorhead played thrash metal or punk before there was any thrash metal or punk at all. His music was definitely ahead of its time. Who the fuck had songs like 'Vibrator' back in 1977? But I even appreciate him more as an excellent lyricist. I would need about 20 pages to give his lyrics a proper justice. His writing style was in your face.

'Orgasmatron' is probably his best work. Among one of his finest lyrical works are: 'The Hammer', 'Bad Religion', 'Love me Forever', 'One More Fucking Time', 'Nightmare the Dream Time', 'Capricorn', 'Jack The Ripper', 'Going to Brazil', 'Bomber', 'Make My Day', 'Dead and Gone', 'Take the Blame', 'Sacrifice' etc. etc.

But I would mark off 'Don't Let Daddy Kiss Me' as one of the most shocking songs of all time. I am assured that not many bands can write something as brutal as that! Lemmy was truly a poet: no one can stay indifferent by his marvelous '1916' song. What I also loved so much about his lyrics is that he had no mercy for politicians; you can hear Lemmy bark: 'Politician scum, you make me wanna puke!' A few years ago, my English teacher asked the class if they could name some of the politicians who are also good people in general. I said to her: "There aren't". She asked me "How come?" but I just couldn't introduce a 55 years old bitch to Motörhead. Lemmy's music is a privilege for a few. However, Lemmy was an idol to 5 or 6 generations and that number will grow over the years forever!   It's kinda weird to know that Lemmy will be remembered by 'Ace of Spades' which is a mediocre song when compared with the rest of Motörhead's catalogue. And band like this definitely deserves more attention when one takes into consideration how big

*Lemmy's contribution to Rock 'n' Roll really is. In my opinion, these albums are pure evergreens: **'Motörhead'**, **'Overkill'**, **'Bomber'**, **'On Parole'**, **'Ace of Spades'**, **'Iron Fist'**, **'Another Perfect Day'**, **'Orgasmatron'**, **'Rock 'n' Roll'**, **'1916'**, **'March or Die'**, **'Bastards'**, **'Overnight Sensation'**, **'Snake Bite Love'**, **'We are Motörhead'** and **'Inferno'** or to be more precise, 16 magnificent classic albums everyone should listen to. I may be a fanboy but that's the way like it baby! I cannot describe how many times I've listened to first 3 records, or the ones from 'Orgasmatron' to 'We are Motörhead' era. Albums from the 90's are among the finest for sure!! (It's kinda ironic that I was introduced to Motörhead with 'Snake Bite Love' and 'We are Motörhead' and not with 'Ace of Spades', haha). Lemmy was a hero. One of a kind. Ljubljana incident shows how great a man he was. Back in 1989, some Slovenian prick joined a dime with a razor and then threw it at Lemmy. That "thing" hit him right in his arm. Even though razor cut his arm and blood was all over the place, Lemmy continued to play and finished the concert. Right after that, he was being hospitalized and the rest of European tour was canceled due to his bad wound. Who the fuck would continue to play the whole concert under such a bizzare event? LEMMY would. And how much he loved his fans approves the fact that he was back in Yugoslavia in a year after this stupid event took place. And I hope that the guy who did that shameful thing rots in hell! That wound could've cost Lemmy his career! In the end, Lemmy got the guts to finish his last tour in such a bad state. 99% of musicians would stay in bed with their family around, but Lemmy kept on playing till the end!*

Words can't describe how great of a loss Lemmy's death is. It really shook the world. I am still in disbelief that the Godfather of Metal, (as James Hetfield named him) the incarnation of Rock 'n' Roll is no longer with us. But his legacy will live on throughout the ages! The world was crying and celebrating his death at the same time! His name will echo in eternity! He was only 70 years old. However, it is extraordinary for him to had lived that long when his lifestyle is concerned. He did so much drugs, that I wouldn't be surprised if his blood and sweat were halluciogenic drugs xD. If Lemmy is in Valhala right now, partying with berserkers from the north, I bet that the Vikings just couldn't keep on drinking with him. A week ago, I was talking to my friend about Lemmy and said, well, he's 'Killed by Death'. And my friend said: "better to be killed by death than to be killed by life". I will never forget that. In the end, everyone dies to break somebody's heart. And Lemmy's

death broke many. I hope that he is looking at the clouds from the other side of heaven!
He will surely be missed."
Miloš Čabraja - Editor of 'Agoraphobic News' (Serbia)

Slovenia

Capital City: Ljubljana
Population: 2,063,077
Currency: Euro
Bands: Naio Ssaion, Leaf Fat, Dekadent, Buldožer

"I am writing you to tell you my story about my experience from Motörhead concert for the book.
The concert took place in Tivoli hall in Ljubljana, Slovenia on 10th of December 2012.
It was the first Motörhead concert in our country since 1989.
Venue was the same. I saw announcement in magazine one day and the next day I ordered ticket on the Internet.
One week later it arrived. I was so excited to go but it was months until concert.
Finally the day came. The concert was scheduled to start at 8pm but because of the opening act, Motörhead started at 9pm.
When they started I was blown away.
They started with "I Know How to Die". I was right at the front but not in the VIP area which was right next to the stage. I felt the raw power of the band and I was enjoying it to the maximum.
Set list included 13 songs, last one being 'Ace of Spades'. Naturally everybody went crazy. After the song they left and came back for encore.
After 'Are You Ready' cover, Lemmy made an introduction of the band, called the names of Phil and Mickey and then Phil introduced Lemmy. Again everybody went crazy.
What followed was 'Overkill', last song ever played by Motörhead in our country.
In the end Lemmy said: "I hope we come back sooner." But that will never happen.
One more thing about this concert. It was only one in our part of Europe and there were many people form other neighbouring countries. We were lucky because next concert was cancelled

because of Lemmy's health."
Nejc Jenko (Slovenia)

Hala Tivoli, Ljubljana
10th December 2012

I Know How to Die
Damage Case
Stay Clean
Metropolis
Over the Top
The Chase Is Better Than the Catch
Rock It
You Better Run
The One to Sing the Blues
Going to Brazil
Killed by Death
Ace of Spades
Are You Ready?
Overkill

Spain

Capital City: Madrid
Population: 46,439,864
Currency: Euro
Bands: Barón Rojo, Obús, Panzer, Haemorrhage

"Very good idea, so the book is great, and for good cause is cancer, I have experienced the death of my father.
I encourage is a brilliant idea.
I tell my story to the great Lemmy.
It was during the tour of '1916', in 1991 they performed in Barcelona, in a venue named Zeleste, and as always risen in the front row on the fence and left the Lemmy and the band.
Lemmy had a cigar in his mouth and then spit, Motörhead to present cigar went straight to my long hair, burning it almost entirely.
After the song Lemmy went on drums and gave me a Jack Daniel's with Coke, then invited me backstage, so I did.
It was the best time of my life ... that no other details would have done and is one LORD."
Miguel Manzano Reche (Barcelona)

"Well My first Motörhead gig was in Zaragoza, Spain, several years ago. I was with some friends in the first line, very close to Lemmy, in front of him.
And I'm sorry, but one of the things that I more remember of that gig was how big was his "package", you know what I mean...? The fuckin size of his balls!!!! I thought, "Maybe he has some socks there, Jesus..."
I'm not gay, but have you ever seen that Simpson's episode when Homer goes to Le Cirque du Soleil and a juggler dance his package close to Homers head? It was something like that, you know...?
When I came back home my wife asked me how it was, and I answered "awesome gig, dear, and what a pair of balls has that motherfucker!!" She was outraged and said that I was sick.

Years later Lemmy and the guys came to play to Madrid and I went with my wife. After the concert she said me " José, sorry but you were right... what a package."
José Carlos Martinez Villamayor (Madrid, Spain)

Monsters of Rock
Zaragoza
June 23rd 2007

Snaggletooth
Stay Clean
Be My Baby
Killers
Metropolis
Over the Top
One Night Stand
I Got Mine
In the Name of Tragedy
Sword of Glory
Rosalie
Sacrifice
Just 'Cos You Got the Power
Going to Brazil
Kille by Death
Iron Fist
Whorehouse Blues

Ace of Spades
Overkill

*"I have met Lemmy a couple of times over the years. He was always the kindest person you can imagine. He influenced my life big time! He was the reason why I started to play music myself in the first place.
In 2007 he signed my Rickenbacker Bass guitar in Munich after a Motörhead Show!
The other time in London 2011 at the Brixton academy. I could spend some time with him and Tim Butcher before the Show in Lemmy´s dressing room listening to Motörhead songs with the big man himself! What an experience that was, I will never forget that! Every time I met him he was a real gentleman. It´s just so unreal to believe that now there wont be any more Motörhead shows. That was definitely the Highlight out of all the Motörhead shows that I was able to attend over the past 11 years. Now there is definitely something huge missing in me and also in the Music scene. It's a gap which can´t be filled.
In January I flew to LA to take part in Lemmy's memorial service at the Rainbow Bar and Grill. That was the least I could do if you consider what this man did for his fans! He gave everything for us! He played until the last moment for us. There will never be another one like Lemmy! He was just the greatest! I will miss him so much! But his legacy lives on!
Thanks you for everything Lemmy!
Rest in Peace."*
Burgi Zerschellt MHB3450 (Barcelona)

*"Motörhead gave me my life back when I was a depressive teenager cunt, but then I started listening to Motörhead, a band that turned me into a man and gave me back my will to live.
Fortunately I attended their last concert in my country and I'm very proud I could see a true legend on stage at least once in my life."*
Daniel V (Spain)

Sweden

Capital City: Stockholm
Population: 9,851,017
Currency: Swedish Krona
Bands: Amon Amarth, Opeth, In Flames, Ghost

*"There will only be one Lemmy.
There will only be one Motörhead.
There will not be any band like that on earth anymore.
But Lemmy and Motörhead's legacy of true Rock'N'Roll will always live in my heart and soul and all Motörhead headbangers all around the world.
So thank You Lemmy. Thank You Motörhead And All Members through all the years for delivering the best Rock 'N' Roll Music in music history in that style. .\m/. .
U did it your way Lemmy and Motörhead.
And you did It "Damn Good ".
Rest In Peace. \m/."*
Flodiz (Mörthzz – Drums - Uppsala Sweden)

"Back in 2005 I travelled to London for the XXX-gig at Hammersmith Odeon. I was able to take two pictures that I think are pretty good, specially considering that I used a simple digital pocket camera."
Peder Lundin MBH-2125 (Holsljunga, Sweden)

*"First time I saw Motörhead was in 1980 (I was 11 years old) in Stockholm, Sweden I was there together with a good friend of mine and my older brother, I have seen Motörhead many many times after that.
I was hooked. I saw Motörhead play in my hometown Sundsvall, Sweden in 1999 on the 'Monsters of the Millennium' gig together with Dio, Manowar and Lions Share.
The only last message I can give to Lemmy is ROCK 'N' ROLL...."*

Ernie Wallman (Skönsberg, Sweden)

*"I'll never forget my first Motörhead gig, 'Iron Fist' tour in Leiden The Netherlands, Stadsgehoorzaal.
It was in the center of the city and we were all in front of the venue hours before they would open the doors.
We were having fun, drinking beer, smoking and making a campfire in the middle of the street :)
The police didn't think like we did so they came with the riot police and beat the shit out of us, spreading all the fans all over the city.
When it was time for the doors to open we all came back.
After getting in the venue it became all a blur in my memory.
I do remember it was LOUD, LOUD as hell, being my second rock concert in my life I got baptized well :)
Still when people don't understand why I don't hear what they say I answer "I saw Motörhead in the '80ties :) that's why."
After that gig I saw Motörhead a lot of times in the Netherlands, always delivering the goods.
My first 'Monsters Of Rock' was also with Motörhead and OZZY, Scorpions, Bad News, Def Leppard and Warlock. Loved it all.
Since 15 years I moved to Gothenburg, Sweden, hometown of Mikkey Dee, and became a local crew chief for Live Nation.
During these years I worked on a lot of Motörhead gigs and got to know there crew well.
Great, great days and memories forever.
Will miss them big time, seeing them live."*
Peter Verhoef (Gothenburg)

*"A few years ago I was writing for a Swedish music site called 'Nyaskivor.se'. I was fortunate enough to get the chance to interview Mikkey Dee over phone.
First time I reached him they were up on a roof in London shooting the video for 'Get Back in Line', I had to call later and then we had a nice chat."*
Mats Johansson, Båstad, Sweden

"Ian Fraser Kilmister is god !!!!"
Isac Buström (Umeå, Sweden)

*"When Lemmy died a huge part of rock 'n' roll died and I'm sure a part of every metalhead died too.
We all miss him very much and I know that we're all trying not to be sad and it's hard. I blast Motörhead louder than hell every day*

and drink some Jack Daniel's. I think everyone should do that to honor the memory of him.
Motörhead forever \m/ "
Sarah Ozzy Rhoads (Malmö, Sweden)

"I saw Motörhead 1986 on a outdoor football field in Närpes Finland. When they walked off stage, on their way to the dressing room, a local reporter screamed at Lemmy for an interview. Lemmy was tired and replied "argh, fuck off".
I was 12 years old and went with my big sister to the gig.
After that gig I was a diehard Motöhead fan."
Mr Loiti Loo (Stockholm, Sweden)

"Back in '92 I went to LA to study music, and the Rainbow became our living room and of course Lemmy was part of the furniture.
He was a true gentleman and one evening, when it was a bit crowded, he didn't mind me asking if I could have a seat beside him.
He was simply a nice guy."
Bo Jonsson (Gustavsberg, Sweden)

"It was a stormy day at the Island of Hyppeln. The water was high so the ferry didn't go as it should, also the buses were cancelled. Just typical for this day, I thought to myself.
When Motörhead should play in Gothenburg, I called for a taxi that should pick me up at Burö. So I got to the second ferry at Hönö Pinan, when my cousin called and said that the buses to Gothenburg were going as they should so I could get there in time.
I was so nervous that I should miss the concert. But the bus came and I got to Lisebergshallen and we got to stand nearest to the stage where they soon would start the concert.
Everything went black and the siren started to sound. The lights go around the room. Then we heard the voice we all were waiting for. 'BOMBER'!!!
And there he stands, the Godfather of Rock 'n' Roll. Lemmy! The show was great and the band really played the best rock 'n' roll I'd ever heard.
The storm outside had no chance against Lemmy's bass playing, it was so high and raw so even a war outside would have no chance. And from this day I just loved Motörhead.
I never thought someone could play as a rhythm guitar on a bass but Lemmy could, he was really one of a kind.

I think everyone in Gothenburg could hear when they started to play 'Ace of spades', 120 decibel pure rock 'n' roll!
This was two of the best hours in my life, so from me to you Lem I hope they got Daniels and cola in the sky, cheers to you!
My favourite song is 'Bad woman', the only rock 'n' roll song I've heard when the piano gets so good in that kind of music.
R.I.P. Lemmy"
John Johaneseen (Hyppeln, Sweden)

Lisbergshallen
Gothenburg
9th December 2011

Bomber
Damage Case
I Know How to Die
Stay Clean
Metropolis
Over the Top
One Night Stand
The Chase is Better Than the Catch
Get Back In Line
I'll Be Your Sister
The One to Sing the Blues
Orgasmatron
Going to Brazil
Killed by Death
Iron Fist
Whorehouse Blues
Ace of Spades
Overkill

```
LIVE NATION
PRESENTERAR
MOTÖRHEAD
INSLAPP 18:30
LISEBERGSHALLEN, GÖTEBORG
FREDAG 9 DECEMBER 2011 KL 19.30
Sektion                    RAD      PLATS
B Vänster                   4        13
PRIS: 395,00 + serv.avg 0,00 ARR. BILJ.
8209408 . Live Nation
ÅLDERSGRÄNS 13 ÅR
KÖPT BILJETT ÅTERLÖSES EJ
```

"First time was 1995 in Gothenburg.
I was 16 years and this was my first concert on my own (thanks mom and dad). What can I say, I was as close to heaven as any living person can be.
15 Motörhead shows I was able to see......what can I say? Thank you for some great memories!
You were Motörhead. You played Rock n' Roll
And I will never let anyone forget you."
Pelle Monat (Sweden)

"Saw Motörhead first time in 1985 in Jönköping Sweden, at an Ice Hockeyarena called Parcahallen.
It was so loud, so the next week the only thing I could hear was the beep from my ears.
Lovely week!"
Jonny Andersson (Jönköping, Sweden)

"I saw them '82 first time.
It was the last gig in Stockholm Sweden with Phil and Fast Eddie. Have seen all concerts in Stockholm since that.
Did meet Lemmy only once, it was Swedish Metal Nights, in a Club called Studion.
I had to borrow an ID card to get in, I was two years too young but I did get in. He was walking around in the Club and talked to everyone and I did get his autograph....then I was happy like a child!"
Michail Wennström (Mälarhöjden, Stockholms Län, Sweden)

9/11-2011 Gothenburg Lisebergshallen it is for me the first time seeing Motörhead live. 2 days before they cancelled a show in Norway because Lemmy had voice problem.
I was so nervous that they maybe had to cancel this show too. That show was a fuckin' great show. It was The 'Wörld is Yours' tour.
They even played 'Whorehouse Blues' and when they kicked the whole place with 'Overkill' I ripped my earplugs out and got fuckin' crazy. I didn't know where I was because of the strobes, I will never forget that night.
The second show was at Sweden Rock Festival 2012 I was standing in the front row to the right where Lemmy's place was it was an hell of a show with Motörhead and The Bomber rig.
R.I.P Lemmy I miss u and it hurts that I am not able to Motörhead anymore with you in the front in this life.
Motörhead 4 ever."
André Nissen (Trelleborg, Sweden)

Switzerland

Capital City: Bern
Population: 8,211,700
Currency: Swiss Franc
Bands: Knut, Gotthard, Celtic Frost, Coroner

"Oh my old brain cells recollect my encounter with Lemmy.
It was at a Reading Rock Festival when the organisers of the Festival made a tour with the mayor of Reading in front of the stage while Motörhead was playing. What a nice timing he he!!
Lemmy's work was very respected by many."
Marcel Kolb (Uetendorf, Switzerland)

"Lemmy or Lem as many used to call him - the Man, the Myth, the Legend – we will miss you.
Your legacy will live on through your art, Rock 'n' Roll at its finest – especially when it's played loud and proud.
The loudest band in the world, that tingling feeling when the lights go down and those words ring out 'We Are Motörhead *And We Play Rock 'n' Roll', from that moment onwards who cares what happens next, it's going to be good, my ears will be ringing and my neck will be in a brace, but as a proud* Motörheadbanger *I wouldn't expect anything less.*
From the first show in Geneva in 1981, I was thrilled to be able to meet the bands, that sort of paced me for the next years of my life, you were so approachable, we had a discussion about linings in leather jackets and what they could be used for.
For 36 years this band have been part of my life, made me live my life as a down to earth Motörhead *fan, I consider myself blessed to have been so passionate about this band to have gone on both Motörböat voyages and have met up with so many dedicated loyal fantastic people over the years.*
My fave position at a Motörhead show is clinging to the front row, barrier steadying me as I bang my head in rhythm to the tunes, whiplash? Sure, regularly, but I am living for the moment, again

and again, having attended close to 100 shows, travelling over all of Europe, even the day I passed my driving license the first thing I did was drive over 3 hours to see the show in Wettingen, am I crazy? Perhaps, I'd call it dedicated.

My other memories including broken ribs, bruises and blisters galore, rain drenched leather jacket, muddy everything as well as the multiple hangovers and no regrets ever, like the big man said, we don't do regrets. I can't believe that sad day has come, where we need to realize that Lemmy is no more, it is almost like losing a family member, and us Metal heads we are a big family.

A couple of meetings with Lemmy I will always remember – The summer of 1986, Castle Donington being the regular annual holiday, he lived in North London and I found his home (thanks to NME, the name of the pub was too explicit and me being sneaky figured out how to find the street address) and trailing along a bunch of Frenchies (that is French guys), one of which was a French reporter from Paris, knocked on your door, you were a bit surprised, and told us that you didn't do that at your door so we should basically 'fuck off', but we were fearless in those days, and you did sign autographs and let us take a few photos, a true gentleman as always.

I did avoid bringing up the subject despite meeting you several times, in case I got banned from all gigs and/or meetings for life. The photo I took of Lemmy in front of his house has been on my wall ever since.

In Zürich when I interviewed you we talked about Kelly and how sick she was, and how women musicians never get the same respect than males do and how it was such a pity.

Meeting at the aftershow party at Hammersmith – 20th and 30th anniversary - I was just another kid in the crowd, but you did say 'hello'; you made me smile all night and for days after.

Or at the Montreux Jazz festival, you were playing with the mighty Dio (Heaven & Hell), while waiting to interview Phil, I got to see you chatting with Dio and discussing a book you were reading, and then when you came to the bar for a drink, you looked at me and smiled and said 'You still here?' 'Yes Lem I'm still here' a bit of small talk about the area and I got you to sign some photographer's photo of you, as always Lemmy was available.

The tour with Rose Tattoo was amazing and seeing you and Angry talking was again legendary.

What will I miss the most? Not being able to put a few Motörhead shows in my Agenda, but thanks for the memories!

MOTÖRHEAD for life!"

Sio (Siobhan) Suzy Inderbitzin Motörheadbanger (Geneva, Switzerland)

"I first heard the song "Motörhead" from "No Sleep 'til Hammersmith" on Swiss national radio in 1981 and was blown away.
Then I bought this monster of a live album and finally got to see Motörhead on the 11th December 1981 in Winterthur when I was 16 years old.
From this day on I became something special, I became a dedicated Motörhead fan, which changed my life forever and became a part of my identity.
Lemmy and Motörhead took me on a journey that has been lasting for 34 years now. In 1986 I became MHB 388.
Even though my daily life is quite unspectacular, I have been and always will be a fan of the loudest and meanest rock'n'roll band that ever existed.
Of course as everyone else I was fascinated by Lemmy's personality, mainly by his attitude, his honesty and the love for books, history, ABBA and the Everley Brothers that I had in common with him. Also Lemmy's ability to write brilliant lyrics has always been a big part of my admiration for him.
Though Lemmy has left us and Motörhead is no more, their legacy will live on forever. I have seen more than 70 Motörhead concerts over the years and had the great pleasure to meet Lemmy and Würzel in the late 80s.
I also had the honour to get to know MHB president Alan Burridge, who kept us fans together before there was Facebook, and many great fellow Motörheadbangers. It was a fabulous journey until now and it will go on, but differently."
Andy Bruehlmann MHB 388 (Bern, Switzerland)

United Kingdom

Capital City: London
Population: 64,716,000
Currency: Pound Sterling
Bands: Black Sabbath, Iron Maiden, Judas Priest

"I have been a bit quiet lately...I was unable to get a visa to go to Lemmy's funeral. I have past sins, which means it takes longer for me to get a visa and with being Christmas, there wasn't enough time...
I watched it online last night. I thought everyone did very well.
Todd did an amazing job as compere. I thought his son, Paul spoke magnificently and Mikkey Dee followed up well.
It all reminded me of what a great man Lemmy was and how much he lived for his music and Motörhead and the fans. It was great to see the picture of the old band with Phil in the middle. They were great days and I miss them both.
I hope you all enjoyed it as much as I did. It was very sad but the message got across about the great man.
Rest In Peace, my old friend."
Fast Eddie Clarke (Motörhead Guitarist)

"I have seen Motörhead a good few times over the years, never got to meet him.
The best one and a big one for me was Maiden, Dio and Motörhead at Maddison Square Garden, New York.
Top gig but as always Motörhead were always the loudest band.
Tim Hanson (Padiham, Lancashire)

"First time I saw Motörhead was when I was 13 at the 'Kerrang! WOOOOOAAARRRGGGHHHHH Weekender' at Great Yarmouth back in '84.
They had just got back from a tour of the states and it was their first UK gig in ages. For the first half dozen songs or so you couldn't hear Lemmy's vocals. Finally when he addressed the crowd he got the message that we 'couldnae hear him' and he

*uttered the words "turn the vocals up Louie".
It was the first time I heard anything by Motörhead and I went straight out when I got home and bought their latest album 'Another Perfect Day'.
Been a fan ever since and I am not shamed to say I cried buckets when Lemmy died."*
Curtis McCraw (Dumfries)

*"Hearing "The Golden Years" EP simply changed my life.
A true original, Lemmy was a force of nature!"*
Mark Charman (Shanklin, Isle of Wight)

"The first Motörhead song I ever heard was 'Overkill' back in '79, but for me he will always be remembered for 'Silver Machine' with Hawkwind. Simply one of the best Rock tunes ever!"
Andy Harris (Plymouth)

"Spending the night reliving so many great moments of the band on you tube so many memories."
Terry Lench (Southampton)

*"I first heard Motörhead in the early '80's.
My neighbour, an older lad who I looked up to, was blasting them out of his bedroom window, whilst playing air guitar. He pointed at me and yelled "headbang Barlow."
I'm now 40 and after hearing of Lemmy's death I thought about the legacy the man will leave behind. I thought about the likes of Ozzy, Mötley Crüe, Keith Richards, Aerosmith etc and realised that they've all had periods of sobriety and clean living. But Lemmy truly lived the rock n' roll lifestyle 24/7 for over 50 years. Jack Daniels, drugs, 40 cigs a day, prostitutes, porn stars and playing metal every night!
There's probably only Al Jourgenson lived as hard. But more importantly his musical legacy, one that inspired many of our heroes, from Metallica to Pantera, will live on. What an immense feat to live that life and make it to 70!
Lemmy, I salute you. A metal legend."*
Lee Barlow (Bolton)

"I saw him at Download in 2010 and he sang with Slash."
Jane McCallow (Ellesmere Port)

"Well that was a mixed bag of emotions watching the tributes to

Lemmy...Brilliant tributes from everyone.
His son Paul's tribute was outstanding, but I had a lump in my throat, tears in my eyes and down my cheeks; and laughter, all at the same time and a lot of memories of the music and the times I saw Motörhead.
Lemmy really made an impact on this world and me. Thank you for pointing me in the direction of being a rockstar, even though I may have done it on a smaller scale.
Lemmy, a true 'Rockstar' and rock 'n' roller.
Lived the dream, lived the life.
As was pointed out, he was a real gentleman with the perfect manners, humour and loyalty; I hope to have installed that in some people/family too. Manners cost nothing.
If I had do half the things in my life too and make such an impact, I'll be happy.
And probably the only thing in life I regret, never meeting the man.
Rest in peace Lemmy."
Andy Rothwell (Coventry)

"Sleep well Lemmy."
Carl Beautyman (Kingston Upon Hull)

"Lemmy you were a Heavy Metal God and you were fucking funny as hell!!!
Sleep well XX."
Sylvia T Thompson (London)

"I used to work in a record shop in Crewe - a plain old Saturday job like you do when you're a teenager but I loved it.
One of our regulars came in every Saturday had a browse went to Crewe Alex watched the footie came back and made his purchase! Well one week in conversation he said he was going to watch Motörhead and was taking his 13 yr old son - I wished him a good time even though a tad jealous!
The following week he entered the store so I enquired how the gig had gone and how his son had enjoyed it - his reply was priceless - he had thoroughly enjoyed it but his son still could not hear - the reason - Lemmy had tied him to a speaker!!!!!!!
His hearing did return but what a memory!!!!"
Louise Bayley (Crewe)

"Seeing Motörhead live was surreal, not only were my ears smashed from one end of the stage to the next but you could feel

the excitement all around you!
There's something about being crushed between thousands of fans in a mosh pit whilst knowing you're all there to celebrate the pure love of Rock and Roll that drives you wild.
My first time seeing them was at Download Festival 2013 swiftly followed by their last ever UK show date at the Eden Project early 2015 right at home in Cornwall.
Blaring Motörhead will always be a favourite pass time, thrashing around the bedroom to Lemmy's iconic and vicious vocals, blaring it loud and proud at work and sippin' back on a Jack and coke in his honour.
Raise a glass for a man who has changed the history of music forever and shaped the future for those to come! And make it a double."
Jazz Urell (Luxulian, Cornwall)

"Well a story that springs to mind and I think shows exactly what Lemmy was like, was on the Motörhead and Alice Cooper tour about 6 years ago.
Myself, my son and my cousin went; my wife and daughter were to pick us up. While waiting Lemmy appeared at the rear doors my daughter who was 12 at the time got a cassette case cover I had in my glove box in fact it was 'No Remorse'. She and my wife went over to what was now a large crowd my daughter managed to get Lemmy's attention and Lemmy's next words were "let the little lady though'. She went over to him asked if she could have his autograph for me which he did then took her back though the crowd to my wife total gentleman."
Kevin Probert (Ebbw Vale)

"In the space of 15 months I saw Motörhead twice, and in two totally different guises.
On April 5th 1982, I saw them with Ian (the author) and a couple of other friends at the Cornwall Coliseum. I have been reminded that we spent the day on Plymouth Hoe, drinking, amongst other things, Blue Curacao! We were very drunk when we got there and although after nearly 33 years, I still remember the large Iron Fist on stage that extended it's fingers out, and on the end of each finger was a spotlight. I remember the songs 'Iron Fist', 'Overkill', 'Motörhead' (don't recall 'Ace of Spades') and the crowd going a bit more mental for 'We Are The Road Crew'. But most importantly, it was the loudness of the gig. To this day I don't think I've heard a louder band!

The next Motörhead gig was July 3rd, 1983 and it was the 'Another Perfect Tour' (in support of 'Another Perfect Day' album). This was a new Motörhead line up which now included Thin Lizzy's old guitarist, Brian Robertson. There was a cartoon on the inner sleeve of the album where Brian's ability to play was up against Lemmy and Philthy's 'inability' to play well.
I remember being with my friend Bill McGougan (there might have been others but I can't remember) as we made our way to the front. We watched the roadies set up Motörhead's gear and thought the twin optic containing a bottle of vodka and bottle of orange cordial, attached to Lemmy's speaker was cool! They played almost all songs from the new album and Bill and I started at the front, messing with a group of punks. But it was short lived as Bill had an asthma attack and we had to get to the back of the venue. Again, it was fucking loud (especially at the front) and to actually say I saw Brian Robertson with Thin Lizzy and Motörhead is quite surreal.
I look forward to Download this year, could be a great tribute to a rock legend."
Theo Christian (Gateshead)

"Following his recent sad departure, I have a couple of personal memories of Lemmy…
c.1985 I was playing with the DTs at Dingwalls in London. Lemmy was in the audience and after the gig he stayed to chat and drink at the bar, we had a right laugh, he was really friendly and said how much he enjoyed the band. He was also complimentary about my guitar playing (which I've never forgotten).
Some four years later in June 1989 I was playing one of my first Feelgood gigs at the 'Town and Country Club' in Kentish Town. It was a sold-out gig and when I walked onto the stage I immediately noticed Lemmy near the front. I remember thinking that he wouldn't remember me…
Back in the dressing room after a brilliant gig – in walks Lee Brilleaux with Lemmy – they were obviously well known to each other. Lemmy came over to me, shook my hand and said 'I know you, you're the guitar player from that band the DTs, I remember seeing you at Dingwalls'…
I was amazed that not only had he remembered me, but also where we had last met four years previously!
Gone but not forgotten – RIP Lemmy."
Steve Walwyn (Dr Feelgood – Guitar)

"I first discovered Motörhead when I was 14. This was 1987 and hard rock and heavy metal had very little exposure in the U.K. at the time.

There was Tommy Vance's 'Friday Rock Show' for two hours on a Friday Night and there was a TV show on ITV called 'The Power Hour' which used to show rock & metal videos in the early hours.

The first Motörhead song I saw/heard was 'Eat The Rich' from the Comic Strip film of the same name. I was mesmerized by them. They were not in anyway commercial and seemed to be playing by their own rules.

They were not your typical 1987 metal fare, no blonde perms, no spandex and no power ballads. Motörhead, in truth, probably had more in common with punk. The more I got into them, the more I realised that Lemmy was not all he seemed.

Yes, Lemmy was very much the rock star turned up to 11. He looked every bit the Sex, Drugs and Rock 'n' Roll archetype. If you dig into some of his lyrics however you will find an intelligence, knowledge and sensitivity that belie the stereotype. The title track from the '1916' album is very untypically Motörhead but it is up there with the last episode of 'Blackadder Goes Forth' in bringing home the sadness and tragedy of the First World War.

Lemmy was also the man who walked off the set of the quiz show 'Nevermind the Buzzcocks' because he thought the panelists were being rude and disrespectful to Bucks Fizz's Jay Aston.

The first time I saw Motörhead live was at the Manchester Apollo. I rather naively stood right near the front. I had been to lots of rock and metal gigs at this point but nothing had prepared me for the sheer volume and the chaos that was about to ensue.

As soon as they came onstage, the mosh pit erupted. People going crazy, wide eyed and wild smiles, limbs and lager all over the place. I will never forget the image of a middle-aged man, in a three-piece suit and holding a briefcase, carried aloft by the fans with the biggest grin you have ever seen. He had obviously just walked into this madness straight from his nine to five office job.

The floor quickly became drenched in lager and treacherous. As I was pushed about by the crowd, I slipped and fell into a giant of a guy behind me. He dwarfed me (and I'm 6ft 5); he was covered in tattoos, piercings and was easily twenty stone-plus. I looked up at him, knowing I had just knocked his pint out of his hand and all over him.

He picked me up and patted me on the shoulder. He said, "Are you ok mate?" Then he smiled and said, "It's bloody mad this innit?" Which just goes to show you can never judge a book by its

cover.
I saw Motörhead *a few times after that. Each time they were brilliant and each time they were deafening.*
I will never forget you Lemmy... (My tinnitus won't let me)."
David Geldard (Nottingham)

"I Live in Wolverhampton, I've seen Motörhead *many times at the Civic Hall. The time they came to Wolverhampton was 3 years ago. I had had a bad accident 2 days before the concert, I had torn the cartilage and ligaments in my right knee. I was in so much pain and was on crutches but I still went to the concert, I wouldn't have missed it for the world.*
Bless you Lemmy I love you man x"
Dawn Blood (Wolverhampton)

"I met Lemmy years ago in St Albans, when the 'Head played the Civic Hall. Nice bloke."
Roger Dighton (Milton Keynes)

"One thing that sticks out in my mind was back in 1981, me my brother and friends went to 'Heavy Metal Holocaust' at Port Vale where Motörhead *were the headline act.*
My brother was sitting on the toilet when Motörhead *took the stage the music was so loud the toilet was shaking and splashing him the next day we spoke to some of the local people and they told us it was so loud that people were complaining about the noise 5 miles away. Lol*
But what a great day it was 'Fucking deafening' Motörhead *at their best!"*
Paul Snow (Dunstable)

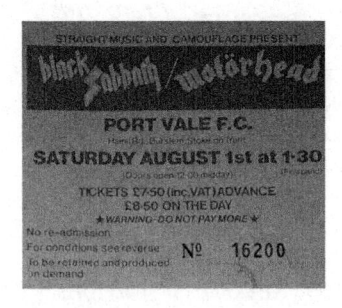

"He gave me the inspiration to take control of my life.
A great man who will be missed by so many."

Terry Lench (Southampton)

"I saw Motörhead at Donington '86. I hadn't particularly gone to see them, but more Ozzy and Scorpions. However, when the band started and had bottles of piss thrown at them, (I think there was a flare as well), Lemmy stop the band and told everyone, "If your gonna throw shit at us, we're going."
A couple more bottles hit the stage, then he laid the law down. "Come up and throw a punch if you've got the balls," he said, "don't throw shit." Nobody took him up on the offer, but lots of people started listening.
He had a massive presence, about him. People took notice of what he had to say. He gained respect massively from me.
I enjoyed the albums 'No Sleep 'til Hammersmith, and 'Orgasmatron' the best."

Andy Carroll (Plymouth)

"I have a small memory of walking to a Motörhead gig at the Regent Theatre Ipswich 2006.
I was walking to a bar nearby when down the deserted High street came three figures. The two either side were large portly men and the one in the middle, in black boots, long black coat and hat, hands in his coat pockets, looked like one mean dude; it was Lemmy!
I guess he was going to find a bar or something to eat. I wish I had spoke to him. I just froze and watched him walk by in amazement."

Nick Wright (Ipswich, Suffolk)

"I lost my Mam in 2008 and my next 'big' birthday was in 2011 when I turned 40.
I most wanted my late Mam to be there, but of course, she couldn't be. So, I had to decide what else would mean the most to me? And finding out Motörhead and my hero were playing in Glasgow, near my birthday - there was the answer! My daughter, Laura and I booked our train tickets and hotel and off we went to Glasgow to see our boys!
We ended up in the front row and I even got one of Lem's guitar picks - now a treasured possession.
Perfect way to celebrate my 40th.
I also took my daughter to her first rock gig, which was Motörhead, at the age of 12.
When Motörhead came on stage, I was that excited I jumped a few rows of seats to get nearer the front. Completely forgetting about

Laura. I thought, 'Shit where's my kid at?' Turned around and there she was, following me over the seats! Proud Mummy moment!
It was that funny. I totally forgot about her and jumped around 5 rows of seats. Took around 5 minutes for it to sink in that she was also with me!"
Julie Stirk (Darlington)

"Another of my favourite memories of Motörhead was in November 2007, when they played with Alice Cooper at the Manchester Evening News Arena.
I mentioned I was going to this gig to a friend of mine, who was more into stuff like Fleetwood Mac, Gary Numan, Status Quo etc. But he fancied seeing Motörhead, so got him a ticket, also!
I warned him it was a world away from those bands, but I still don't think he was ready for what was to come!
The band took to the stage, Lemmy belts out the immortal words 'We are Motörhead, and we play rock n roll!' and break into 'Doctor Rock'!
The crowd went nuts, his face was a picture! haha. Lost him about 10 seconds in! Found him again after about 6 songs! He just gave us the thumbs up with a shocked look upon his face! Hilarious!
He loved it in the end, I ended up with a converted Motörhead fan! Result!"
Rob Bray (St Annes, Lancashire)

"Played the Marquee in London with 'Legend ' NWOBHM band, 1984 - I think - came off stage and said to my bro I need a pint. Went into the bar at the back and Lemmy came up to me with a copy of our 'Death in the Nursery' album, said I was an aggressive player and asked me to sign it and bought us a pint each. Then he said 'do you want to go outside?' so we did.
He lit up a joint, the three of us got slightly stoned and then he took us to a club somewhere in Soho. I think Rock Goddess were there and Phil Collen (who was in Girl at the time) but went on to join the Leps. We got completely hammered and when I got back to my hotel room (The Regents Palace in Piccadily) there were 14 people in it!"
Peter Haworth (Jersey, Channel Islands)

"First time I saw Motörhead was a few years back at Download and I didn't know what was going to happen.
That feedback from the bass and the iconic line from Lemmy "we are Motörhead and we play rock and roll" that's when life was

complete and also a slight ring in my ear still now and then from his shows!
Rock in peace Lemmy thank you. \m/"
Jamie Wyn Edwards (Ruthin, Wales)

"Only saw them once Download '05.
My memory of them and specifically Lemmy, was after a day of bands backslapping and shouting out to each other, they just walked out on stage "Hello, we are Motörhead and we play rock and roll" which is exactly what they did.
They played a blinding set, with the traditional "is it loud enough/turn it up Dave" banter with the crowd.
Great man, great band."
Liam Kelly (Plymouth)

"I first properly discovered Motörhead about 15 years ago. Naturally 'Ace of Spades' was the first song I heard, which soon became one of my all-time favourite songs. However, it wasn't until I heard the song 'Overkill' that I REALLY got what this band was all about. Loud, fast and powerful.
That song in particular, with it's constant double bass drumming thundering away like a Sherman tank about to crush you to death, and the 'fake' endings, where you're never quite sure if it's all over yet. I bloody loved it.
It was one of the very first songs I ever learnt to play on drums, and one I actually played for the first time on my debut live appearance. Musically Motörhead were certainly one of my first inspirations with regards to playing music and forming a band.
Lemmy's attitude towards life has in itself always inspired me, he does what he wants, drinks what he likes and says it how it is. I never had the honour of meeting him but he always came across as an honest, loyal and genuinely down to earth guy.
The word 'Legend' is used a lot when someone dies, but in Lemmy's case it is more than justified, he is the true epitome of a rock 'n' roll legend and the world is going to be a much quieter place without him being part of it."
James Balcombe (Braintree, Essex)

"I saw Motörhead in 1978 at the Rhodes Centre Bishops Stortford. I didn't know who they were really and didn't realise that one of my fave records of all time, 'Silver Machine' was Lemmy.
I remember it being so loud and I was near the front and Lemmy spat into the crowd and it just missed me by a whisker.

That's my one experience I'm afraid."
Penny Larkin (Newton Abbot)

"We met Lemmy, thanks to Phil Campbell and Tim Butcher, in Calgary Alberta Canada, when they played at 'Flames Central.
Lemmy and Phil signed my husband John Evan's back and then he got it Tattooed.
Lemmy was awesome! He put up with us wanting photos and chatting to him, when all he really wanted to do was go back to bed and sleep!"
Ginja Red (Cardiff, Wales)

"Years and years ago, when I was small, I saw a band on a comedy show (The Young Ones) that changed everything. I must have been 7 or 8 when I saw the episode - never saw it when it came out in '84, because I wasn't born until November, and it had aired in May of that year.
The show was well known for having guest acts perform in the middle of the episodes, but this time my mind was blown away by the speed, heaviness, and the cool motherfuckers on the screen. I knew at that moment that's who I wanted to be, that's what I wanted to play.
As the years went on, my tastes in music got heavier, I ended up listening to black and thrash metal a lot, but in the end it always came back to "Motörhead play fuckin' heavy, and they play fuckin' fast, and I'm fuckin putting 'Bomber' on as loud as my speakers will go!
My favorite Lemmy moment was at Wacken 2014. Motörhead had played a few already and were talking about the new album and Lem goes:
"We have a new album out, it's called 'Aftershock', I hope you've all bought it! Ahh who am I kidding, you all probably downloaded it, heh heh heh."
It was brilliant to see his sharp sense of humor undiminished by his health problems, and of course great to see him back on stage after he had to cut the show short the previous year.

The world really is less cool these days ☹"
Myrròen Vagonbrei (Glasgow)

"1972 I was one year old and my dad Robbie Simpson worked at The Round House in Camden doing stage and lighting.
My mum thought it would be a good idea if he took me to work to

have some "bonding time" my dad was busy preparing for a gig, Hawkwind.
My dad gave me to someone to hold for a minute while doing something and got busy and forgot all about me. A few hours later my mum arrives to collect me and I am nowhere to be seen so after much searching and panicking I was found in the bar with Lemmy, my dad gave me to Lemmy to look after me!
There you go.
Anyway now a Motörhead fan and always will be, took my kids to see them play last year at Wembley and my then 6 year old fell asleep midway through; who falls asleep mid way through a Motörhead show??
And I went to LA this weekend to say goodbye and stayed on Sunset with my incredible fiend Cherry Bligh, just got home to let it all sink in.
RIP Lemmy."
Ned Kirkham (Berkhamsted)

"Motörhead were one of the first heavy bands I listened to (maybe even the first!), which got me into heavy metal (amongst other bands).
I always used to play a skateboarding game on either the PS2 or Xbox when I was about 8 and 'Ace of Spades' would always come on and I remember hearing it for the first time and going insane! I'm 17 now and I still love the song so much (and will do for the rest of my life).
Lemmy was, and still is a huge role model to me and an inspiration. I look up to him.
I have all vinyls, cd's, tshirts, posters everywhere!
They're one of my favourite bands of all time!
I had tickets to go and watch Motörhead this month, the 26th January but unfortunately I can't now due to the passing of Lemmy.
I've always loved Motörhead, but I've always loved Lemmy too. He's a massive idol and inspiration.
Rest in Peace! "Born to Lose, Live to Win"
Owen Alderson (Wigan)

"So its 1982, Leicester De Montfort Hall, 'Iron Fist' tour, at the tender age of 15.
Me and a few mates are hangin' around outside, trying to get autographs. It's fuckin' freezing, snow everywhere. We start throwing snow balls at the window, when "smash!" A window goes

through and out pops Philthy's head.
"You fuckers, your'e gonna get it now".
Everyone scarpers, as a group of burly roadies come running out. Me and a friend just walk casually, all innocent like, when the big man himself comes out.
"You not with that bunch o' twats then?"
"No Mr Lemmy."
"Fair do's." We then get invited in and get all of the bands autographs ☺ we did feel a right pair of cunts though.
Thanks Lem, we love you.
Jon Simpson (Penmaenmawr)

"Way back in 1991 after Motörhead *cancelled the gig at Aston Villa Leisure Centre, the show was a go.*
It were before decibel limits and they were so bloody loud me and my uncle Ray was at the barrier at the front and at the end of 'Ace of Spades' my uncle looks to me and shouts in my face
"THAT WAS ACE OF SPADES."
You see it was that loud, it was just noise lol!!
But despite being deaf for weeks after, it was a night I'll never forget and me and my uncle still talk about it to this day.
Going to be very quiet in the metal world without Lemmy."
Pete Matthews (Telford)

"I was born in 1964 but as a kid/teenager I wasn't really into music (being obsessed with football & cricket) until I was about 14/15 when I started to take notice & listen to stuff which was in the charts such as The Police & Dexy's Midnight Runners.

I didn't really have a specific genre that I liked.
However at about 15 I started to hear my best mates brother's music Lizzy, UFO AC/DC etc.
One band stood out and I was drawn to a group with 3 band members that looked cool as fuck but hard as fuck too.
It was an added bonus that band leader Lemmy came from my place of birth Stoke on Trent!
I bought 'Overkill', 'Bomber' & the 'Beer Drinkers and Hellraisers' 12" EP on blue vinyl with birthday money (along with 'Down to Earth' by Rainbow).
I fell in love with Motörhead from then and they've been a constant in my life ever since.
I loved everything about them their heaviness speed lyrics and especially their volume.
I can remember buying both 'Ace of Spades' & 'No Sleep' the day they came out from a local small independent record shop called 'Town Sound' in the town where I live (Sandbach in Cheshire). Now sadly a kebab shop!
I missed the 'Ace of Spades' tour as it happened just before I was allowed to go gigging.
Some of my mates went (bastards) and I listened in awe of tales of the frightening levels of volume at the Victoria Hall Hanley Stoke on Trent.
The urban myth doing the rounds is that several fans had burst eardrums and left the gig with bleeding ears!
The next gig I was missed was the 'Heavy Metal Holocaust' at Port Vale in 1981.
By this time I was gigging but had been booked on a family holiday to, wait for it, fucking Switzerland on a coach trip!!!!!!!!
At this time Motörhead were one of the biggest bands in the country and therefore big news locally.
Although I didn't go I lapped up all the available info about the gig.
There were local objections about the gig taking place in a built up area and as a compromise the promoters took the mainly elderly residents on coach trips to Blackpool for the day!!
Apparently the gig was so loud it was heard 10 miles away and there were reports of people listening to in their gardens.
One old guy complained he could hear it all day working on his allotment!
I finally got to see my heroes on the 'Iron Fist' tour at the Deeside Leisure Centre just outside Chester on 21st March 1982 for the princely sum of £4.50.
Support for the gig was Tank & Raven but this was back in the day

when nobody could be arsed with support bands and from memory they both got a rough time.

They came on to the song 'Iron Fist' and the volume was amazing. By this time I'd seen quite a few bands Maiden, DC, MSG, Saxon, but heard nothing this loud.

I've still got my tour t-shirt that has since been worn by my ex wife son & daughter after my waist expanded! It's still in very good condition and won't ever be thrown out!

I can remember being gutted when Eddie left but still obviously followed the band and bought their LP's and continued to see them on tour.

I had a ticket to see them on 'Another Perfect Day' tour in Stoke in '83 but for some reason the gig was cancelled and never re-scheduled.

I saw them at the Apollo in Manchester on the 'Orgasmatron' tour in '84, MOR '86 and again in '86 with Zodiac Mindwarp as support.

At this gig I went backstage with my ex wife and met them for the first time. I got my denim cut off signed, which I've still got and took several photos of the band. To be honest the only one I really wanted to meet was Lemmy and he was as good as gold chatting to fans and signing anything and everything!

To be honest after '86 they kind of dropped off my gig & buying radar.

The new version just wasn't as good as the classic line up!

My interest was re-awakened by my son when he 11/12. I'd always played rock/metal in the house and car all through his life.

I remember him asking me "dad can I go and see Motörhead with Jack & his dad?" I obviously said, "yes" although I was concerned about what the volume might do to his delicate ears lol!

In 2005 my son persuaded me to go to Download for the first time and off we trotted the first time back at Donny since 1996!

From memory Motörhead were headlining the 2nd stage, which was a tent in those days, so me and my son headed off to get a good spot in the tent before they came on.

MC5 were on before and it was great to see and hear Lemmy join them for a rousing version of 'Kick Out the Jams' before their set.

When Motörhead finally hit the stage they were awesome even though they were only in the tent they were the loudest band of the weekend with Lemmy constantly urging the sound desk to turn it up!

I was back home both at Donny and with my first musical love!

After that gig I've been to see Motörhead on most of their tours and started buying their albums again as well as some of the back

catalogue which to be fair is pretty good although not 'Overkill', 'Bomber', 'Ace' good!
In the years I'd not been seeing the band Lemmy had changed from a 'biker scary as fuck rocker' to an 'elder statesmen of rock/metal'.
What he had maintained was his great sense of humour I loved his mid set rants against the 'X Factor' and new bands always being on laptops on the road.
I remember him say jokingly "I wish everybody who bought the t-shirt bought the albums" in response to all the teenage kids wearing t-shirts bought from Top Shop etc!
When it became evident that his health was starting to worsen I always stood to the right of the stage as close as I could to see him close up and I always watched him go off stage at the end of a gig until I couldn't see him anymore kind of knowing it could be the last time I'd ever see him!
I saw Motörhead at Hyde Park on July 4th 2014 with Sabbath, this was the first gig back after he'd been really ill and he looked dreadful. I was shocked by how ill he looked.
To be honest that day they were just ok for obvious reasons.
I went to the mini tour in November 2014 thinking it would be the last time I'd see them (it was) but I was pleasantly surprised he looked a lot healthier and they played a blistering set full of classic era songs.
I thought he was on the mend.
Strangely I lost the ticket for this gig on the walk back to the station, it's the only ticket I've not got in 35 years of gigging!
I had a ticket for this months gig at the Apollo and was looking forward to seeing him at Download this year.
The morning after he'd died I looked at my phone and had a text off my son saying "Dad you may not want to check FB or look at the news this morning"
I knew instantly what had happened.
I was absolutely gutted still am to be honest I've played Motörhead virtually non stop ever since.
That night me, my lad and a mate went for a few. I even had a JD & coke and I fucking hate the stuff!
Out of all the icons that have died this one has upset me the most.
He was one of us not a rock star that lived on a different planet just an ordinary guy who loved what we all love!
I watched his funeral on Youtube on Saturday and it was superb (if it can be) his son was fantastic and so were many others!
Steve Bendall (Sandbach)

MCP PRESENTS
Motörhead
Plus Guests
DEESIDE LEISURE CENTRE
Sunday March 21st 7.30pm
Tickets £4.50 (Standing)
Official merchandise is on sale
only in the Hall

N° 1527

"Lemmy had that face of a hard man yet underneath was a gentleman going by the recent feedback from the people who knew him.
Motörhead *and Lemmy became rock legends and to see them live in their latter years at the Download Festival proved they were master musicians.*
Lemmy leaves a void in Rock music.
R. I. P. Lemmy."
Mark Jewitt (Plymouth)

"Reflecting back on the last 40 years, I think that rather than just memories of great music / great concerts and the buzz from the sound of Lemmy's bass hitting you in the face (I can't say I have ever 'felt' sound anywhere else in my life) it has been about a way of life. From my late teens I identified with the music, the image and the comradery amongst like minded people.
It didn't matter where you were from or what you do or look like, Motörhead fans have to be the best in the world.
My first gig was in '82 when I was 17. Venue was Queens hall Leeds with some mates. I remember the police walking up and down the queues with alsations. God knows what they were expecting! The crowd was a mixture of rockers and punks who were sporting huge, brightly coloured Mohicans. Everyone got on and it was a fab night and I got to see my idols! Lemmy, Philthy and Fast Eddie!
Since then I have dressed in the same style, leather jacket / Motörhead t-shirt and jeans.
I reckon I have seen Lemmy and Motorhead 25+ times. The Head Cat at the Garage in London was fabulous, small crowd and a fantastic atmosphere. Lemmy was on top form and it is a night I will never forget. It was more of a party with everyone dancing and

considered noise, I fucking loved it.

I walked in our room one Saturday afternoon and the stereo was on, "On Parole' was the track that got me hooked on Motörhead and is still my favorite track, something about the mocking the system or the fuck you intent with that bluesy rock 'n' roll and humour just dragged me in.

I listened to the Motörhead album over and over, ever since then I needed faster, harder, heavier. Every time I was down Motörhead dug me out of it and kept me sane, kept me alive, no fucking joke!

I have seen the band live 10 times; the last time was at the Manchester Apollo with the Damned and the Bosshoss. That night will be the highlight gig of my life, it was sublime, 'Overkill' was the last song as Lemmy stood his bass against the Marshall stack giving the usual last blast, the light faded on the backdrop and 'Snaggletooth' disappeared I leant in to my eldest son and said "that'll be the last one", just a horrible cold feeling, and it was.

"I was in Soissons on the 29th of Dec, I woke up to the missus saying Lemmy was dead, so I kept my Motörhead shirt on.

We went into Paris to shop, wombling around with Motörhead blaring through my headphones upset and kicking my feet behind my lot, a guy walked past tapped me on the shoulder and said 'R.I.P. Lemmy' shook my hand and walked off.

It cheered me up a bit as the guy was maybe 20 or so and that is a good sign for the future, anyways we stop outside a posh clothes shop and in my current state I couldn't face going in so me and my eldest just hung around outside. After about 10 mins of conversation at how we couldn't believe it had happened this older guy came out of a crowd walking past and patted my t-shirt saying 'R.I.P. Lemmy' and gave me a hug, now I'm not talking about people you would assume liked Motörhead this guy wad extremely well dressed had a briefcase really posh looking bloke, it fucking blew me away, all day and into the night this continued such a great feeling, cheered me right up."

I love that band as strong as I have ever loved anything; they gave me everything I needed to survive. Made me a better person, listening to every word those albums utter and every interview gleaning wisdom and strength time after time, those guys will never know how much they mean to me, but that's ok, I know, R.I.P. MOTORHEAD YOUR LEGACY WILL LIVE FOREVER! \m/ "

Conrad Barnes (Bolton)

"Motorhead caught my attention in the early '80's when I heard Lemmy describe his band as a punk band.

Back then I had no time for heavy rock and metal as it all seemed very pretentious and lacking substance. I remember hearing 'Iron Fist' and being very impressed with the urgency and power that was so reminiscent of the punk bands I was listening to and I immediately went out and bought the album. From then on Motörhead stayed with me and opened me up to metal and how it began to fuse with punk.
Live they were great and I had the pleasure of seeing them 4 times and ironically on two of these occasions supported by the Damned, the UK Subs and the Anti Nowhere League, 3 top drawer punk bands.
I hope Motörhead and Lemmy will be remembered for the huge role and impact they made within rock music, especially for its honesty and total lack of bullshit."
John Caithness (Plymouth)

"I haven't personally met Lem nor have I been to any concerts (I regret it very much) but Motörhead's music and in a way Lemmy himself, have helped me in a time when I was very down and close to hitting bottom.
Bartösz Kunatowski (Aylesbury)

"During my days in the clubs in London from '82-'91, Lemmy was always "about". Like Charlie Harper he was simply so down to Earth, I forgot how famous & influential he was.
On occasions when Northerners & the likes came to the club, totally shocked that the great man was just standing there, having a drink, or playing the fruit machine. He always had time for ALL of them.
I never saw him flustered or pissed off, just one of the crowd.
A couple of times he came to the club early for a quiet chat (the clubs were usually empty before the pubs closed at 11).
On occasions he would give us his latest demo tapes and I was honored that "Buttz & Spikes" would be the first club to play the latest Motörhead tunes.
We often discussed the "Titanic" and why it really sank, also everything Dambusters and D Day and did Hitler survive...?
He was an intelligent, educated man. Like everyone else, I thought he'd live forever. I know hundreds of people who call him a friend and he was.
The World's a much quieter place without him. Truly the last great Rock 'N' Roller... R.I.P. Lemmy."
Buttz (The Babysitters)

"It was 1979, I was a 14 year old Rocker desperate to go to a gig, a few friends had already seen a couple of bands & the next on the list was a band described as the Loudest & Heaviest band around. Motörhead, *I didn't know much about them & only realy knew one song… 'OVERKILL'.*
I sat there on the back of my chair centre stalls of the Birmingham Odeon, filled with nervous fear & anticipation of what was to come, the concert programme advertised hearing aids & had stories of fans leaving gigs with their ears bleeding, which didn't help me one bit.
They came on & finished with 'Overkill', which I was very pleased with, they kept their promise of being very very loud & Heavy.
I remember Lemmy saying it wasn't loud enough & every other track he'd go to the amp & turn up the volume, I can honestly say it's the only time I've been scared & happy at the same time.
I saw Motörhead *4 times in the next 2 years & got a little obsessed.*
I'm so glad I can say to people that the very 1st Rock star I ever saw was Lemmy… thanks for setting me on this metal/Rock path I now walk on… R.I.P."
Andrew Belfort (Halesowen)

"I've been very fortunate with my meetings with Lemmy and members of Motörhead over the past 36 years.
Feeling somewhat whimsical and with many Motörhead memories, my Motörhead brother flew across from Milwaukee, Wisconsin for his first visit to Glasgow with me being his guide.
Mr Steve Sharp (Milwaukee Wisconsin USA) had made his first trip to the daunting city of Glasgow, he along with his mate, also called Steve but nicknamed Rasta, were staying in the Ibis Hotel Pit Street in the city centre (right across the road from Pit Street police station).
Motörhead were to play the famous Barrowlands ballroom that evening, Steve, Rasta and my good self were at the Barrowlands that afternoon and had a candid chat with Lemmy out side the venue (at this point may I inform the reader of the rather large spliff I had in my leather jacket). Two other Motörhead brothers joined in with our 'motor' get together namely Matt Armstrong and a enormous Viking (6ft 7inches of him) sent over by Peder Lundin I believe this Munster went by the name of Egor not surprisingly enough I may be wrong.
Lemmy chuckled too himself as he witnessed my Groucho Marx

impression with my spliff.
The idea was after our meeting with Lemmy the 5 of us made for a booze outlet and loaded up with local fair (lager, lager, Buckfast tonic wine and more lager...when in Glasgow eh!).
We started our afternoons celebrations after leaving the east end cheap drinks emporium and I informed the Americans it's perfectly legal to drink on the streets of Glasgow but just don't publicise the fact.
We made our way some distance to Steve's hotel where more booze was enjoyed, at this point Rasta (the quiet one) said something about writing some post cards for the folks back home down in the lobby as they call it as it was getting a little noisy in the room with the 'Yankee, Swedish, Edinburgh' accents and gob shite here all trying too slur there point across.
So with one body less in the room I recalled my HOGS LEG SPLIFF just itching to join in on the fun (much to Steve's drunken enthusiasm).
At this point I can't recall Matt or the Viking wishing to partake but Steve and I started suckin' on this thing trying to put Monica Lewinsky out of business. I'm not sure if any of you guys reading are familiar with the strict 'No Smoking' policy we have here in the U.K in hotel rooms! Anyway as hilarity ensued the automatic fire alarm kinda kicked in.
Steve came up to me and said 'you mother fucker you set off my room alarm'. I quickly came to terms with how automatic fire alarms actually work and informed Steve that it's more than probable that the whole hotel alarm system was informing the hotel that there was a fire in the building, Steve at this point immediately sobered up realising the implications of his name being on the hotel guest list and no doubt the fire alarm isolating his room as the source of the incident. In somewhat of a panic Steve now wide eyed and opening all windows tried to tell me what a 'murther fuckin' son of a bitch' I was and possibly the best Idea would be to extinguish my spliff and (shock horror) throw it out the 15th floor window (how very dare you sir!).
Almost immediately the door knocked and members of the Ibis Hotel staff were rapidly informing all guests, no matter what state of undress they may be in, to go to the fire meeting point some distance from the hotel entrance.
I along with a Viking and Mr Armstrong collected our cans and carried Steve down the stairs (his legs seemed to have stopped working correctly). As it looked we were the last ones to walk out into the cold November air as a congregation of hotel guests (quite

a number if memory serves me correctly) stared back at us with a eye of suspicion.
Rasta (who'd been one of the first to evacuate the building) walked up to me and said quickly and to the point 'You fuckin' bastard Dunkster'. At this point I'd realised my name was not on the hotel guest list and for all purposes I was 'invisible'.
The three fire engine sirens rapidly making there way to our location kinda put the two Americans in a state of sheer panic and I asked them both 'have you got your wallets and passports on you !' I think at this point Matty thought it a good idea to fuck off sharpish (Matty I'd love to meet up with you again some day mate for ole time sakes).
With three fire engines on site and uniformed fire personnel making there way into the hotel I saw the station officer (white helmet usually in charge) sitting patiently in the front of the lead engine, I strolled up to him introduced myself and informed him that my foolish American friends thought it was ok to smoke in their room. The station officer said 'who's on th' neet?'
'Motörhead ' I informed him.
'Fuckin hell man great I'm on till 9.00 th' morra'.
I asked again is everything cool here !!!!!!!' ....'fuck eye son it's only a fire alarm enjoy the night ya jammy bastards.'
With the good news in my head I rapidly ran up to the two Americans who at the time were contemplating a night in the police station cells a short distance from where they stood I barked 'ffs Steve you best fuck off mate there's a fuckin' massive call out charge to be paid here and they are sorting out what room the alarm started in.'
Looking like marble at this point Steve grabbed onto my jacket and spluttered 'what the fuck we gonna do!'
I said 'I'd love to help but I'm not on the hotel guest list Steve', I ask the reader have you ever seen someones dream of seeing Motörhead in a different country rapidly go to despair within a few short moments!!!! And the possible incarceration in a Glaswegian police cell followed by a hefty fine from Strath Clyde fire service for a call out charge for 3 units and all there personnel, not to mention the cleaning de fumigation bill at the Ibis Hotel!
At this point I thought my American brothers had suffered enough and propping up Steve I informed him of the good news that 'shit happens and the fire station officer was more interested in Motörhead than perusing the culprits', still shaking Steve and myself went too the hotel manager and blamed Matty for lighting up illegal smoking material and promised the hotel not to bring him

back to the Ibis in Pit Street .
Steve seemed to flout for the rest of that evening and as per usual MOTÖRHEAD WERE AWSOME!!!
Sometimes what went on prior and after the shows was more informative than the actual show itself, after an afternoons entertainment like that Motörheads show was something to remember.
Here's another cracker from the 'Iron Fist' tour 1982.
My beautiful girl (Julie Munn) and I had seen Motörhead on their Birmingham dates of the 'Iron Fist' tour at the famed Birmingham Odeon .
Along with a few others we waited patiently at the side entrance at the rear of the building.
Around this time Motörhead had a rather large security guy that I'd seen on the inner sleeve photos of the live LP of Motörheads 'chart topping 'No Sleep'. This guy was walking down from New Street towards us waiting at the stage door. He abruptly said 'the bands not here you might as well fuck off ' after a few moans n groans everyone bar Julie (Jools) 'n' me had done just that.
I said too Jools 'if the band ain't here, why is he here then ...let's give it a bit longer', so after a few cigarettes the stage door opened and the same security guy poked his head out and looked up and down the dimly light side road and nodded saying 'ok'.
The door opened and we saw a pair of white stack heeled boots appear along with the same black 'Ace of Spades' studded jeans and leather jacket Lemmy wore on the the cover of same LP and Lemmy was indeed inside them.
With Jools 'n' me being the only ones there Lemmy came up to us as I handed him a photo of him and myself in Brussels Belgium the year before. I asked 'remember me in Belgium?'
Lemmy looked and with a grin said 'fuckin' yeah', I then asked 'any chance of Jools 'n' me coming back to the hotel for a few drinks?'
Lemmy took one second and asked the security guy 'what's it like in there?' A none too impressed reply came back informing Lemmy 'it's fuckin full' one more second past and Lemmy looked at Jools 'n' me and said 'fuck it your with me let's go.'
We walked up the side of the Odeon onto New Street, Lemmy was stopped by a few guys who asked him to sign some stuff and as Lemmy always did he obliged then again he turned to Jools 'n' me and said again 'come on let's go'.
The Midland Hotel was directly across the road from the Odeon so within moments all four of us were in the hotel lobby where the staff insisted no guests are allowed, Lemmy point to Jools 'n' me

and informed the staff 'these two are with me' the staff stepped aside.

All four of us squeezed into the smallest lift I ever been in (I'm putting that down to the security guy being somewhat on the stout side, but at this point I thought I'd keep that to myself).

So there we were, Jools facing the security guy and me facing Lemmy so close you could smell them I looked at LEMMYS rings on his fingers and looked at my own pewter skull rings and said 'my rings are better than yours LEM', Lemmy dryly looked at his and said 'yours silver are they?'

Thankfully sparing me of making an even bigger knob of myself the lift doors opened into the hotel bar, Lemmy tapped me on my shoulder and told us both 'go knock yer selfs out.'

We were mixing with fast Eddie and just pinching ourselves trying to come to terms where we both were and there was Philthy sitting on his own in a large leather sofa chair, we walked up to him and introduced ourselves to him not knowin' what his reaction would be, Phil was great we chatted for a while about the meeting I'd had with him the previous year in Brussels.

I then said to Phil 'Jools fancies you. Any chance she can suck your face off.'

Phil and Jools then had a few moments snogging, not wishing to be fucked over I thought it only fair I nicked his drinks ... So I did all of them.

We spent some time with Phil it was a great time for Jools 'n' me a moment in time we cherish."

Duncan Nixon (Glasgow)

"We knew it was coming, it was inevitable, as much as Lemmy had built up an indestructible image of himself as the man who could calmly walk out of the mushroom cloud of Armageddon with a glass of Jack Daniels in his hand and a Marlboro hanging from his mouth, the truth was becoming clear. Lemmy was ill and the realisation that he was not immortal was becoming evident.

That realisation became clear to me when I was at the Wacken Festival in 2013 on a incredibly hot scorching day, Lemmy only lasted six songs before he had to bow out with heat exhaustion. I honestly thought that would be the last time I would ever see my boyhood hero up there on the stage. But Lemmy was made of stronger stuff than others. His bloody mindlessness of 'never letting the bastards grind you down' made him carry on touring and even recording new studio albums that defied all non believers.

Lemmy only knew one life and that was rock 'n' roll pure and simple, Lemmy was determined to go out in a blaze of glory. Despite shows being cancelled due to his ill health, Lemmy would get right back up and carry on regardless. It was if he was wishing to do a Tommy Copper and die on stage.

I've only ever cried twice before over the death of a rock star, Phil Lynott and Freddie Mercury both who left this world too soon. This time though it was different, I was expecting it but was hoping that Lemmy could defy all and just keep on going. But at 12.30 am on Tuesday morning rumours were flying around and then it was confirmed, first by Eddie Trunk and then by Ozzy Osbourne, my heart sank, I was completely numb and void. I poured myself a large JD but couldn't even drink it; it was if my own soul had been ripped out of my body. I didn't know Lemmy on a personal level but it felt like I've just lost a very special friend.

You see, Lemmy has been a valuable part of my life for 35 years and most probably will still be until the day I die.

My parents went through a very messy and damaging divorce in 1979, a rare thing in those days. I was eleven years old and soon became disillusioned with school, home and life in general.

I lost all interest in football too but a year later I was starting to enjoy pop music especially the louder stuff. Even when I was six years old, I was always got excited whenever bands like Mud or Sweet were on Top Of The Pops.

Now at the age of twelve I made sure that I watched Top Of The Pops every Thursday and also listened to the Top 40 rundown of the charts every Sunday on Radio 1. As I've already said, it was the louder stuff that struck a chord with me. Siouxsie & the Banshees, Blondie, The Specials were the bands that I was taping on my cassette player but my ears were also perking up to the sounds of Rainbow, Gillan and Whitesnake but the real epiphany moment came when I saw Motörhead and Girlschool on Top Of The Pops with their version of 'Please Don't Touch', a Top 5 single no less. By now I got myself a paper round so I could finally have some money in my pocket and treat myself to buy music magazines like Flexipop which covered metal, goth, ska and the whole alternative scene.

The first heavy metal single I ever bought was 'Motörhead (Live)' with 'Over The Top' (Live) on the B-Side for 99p from Boots superstore in Chatham, Kent. It was a life changing moment and I played that racket to death. Motörhead were also on the cover of Flexipop which had free Flexi-disc of Motörhead's live version of 'Train Kept A-Rollin', I then immediately went out and bought my first album 'No Sleep 'Til Hammersmith' which was Number 1 in *the album charts.*

I was hooked on Motörhead, that cranium crashing sound where I could turn the sound up on full blast and annoy the hell out of my neighbours and I didn't care less, I wanted the world to know. I look at the inner sleeve of that iconic live album and there were these Polaroid photos of Motörhead on the road with Girlschool, photos full of beer, birds and debauchery ... This was the life for me when I grow up I thought, I was on a mission in life.

Motörhead soon become the first of everything for me, my first single, my first album, my first Flexi -disc, my first ten inch EP, my first poster on the wall, my first patch, my first pin badge ... The list went on. I still remember strongly how proud I was of my first band t-shirt which featured Motörhead's iconic logo of Snaggletooth on the front. It was only an unofficial iron on transfer, but it didn't matter. At last I had an identity in life. I was a Motorheadbanger!

I backtracked and bought all of Motörhead's back catalogue of singles and albums. Motörhead well and truly opened the floodgates for me as I was now getting into the sounds of the NWOBHM getting heavily into bands like Saxon, Tygers Of Pan Tang and Iron Maiden. I no longer listened to the alternative scene, it was metal all the way with a little splatter of punk.

It wasn't until I left school and got a job that finally I could go to concerts. My first live experience of Motörhead wasn't until 1986 at the Monsters Of Rock festival at Castle Donington. By then Fast Eddie Clarke and Philthy Phil had left the band and Motörhead had became a four piece but the message was still loud and clear. Lemmy took no shit at that show when someone shot a flare onto the stage forcing Lemmy to stop mid song and offer the 'fan' up on stage for a knuckle sandwich.

But the real Motörhead experience is witnessing them at one of their own shows. The first show I saw was at Folkestone Leas Cliff Hall, an intimate venue by Motörhead's standards but one that they often returned to. On this occasion the volume was fully turned up way past the max, not to 11 but all the way to 14. It felt as if my ears were about to bleed, I went to the bar just to escape the cacophony of sound and all the windows in the bar were shaking violently with the volume. The bar staff looked terrified.

Over the years I must of seen Motörhead about 50 times at their own shows and various festival slots, but going to see Lemmy and his gang in action was a totally unique experience. It was a united bringing together of both punks and metalheads all fuelled up on beer. Lemmy would stand their with his Rickenbacker bass played like a lead guitar, head held upwards as he growled into his microphone as the band smashed all sensibility out of your brain, flattening it into a pulp.

My most memorable live performances from Lemmy was over a weekend in 2000 when on the Saturday night at the Brixton Academy he performed some songs on an all nighter gig from his former band Hawkwind followed by Motörhead celebrating their 25th anniversary at the same venue a night later in a varied set that included guests Doro Pesch, Whitfield Crane, Brian May, Fast Eddie as well as his own son Paul Inder.

I've been fortunate enough to meet Lemmy on three occasions. The first time I was a complete fan boy and I managed to blag my way into the aftershow after a mind blowing sold out performance at the Astoria in London. It was the stuff of dreams, the whole of Girlschool were there as was Fast Eddie Clarke. I nervously approached Lemmy and I told him how much his music has meant to me over the years. He looked me into the eye and promised, "I'll never let you down."

The last time was only last month at the Classic Rock Awards when I was working on the red carpet. Lemmy looked frail and walked in with the use of a walking stick, which he soon handed over to his minder. He still looked the epitome of cool dressed dapper like a true rock 'n' roller. He ignored questions about his health only wanting to talk about the music.

When he left the building towards the end of the evening, Lemmy looked over at me and slowly lifted his hand to wave goodbye. It made my night, although I had an eerie feeling that that would be the last time that I would ever see Lemmy. Sadly that proved to be true.

Ian 'Lemmy' Kilmister, you most certainly have never let me down. A man who really is the stuff of legend. You walked it like you talked it. Thank you for the wonderful years of music and insightful intelligent interviews.

You music and attitude in life is immortalised in us all.

I couldn't write this article the day after Lemmy's death, it was still too soon. Instead Cliff Evans the guitarist in Tank called me up and said we should go down to Hammersmith Odeon (that's what it always will be called as far as I'm concerned) to have a drink in Lemmy's honour. MetalTalk's Steve Goldby joined us as did friends Steve Barker, Tim Rahman, Mark 'Woody' Wood and Andy Rawll.

After polishing off a bottle of Jack Daniels on the steps next to a poster advertising Motörhead proposed shows in January at this venue which has witnessed so many glorious nights from

Motörhead.
Afterwards we adjourned to the Duke Of Cornwall pub next door where they were playing the music of Motörhead non-stop in his honour. A full nine hour drinking marathon ensured way past closing time ... I woke up with a full Motorheadache ... Lemmy would've been proud."
Mark Taylor – MetalTalk Website (Chatham, Kent)

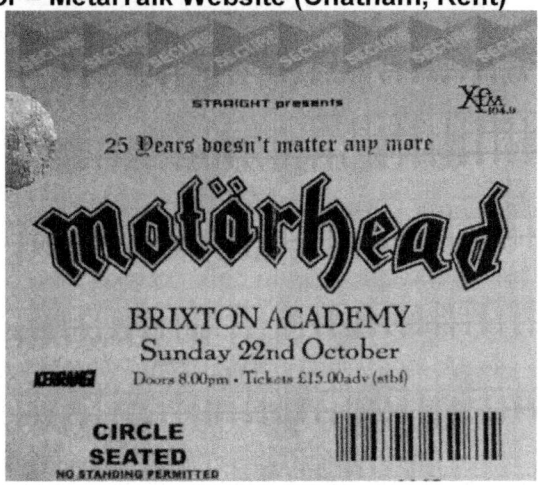

"He may have not been everyone's taste but whether you loved, loathed or were indifferent no one can deny he was the real deal.
It's always been a love thing for me with Motörhead. As a kid I grew up on metal from early teen formative years, Quo were my first, Rainbow were the most influential, I was 11 in 1979 and everything was dropping into place. Steve Lawnmower got me introduced to Bonce though. They were his band. I used to go around his house, years before we formed and listened to early Bronze recordings. But when 'Overkill' was put in the mix that was it. Job done. Those vocals, that bass line, and of course those double kicks which defined it. It's still one of my favourite all time albums, it's that important, it's that listenable and it's that killer.
They are the band I've seen more than any other over the years. 16 times. To be fair they weren't always great. The last time I saw them they were awful, the time before that, in Blackburn, I've never seen him so happy. No one plays Blackburn and there is nothing to be happy about, but they were out of the park that night, killer set and just great to see him in such fine form.
But the ultimate memory is my first. Nottingham concert hall on the 'No Remorse' tour. The band were firing on all cylinders with

Wurzel and Phil having just joined, they had the new energy and even now looking back you could see why. I was 15 or 16. Steve, Chris and I (all Lawnmower) bunked school for the afternoon as we sometimes did when gigs were in town. We hung around outside the stage door. We waited for hours, we even met Eddy Large whilst we were waiting! But it did pay off, we got invited in and spent time with the band. They signed stuff, we got to chat and hang out, and we got to drink Cinzano with Lemmy. It may not have been Jack and Coke on the strip but when you're this age who cares, we didn't even know about LA! I seem to recollect the conversation was mainly around them playing on 'Saturday Morning Starship' (kids programme on ITV) the next morning.
I'm still sad about the whole thing. Let's be honest, no one was surprised, it was well broadcast about his illness and we knew it was coming, but I wasn't expecting such a void. Of course it's a monumental passing, he defined icon, but there is no Motörhead. It's gone, it's bigger than one man, it's a whole bigger thing having no Motörhead. After 16 shows of not seeing the 'Bomber' now I never will.
The one band Lawnmower always wanted to support was Motorhead, that will never happen. We've done Download five times now and many other festivals but would have given these all up to do Hammy with him." **Qualcast "Koffee Perkulator" Mutilator 'Pete Lee' -**
(Lawnmower Deth – Vocals)

"I went to the 'Ace Up Your Sleeve' tour at Hammersmith in 1980 and this proves how sharp Lemmy was even on stage!
They opened with 'Ace of Spades' and as he got to the part of the song where he sings 'you know I'm born to lose and gambling's for fools' someone threw a bottle on stage and just missed Lemmy. Without missing a note he sang 'who ever threw that fucking bottle he ain't gonna live forever' and don't forget the joker!! Quite impressed with that one and not forgotten it to this day!
Met Lem at Manchester I think 2011? He was signing autographs and doing pictures I wore my 'Pisshead' T-shirt. When I met him he looked at my shirt and said
"Pisshead' I like that!!"
Nigel McHugh (London)

"I have met Lemmy a few times over the years but the first and most memorable occasion was backstage at Manchester Apollo. Managed to get 'Access All Area' passes through Wurzel just

before he left.
All the warnings about never meeting your heroes were running through my head.
After meeting Phil and Mikkey we were shown into Lemmy's dressing room - at this point all the words I knew had somehow left my memory bank rendering me speechless..........
Lemmy greeted us with "hello lads come in. What did you think of the show"? I babbled something that meant great and he said "good I'm glad you enjoyed it".
I'm still trying to comprehend the fact that this massive rock star actually cared what a 24 year old kid from Stockport thought about him and the show when he hands me a spliff and says "get that down ya!"
After some photos and autographs it was time for the next wave of fans to meet their hero. We were escorted out to the stage door and went to the bus stop when my mate said to me "erm you might want to put that away" pointing to the spliff I still had in my hand...........it now resides in a frame with a signed photo from the guys including Wurzel and Philthy."

Dave Kirby (Manchester)

"First I heard of Lemmy was on a single by The Damned – 'I Just Can't Be Happy Today', on the b-side was a cover of 'Ballroom Blitz' by the Sweet – 'Bass by Lemmy'… Who's Lemmy I thought at the time.
As the years went by we all knew who Lemmy was…A LEGEND."

Geoffrey Harris (St Austell)

"Lemmy Kilmister- Rocker, great conversationalist, brilliant military historian (pointed out mistakes in a WW2 film), outstanding musician (played the bass guitar in new and unique way) and songwriter (whole range of subjects from war to sex & drugs & rock 'n' roll in fact most aspects of the human condition), comedian (with a dry sense of humour), a flawed but decent human being.
I personally never got to either meet Lemmy or see Motörhead 'live' (just one of those things), but their recorded music left an indelible impression on me. Lemmy's interviews whether written or on radio/television made me feel like he was a long lost uncle, the black sheep of the family.
You could say in some way I would not be who I am today without Lemmy and his massive contribution to the world of rock music be it through Hawkwind or Motörhead.
Thank you Lemmy for being you, but most of all thank you for the

music, and the mid digit to 'The Man'!"
Keith Bray (Amesbury, Wiltshire)

"It was good. Just the sort of thing I like.
At first the music was quite over the top, outrageous, but over the years a lot of other groups got far more heavy, but Lemmy's music stayed basically the same. At the end it sounded quite mainstream."
Gary Dyer (Crafthole, Cornwall)

"Unfortunately never had the pleasure of seeing Motörhead as they always clashed with other bands at download. However I do remember 'Ace of Spades' being on 'Tony Hawks Pro Skater 3', I'm sure that many a teenager was introduced to classic metal as a result.
In fact I also remember at about 13 my uncle got me Hawkwind's 'Greatest Hits' for Christmas and I remember it being the most surreal hour of music I'd ever listened to, took about a week to feel normal again afterwards."
James Hargreaves (Birkenhead)

"I saw Motörhead play at the Cornwall Coliseum in the 80's.
A group of us arrived at the gig early and grabbed a Wimpy, then had a stroll on the beach. To our surprise, 'Philthy Phil Taylor' was walking towards us. We had to have a chat with him, and he did just that. He asked us if we were going to the evening gig, and were we local. As crazy as the great drummer was, he was fascinated by the beach, and how close it was to the venue.
The evening eventually arrived, and the time had come for Motörhead to take the stage. There were no disappointments in their delivery of music. They were loud enough to witness items bouncing on the bar. This was the original line up with Lemmy leading the vocals. The only other band as loud was The Who.
A great night was had, playing all their great songs that they had penned together.
It was only years down the road that I learnt that Lemmy sung vocals on Hawkwind's 'Silver Machine.'
RIP Lemmy, you played a huge part in the music industry, we shall all miss you. You may be gone but your music is with us in our vinyl/CD collections. 'Ace of Spades', 'Bomber', 'Overkill', 'Motörhead', 'Speedfreak', '(We Are) The Roadcrew', classics!"
Paul Deacon (Bodmin, Cornwall)

"My favourite Lemmy moment occurred while watching Motörhead at 'Monsters of Rock' some time in the mid 80's.
Some idiot shot a flare gun over the stage causing the man to bring whatever they were playing to a screaming halt.
He then proceeded to give a roughly 70,000 strong crowd a thorough bollocking, threatening to leave if anyone did it again.
We stood there, sheepish as if being told off by our 'metal dad', before they launched back into the song.
Good Times were then resumed."
Andrew Freudenberg (Ilminster)

"Lemmy's sad passing was a real shame for rock and roll and indeed the world. A true legend.
My first gig as a lad was at Bingley Hall, Stafford with Motörhead, Saxon and Girlschool. I was due to take my lad to HIS first gig in January 2016 which would have been, yep, you guessed it, Motörhead, Saxon and Girlschool. It would have been poignant but, sadly, was not to be.
From that first gig in '79 I was hooked on Motörhead and through time, Lem osmosised from hero to living legend to legend. They never let me down or disappointed. A constant throughout my life and I was fortunate to see them many times around the UK and Europe.
Heroes die, but legends live forever. ♠♠♠"
Richie Addison (Abingdon, Oxfordshire)

"I never met the bloke, but I'm sure we would have got on…"
Carl Parsliffe (Plymouth)

Monsters of Rock – Donington Park 16th August 1986

Iron Fist
Stay Clean

Nothing Up My Sleeve
Metropolis
Doctor Rock
Killed by Death
Ace Of Spades
Steal Your Face
Bite The Bullet
Built For Speed
Orgasmatron
No Class
Motorhead
Bomber
Overkill

"My memories of Lemmy start when I was about 14 and I heard 'Ace of Spades' for the first time. It was blasting though the bedroom door of my best mate's brother's bedroom.
I'm like "HELLLOOOOO, WTF WAS THAT!!!!" I was sold. Whenever Motörhead was on at Donington I made sure I was front and centre for their set. When they came to Derby in 2010, my sisters, brothers in law, husband and I celebrated our anniversary at the gig. I woke up totally deaf in my right ear, ringing in the left. Took weeks for me to get my hearing back. Yep. Louder than anything else.
End of an era and 30+ years of ear bleeding pleasure. Cancer gallops through my family. My uncle got 6 weeks notice when we discovered he had brain tumors. I'm so glad that it wasn't protracted like that for Lemmy.
Cancer is a b*****d...."
Karen Whaley (Derby)

"I first heard Motörhead in early 1982 when someone lent me a tape of 'No Sleep 'til Hammersmith' which was the heaviest music I had ever heard and they became alongside Quo, AC/DC and Iron Maiden my favourite band.
Motörhead were and are unique, a band you didn't like for 5 minutes, you loved them for life...and they became a part of life, dependable, always out there somewhere playing shitkicking rock 'n' roll.

As soon as I got the chance to see them in 1984, I went with my school friends and that tradition continued to the last time I saw them at Hyde Park in 2014, my 18th and final time with the same friends. I had seen the band in Melbourne, in Munich, in Brixton, at Hammersmith, or at Donington and the crowd were always the same... metal-heads, punks, skinheads, rockers... Motörheadbangers who loved, lived and breathed the band.

Lemmy to me was like a grumpy uncle, a man nobody messed with, but if you were on his side, he was your ally for life. Motörhead gigs were a celebration and hearing, 'Going to Brazil', 'Overkill' or 'Ace of Spades' live was all the confirmation we needed, we had picked the right band because that band was Motörhead and they played rock 'n' roll and they played it Louder than anyone else.

Rock in Peace Lemmy."

Andrew Simm (Dawlish, UK)

"I went to his hotel to pick him up one day after Reading Festival. He had asked me whilst we were in the backstage bar if I would give him a lift.

I got to his room at about 7 am. Lemmy opened the door and said to me "do you want some breakfast before we leave? "

"Ok" I said, "what did you have in mind "?

Lemmy looked at me and said:

"Well I've got Jack Daniels or I've got speed. What do you fancy? "

I had the Jack. What was I gonna say, no?"

Noel Ratty Wyatt (Bristol)

Reading Festival
24th August 1979

Overkill
Stay Clean
No Class
I'll Be Your Sister
Metropolis
Step Down

**(I Won't) Pay Your Price
Iron Horse/Born to Lose
Too Late, Too Late
Capricorn
Train Kept A-Rollin'
Limb From Limb
Motorhead**

"I remember seeing him in HMV London buying LP's.
I'd gone to see MSG at Hammersmith. He spent quite a few quid and the guy on the till remarked at the amount, then asked for his autograph, at that another 10 people appeared and he said "right boys 'n' girls I'm off for a fag n a gargle, might look in at Schenker later, young un" at that he left and winked at me."
Andy Brown (Leeds)

"I first met Lemmy like many others when Motörhead played the Coliseum in 1980.
He was up in the arcade above the Wimpy playing the machines! I interrupted him as an annoying 15 year old would! Something he remembered a few times years later! He signed autographs and was very friendly though.
Three years later and I was living in Cardiff with new band Persian Risk and got a call from Rob sanders on asking us to support Motörhead at the Coliseum!!! Anvil were supporting but had to return to Canada early!!!
July 83' we did the gig, Lemmy was extremely friendly again and commented on me interrupting his game 3 years earlier!!!
1984 and Phil Campbell (my guitar partner in Risk) got the job in Motörhead!!!
We were in Dingwalls at Camden Lock and Lemmy came up and in his gruff vice "How would you boys feel about supporting us on the British Tour"?!!! Silly question!!! We were in!!! Lemmy helped me out a lot on the 15 date tour, encouraging the band and personally slipping me a few quid here and there as I was skint as usual!!! We had use of a little green mini van and a roadie from our manager Mickey Miff, and we'd often call round to the Motörhead house to pick up Phil and Lemmy to go to places like Hammersmith Odeon etc. Stayed at the house a couple of times

(up all night!!) And Lemmy would come in at 8.30 or so and immediately be on large glasses of Blue Smirnoff and Orange!!! Few years later, 1988 January 23rd, we (Paul Dianno's Battlezone) were on tour in the USA, A gig in Providence Rhode Island, it was Steve Hopgood's (our drummer) birthday, Motörhead were also in town supporting Alice Cooper, they came to our gig after they'd played and got on stage with us to help cream pie Steve for his birthday!!!"
Graham Bath (Persian Risk)

"Motörhead are my favourite band, I have seen them at least 5 times and every time they blew me away.
I am very sad that Lemmy has passed away; I have taken almost all of my immediate family and my friends to see them. The first time I saw them I was deaf for a week and had my driving test the day after, which was eventful.
RIP Lemmy I will never forget you and I will always listen to your music."
Clair Trigg (Plymouth)

"I've many memories of meeting Lemmy - the first time I spoke to him was at the Marquee Club in Wardour St, Soho aged 14... yeah, I'm sure many of your readers will recall Lemmy at the fruit machine in there - he was a regular and it was as if it was the most normal thing in the world to walk in and chat to him, as simple as that.
He left a huge impression on me in more ways than one and over many years of going to see Motörhead I never tired of seeing Lemmy's band. One gig in particular I waited over 20 years for, when they played the Bulldog Bash in '09.
The man was a one off, genuine, unique and sound. I'll miss him."
Essex Girl

The Bulldog Bash
8th August 2009

Iron Fist
Metropolis
Over The Top

**Another Perfect Day
Killed By Death
Bomber
Whorehouse Blues
Ace Of Spades
Overkill**

"Sheffield City Hall, mid 90's I think!
Some complete prick spat at Lemmy.
So Lemmy stopped the music, while the spit was rolling down his hair. Lemmy points at this guy and says – "Listen boy, I can wash my hair tonight, but you'll always be a WANKER!"
Then the wanker was thrown out! PMSL!
Lemmy = Legend, RIP"
Bret Bowman (Barnsley)

"Lemmy's music not only inspired Metal it inspired the rock world in general Punk, Rock and Roll, Black Metal, Thrash, it doesn't matter.
Whether you're Metallica, The Exploited, Venom or Iron Maiden you owe Motörhead for the reason you sound like that.
Lemmy lived his life to the fullest even into his 70's and literally played until he could play no more.
You owe yourself and everything you stand for if you're a Metal fan to go check out his back catalogue with Motörhead and as a person lucky enough to see them live, there was never quite an experience like a Motörhead live show."
Bradley Cassidy (Crewe)

"My earliest memory of Lemmy is seeing Motörhead on 'Top of the Pops' way back in 1980 and they just blew me away with their look and energy.
Just over a year later I saw them in concert at 'The Heavy Metal Holocaust' festival at Port Vale football ground. It was the first heavy rock show I had been to and what an introduction to live rock concerts that was to me. To see a band I was introduced to less than a year before on the telly and then to see them in person with the full 'Bomber' lighting rig and wall of sound just blew my mind and has stayed with me from that day to this.
Of course, I would see them many times later on various tours, but

what struck me about Lemmy was even watching as an audience member, you could see how natural and genuine the great man was and how much he really cared for his fans. He always gave 100% whenever I saw them live. Such a fabulous presence and charisma, he only had to stand there and the audiences would be cheering and calling his name, it was a sight to see.
I thought he was a one off original that said it like it was and lived his life exactly how he wanted it to be.
An icon of British rock music that will be with us forever."
Martin Evans (Llanelli, Wales)

Heavy Metal Holocaust
Port Vale Football Stadium
1st August 1981

Ace of Spades
Stay Clean
Live To Win
Over The Top
No Class
The Hammer
Metropolis
Leaving Here
Jailbait
Iron Horse/Born to Lose
Fire, Fire
Too Late, Too Late
Fast and Loose
Dead Men Tell No Tales
(We Are) The Road Crew
Capricorn

Train Kept A-Rollin'
Bite The Bullet
The Chase is Better Than the Catch
Overkill
White Line Fever
Bomber
Motorhead

"Saw Motörhead in 2010 At Download. It was my sons 1st time at Download, he was 10 and couldn't wait to see them! They were amazing, and Slash also came on stage to play! Lemmy was an absolute legend, can't believe he's gone ☹"
Louise Goodenough (Botley, Southampton)

Download Festival
13th June 2010

Iron Fist
Stay Clean
Be My Baby
Rock Out
Metropolis
Over The Top
The Thousand Names of God
Cradle to the Grave
In The Name of Tragedy
Just 'Cos You Got the Power – Featuring Slash
Going to Brazil
Killed by Death

Ace of Spades
Overkill

"Me and a mate Andrew Cheeseman was in the 'Wap' on the Friday afternoon an *Motörhead* was playing the Sheffield City Hall that night back on the '1916' tour back in '91 and Lemmy was also in the 'Wap' playing on the bandit drinking 'Newky Brown' and JD chasers.
He had no security with him and if people didn't know who he was they would have thought that he was a normal Sheffield rocker having a drink and not a rock 'n' roll legend about to play the City Hall in a few hours as nobody bothered him as he had been in the 'Wap' loads of times.
 As we were leaving Lemmy was also going up the stairs and Lemmy asked Andrew where the nearest chippy was, so we told him and he went off for his fish 'n' chips and we went off towards the City Hall and we then said 'why the fuck didn't we go with him to the chippy!!!!! And we should have said to Lemmy in fact we are going come with you' what a chance we missed to dine with the great man himself!!!"
Mark Lindley (Sheffield)

"That all I got, I never had PIC with Lemmy I wish I could I only see Motörhead one time in my life was my b'day present in the park London
I was very happy, they was amazing couldn't believe I was seeing them play, my best gift b'day of my life."
Nella Bellinzoni (Fleetwood)

My first memories as a fan of Motörhead was probably seeing them for first time at Hyde Park supporting the mighty Foo's...
Now Motörhead don't really play in the day, they're more like a sweaty sawdust room kinda band, oh wow they were loud and just so on it in every musical loud note it was like a plane taking off I loved it. I still have some vid footage on old phone somewhere but the highlight was 'Killed By Death' with Juliette Lewis as guest vocals, she was dressed as an Indian girl native, that is well Lemmy was always the chief \""/ ...
I was also lucky to see Lemmy come on as special guest to Metallica at the O2 in London '09 and tear through 'Overkill"
Dave Morrissey (London)

Hyde Park Supporting Foo Fighters June 17th 2006

Doctor Rock
Stay Clean
Love Me Like a Reptile
Killers
Metropolis
Over the Top
I Got Mine
In the Name of Tragedy
Dancing on Your Grave
Just 'Cos You Got the Power
Going to Brazil
Killed By Death
Ace of Spades
Overkill

"I have fond memories of seeing Motörhead on the 'Bomber' and 'Ace Up Your Sleeve' tour.
The 'Bomber' tour in 1979 when I was 13 is more memorable as a friend and myself wagged school to go and see Lemmy, Fast Eddie and Philthy at Blackburn King Georges Hall.
We spent the day at Accrington market on my friends Dad's record stall, a great time for music and remember The Jam's 'Going Underground' and PIL's 'Metal Box' being amongst the stock of the day...on vinyl of course.
The gig was incredible, the loudest thing I have ever heard in my life only bettered when we went to see them on the 'Ace Up Your Sleeve' tour. My ears were ringing for several days afterwards and my love for this band was confirmed.
I remember Lemmy playing his Rickenbacker on the 'Bomber' style

lighting rig which also added theatre to the show.
My friends Dad was in the bar for the whole gig but he still walked out saying 'I'm fuckin deaf after that' I feel very lucky and honoured to have seen in my opinion the best line up of the band.
Happy days indeed. RIP Lemmy."
Steve Walmsley (Blackpool)

"Losing Lemmy has hit a lot of people. I do not usually find myself distracted by the passing of "celebrities", but I think Lemmy was a little different, so say the least.
After Motörhead's Afan Lido gig in Port Talbot, West Wales on 1st April 1982, my mates and I hung around outside for a while hoping that my mate's "mislaid" bullet belt would turn up.
We were fresh faced 18 year olds and pretty new to the gigging game, so when after a while someone came out to say that the band were happy to say hello if we wanted, we and a small group of others jumped at the opportunity to say hello (albeit very briefly) to Lemmy, Phil and Eddie.
Maybe they always did this, but to me it said a lot - we had not requested to see them - they offered to say hello to us! This was not for the media or anyone other than to say thanks to some fans that had turned up on the night. True gentlemen.
A few years ago at a Motörhead gig at the Colston Hall in Bristol, during one of the songs (I don't remember which) someone in the audience (in punk-style) coughed up and spat at Lemmy, ending up (let's say) with a new addition to Lemmy's hair-do.
Lemmy responded by stating, in his typical growl that in the morning he would once again have clean hair, but the offending gentleman would still be a c**t.
As they say here in Brizzle "it made I larf!"
Ian John (Bristol)

"We'd seen Motörhead at the Colston Hall in Bristol and waited in the reception after the show to hopefully meet the band, - only three of us there!
After some time Phil Campbell came out first and said "Fuckin' 'ell, I fuckin' wish somebody had fuckin' told me people were fuckin' waiting I'd have fuckin' come out earlier!!!!" and he stayed for a chat and pictures.
Mikkey Dee came shortly after and did the same.
Then, Lemmy's boots were carried through by a member of the crew and taken onto the bus, and a few minutes later Lemmy came through. He didn't stop, he looked pretty tired, but he

casually walked between us and as he passed me he looked up, gave a little nod and said "Goodnight".
I'm sure if I'd asked for a photo he would have obliged but I was too polite (or shy) to ask!"
Simon Court (Bleadon, Somerset)

"My big sister took me to see Lemmy in Plymouth, he made me really want to listen to rock music.
I will miss him dearly as I really wanted to get the chance to see him again. He was a rock God and will never be forgotten."
Joanna Trigg (Plymouth)

"I was fortunate enough to experience Motörhead live in 2014 when they played the British Summer Time Festival in Hyde Park. Lemmy kicked off proceedings by stating "we're Motörhead and we play rock and roll " and by god they did!
No gimmicks, just full on rock and entertaining as hell.
Arguably maybe not the most charismatic; but definitely one of the most iconic front men in rock. He will be missed."
Sophie Alexandra Hall (Cantebury)

Hyde Park London Supporting Black Sabbath 4th July 2014

Damage Case
Stay Clean
Over the Top
Lost Woman Blues
Doctor Rock
Going to Brazil
Killed By Death Feat. Whitfield Crane
Ace of Spades
Overkill

"I've never met Lemmy but he is one guy I would have loved to have done so. He had such a huge character and what you saw with him is what you got...nothing false whatsoever! Typical of someone of that style I suppose. Somebody who I would liked to have a party with (if I could remember much about it!!) and he partied hard! I particularly loved his style especially the position of the microphone, which saw him look to 'heaven'. He also sang with Hawkwind on the rock classic 'Silver Machine'.
That was also his trademark along that long hard never say die style of playing. Rock n roll without him would not be the same. Hope this is some help for your forthcoming book. I myself suffered a cancer 18 years ago on my lower left calf muscle. It was known as a Liposarcoma tumour and it nearly killed me. Luckily, they found it in time and since then have had a high dose of radiotherapy. I am in now in the clear. The tumour itself was about the size of a melon. I was carrying that tumour for over a YEAR before I got the suspicious lump checked out. I thought that I knocked the leg!!
Gary Cocks (Falmouth, Cornwall)

"He wasn't just Ace of Spades. He was much more than that.

He was a new album of dependable Rock & Roll, every couple of years throughout your adult life.
He was an annual gig in my home town, a night of blistering beautiful Rock & Roll, the way it should be.
He was the simple balladic poignancy of "1916".
He was storming off the Never Mind The Buzzcocks set because he felt the mob were unduly ripping the pish out a naive young woman.
He was the direct link between the Beatles, who were his influence, to all the thrash/death/industrial/hardcore hybrid metal bands who he influenced.
He was a bass sound, along with a drum sound, that made "Locomotive" sound like you were actually really inside a fucking steam engine.
He was the stark, serious social commentary of "Don't Let Daddy Kiss me".
He was the pure joyous boogie abandon of "Going To Brazil".
He was the ex-Hawkwind hippy who embraced Punk, taking the Damned on tour, paying homage with "Ramones", bridging the territorial gap between the cultures, reminding us we are all just the bastard sons of Chuck Berry.
He was an evil looking bastard, bathed in green light, growling out "Orgasmatron" at the Glesga Barras.
Talking 'Bastards', (another fine album), he was the father figure that I adopted for myself.
Cheers da.

" . . . All your life's a cosmic joke
Fill your days with piss and smoke
The wolf waits at your door." "
Shaun Moore (Glasgow)

"Please Don't Touch" with Girlschool. Brilliant track!"
John Borlase (Exeter, Devon)

"What you see is what you got and if you didn't like it he would tell you 2 fuck off."
Danny Robert Williams (Bognor Regis)

"It was the year 1979. I was young, it was my first concert, and I was extremely excited, the 'Bomber' tour, Ipswich.

I was with a few friends who I worked with, two of them were brothers who had met Lemmy several times before, who often spoke of how they used to help load the bands equipment on the van after a concert at West Runton Pier, just prior to them hitting it big. They promised me that I would meet Lemmy, Phil and Eddie after the concert, so you can probably imagine how I was that night, fuelled with alcohol I was off the chart!
The gig did not disappoint. I was head banging all through, cheering and all the usual stuff. At the finish, I was still bounding with energy, sweating, ears ringing, and a strained voice I was ready to meet my idols.
True to their word, we were led back stage into a room, and there they were, and Lemmy in all his glory. He looked at me and grinned, in that famous gravel voice he said "Enjoy that, did you?", I just nodded, dumbstruck, not quite believing I was actually there, in the presence of Lemmy, all I could do was stare at him, his physique, his lovely long hair, the signature mutton chop tash, and his handsome face.
I remember him being warm, friendly, and humourous. I can't remember the conversations, but my t-shirt was signed by the band.
I do remember Lemmy laughing that across my chest, Eddie wrote "Fast Eddie likes these"!!
The time came for all of us to go, we walked out with Motörhead. Outside a crowd was waiting, not hundreds, but a crowd none the less, boy did I feel special. A young lad in the crowd shouted "Lemmy, why do you sing so loud"
"Coz I'm deaf" he replied, the lad then shouted
"Why are you deaf?"
"Coz I sing so loud" came the reply, there was some laughter at that, then Lemmy said
"I had better remember that, that was quite good, wasn't it"!.
That was my first time meeting with the man himself, and Motörhead.
The second time, was 1983, in Glasgow, it was the year before my son was born.
I had a bit of a following of young lads, I had a partner, but for some reason I was a bit of a celebrity!?
Anyway, long story short, my partner would have been one of the 'arseholes' Lemmy would have politely called a bastard.
He, to make himself look good, used to exaggerate, so to these lads, he said about how I knew Lemmy personally, and we were good friends. If they wanted to meet the band, stay with us and I,

(me) would sort it. They got so hyped up, I didn't have the heart to tell them I'd only met him once, 2 -3 year previous.

Another brilliant concert, was enjoyed by all, everybody was shouting at each other afterwards, because we were all rendered deaf with tinnitus, the lads were waiting for me. Shouting louder than most, they couldn't contain their excitement wanting to meet Motörhead .

Well, me being me, and not wanting to look as stupid as my now long gone ex wanted me to, I said follow me.

I marched back into the concert area, all the lads in tow. I was met by a burly bouncer, being 5ft, I was dwarfed by all around me. I said full of confidence, "Can you ask Lemmy and the guy's to come out please?"

The bouncer said in a broad Glaswegian accent "An ye wey, oot all o ye" ... Seeing the disappointment on my friends faces, I stood my ground, and heard myself saying "Lemmy would want to see me, tell him Tracey from Norfolk is here, he knows who I am."

Well, the bouncer went off, a few minutes later he came back, and said, he'll be here in a bit.

Sure enough, like a vision appearing through the smoke, came Lemmy, flanked by the rest of Motörhead.

"What are you doing up here"? he said looking at me, I couldn't believe it, he remembered me! Lemmy actually remembered me, ME!

He spoke to my friends, signed their posters etc. I asked him to sign my cut down, as he was doing so, he asked where I got it from, I had painted "Snaggletooth" on the back.

Confused, I asked why? It was an old Levi jacket my brothers mate gave me, I cut the arms off.

"So you didn't buy it like that then, with the Motörhead on the back"? Lemmy said, I laughed "No, I painted that". To which Lemmy shouted "Fuckin hell, that's brilliant, look at this she's done", he said to the band, swirling me around, "That's fucking spot on eh fellas".

One of them laughed, and said, "was you thinking of suing for copyright?" I gulped and asked if I'd done something wrong, (I was a bit naive) Lemmy just laughed and assured me not. He said I had a great talent and to keep the art up, and I have, to this day.

I just want to finish this off by saying Lemmy is everything people say he is. He is my Hero, I love him for all he is, as the person, a kind, intelligent, humourous, warm, thoughtful being, and the Rock 'n' Roll star, faster and louder than anyone else, who never put himself above his fans.

I for one will miss him terribly." Love you always big man."
Tracey Horn (Yarmouth)

Apollo Theatre, Glasgow June 18th 1983

Back at the Funny Farm
Tales of Glory
Shoot You in the Back
Marching Off to War
Iron Horse/Born to Lose
Another Perfect Day
(Don't Need) Religion
One Track Mind
Go to Hell
America
Shine
Dancing on Your Grave
Rock It
I'm Your Hoochie Coochie Man
I Got Mine
Bite the Bullet
The Chase Is Better Than the Catch

"I remember seeing Motörhead down Cornwall Coliseum when they were promoting the 'Ace of Spades' album in 1980.
I remember they had a massive WW2, 4 engined bomber which they lowered over the crowd. It also had spinning spotlights for the 4 engines and the roar of the Lancaster bomber blasting over the load speakers, whilst they performed the song 'Bomber'."
Roger Lewis (Plymouth)

"Seen Motörhead at the Plymouth Pavilions & they were that fucking loud, my ears were ringing for a week!!"
Chris Adams (Plymouth)

"All I can say about Lemmy is, although I did not ever meet or see him or Motörhead, that man changed my life completely.
I'm a guitar player, but Lemmy started it all for me: the style, the attitude and just generally being a great guy. His music completely changed what I listened to and watching him perform with other artists like Slash and Metallica just made me want to be in band more than ever.
His music and personality have changed me and my career aspirations. My only regret was missing out on seeing a legend."
Ben Haslehurst (Blackpool)

"Lemmy was a great man who lived by his own rules. I never had the pleasure of meeting him or seeing Motörhead play live, however I can tell you Lemmy was the definition of rock 'n' roll.
Motörhead was one of the first 'heavy' bands I ever heard. Along with ACDC they kicked off my love for metal and rock music.
There has never been another band like Motörhead and I don't think there ever will be. The same goes for Lemmy, there will never be another like him, he was one of a kind.
I will remember Lemmy for the way he lived his life and how he would not let anyone tell him how to live his life. His rock 'n' roll attitude and life style will live on in all of us.
Most of all I am grateful of what Lemmy did in his life. His music means so much to me and to millions of other people. Whatever mood I'm in, I will always want to play my Motörhead records. They were Motörhead,
and they played rock 'n' roll!
Born to lose, live to win!!!"
Harry Long (Blackpool)

"I'll share an amusing story from when a team of us travelled down from Wick in the far north of Scotland to Glasgow to see Motörhead on the 'Overnight Sensation' tour 1997.
We went to the Cathouse after a blinding gig by Motörhead. As we stood at the bar Mickey Dee came in with 2x stunners on his arm.
We went over had a wee chat with him, got the gig tickets signed etc then went back to our pints.
One of the lads 'Gordy poop' went off to the toilet for a pish.
As soon as he had left Lemmy appeared at the bar. We weren't sure whether to bother him or not, so we said "fuck it let's speak to him."
We went up to him and he was so cool. Got our tickets signed and fucked off back to our drinks.
Gordy poop was returning from the bog just as Lemmy had been served (I shit you not) 2x pint glasses of JD 'n' coke.
Gordy says "Lemmy can ah shake yer hand" bear in mind Lem's got 2 pint glasses.
Lemmy says "FUCK OFF!"
Poop looks stunned as Lemmy walks away.
Poop then shouts at Lem as he's walking away to the VIP area "IF YE EVER COME TO WICK BIY. YER GETTING A KICKING!! "
We we're stunned Lem kept walking away laughing. Never did see Lemmy up in Wick, maybe it was Poops threat that kept him away!"
RIP LEMMY
MOTORHEAD FOR LIFE
Gary Begg MHB3506 (Wick, Scotland)

"Still unable to grasp Lemmy's passing but here's my memory…
Four years ago my then 12yr old daughter Amy walked through the living room as 'Ace of Spades' wason the TV, a Motörhead obsession was born. She listen
to, read about and gathered as much info as possible on them and Lemmy became her hero and inspiration.

Nov' 2012 Motörhead played at Leicester de Monfort Hall.
I got tickets and sent a letter addressed to Lemmy to the box office, long shot that it would get to him but worth a try!! I basically said how much he meant to Amy, to
thank him for still touring and for making it affordable! Told him we'd be in the stalls and to give Amy a nod. Went to the concert, Amy fainted several times and I hoped Lemmy had got the letter because I wanted him to know what he meant to us.
Fast forward a couple of weeks, getting ready for the school run and a parcel arrived.
My tum did a wee roll.
Opened it and found a letter, a letter from Lemmy! And three t-shirts.
And the offer of tickets for the Download rock festival. After I'd regained consciousness I called Amy to show her.
I can't really explain her reaction, shock, tears, total elation, disbelief. The same went for myself and her dad.
1. He'd got the letter
2. He replied, personally, how amazing is that??!!
3. Tee shirts, the offer of Download tickets.
I mean this was Lemmy, rock 'n' roll icon!! But this is why I was so proud of Amy for choosing Motörhead and Lemmy, a true honest gentleman.
6 months of major excitement and telling everyone who would listen and many who wouldn't about all this,
the Lawrence clan arrive at Download. Email sent by Motörhead team said that tickets would be at the box office on site. Several trips to the box office, nothing there. Around 11am they arrived! Not just tickets tho, VIP 'Access All Area' tickets. More delirious meltdowns from us.
So, in a daze we go everywhere, because we can. VIP loos were used, Bar was frequented, syrup sponges were ate in the artists catering tent.
But we had access to the artists area, we found Lemmy's dressing room.

We waited.
His girlfriend appeared on the steps, I complemented her boots and showed her the original letter from Lemmy which she took inside. Minutes later she reappeared and beckoned us in......
At this point I had to remind Amy to breath. I guided her to the door and in we went. There sat Lemmy. He stood up and offered his hand. He was then pounced on by a delirious woman (that was I) who hugged him and thanked him profusely, calling him petal......
Once he'd got over the shock he sat with Amy, looked at all the patches on her jacket, spent time with her. Photos were taken. Time Butcher came in to say it was sound check time, more handshakes and hugs. Lemmy checked we'd been given the full VIP tickets and then it was time to move on.
Amy came out of there shaking, sobbing, but forming the best memories ever.
For all of that I love the man, no-one in the industry will ever come close.
I've just re read my ramblings and my eyes are leaking slightly. The pure joy of that day returns. It was obv then that Lemmy was feeling ill, he spoke about his operation to fit a defibrillator. He still took time for us. I told him Amy had been called a freak because of her taste in music etc, 'what's wrong with being a
freak?? Wouldn't want to be fucking normal!' Sound advice.
A short time in Lemmys company was like sitting with an old friend."
Bridgette Lawrence (Leicester)

"I think I was hooked on Lemmy and Motörhead from the first time I heard them, I think I was about 8/9 1983? when I heard 'Ace of Spades' and my Dad banned me from listening to this "devil music", fair to say from that point I listened more and that's where it all started.
I never got to see them on their own, but saw them for the first time in 2013 at Download and they blew

me away! Excellent. I'm so pleased I got to see them there. Just amazing.

I think Lemmy has had a massive influence on many of our lives as he was the daddy of rock and roll that we all wished we had! No one will ever be as rock and roll as Lemmy. He lived the life we wished we could, I guess their music was an escape for a lot of us. I'll never forget him, what an amazing man.

We were lucky enough to have a friend (Chrissy) who went to his memorial service and took our roses and messages for him (she got invited in, one of only 6 non celebrities to be in there) so that made us feel part
of it. What a wonderful thing to do for us all.

It was nice to know when we watched the memorial that our roses and messages were there. In a small way it was like we were there saying goodbye to our hero."

Amanda Young (Grimbsy)

"I've met Lemmy a total of three times but before I go in to that I'll give you a brief history of my Motorcareer.

I was brought up by my Grandmother from a baby and during the 1970's was an overweight, under confident child with zero social skills. In fact my Grandmother had
such trouble finding clothes to fit she actually made me write to Ronnie Corbett at the BBC to see if I could blag a few of his tank tops etc.

In 1979 I was given a tape recorder as a gift but had nothing to play on it. I bought a 3 pack of blank cassettes and gave them to my older cousin to record some of his albums. He duly did and this included the albums: 'Motörhead', 'Overkill' and 'Bomber'. I was completely blown away by this and especially the 'Overkill' album. My life totally changed from that moment. I grew up. 1980 I grew my hair, bought t-shirts and owned my first pair of Levi jeans and a leather jacket.

I then went to my first Motörhead concert in November 1980 – my 14th birthday.

I've gone on to be an outgoing, confident, successful man – still long hair and numerous tattoos etc. I have seen Motörhead over 40 times now in several different countries – most of mainland Europe and even as far as Australia.
The first time I met Lemmy was in July 1987. Thames TV, as it was, did a report on rock music in South London and decided to feature my friend's band at a pub in Croydon. The film crew turned up, a load of cash was put over the bar and we proceeded to enjoy said freebies. Then low and behold there was Lemmy in the pub. The film crew were concentrating on the band and the beer was flowing. I eventually plucked up the courage to talk to Lemmy.
I found him very friendly and approachable, we had a chat about music and I showed him my 'Born to Lose, Live to Win' tattoo which is the same as his. He rolled up his sleeved, placed his bare arm and said tattoo against mine announcing that we are 'tattoo brothers'. I nearly fell through the floor with the honour of it all.
The film crew then went on to interview him about music, with the infamous Danny Baker asking him inane questions. One of which was "do you bath???"
Lemmy replied – "yes at least once a year whether I need it or not, it's the scraping that's the hard part."
He left by taxi soon after and we as rock fans were interviewed by Danny Baker –not making much sense as we had been at the free bar for some time.
The second meeting was several years later. It was my 27th birthday myself and two friends had been at The Astoria in Charing Cross Rd to see a band and then we went on to the St Moritz Club in Wardour St. We settled in at the bar with a drink and were chatting away above the music. My fiend then pointed

out that Lemmy was there playing on the one armed bandit. I thought back to the time in Croydon and decided I must say hello.

Not wanting to say obvious things like 'hey man 'Ace of Spades' is great' or 'what's the real story behind finishing in Hawkwind'. I, like him, have an interest in the 2 World Wars so my approach was –

"do you think after the Battle of Arras that the Germans more or less let us go still thinking they may broker a deal with Britain?"

He froze, turned around, looked me up and down (I was terrified haha), then began to give me his opinion which was very similar to the question I'd asked.

We then went on to talk about many things First and Second World war related, amongst other things, none of which was music, Motörhead or anything along those lines.

After about half an hour he asked what I was up to in London that evening. I said I was celebrating my birthday with friends and had been to a gig at The Astoria.

He proceeded to get a £20 note out of his pocket and said "get yourself a drink, are those your friends over there?" which they were, he said, "get them one too".

As I was leaving for the bar he shouts out – "get me one too!"

I returned with the drinks and we chatted more for another half hour then I thought it best to leave him to it. I was once again, taken aback by his friendliness and willingness to chat with people. And as to being bought a drink, well, that was just awesome.

The third time was just very briefly.

When his biography was released in the early 2000's I was working in Central London. I got wind of the fact he was doing a book signing at a store in Oxford Street.

I went along after work, bought the book and duly queued up for a signing. Lemmy was

*forever gracious with all the thronging masses
asking for signatures and posing for photographs.
I got to my turn and he signed my book, shook
my hand and wished me well.
I never expected him to remember me, but when I
said to sign it to Squid (my nickname since birth),
he said "I know that name". I said briefly that we'd
met before a couple of times and I was given one
of those extraordinary Lemmy grins. We were all
being hurried through by the book shop staff
so I had to get on my way.
Lemmy was an enormous influence on me and
my life and will always continue to be. I was
deeply honoured to have met him those times. I
will miss him and the Motörhead concerts terribly.*
Gareth 'Squid' Goodall (Rugby)

*"I've never met Lemmy but I have been a die hard
fan and MHB since 1988.
I first saw* Motörhead *live on the 1916 tour.
February 4th 1991 @ Guildford Civic Hall. That*
Motörhead *ticket was like holding the Holy Grail of
Rock in my hand.
The support band was The Almighty and my
anticipation was heightened by the interviews
in Kerrang! and Raw magazine.
So came the night of the gig and the car journey
to Guildford (approx 30 miles). We arrived in plenty
of time to catch The Almighty and they were
awesome.
Off go The Almighty and after a brief wait and
watching the roadies flying around the stage
the lights dropped
and on they walked.
Motörhead ...larger than life and bursting into
action. '1916' is an awesome album and I
loved every minute of that gig.
Philthy Animal, my main drumming influence and
the two guitar attack blowing all expectations.
I got home that night totally exhausted, my hair
dripping with sweat from the headbanging.
Next day I'm back at school ears still ringing*

for the next three days.
I missed one London date between 1991 and 2014.
I remember one gig around the 25th Anniversary gig at Brixton Lemmy spoke to the crowd and said something along the lines of 'Ah I see some familiar faces tonight'. Although his eyes scanned the crowd I know his eyes met mine and you could see that he appreciated our support of his band, his baby.
That man will never be forgotten...and for all the RIGHT reasons."
Grizzly Pickett MHB 933 (London)

No Remorse, No Reprise

Life was like Overkill?
Anthemic, high and mighty,
a glorious, epic journey,
that left you,
drained and happy

. . . And then, as the last chord stops ringing,
it seems your song is over, your story ending . .

drummer pummels the pedals the power still pounding
double kicking the cracking cacophony off again,
and you get to surf those sonic waves,
feel the living wall of sound once more.

Just one more fucking time.
Or maybe twice, on a good night thrice,
that's if the band,
has enough in the tank,
and the crowd, or God,
is still on your side.

But all you got is one short life,
a single track that sounds more like . . . . .
R. A. M. O. N. E. S.

quick step fast pace rapid race
a stunted sprint a darting dash
that flies right past a flight too fast
at redline white hot feverish speed
it's fast and loose and short and sweet.

No sooner started than it's over and done,
you're born to lose, but you better run,
live to win till you're dead and gone,
till the end when you crash and burn,

no remorse, no reprise, no encore,
no slow dance when you hit this floor,
rock out, join the chorus, jump in the pit,
rock out, shake the world, stamp your feet,
rock out, make some noise, punch the air
because all too soon, we're all leaving here.

And it's too late too late, the party has passed
the thunder and lightning has hammered it's last,
no more familiar figure
upstanding, chin jutting,
teeth snarling, face looking,
up towards the lights
grizzled and growling,
into pointing down mike.

The end of time, the show is over,
a terminal show, stone dead forever,
killed by death there's nothing left,
you won't live to see another perfect day,
and in the wings, the roadcrew pallbearers,
wait to carry the silent Murder One away.

And up against the Marshall stack,
the stricken Rickenbacker
is laid to rest,
with limp and hanging strap,
feeding back, feeding back, feeding back,

the tortured ghosts,

of his last notes,
wailing and howling,
like the mourning of a million,
other fallen angels.
Shaun Moore (Glasgow)

"I saw Lemmy 2 or 3 times a week during the 80's, drink in one hand cigarette in the other playing the slot machines at either the Marquee club or St Moritz.
It didn't mater how rock 'n' roll we thought we were, we weren't as rock 'n' roll as Lemmy.
I was proud to get a nod from him as I staggered from club to club back in those days. It was at the St Moritz club I was trying to get him to come up on stage with us to sing 'Overkill', that was when he said "it's a good version, for a group of Nancy's".
Last saw him in Hollywood about 7 years ago, he looked good and asked what I was doing there? He didn't stop to hear a reply.
First saw him was at the Reading Rock festival in 1979, after punk Motorhead was the best sound I'd heard from a metal looking band with long hair.
We played 'Overkill' in the Babysitters and 'Bomber' in my time with Demon Preacher where we all put money in to get the double bass drum setup for Razzle so we could play that song.
Back then I had no idea I would one day play same stage as Lemmy."
Jimbo Gimson (The Babysitters)

"All I can say about Lemmy is, although I did not ever meet or see him or Motörhead, that man changed my life completely.
I'm a guitar player, but Lemmy started it all for me: the style, the attitude and just generally being a great guy.
His music completely changed what I listened to

and watching him perform with other artists like Slash and Metallica just made me want to be in band more than ever.
His music and personality have changed me and my career aspirations. My only regret was missing out on seeing a legend."
Ben Haslehurst (Blackpool)

"Done the Motörhead tour with the UK Subs few years back.
Met Lemmy near end of tour me and Darren went in to the dressing room to find Lemmy on his fruit machine, it was set up to not talk 2 him when he was on it, so we stood there for 4-10 mins like 2 little school boys then he turned round and smiled.
Took a pic with a chuck away camera. Lemmy said "what the fuck is that?"
Then said "proper punk rock camera that is!"
Chris Long (Cam, Gloucestershire)

"Never got to meet Lemmy or the band.
My dad took me to see them when I was about 13 I think.
We went to see them at Newcastle about 6 times after they were the first proper band I had seen and fuck it was loud, fast and raw it was fucking great.
I went with a friend a few times after as well. But I will never forget the time me and me dad took my brother for the first time the look on his face when Lemmy walked on was great, he was speechless.
I was hoping to be able to take my own son he's 4 and a massive Motörhead fan. I would of loved to say thank you for all the great fucking times Motörhead give me with my dad and brother I'll never forget that…
Sam Dawson (Durham)

"Me and my girlfriend Liz were so fortunate to see Motörhead *nearly 200 times all over*

the world. As you can imagine we have so many great/funny stories. Just a few that immediately come to mind are we went to Graz and Vienna to see them in 1998 I think. They set up and soundchecked in Graz and Lemmy was really unwell. They said they had all been hauled off the bus in the early hours in sub zero conditions by the border police while the bus was searched, I have no idea how the police didn't find anything BTW !

After the soundcheck Lemmy deteriorated so a doctor was called in who immediately told him to cancel the gig. Lems response of course was "fuck off, if I'm going to die I want to die on stage."

The doctor apparently said "OK I will give you a booster" but actually sedated him so he went to sleep and they pulled the gig.

Fortunately the venue had a recording studio above it so while Lemmy slept Phil and Mikkey recorded everything except the vocals for what turned out to be 'The Game' and we sat in and listened.

It was funny as Phil just could not play Lem's Rickenbacker at all so used one of the support bands Fender Precision basses.

The Vienna gig also got pulled but Lem went on to live another day.

We went to see them in a tiny town In the middle of Italy called Pordenoni. Only about 100 people turned up. We booked into the only hotel in town and were having dinner when Lem strolled in and said hi, then went upstairs to his room. I asked if the band were staying in the hotel and the answer was no, but Lemmy sometimes books a room in a hotel just for a couple of hours so he can do his business in comfort with a newspaper for company! We asked reception to get us a taxi to the gig and all the way the driver was looking in his mirror, talking Italian, punctuated with 'Lemmy', 'Motörhead ' of course we kept on just replying 'yes' thinking he was confirming that is where we wanted to go, to the Motörhead gig. When we got there he refused our money, then thrust out a piece of paper for an autograph, it was only then I *realised he thought I was Lemmy ! Did I sign? Of course I did lol! We wandered into a room backstage at a gig in Ventura in the USA in 2003 to find him sat by himself reading a book and drinking soup through a straw, that is when he was half way through having all his teeth fixed. We expected to get our arses kicked, but as always he was the perfect gent and said it was OK for us to come in for a chat. I could go on and on.... Just feel so privileged to have had so many great times and to have met him so many times. I only had my picture taken with him once and that was bang on Me and Liz went to LA for the first time in 2001, we went straight after Xmas to spend the New Year there. We went up to 'The Rainbow' several times as we knew Lemmy always hung out there, but after a few visits at various times and the bar staff saying how unusual it was that he had not been in the last few days as they knew he was in town we were feeling a little bit despondent as we were heading home in a couple of more days.*

Anyway we went for the last time we could which was actually 31st December to see New Year in. The place was busy but not heaving like we expected it to be. There were a few crazy guys running around with a professional looking shoulder held camera, putting it in everyone's faces and when I went for a piss upstairs they were on the stairs filming up women's skirts, I had no idea at the time it was the 'Jackass' guys as I had not really seen the show at that point.

Anyway midnight loomed and drinks flowed and we had pretty much given up on seeing Lemmy and then right on the stroke of midnight he appeared in the back room. Of course we pounced on him and right as the clock ticked into 2002 I got the perfect picture, by pure luck Liz managed to capture the wording on the machine right behind him in the split second before he got mobbed by other people, He still had chance to wish us 'Happy New Year' and kiss Liz as he always did before he disappeared with his entourage down the road to the Whisky.the stroke of midnight at the Rainbow, New year 2001/2002. Hard to think we will never see him and Motorhead ever again. I was given a collection of various Motörhead laminate passes a few years ago. They belonged to a friend of mine Paul Hadwen who lived in Leeds just a mile or so away from me.

He used to run the fan club with Helen Taylor and I used to go round to the office now and then mainly to eyeball the gorgeous Helen lol. Paul worked as a PA for the band on and off and also did the artwork for the magazine along with other bits and bobs. He did the artwork for the 'Ace Of Spades' and 'Bomber' tour shirts by cutting up individual letters and pasting them together. He did the cartoon artwork on the inner sleeve of 'Another Perfect Day' album. He also did the artwork for a few of the passes. Unfortunately he passed away at a very young age, his flatmate found him dead in his chair after he had been complaining of man flu.

The collection is interesting on many levels, its hard to believe now that these were the official passes used by band and crew as they are in essence just bits of card cut up and laminated by hand with a clip added. The 'Ace Of Spades' one in fact has a hole punched and was fastened with a piece of string!

There is one from when they appeared on 'The Tube' TV programme, one from the 'Kerrang Wooarrgh Weekend', one from when they did a one off gig in a ballroom in Covent Garden. The 'Another Perfect Day' tour was renamed 'Another Perfect Penguin' tour for some reason?"

Nomis and Liz (Leeds)

"I first heard Motörhead in the early 2000s when I heard a Now! 1980 CD. The song was of course "Ace of Spades". After hearing the classic song, I was hooked from that moment.

On 19th November 2004, I attended my first Motörhead concert at the age of 14. The venue was Southampton Guildhall and the support band was Sepultura.

*The following year on 23rd November, I saw them on their 30th anniversary tour. They were supported by In Flames and Girlschool.
In 2007, I saw Motörhead for the first time as a support band for Alice Cooper at the Bournemouth International Centre. I also saw them live in 2008, 2009 and on their 35th anniversary tour in 2010.
In 2011, I made my first attempt to meet Motörhead, particularly Lemmy. So I arrived in Southampton, England really early in the hopes of meeting my beloved band.
Well, I waited for the best part of three hours to no avail. I was growing hungry so I went off to the KFC nearby to purchase a quick wrap. I was only in store for around 10 minutes.
I rushed back to the venue, not far from the band's tour bus where I had been standing beforehand. Another big Motörhead fan then informed me that in the ten minutes or so that I was gone, Lemmy had already met the people waiting there for pictures and autographs and had already entered the building for soundcheck.
I was gutted about missing my opportunity to meet the great man himself. But at least I watched the soundcheck from the windows of the main doors, and I heard them play 'Cat Stratch Fever' during that soundcheck.
The following year I crossed my fingers and damn hoped that my persistent effort and dedication would pay off. The date was 14th November 2012, and the venue was Portsmouth Guildhall.
I waited by several tour buses and gear trucks for several hours to try and meet the band again. Initially I only saw Joey Belladonna of support band Anthrax and the roadies unloading. After several hours passed by, another tour bus pulled into the parking bay, and this time I thought this is it, here come the mighty Motörhead!!
Sure enough I was right, first off the bus was drummer Mikkey Dee who was really friendly and happily posed for a picture with me. Next off the tour*

bus was... Lemmy. I am not ashamed to say it, but I was starstruck at seeing the legend right before me in the flesh, clad in his iconic black attire and iron cross necklace. Lemmy was really cool and didn't mind posing for pictures. I did get a picture taken with him, and I am glad I did. It's one of my most cherished possessions. One of the best moments of my life.

It was three years before I got the chance to see them again, because of course Lemmy had health problems which restricted the touring schedule. One day in early 2015, I received a phone call from my cousin who lives in Cornwall. She informed me that Motörhead were playing the Eden Sessions in June, and they were supported by The Stranglers. I eventually managed to get a ticket after a long delay at the booking office.

I was really pleased about getting the chance to witness Motörhead for the ninth time. From my small town in Hampshire, I travelled approximately 180 miles via train to St. Austell in Cornwall to attend the event. It was the final time I saw them live, and it was a great experience.

One of the pictures I took of Lemmy shooting the crowd with his Rickenbastard bass during the end of 'Overkill', was featured in the 40th anniversary edition of the Motörheadbangers fanzine. I am proud to have been a dedicated Motörhead fan for over a decade now, and I always will be. Lastly, I wish to say rest in peace to Lemmy, Philthy Animal Taylor and Würzel."

Shane Pike (Andover, Hampshire)

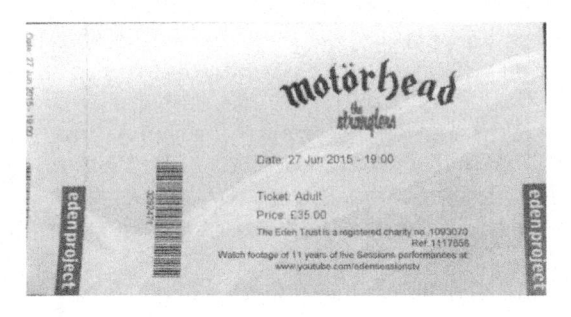

"Lemmy was a great hero to me, he was the embodiment of rock 'n' roll, his heroes were the greats of the original rock 'n' roll explosion of the 50's whom he was around to witness, people like Little Richard, Buddy Holly, Eddie Cochran, Gene Vincent and Elvis Presley.
I loved Motörhead, especially the early days on Chiswick records when they were the scruffy Ladbroke grove bikers who emerged out of that great radical scene that existed in the late '60's and early '70's typified by great bands such as the Deviants, Hawkwind and the Pink Fairies.
Lemmy was spot on regarding rock 'n' roll, he lived the life, it wasn't an act it was who he was, he never took notice of trends or the critics, he just carried on doing what he'd always done regardless.
Hawkwind were at their best when Lem was in them, their best albums featured his unique rumbling bass sound, it was a big mistake firing him but at least it led to the creation of Motörhead, Lemmy's vision of a UK version of the great MC5, a city, dirty, raucous rock 'n' roll band who took no prisoners.
The original line up of Larry Wallis and Lucas Fox looked the business, they could have been great but it wasn't to be, Lemmy recruited Philthy Phil and Fast Eddie and the legend was born, the band went from strength to strength after a false start, the mighty Chiswick records signed them and their boss Mr Ted Carroll had belief in them and it all mushroomed from there.
I never met Lemmy but I feel that I knew him somehow, his unshakable faith in rock 'n' roll and how it should be was the gospel to me, Lemmy was real, a great raconteur, a fiercely intelligent man who devoured good books and to whom good manners were paramount, a true gentleman despite his hells angels image.
Lemmy will never be forgotten, I will never forget seeing Motörhead as I did a few times over the years, Lemmy led me to discovering some great rock 'n' roll. His kinship with the early punks such as the Damned, the Adverts and people round the Roxy club was very special, I loved punk and through my love of Motörhead I got into Hawkwind and the Fairies, thank you Lem. I also discovered the mighty Mick Farren (RIP) through Lem and I am deeply grateful for that.
My Favourite was 'Motörhead' the original Chiswick release from

'77. It sums up what they are about to me, scruffy, raw rockers, Ladbroke Grove dossers beloved of angels, speed freaks, nascent punk rockers and general freaks. The whole philosophy of Lemmy is encapsulated in this great song which was originally recorded by the great Hawkwind of course, the anthem of uncompromising rock 'n' roll.
Lemmy was a one off, we wont see his like again, he came from the '50's and '60's, a lost time when rock 'n' roll mattered, his spirit will burn bright for ever and Motörhead are one of the truly great rock 'n' roll bands, thank you Lemmy old man for everything, an inspiration, hero, rocker, scholar and gentleman.
Lemmy is my hero like Gene Vincent, Joe Strummer and Mick Farren, my memory above all of Lem will be his utter belief in the power of rock n roll and his rejection of the bullshit that society forces upon you, Lemmy Kilmister, a legend of rock 'n' roll.
Simon Prodhan (Barrow-in-Furness)

"Forever so grateful that I got given a chance to live my dream and share a stage with Motörhead with my band King Creature, it even ended up being there last show on home turf here in the UK. Motörhead was the first band I ever saw in 2006 and ever since they have been my favourite, any one who knows me know much love I had for Lemmy and the band.
I've read many stories over the internet today and yesterday about Lem and they all show what an amazing person he was, and how many people he made happy with his generosity and wisdom!
He certainly made my dream come true. Words cannot express how much Motörhead and Lemmy mean to me. And I feel truly privileged and honoured to have seen and shared stages with them, the things I could say about the impact they have had is endless.
It feels weird that I am now in a year knowing that Motörhead is over, but the music will forever live on.
Here's to the man himself! Raise a glass and celebrate the life of such a fucking amazing person! See you on the other side Lem!

Much respect

♠Deaf Forever♠"
Jack Sutton-Bassett (King Creature)

"I think I may have shook Lemmy's hand after a concert in Llandudno North Wales on 'The World Is Yours' tour. I can't be too sure as I was shitfaced at the time on whiskey.

Best gig I ever went to was Motörhead on the 'Aftershock' tour in Birmingham. Was helped by two great support acts...The BossHoss and The Damned who primed the crowd for Lemmy 'n' the boys who bounced the roof and shook the ground. Best crowd too 'n' a damn good mosh.
I will miss Motörhead. Lemmy lives on in us all."
Matthew Wilkes (Tywyn, Wales)

"I first saw Lemmy at Plymouth Guildhall on early '70's with Hawkwind and was blown away by his gravel toned voice.
I then saw Lemmy and Motörhead at Cornwall Coliseum in about '83. Was so loud and packed! My ears rang for 3 days after!
Lotta shouting... much to the displeasure of my wife (Now ex lol)!!
Have followed Lemmy every time they gigged in Plymouth!
Even introduced him to my grandson! And so we both used to go see Motörhead as "Our Gig"! Will miss these 'nights out' and hearing Lemmy rasp out old classics and new!!
I think his time with Headcat was amazing!! A true Rocker in all ways man!! My fave track is his version of Metallica's 'Enter Sandman', sounds like the Vincent Price of Rock 'n' Darkness! R.I.P. Lemmy! (ROCKIN' IN PARADISE!)."
Taff 'Rockin' Bear Evans (Plymouth)

"A Stoke Graffiti artist paid tribute on A500 main road into Stoke, what a brilliant way to remember him. At the bottom he wrote "RIP Lemmy a local legend."
Doug Earle (Liverpool)

"I never got the chance to speak in detail to Lemmy about the tough times in the army that Motörhead helped me through. Travelling to some of the world's nastier places and seeing what humans can do to one another often needs something more than a stout heart and a stiff upper lip to see you through a tour of duty. Motörhead often provided that missing something and I will be forever in their debt for this.
Lemmy's passing has left a huge hole in the world and in many of our lives but when he died, he unknowingly gave me a very precious final gift by enabling me to grieve not only for him but also for my Mum, Gran and Dad as well as several friends I have lost in the line of duty, which I had been unable to do previously.
I am now slowly being able to deal with these losses that go back to 1982. Here then are my memories of significant Motörhead moments for you, my friends, brothers and sisters of rock and roll to

help you through this difficult time.

Promoting their 1987 album 'Rock 'n' Roll', Motörhead played at my local club, the Jovel in Münster, Germany, where I was serving in the Army. I was fairly new to any 'guitar heavy' music, having been brought up on jazz and big band which were what my Dad played and this was to be my first Motörhead show.

My mate was a Cheltenham lad and had known of Würzel so we duly made a banner and went along to the show hoping to maybe get a wave from him. Support bands were German thrashers Destruction who opened and then King Diamond but of course, it was Motörhead we were waiting for!

Positioned front centre of the barrier, we were right in front of Lemmy and after a few songs, he reached out and took the banner off us and had it put on top of his amp! By that time we had already made eye contact with Würzel and enjoyed the show all the more for those little touches. After the show, we just hung around at the front as when the live bands had finished their gig, the place became a normal nightclub again. I can't remember whether some of the crew got chatting to us or Würzel just came out to see us, but we ended up having a really good chat with him and Phil Campbell.

We didn't get to meet Lemmy or Phil Taylor but it was a very special evening nonetheless, especially I imagine for Würzel as we compared how times had changed in the Army since his day and talked about his home town.

Still in Germany, I think it was on the 'Inferno' tour that I saw Motörhead at the PC69 in Bielefeld. Another small club which, for my money, are the best venues to see live bands. I was on my own this time and again just hung around after the gig with a load of others, trying not to get thrown out as the staff cleared up.

This time Lemmy came sauntering out and was immediately thronged by very exuberant German fans. I just hung back and patiently waited my turn and when I got to the front, just said that I was sorry I had nothing to sign but I just wanted to shake his hand and thank him for all the years of entertainment and enjoyment his music had brought me. We chatted for a short time and at one point, a drunk or excited fan leaned in and started singing 'Ace of Spades'. Lemmy leaned back, gave 'that look' and said, "You've had your turn, I'm talking to this guy now, don't be rude!" and carried on the conversation. After that, he went to the bar at the front of the club and played pinball, just moving through the crowd like a regular guy. No airs and graces, a normal bloke on a night out.

In 2009, I booked tickets to see Motörhead in Bournemouth as I was serving in Winchester by then. Support was Girlschool and The

Damned. My daughter was ten and was still very influenced by the music I listened to. Having taken an interest in playing guitar, she was very keen to see Girlschool but also knew all the words to 'Iron Fist', her favourite rock song since she was 6!!!

On arriving at the venue, I took my booking form and exchanged it for the tickets, lined up to get in and then got stopped at the door. "How old are you?" said the lady on the door to Poppy. "Ten." Poppy replied. I was then told that it was 14 and over only!!! I stood my ground and stated that at no time during the booking process was this mentioned and the earliest I had been made aware was when I had collected my tickets 3 minutes prior. Having short 'army' hair and looking fairly respectable, she said I was obviously a responsible parent so we could go in, but to stay at the side as it was quite a loud band playing. I agreed, went in and we immediately made our way to the barrier – front centre which is the only place for me at a gig.

Poppy loved Girlschool and was chuffed to bits when Jackie Chambers waved to her and she got plenty of smiles from the others too. She was a bit bemused by The Damned and as the crowd was getting a bit rough for her, we stood behind the crush for Motörhead, about 10 rows back. Imagine her delight when they opened up with 'Iron Fist'. I lifted her high and she sang every word with them!!!

Although she has moved on in her musical preferences now and possibly doesn't really appreciate the significance of it, it is one of my proudest moments as a parent that she came to see Motörhead with me.

"At the back end of 1990 along with many others, I was deployed to the Middle East to help kick Saddam Hussein's arse. This was very different from say, a 6 month tour of Northern Ireland or the Falklands. On this occasion, we were there until it was finished one way or another so none of us knew at that stage when we were coming home - or indeed IF we were coming home.

In early 1991, I was sent a cassette of the newly released Motörhead album, '1916' and remember listening to it on my 'Walkman' in the Command Post for the first time.

When I heard the song '1916', I have to say it scared me half to death. There was I, waiting to cross the border from Saudi Arabia into Iraq the very next morning heading into goodness knows what and Lemmy is singing about the slaughter of soldiers by the thousand, soldiers just like me and my mates.

Our Sergeant Major looked over and must have seen me wipe a tear from my face and noticed the vacant look on my face. He asked what was on my mind and so I played him the song too.

Now he was a bit of a dyed in the wool type and a touch strait laced too - I suppose just as a Sergeant Major is supposed to be but he listened to the song and when it was finished, he took the headphones off, looked me straight in the eye and said, "That fella can tell a bloody good war story and I can imagine that's just how it was back then. But this time, it's going to be different. It's them bloody Iraqis that'll be calling for their mothers before the day is out, you mark my words. You get some sleep now and put some of his other stuff on in the morning to see you through. It'll be a fine day for Motörhead tomorrow!"
Well, I did as he said and put on the album when I woke up. Sure enough, I got through that day and many others like it, standing tall and proud with Lemmy's voice in my head telling me "I'm so bad baby, I don't care."
I never knew my Sergeant Major was so worldly wise, but again, that's how he's meant to be. His job is to know his lads as well as his own sons and I suppose that's the way I always felt about Lemmy.
He always had a song for every occasion in my life and I never got chance to tell him this particular story but one day, I hope to meet Phil Campbell, very sadly the only surviving member of that particular album, and tell it to him. No doubt I will have another tear or two to wipe away at the end of it all!"
Dave Mitchell (Withernsea, East Riding of Yorkshire)

"I was lucky enough too see Motörhead back in the late 70's early 80's on the 'Overkill' and 'Bomber' tours.
I still reckon my ears have never recovered from the belting they got.
I am now in my middle 50's and hadn't been to a concert for over twenty years until I seen Motörhead at the NIA in Birmingham. Wow what a night.
As I am only 5 foot tall I thought I wouldn't get too see much but I managed too get to the front, right in the middle. As I was in the mosh pit I got kicked in the head so many times by people being carried out, but every kick was worth it.
To round a perfect concert off Lemmy introduced Fast Eddy and Philthy Phil onto the stage.
Rip Lemmy and Phil."
Keith Wilkins (Tywyn, Wales)

"I never got to see Lemmy. Man I wish I'd met him though.
He seems to have been part of my life forever. Since the age of 7

or 8 my older brother would be blaring Motörhead, Saxon, Judas Priest, Iron Maiden and the like from his bedroom.

I don't know why, but Lemmy stood out miles above the rest. Be it 'Snaggletooth', 'Killed by Death', 'Louie Louie', 'Silver Machine', 'Dancing on Your Grave', 'Love Me Like a Reptile', 'I Am the Doctor' and of course 'Ace of Spades'. That voice, that sound, the whole persona was perfect.

'Snaggletooth' is my all time favourite track and I can get lost (and do) listening to my very crackly album 'No Remorse' and staring at the album sleeves...

I suppose Lemmy is a hero. My hero.

He didn't care for the glamour. He was easy, down to earth, never forgot his roots and lived in the real world. That is what makes him soar so far above the rest and be just so special, to me anyway. He might have been born to lose but he certainly lived to win.

I've always joked that my brother modelled himself on Lemmy. He even does that look - with the raised eyebrows and slightly menacing grin... But here I am, 43 and feeling like I've lost a part of me. Sad sad days indeed, but Lemmy will never truly die. Not as long as we have him in our hearts and amps. You can never truly lose a legend."

Mandy Short (Towyn, Wales)

"I became friends with the Rocking Vicars just after Lemmy arrived with the band, about a week after. I saw them supporting the Who in 1966 and also saw that one of my old school friends Mogsy Morris was playing bass for the group. I had seen the group many times before but they had reformed with new members.

The singer Reverend Black (Harry Feeney) was always the vocalist and he was really good. As was the drummer Ciggy Shaw he was awesome on drums. However I saw my old school mate Mogsy and Lemmy were with the group. I found Lemmy awesome he was like Pete Townsend he would pick up one of the drummers cymbals and rub it along the guitar strings making this fabulous noise and then he would hurl it across the stage.

He would also put the neck of his guitar through the front of the speakers and rub his guitar across the amps and speakers and Harry would hold his microphone in front of the speakers to get great feed back.

I was mesmerised by this performance and asked my mate Mogsy who this new guitarist was. He told me he was called Lemmy and he joined the band in Manchester a few days before as lead guitarist.

He also told me that they were playing for the summer at Beat City which was in the Palatine Hotel on Blackpool Promenade. So I said I would see him the next night and come and watch them again. Thinking they might have just put that great show on at The South Pier because they were supporting the Who.

I arrived at the Palatine and knew when I saw their van with the cross on the top that I had the right place as I read some of the comments on it I saw spray painted down one side of the van 'LEMMY' - the van was like a huge travelling wall of graffiti. This was 1966 and nothing crude written just initials and names of the many fans who followed this band which was years before their time.

I was just going to pay to go in, which was five shillings and was quite a lot of money for a young lad like me in comparison to my wages, but I heard a voice shout to me and it was my friend.

"Don't pay, come this way" and he showed me through a side door into the small ballroom where they were to play.

All their gear was being set up their roadies (they had 2) and one of them was nailing a drum kit to the floor. I was told it was because they kept ending up all over the stage.

Then they came on to play when I heard the sounds of the 'death march' start up from Lemmy's guitar; I knew this was the group I had seen at the South Pier, this was their signature tune played at the beginning of their set and at the end every time.

I was soon relieved that this show would be as good as I had seen them at the South Pier and Lemmy was bang on form with his performance of 'Rocking Pneumonia' with a great guitar solo and cymbals being hurled across the stage and his guitar being rubbed over everything from Mike stands to speakers and the neck of the guitar rammed through the speaker fronts.

After the performance the stage looked like a war zone. But I was hooked and spent the next two years of my life following my hero everywhere they played.

I went to my mate after they finished and told him how awesome I thought Lemmy made the band and he said "would you like to meet him".

"Hell yes" I said. So he took me and introduced me to him and we got a whiskey and coke and spoke most of the night about the Yardbirds a group I loved because of Eric Clapton and Jeff Beck and had just seen them live on the North Pier a couple of weeks previously.

I found we had the same interests in groups and guitar players. I used to see Lemmy most nights and never missed a performance.

I was then asked "hey man do you fancy taking me to Bury Palais tomorrow night? We have a transport problem."
I said "yes anytime" and from then on my friend and I would take him to gigs from the Cavern in Liverpool to the Oasis in Manchester. I was probably his most ardent fan and a few months after meeting Lemmy I had taken up with this girl who lived next to my friend Dave and her mother didn't approve of me because I hung out with the Rocking Vicars.
On New Years Eve in 1966 we were having a party at my friend Dave's house and asked the band if they fancied coming. Lemmy said yes straight away and Harry also said yes. So off we went to my friend's house. Next door at my girlfriends house they also were having a party and my girlfriend Margaret was not allowed out with me to see the group and I told Lemmy and he said "I'll get her man" and he knocked on their door and asked can Margaret come next door to a party. Her mother went mad at him and slammed the door in his face.
I was really down and he kept trying to cheer me up and giving me drinks but it didn't seem to help. Next thing him and Harry had gone into the back garden and they had somehow managed to attract her attention through a bedroom window telling her to get out onto the flat roof and they lifted her down into the garden and she came running into the house.
She said "Lemmy just got me out of a window."
We were only in the house for about ten minutes and her mother burst in and slapped her and dragged her out giving everybody a mouthful and saying she would ring the police if we didn't leave them alone. So that was it we all got pissed and Lemmy and Harry left about 4 am and whoever were left crashed out in chairs and on the floor.
I ended up marrying Margaret and am still married to her 49 years later.
Lemmy stayed with the group quite a while and we had so many great times both going to gigs and getting pissed in the Palatine Hotel whenever they weren't playing. Or we would go on the slot machines on the Golden Mile.
I remember Lemmy going to see Jimi Hendrix at Blackpool Odeon he asked me if I fancied going but I had something going on with Margaret and didn't go.
I never saw him again until a few years later when I was in London and ran into him he was playing with a group called Sam Gopal and gave me an L.P. they had done on which he was the vocalist.
The next time I saw him was at a Hawkwind concert at Preston

Guildhall in 1975. The support group was Motörhead and I met Lemmy again at their merchandise table. I was a great Hawkwind fan but that night Motörhead became my favourite band.
Then I didn't see or hear from Lemmy until 1985 when I heard he was playing with Motörhead at this venue so wrote to him asking him if we could meet up. He told us to come over and let the security guys know we were there and he came out and took us in to his dressing room. He asked me if I still drank Vodka and orange juice and I said yes sure and he poured half a pint of vodka into a pint glass and gave it to me. I looked at him like he had gone mad. He said oh yes sorry you need the orange and he topped the other half pint of the glass up with orange juice.
I truly had many great times from knowing Lemmy and the Lemmy years in Blackpool were the best of my life. He was a really nice guy to know and a great friend. I know he will be well missed
Jim Marsh (Weeton, Nr Blackpool)

"The first time I saw Lemmy & Motörhead was at the Cornwall Coliseum I think it was 1983, it was after Fast Eddie had left, Brian Robertson was on guitar.
My hearing was all to hell for a couple of days.
I used to go to the Coliseum a lot back then as I have lived in Cornwall all my life. After the gig me and some mates were outside waiting for the mini bus and Lemmy came outside and spoke to us, can't remember what he said as we were awestruck and didn't know what to say.
Also saw them at Donington 'Monsters of Rock', and at the Eden Project in June of last year.
RIP Lemmy."
Graham Perryman (St Austell, Cornwall)

"The first time I came across Motörhead was at a 'Hook a Duck' stall at Barmouth fair where you could win a Motörhead 'Ace of Spades' picture with the writing in red. The picture, more or less, was the same as the Record cover which I never knew at the time. I just wanted it and after a few attempts I won it.
Then I went to Porthmadog and saw the same picture on this record in Cob Records shop so I bought the record, went home, put it on the record player and could not believe what I heard it was Ace.
That's the first time I came across Lemmy Phil and Eddie the rest

is history and a good one."
Simon M Short (Barmouth)

"Everyone remembers their first truly life altering Motörhead experience, for me it was Glasgow Barrowlands, April 1991...
For some others it was later...
On 1st June 2004, a considerably younger Motörheadbanger with a huge bag packed with enough sunscreen, spare socks and deodorant to choke a marauding war-pig set off for a 13 week trip to work on a small island off Nigeria called Bonny.
A fully laden CD wallet, Walkman and small but powerful speakers went with me as always, for my sanity, and I settled into my Nigerian life of working, eating, drinking and sleeping, with occasional bursts of malaria, strange food, food poisoning, burglary and murder thrown in for good measure.
On frequent outings to various local humid, colourful and very noisy bush bars, I was accosted by curious locals who wanted to know why I wore a monster on my t-shirt. It turns out they had never heard of Motörhead or seen a real war-pig / snaggletooth before.
When I introduced my new friends and work colleagues to the subtle delights of Motörhead, there was much wailing and gnashing of teeth, "Too loud, too fast, too harsh" was the cry from some as they fled, but there were a few who seemed to enjoy it.
When I eventually left (after 2 years) I bequeathed my CD collection (having discovered the delights of MP3 by then), and t-shirts, to some of the local guys who worked with me. They were over the moon, especially as I had washed the shirts first!
I still remember with a smile how I spread a little Motörhead love, or fear in some cases, to a small island off the coast of Nigeria, and still like to imagine that, as I was driven past my favourite bush bar in a battered old Toyota, to the waiting river boat, I could hear 'Ace of Spades' playing as I was waved and jolted off into the sunset.
To this day I wonder how their neighbours lawns are doing...That'll teach 'em!"
Greg McCallum Motörheadbanger 3179 (Dufftown, Scotland)

"I first discovered Motörhead through my enjoyment of professional wrestling. Triple H had always been my favourite wrestler and when he changed his theme song to "The Game" I knew I had to find out more about his band.
As luck would have it, the very next day on BBC2, 'The Young

Ones' aired. Just as soon as Mike cues the music, the thunderous riff of 'Ace of Spades' was heard for the first time by a young Spuggy. The very next day I went out to my local music vendor and purchased 'Ace of Spades' and 'Overkill'.

My local music merchant became used to me coming in for Motörhead and even managed to get me a promo copy of 'Hammered', a few weeks before its release. Motörhead got me through school, which I am sure as for many, were not the happiest times but I could rely on a little Motörhead to help me get through.

I have seen the band a few times, in fact one of my friends refused to come again after the first time as her hearing did not return to normal for a while.

In 2014 I saw them for what is to be the final time but I made some great friends in the Motörheadbangers. These people have had a profound effect on my life and I am truly grateful to know them. So through Motörhead's and Lemmy I feel my life has been enriched by fucking great music and meeting some of the best motherfuckers walking this place we call home.

Thank You Lemmy, you were one of the good ones."

Spuggy - MHB 3774

"I was only 12 years old but I still remember walking into my local record store and buying the 'Bomber' single, I knew of Motörhead as I'd read about them in the great music paper of the time 'Sounds' but I wasn't over familiar with them at that point as I was just getting into Rock Music, it was however a life changing moment.

From that day I was totally hooked and obsessed with this musical monster. Within weeks I had a six foot 'Snaggletooth Skull' painted on my bedroom wall and started collecting anything and everything to do with the band.

I joined the 'Motörheadbangers' just after Alan Burridge started it and was fanatical about the band.

I was lucky enough to see the original line-up on both the 'Ace of Spades' and 'Iron Fist' tour's at Bristol's Colston Hall, the energy of those shows was mind blowing, I was 13 and 15 respectively and I had never witnessed anything like it in my life, the volume was intense, I never knew that a bass guitar could make your trousers shake and your eyeballs rattle.

Lemmy was my hero and role model back then (any parent's nightmare surely?) and he continued to be throughout my life.

I remember seeing the band on the 'Another Perfect Day' Tour at a

small club called Gold Diggers in the small Wiltshire town of Chippenham in May '83, it was chaos, Punks, Metalheads and Rockers all in together going crazy, I loved it and couldn't get enough. In the late 80's I was a roadie for a band and one night we were playing at London's famous Marquee Club, I was walking past the bar and there was Lemmy, just stood there having a drink with friends, I couldn't believe it, I walked up to him and shook his hand, sadly I was pretty drunk that night and understandably he didn't really want to engage in conversation with me (hahaha, why the hell would he?), despite my persistence to try and talk to him he was very polite when he probably should have just told me to 'Piss off', in the end I was dragged away by a friend. I look back on it now and cringe, it was an honour to meet him and I blew it.
I got to see the band nearly 40 times over the years and started the website 'motorheadengland.co.uk' over ten years ago, through that I've met many wonderful people all with the same passion and love for the great man.
Not only do I have Lemmy to thank for Motörhead's music, but also for opening my ears to the Rock 'N' Roll music he grew up with like Chuck Berry, Jerry Lee Lewis and Little Richard etc. In later years it was great to see him become the 'Living Legend' that we all knew and loved, it was wonderful to see him obtain recognition as an icon of modern music, an innovator, a leader. His straight talking, his anecdotes, his humour and his whole persona are something that makes the world a sadder place now that he's gone. Thanks for the music Lemmy, I'm gonna miss you."
Steve Hoare (Bristol)

"With Motörhead being in my life since I can remember, they've had a massive influence on me.
I remember the first time I saw them live, the anticipation of waiting for them to come out on stage was immense. Knowing they were all sat back stage, that I was in the same building as them.
The electricity when they came on stage was something I'll never forget. The energy from them surged through the audience, it's a feeling I can't describe. The sound of the drums, the guitar and of course Lemmy's legendary bass sound and his gruff voice.
The crowd at a Motörhead gig has always been the best crowd from any gig. Everyone is so respectful, it's like Lemmy's persona of not only being a rock and roll icon, but also a gentleman rubs off on people. Motörhead have and will always be a big part of my life. Long live Motörhead and long live Rock 'N' Roll.
I also remember meeting Phil at the Waterfront in Norwich. He was

at the back of the room watching the support bands. He was such a nice guy, someone that was happy to spend time with the fans.

I also remember when I saw them in Brixton in 2012, I was across the road having a few drinks before the gig and not a single person in the bar didn't have a Motörhead t-shirt or jacket on.

People were talking to strangers, exchanging Motörhead and Lemmy stories and I also remember we drank the bar dry of pint glasses, they couldn't wash them quick enough.

I'll not only miss the gigs, but I'll miss the crowds, the drinks before, meeting new people.

I'm glad to see people are keeping Lemmy and Motörhead's memory alive though as they'll never be another band like them."

James Grimes (Norwich)

"From the off when I was getting into rock, metal and punk Motörhead stood out.

I was about 13 years old when I bought the 'On Parole' album from a little record store on Arnold Market in Nottingham. I was soon painting their logo on my rucksack for school and embroidering their moniker onto my denim jacket and was hooked for life.

I see the phrase 'Motörhead for life' everywhere these days but if you stop and think about it, it is true. The songs are timeless and they have left us with a legacy of music that will never die.

We all have that one song that wherever you are, in the car, on a beach with headphones on, at home on a stereo, watching a DVD you just always reach for the volume button and crank it that little bit more; well my one song is 'Overkill' by Motörhead. I must have listened to that song thousands of times and I still reach for the volume up button every single time.

This leads me nicely into my favourite Motörhead memory.

Although I never had the pleasure of meeting them I have seen them live many times. The tour was the '1916' tour I believe and the venue was Rock city in Nottingham.

They left 'Overkill' until the end and the place errupted. I mean one big dance floor packed solid and during that song I and I guess about a thousand others, covered every inch of that dance floor.

One minute in the middle, the next you are stage centre at the front and then in a breath right at the back near the sound engineer and back to the front again. Then when you think it is over those drums start up again and you are off again.

The performance was that good every single person on that floor moved en masse. Not just a handful or a quarter of the crowd, every single person; this I have not seen since by any band.

Now I have been to many shows for many bands but this memory sticks with me and I guess it is this memory that partly makes me reach for that volume button every time those drums start belting out."
Schizo Rotary Sprintmaster 'Gavin 'Paddy' O'Malley' – (Lawnmower Deth)- Guitar

"The first time I listened to Motörhead it felt strange, like I'd discovered a whole new world. It made me feel different, made my heart beat and I felt so alive.
I knew from that moment when I was 14 years old that I was hooked. No matter what happened in the day, if I put some Motörhead on or wore a t-shirt of the band, things seemed better.
I walked down the street with my Motörhead top on with pride and continue to do so. Throughout my life my love for Motörhead grew and changed.
From listening to their CD's in my bedroom, in my car to get me ready for the day, to dragging a friend along to a yearly gig in Manchester, being brave enough to go to gigs alone, meeting Motörheadbangers, doing multiple dates on the tours, travelling all over the UK and Germany to follow the band with the most amazing people - my Motörheadbanger brothers and sisters.
I was lucky enough to be part of the 'Aftershock' special edition DVD, in the audience at 'Download Festival' and I treasure this DVD as my personal memory immortalised on disc.
The feeling that I get from Motörhead has always made me feel alive and that everything was OK, but the feeling of being with the Motörheadbangers in Germany on tour is the most amazing feeling in the world, apart from the pure rock 'n' roll, fun loving energy of the band and the fans, it is the real sense of family. It is sad that I will never get to feel again those moments waiting for the band to come on and the pure adrenaline rush of them coming out and beginning to play.
I feel so lucky and thankful that I have those memories of the best rock 'n' roll band in history and some amazing people. Pure rock 'n' roll fun.
Motörhead will never be forgotten and never be replaced."
Lindsey Turner (Crewe)

"I always liked some bits of Motörhead but I never got properly into them until about 2004 or 2005 after hearing 'Overkill' on Planet Rock in work (which many of my team hated!).
I went to my first Motörhead gig in Liverpool where I was born and

bred and tried to meet Phil, Mikkey and of course Lemmy.
I met Phil after a long cold wait behind the venue (I also made a now life long friend in the process).
One by one people started disappearing and I was the last one left. Now the building known as Mountford Hall has quite a bit of glass by the stage door. I'm stood on my own after a long wait and can see the band. I'm hitting the glass door trying to signal that I would like an autograph on my 'Inferno' booklet but I didn't realise they were going on stage. Lemmy smiled and gave me the thumbs up! I was made up and it would do for 'this round' however I would have to meet Mikkey and Lemmy too.
So fast forward a year and similar scenario but in Manchester Apollo but after the gig at some silly hour in the morning.
I met Mikkey and the man himself too (who I might add was always warm and witty). At this point I was tired, cold, thirsty, hungry and of course deaf!
Now when I speak to Lemmy I ask to get a picture and he happily obliges. I also asked for an autograph and again he happily says yes. At this point I am trying to undo my Motörhead red and black cowboy shirt pocket and just couldn't get it out. Eventually I get it out after what seemed ages but no more then 20 seconds and Lemmy turns to me and says "you didn't rehearse this well did you?" Then laughs and gives me his autograph.
I will treasure the autograph but more importantly this memory as having the piss taken out of you by your musical idol is something I personally can never forget
Lemmy was a true hero and inspiration for me. The music he helped create has helped me through both good and bad times."
Gareth Southern MHB 2485 (Liverpool)

"Not had a pint with him in "Sun in Splendor" Portabello Road for years but he would be pissing him self laughing at the wankers CASHING IN ON HIS DEATH!"
Steve Howse (St Austell, Cornwall)

"My little story re Uncle Lemmy....
My dear wife is not a metal fan but for some reason, and with exceptionally discerning taste, loves "Ace Of Spades". I took her to see Motorhead for the first time in 2010, at Bristol, for the 'World Is Yours' tour.
Great show! Louder than an artillery barrage, Lemmy threatening to beat up the idiot who was chucking beer on stage and the obligatory encore of my wife's favorite track. We loved it!

Walking back to the car she commented that she'd really liked the 'Bummer' song as well. "The 'Bummer' song love, not a clue which one you mean?" "You know", she said, "It went....It's a 'Bummer', it's a 'Bummer'.......".
Andrew Ingall-Tombs (Haydon, Somerset)

"Lemmys lyrics helped me through a bad patch of my life, by listening to Motörhead songs I overcame an addiction, I talk to lots of Motörhead fans on Facebook, its been a battle, but a battle I won."
Robert Thomas (Liverpool)

"I never met the God that was Lemmy but saw him over the years always at the Apollo in Manchester as he seemed to have liked venues where you could see the audience."
Jo Casson (Manchester)

"My first experience of Motörhead was at Liverpool Uni's Student Union.
I knew of Motörhead through 'Ace of Spades' and 'The Young Ones' (yes THAT scene) but 'live' was what hooked me.
As they walked out the crowd went quiet and Lemmy's gruff voice barked "We Are Motörhead" and the opening riffs of 'Bomber' came crashing out.
Better than any drug in the world.
Thanks Lemmy. Many a Jack 'n' Coke (now known as 'A Lemmy') will be drunk in your honour."
Ant Yank McKenna (Liverpool)

"First time I saw Motörhead was on the 'Bomber' tour at Southhampton Gaumont.
I was stood right by one of the speakers at the front of the stage. I

could not hear properly for a week after. The place was rockin' so much with everyone that the spotlight cables that were stretched across the whole auditorium ended up with a 3ft stretch after the gig."
Ian Barton (Airdrie, North Lanarkshire)

"I spent loads of money entering a competition and was lucky enough to see Motörhead play at the Royal Opera House, it was an amazing gig!
They started off all dressed in Tuxedo's then after the first song ripped them off!!"
Terry Barratt-Mills (London)

"Lemmy for me, is home."
Maggie Bevan (High Wycombe)

"My favourite song was 'Please Don't Touch'! Cracking. I only ever bought about 15 singles back in the day (I always bought albums), but this this was one of them. B-side was covers of the others songs."
Andrew Carroll (Plymouth)

"My favourite song is 'Bomber'. Raw power great lyrics, speed and it's Motörhead! Never tire of it."
Simon James George (Newquay)

"Lost Woman Blues", because it's just so true. Great and honest lyrics with smooth and sexy sound."
Marta Zajaç (London)

"Saw Lemmy and Motörhead live at the Reading Festival 1979, they blew Reading away, it was awesome!
Have seen them so many times since then finally saw them at 'Graspop 2015' sadly it was to be the last time.
They may be gone, but will never be forgotten… the music will live forever.
Lemmy will always be remembered for Motörhead but we should also remember the stuff he did with the likes of Headcat and with various other musicians.
He was truly one of the greatest talents of his time and because of Motörhead he probably didn't get all the recognition that his talent demanded."
Pedro Runcieman (Taunton, Somerset)

"And being the fine father he is, he took me more than a few times too.
I remember seeing them at The Astoria in London on (I think) 'The Overnight Sensation' tour.
We got right on the barrier at the front... in line with Phil. That was the first mistake. I remember Lemmy hitting the strings on his bass and the sheer volume from the PA was like being punched in the guts....
I remember bodies flying everywhere and not being able to hear properly for days.
Never seen Lemmy give less than 100% at any gig, we won't see his like again that's for sure.
Ps. Still got your old Motörhead vinyl dad and no, I'm not giving it back haha!!"
Peter Runcieman (Bridport)

"Seen Motörhead a few times.... they played venue Cymru in Wales 2010 which was a rare occasion.
As they came on Lemmy barked "I used to live round 'ere, bet you get more pussy than I did" then straight into 'We Are Motörhead".... very funny and fondly remembered.
Believe it or not I've always loved 'Loser' from 'Iron Fist' such a well structured mid paced rocker with great solo fills from fast Eddie and Lemmy's acidic but comedic lyrics. 'I'm a loser that's what they said...now I got their women lying in my bed, buy me a drink wishing I was dead' wonderful stuff."
Peter Warder (Menai Bridge)

"First band my big brother ever saw live.
I remember he was deaf for about a week after admitting he spent the entire concert headbanging in front of a massive speaker!"
Vanessa Cook (Bristol)

"Introduction to Lemmy and Motörhead - 'No Sleep 'til Hammersmith'
I made the crucial mistake of reading the CD cover and it said to play it loud, I was deaf for a week but was well worth it!
RIP LEMMY AND PHILTHY."
Stevie Ruffs (London)

".....followed them before they even existed.
Read in Sounds about Lemmy forming the loudest most horrible

rock 'n' roll band in the world and thought I'll have some of that.......
January 1978, Woods Centre, Plymouth, billed as 'Ex-Hawkwind Motörhead'.
Lem sitting at the bar with a drink and a fag, my shy 17-year-old self didn't dare approach him, Phil Taylor in his motorcycle boots looking mean.
We were at a table immediately left of the stage side-on to it and didn't get the full onslaught and man it was LOUD!!!
Audience a seeming mixture of bikers and punks.
Lemmy opened with an intense, maybe speed-fuelled, rap ending ".......ladiesandgentlemenWEAREMOTÖRHEAD!!" and straight into 'Motorhead'.
I remember 'Keep Us On The Road', 'Lost Johnny' (introduced as 'Misplaced Durex').
Lem acknowledged each bout of applause with "Thank you kindly!" Phil Taylor changed into a pair of Clarks Polyveldts to drum in, I kid you not.
Lemmy: "Just going to have a drink of water!!" (indicates pint glass of water perched on top of amp)- crowd: "WATER?!??" Lem: " YEAH, FUCKIN' WATER!! S'alright for you bastards out there drinking Southern Comfort, I'd be flat on my back!!"
Scuffle breaks out bit later, Lem: ".......if you don't fucking stop that I'll come down there and I'll brain you with this!!" (indicates very heavy Rickenbacker bass).
Ended with 'Motörhead' again "in case anyone doesn't know who we are yet!!"
Great night, the first time."
Ian Barnett MHB2195 (Kingsbridge, Devon)

"When Lemmy entered a room, he had this incredible energy around him, everyone and everything just stopped.
Forever Missed Always Loved and Never Forgotten..."
Pink Zuzini (London)

"I met Lemmy a couple of times, always a complete gentleman, straight to the point and never shy of expressing an opinion when needed.
First time I met him was in '82 in Edinburgh, backstage door at the Playhouse, talked for 5 or 10 minutes, signed a few things and the bit that made him a prince in my eyes, asked what age I was, I was 11, and asked where I lived and how I was getting home, told him I was walking it was only a few miles away.
"Fuck that" says he and gave me a fiver for the bus!

I was in Uphall at the time in '82, 12 mile walk from Edinburgh, you understand now why it stuck. I am a big guy, was 6'2 back then but he knew it wasn't right walking, that's what stuck.
Back in the days before the world went mental and bands had to separate themselves from crowds for their safety, good times."
Saw him a couple of times after and tried to give him it back, always to be greeted by that chuckle and always the same response, "fuck off, I don't want it, buy yerself a drink".
Still owe him that fiver though, sadly, I'm going to post it to the Rainbow I think, buy the Man the drink I never could when he was here.
Nigh on a month and in all honesty I'm still reeling, even seeing him so frail and knowing, still feels like we lost the "best" uncle, brother, mate we ever had. Not a bad legacy for a noisy bugger I would say.

Dave Coburn (West Lothian ,Scotland)

"I bought my first bass off Lemmy, it was for my 16th birthday so I think I would have been 15.
I met him at Dingwalls, he was a friend of my mum's from a musos club called 'The Funny Farm' and I was wearing a Motörhead t-shirt, which went down well.
Anyway he said he had a bass I could buy, it was one he'd been given from Pete Way of UFO.
I got the tube to his place which was exactly how you'd expect it to be, Motörhead stuff everywhere. A Snaggletooth/Warpig sculpture on the wall, optics on the mantelpiece, JD for Lemm and vodka for me.
It was Sunday evening and Rusty Lee was on TV laughing away as she does and he said people like that restore you're faith in humanity.
He pulled out a bag of speed and laid some out on a knife and asked if I did drugs. When I said I didn't he said,'Well I aint starting ya' and kept it to himself.
We shared a cab to Camden and he invited me down to Ezyhire where Motörhead were rehearsing with Phil, Wurzel and Pete Gill to get some new strings for it so I got to see them rehearse, which largely consisted of a jam session with Lemm on guitar and I think it was one of Uriah Heap on bass.
This was so cool for a 15 year old kid.
He never treated me like a kid, just a person. Over the years I used to see him often at The Ship, St Moritz etc on the fruit machine. I got him change from the bar loads of times.

There was one time at the Ship and it was quite early, maybe 5pm and just me and him chatting.
He was asking about how my life was being brought up by a single parent, told me I'd turned out alright then talked about Paul and Tracey.
No ego, just honest person to person stuff. It also stuck in my mind that the landlady, they were a seriously take no shit, Irish lot that ran the Ship, brought him out a boiled egg!
Lost touch when he moved to L.A but was hoping to catch up this month in Swindon (my brother works at Planet Rock so I should have got back stage passes).
Anyway, I'm totally gutted that he's gone. I'd been playing 'Bad Magic' that week.
The first time I met him I was 15 and wearing a Motörhead t-shirt, the day he died, I was 46 and wearing a Motörhead shirt.
Garon Wendels (Westbury, Wiltshire)

"The first time that Motörhead really registered with me was the infamous appearance on 'The Young Ones' playing 'Ace Of Spades', while I was aware of their existence previously, this was the moment that it all clicked.
However it would be the turn of the decade into the 90's before I would be battered by the live experience and even this first time was almost destined not to be.
It was the '1916' tour and myself and my good friend Richard Wilson had set off for Glasgow's Barrowlands from Stranraer in his Mk3 Ford Granada (nicknamed "The Grenade" for it's engine's habit of exploding).
A mere 20 miles into the 90 mile journey the car lived up to it's nickname and in a cloud of steam and a cacophony of mechanical noise, it exploded itself again. It soon became clear that we would not be making the gig in time and we resigned ourselves to being towed home and not seeing the 'Head this time round.
As it turned out, the next day we found out that Motörhead had cancelled the gig, for reasons that I have long lost in the haze of time, and as it turned out they would reschedule for the following April.
Richard and I both made it to the Barrowlands that April and with another friend, Robert Alexander in tow, and despite an incident involving a broken nose, we all popped our Motörhead cherries in glorious cacophonous style and Lemmy commanded that stage and crowd like no other. I would go on to see Motörhead and of course Lemmy several times , including taking my son to see

Motörhead on the tour they did with Alice Cooper and Joan Jett in 2007, a pleasure to introduce the next generation to such legends of rock, but Lemmy would make the biggest impression on him of the lot, as will become clear at the end of my tale.

It would be another 4 years until I would see them again, at Knebworth playing 'Sonisphere Festival' and I have to say how taken aback I was by how subdued they were, in particular how low the energy projecting from Lemmy was.

Of course during the course of the set we learned that Wurzel had passed the night before, so this was understandable. It had a profound bearing on how I would see Lemmy for the last time though.

Donington 2013, while I was perusing the stage times, I came to the decision that I would pass on seeing 'Head as I had started hearing of Lemmy's failing health and I wanted to remember him and Motörhead at the top of their game.

However as I was walking between stages, I stumbled across Motörhead finishing their set and there he was, THE One and Only Lemmy, snarling on stage, holding a crowd numbering in it's many tens of thousands in the palm of his hands and doing what Lemmy has always done, playing Rock 'n' Roll and playing it damn loudly with that sneering grin on his face and that was it, the last time I would see the man in person.

The mark of respect that the great Lemmy was held in and the impression that he made on all those that had seen Motörhead hit home on the night of his death.

I was asleep and my son Ryan was out 'on the town' when he heard the news.

He burst into our room on his return home and pleaded with his mum to wake me as it was a 'biggie'. He wanted me to tell him it wasn't true but I could not reassure him as I hadn't heard the news myself, so I checked and it was true and that was when it hit me Lemmy was dead and the world of rock and metal would never be the same again.

His name was Lemmy and he played Rock 'n' Roll.

Matt Halliday (Kirkcolm, Scotland)

"First live band I saw in 1980, Girlschool were supporting. Saw them 46 times in total, should have gone to Newcastle on Saturday 23rd January, but sadly wasn't to be"
Darren Leeson (Burbage, Leicestershire)

"Lemmy always played the way he wanted to play. True rock 'n' roll - loud & proud.
I feel privileged to have been in the company of the legends Motörhead on so many occasions around the UK. From the late '70's to the last tour they played at Wembley arena.
There will never be another band like Motörhead. There will only be one Lemmy - I will never stop playing their music, truly missed but never forgotten - rock 'n' roll has lost a legend."
Geoff Long (Bury St Edmunds)

"First time I saw them was at The Astoria in London in 1999.
They opened the show with 'Bomber' and it was the most amazing feeling I'd ever experienced. The volume and the speed was everything I wanted.
Nearly every year after that I went too see them with my Mother (who is 6 months older than Lemmy) and two of my nephews, the youngest being about 10 at his first Motörhead gig. Three generations of a family enjoying the band says it all.
Lemmy will be missed, Motörhead will be missed. Never be another band like them but I'll never forget being at the shows.
Will be played loud forever."
Stewart Fryers (Rochester, Medway)

"I met Lemmy once.
Motörhead were playing St Albans Civic Hall I think.... nice bloke. He bought me a JD&COKE!!!!"

Roger Dighton (Milton Keynes)

"I've was lucky enough to see Motörhead 3 times, twice at small indoor gigs where everyone in the building seemed to be drunk and the music was fucking loud. I've still got my tickets for those gigs.
The last time I saw Motörhead was in 2010 at Download Festival, where we all stood in torrential rain and mud, but it was well worth it to see Motörhead.
The only other Motörhead story I've got is when I entered a competition on the Radio 1 Rock Show in 2005, they were giving away a free double DVD of Motorhead's 'Stage Fright'.
They asked the question "How long have Motörhead been together"? And I answered the question correctly with "30 years". I won the DVD and they announced me as the Motörhead DVD winner on the Rock Show.
Almost 11 years later and I'm still bragging about that and showing my DVD off.

Motörhead fan until I'm 'Killed By Death' \m/"
Lynne Dogue Walsh (Bolton)

"First one ....April 1977 Castaways Club Plymouth. 5 Punks off to see Motörhead at a gig surrounded by the Local Biker Club, who were baying for Punk blood as the 'past-time' of the day was 'beat on a Punk'.
Lemmy told them to "Fuck Off" and leave us alone. We saw the rest of the gig then ran for our lives once outside.
2nd... a sad story.
November 2015 arrived in Paris for the on 13th for the gig on 15th. Went for a walk and passed some resturants looked in and saw the happy people enjoying their meals. Twenty minutes later they are gunned down by terrorist.
Of course we know this was not the only place that tragedy hit. The gig was postponed until Feb 2nd 2016. Of course with the passing of Lemmy it will not be.
Remembering the folks faces as I passed by is still with me and with the passing of Lemmy it has changed my life.
I always used to be a person that didn't care what was happening in the world long as it did not affect me I was fine. But now I cannot forgive terrorism as it has left me with memories of people in everyday life that will never see tomorrow and robbed me of that last chance to see Motörhead

I am also running a group on FB trying to get a 'Tribute Concert' in the UK."
It would be magic to have a massive celebration of Lemmy's life, with contributions from all of the bands Lemmy has collaborated with/influenced. Yes, we are talking Metallica, Foo Fighters etc etc. Not only would it be a celebration, but contributing in the fight against cancer."
Peter Lang-Stephens (North Berwick, East Lothian)

"The only rock star I ever wanted to be... on and off stage... top bloke."
Geoff Wlodarcsky (Shoreham-by-Sea, London)

"I had my ticket to see Motörhead tonight but as we all know now it is not going to happen! Gutted!
So instead, drinking the Lemmy and listening to Motörhead loud and so are my neighbours!
Lemmy the legend!"
Kasia Winskiewicz (Scotland)

"The mother fucking Motörboat and countless gigs.... Life will certainly be different without Lemmy and Motörhead.... I'm sure many many fans can relate to that.... R.I.P. Lemmy...."
John Lang (London)

"RIP Lemster.

First time I met him, I was working for his press agency, in the 90's.
I got sent out on my first ever press day, with him, he came down to the hotel bar to meet the first journo, he didn't even turn around or look at anyone, puts his hands on the bar outstretched, ordered a double whiskey, slammed it, turned around and said "ok then you mother fuckers lets go".
The last interview of the day was a newly appointed Kerrang! editor (wish I could remember his name).
Lemmy suggested we took it up to his room, so the 3 of us went up. He proceeded to pour half pints of 'Knob Creek' and stuck a grubby pinky nail into our mouths filled with industrial grade base speed, stashed in the fold up on his shirtsleeve.
The interview never happened, we talked about Nazi memorials for a bit, and then he suggested we went to Stringfellows.
We went out to hail a cab and in slow motion, I'll never forget it, the

Kerrang! dude looked at me, looked at Lemmy, looked at me, looked at Lemmy and said, "I can't do this" and just ran. Ran off down the road. Just legged it!!
I remember thinking, shit this is my first press day and I've lost the editor of the biggest magazine at the time and the interviews have been aborted to go to a strip club, this hasn't gone well.
So just him and me dashed off in a black cab to Stringfellows... a lot of blanks....
And me getting fired!!! I always wondered why the sent me?"
Chloe Le Fay (Heathfield, East Sussex)

"I remember Lemmy being in the star bar at the Hippodrome in the '80's. Was a great fan then and I still am. The man was a legend and thankfully the music will live on!
RIP big man!"
Simon Ebdon (Southend on Sea, Essex)

"My first memories of Motörhead are my dad coming home from the pub, and going to sleep on the sofa with these huge old headphones on, asleep while Lemmy and Co amongst others blasted out.
Later in life, being the fine father he is, he took me to see them more than a few times too. I remember seeing them at The Astoria in London on (I think) 'The Overnight Sensation' tour.
We got right on the barrier at the front, in line with Phil. That was the first mistake.
I remember Lemmy hitting the strings on his bass and the sheer volume from the PA was like being punched in the guts.
I remember bodies flying everywhere and not being able to hear properly for days. Great times."
Pete Runcieman (Bridport, Dorset)

"Rock 'n' Roll!!!!"
Nick Fernandez (Slough)

"I was at a gig at Hammersmith in the '80's, think it was a Ozzy show.
Anyway I was at the upstairs bar getting a round in and as I was ordering this voice behind me asked "can I have a can mate?"
I turned around and it was Lemmy I was wearing a Motörhead back patch so I said "ok" and he stood there for about ten minutes talking then said he had to go and thanks for the drink.
Then a few years ago I heard he was coming into my work and my

mate told him I was a fan of the band. So just before I finished work I looked up and there was Lemmy walking across the shop floor asking where I was.

He then came over, we shook hands, he signed a bit of paper I found and we talked for ages about his new bass guitar, the wooden hand carved one. He was really proud of it then in 2013.

I was standing on the side of the stage at Download as they were going on and as Lemmy walked past to start the show he looked at me and said "I remember you do you still like the band?"

I said, "yeah always will do" and he looked at me and said "thanks" then walked on to the stage and started the show."

Steve Hill (London)

"They played the Hammersmith Odeon early '91 I think on the '1916' tour.

My mate and me were told we were on the list and there were tickets at the box office. Turns out we weren't, and there wasn't. But we didn't know so we wouldn't budge. Next thing he (Lemmy) walked past and stuck his head into the room.

He said to the staff "what's up?"...then he said "well fucking let them in then...."

Michael McAleer (Belfast)

"I heard Motörhead for the first time when I was 9 years old. I'm 41 now.

Immediately I fell in love. Lemmy's voice has helped me when I'm mad, happy, sad and anything in between.

There will never be anyone who can compare. Ever."

Janine Larkin (Manchester)

"The question, Where were you when you heard Lemmy passed away? Very similar to the Question asked when Elvis passed away or Kennedy was shot hence why I wrote the following as the news was breaking.

The news came to me via a Facebook message, from a friend, at 12.35am 29th December 2015... I was half way through watching an episode of TV crime series 'Luther'. I was drinking a glass of port at the time, after previously drinking a glass of Jack Daniels and Coke. I don't normally drink JD and Coke but on this occasion my wife Panee had bought some home from work. As a coincidence JD and Coke was Lemmy's favourite drink. I proceeded to go on line and check out the news on the internet sites, FB etc. I turned the TV channel over to Sky News, to hear the news breaking and sat watching and reading the shock news of the sudden death of Lemmy...

Earlier in the evening I'd also thought to myself that the last Motörhead album should be in my list of favourite albums of 2015. As I'd made comment on it's release that if this was the final Motörhead album, it was a great swan song to go out on, and the final track seemed to say it all. Lemmy knew he was on his way, I believe, and it was his way of saying he was coming, so have 'Sympathy for the Devil'. Things down there would never be the same again. Rock 'n' Roll Hell.

I vaguely remember, while tidying up the house, earlier in the day, hearing Planet Rock radio playing the song that for me was probably my all time fave as it probably is for most Motörhead fans, 'Ace Of Spades'. Another coincidence that something was going to happen later.

Another rather strange coincidence was receiving a Motörhead mug for Christmas.

I've not been the biggest fan of Motörhead in latter years as my musical tastes have changed but it seems strange that I got a mug of a band that I was very fond of when I was in my teenage years and following the Classic line-up.

But it seemed to be very sad news for me to hear, as we approach the end of what has been a rough year for me too in my personal life. We also lost Philthy Animal Taylor this year too.

The Classic line-up of Motörhead, that also included Fast Eddie Clarke also, was a band that influenced me and my venture into the world of playing music. That classic band also introduced me at the time to one or two other bands, live. I got to see Girlschool, Saxon, Tank and Twisted Sister via Motörhead. And as a youth it was always a pleasure to see Motörhead shake up 'Top of the Pops' amongst all the bland pop bands that appeared on the programme at the time.

A personal highlight from back in the day was to see Twisted Sister at Reading Festival with Lemmy, Fast Eddie and Pete Way joining them on stage. I also got into the Punk side of things when picking up and hearing Lemmy play with The Damned on 'Ballroom Blitz', the B-side of one of their singles. Which was a double whammy as I was a Sweet fan too.

I watched the Lemmy Memorial live on YouTube as it was beamed around the world for us all to see and be part of. It truly was a mixed bag of emotions watching the tributes to Lemmy... Brilliant tribute from everyone...

His son Paul's, tribute was most outstanding... But I had a lump in my throat, tears in my eyes and down my cheeks and laughter, all at the same time and a lot of memories of the music and times I saw Motörhead. Lemmy really made an impact on this world and me. Thank you for pointing me in the direction of being a rockstar, even though I may have done it on a smaller scale.
Lemmy, a true Rockstar and Rock 'n' Roller, lived the dream, lived the life.
As was pointed out he was a real gentleman with the perfect manners, humour and loyalty. I hope to have installed that in some people/family too. Manners cost nothing, If I had done half the things in my life too, and made such an impact, I'll be happy.
And probably the only thing in life that I regret, never meeting the man...
 I went out and bought a Rickenbaker bass guitar (or at least a copy) back in my youth and also emblazoned it with a Motörhead sticker, as the need to be a copy of Lemmy back then seemed to be the way forward. We tried as a band writing Motörhead style songs in my 1st band 'Phaze 4'. Everyone thought we were crazy wanting to be in a band and even more so when we tried to be like our idols Motörhead. I played bass and sang for a few years and tried imitating Lemmy with his style of bass playing.
I later moved over to just lead vocals upon joining my 2nd band... But upon joining my 3rd band, who were another biker rock style band, with a Motörhead kinda image, long hair leather jackets n jeans etc I got the push for liking Twisted Sister and wearing a red leather jacket. Even though Twisted Sister were a band that Lemmy liked, they were too glam for the band.
My only regret, as I previously said, was as per my bucket list, not getting to meet or getting a selfie with Lemmy.
I had already met another idol, Phil Lynott around the same period in the 80's, when they had played the Coventry Theatre.
I do remember on the 'Bomber' tour, that Motörhead played Coventry theatre twice on this tour and one of those gigs they played on Top of the Pops, and I'm led to believe, from memory, that they had to fly via helicopter from the London BBC studios, to play the gig in Coventry.
A very sad loss to music on this day. Thanks for the soundtrack to my youth...Lemmy... You will be missed RIP"
Andy Guttercat (Coventry)

"King Lemmy!"
Bret Bowman (Barnsley)

"I met Lemmy several times in the early eighties.
The Royal Court in Liverpool. Each time.
The guy always had time for the fans. Even the spotty, teenage geek with Motörhead album covers and singles covers. And he signed them all!
There, was one true gentleman of rock.
I will miss him. I might just get a new truss rod cover in brass for my Rickenbastard."
Mark Gilbertson (Appleby Bridge, West Lancashire)

"I was going to see Motorhead tonight but as we all know now is not going to happen!
Gutted!
So instead drinking the 'Lemmy' and listening to Motörhead loud and so are my neighbors!
Lemmy the legend!"
Kasia Winskiewicz (Scotland)

"I'll never forget my first festival (BST Hyde Park, London, 4th July 2014) in which Motörhead performed during my first mosh pit experience (and last).
Lemmy was kind enough to give me a wave as I sat above the crowd on my brother's shoulders. I felt like my life had been blessed and I'll cherish that memory forever.
Lemmy's music and character helped me overcome heart break, self esteem issues and left a mark on the world that will never be forgotten.
I remember first watching the 'Lemmy' movie and being awestruck: I'd never seen anyone like him.
He set the grand example of being confident in your own skin without giving a toss about what others think. And yet he was still a friendly, generous, loving individual. Inspiring millions of people all over the world, he can never be replaced or forgotten."
Iona Woods (Chester)

"First time I heard Motörhead was in 1983. I was 15.
My mum's house was a bikers/metalhead clubhouse. The bikes would be lined up outside and the metal playing full blast on the stereo. Our neighbours hated us.
'Ace of Spades' was played night and day.
My mum would be doing tattoos or piercings and sewing patches on jackets and cut-offs. It was a crazy time.

My daughter Gemma Greenwood came along a few years later and loved it.
At 3 she had her own jacket with patches and studs. She grew up with a major appreciation of metal and we all go to Download every year and were hoping to see Lemmy for the third time this year.
My mum was a metal fan and she loved Lemmy but she never got to see Motörhead.
When we told her we were going to see them she started singing 'Ace of Spades' and headbanging which was amazing considering she has dementia and doesn't know who I am most of the times. Music really does bring back memories.
When Gemma woke me to tell me that he'd passed we both cried. She shared her birthday with him, 24th Dec. She did her own tribute to him for New Year by dressing up as him in her rock bar in London and we had a Jack D & Coke in his honour at midnight.
He'll always be a part of our life."
Donna Greenwood-Miller (York)

"I haven't seen Motörhead in concert, but I did see Lemmy before an Iron Maiden concert. Hubby did buy tickets to see them last Saturday alas it did not happen.
Sandra Nascimento (London)

"Well my first Motorhead show was in April 1979 at the Portsmouth Guildhall on the 'Overkill' tour.....
I was 13 years old and from those first rumblings of Lemmy's Bass to the constant ringing in my ears at the end of the show, I was totally hooked. So much so, that later that same year I saw them twice on the 'Bomber' Tour at the Hammersmith Odeon and the Bournemouth Winter Gardens, and I've not looked back since.
As I have got older, I've travelled further and further afield to see them, various road trips to festivals in Europe and I have even been known to take annual leave to go on road trips around the UK and Europe to take in every date of a tour or three. Even getting married and becoming a father hasn't stopped, or slowed me down any from seeing them, as my wife and two children have come with me to see them on a number of occasions.
I've lost count of the number of times I've seen them, and I have so many great memories to cherish, such as the 10th birthday show, their 25th anniversary at the Brixton academy and the 30th anniversary show at Hammersmith, but my favorite memories are from those early days. As a not so tall 13 year old kid dressed in

his denim and leather pressed up against the barrier at the front with his school mates at those early shows. It's where we always felt safe, the bigger guys always watching out for you down the front, they looked after their own, as we still do today, that's what's so great about heavy gigs!!

Two years on from '79 and it's the summer of 1981, I had just celebrated my 15th birthday in the July, with a party, at which my two best mates had given me a joint birthday card, now I know that's not unusual, but it's what my mates had put inside the card as my present that really matters. I remember to this day being given the card, and my mate Paul whispering in my ear as he handed it to me 'don't let your mum see it'. So I looked round and saw that my parents were busy making sure everyone at the party was being fed and watered, I turned my back on them just to make sure they couldn't see and I opened the envelope and pulled out the card.

Tucked inside it was a cream coloured ticket, printed on the top of the ticket within a solid red background were three words, **Black Sabbath / Motörhead,** the venue was Port Vale FC, in Burslem, Stoke on Trent and the date Saturday 1st August, and as you may know this was billed as 'Heavy Metal Holocaust'. Now I knew why I was to keep this from my mum, you see we lived in Sunbury a town on the River Thames, a town that's only a bus ride away from West London, so the only gigs we were allowed/supposed to attend on our own due to our young age were those in and around London and the South.

My mates and I had been talking about this gig for weeks as more bands were announced the more we wanted to go, you see it wasn't just Motörhead. Although they were the main draw for us, we had seen Riot the year before supporting Saxon and thought they were superb live, also Vardis had been down the road from us at Shepperton Studios rehearsing and recording, and we had got in there to see them, as well as catching them at a few London dates, with these two on the bill as well as Ozzy being announced as the replacement for Sabbath who had pulled out, this was going to be an awesome day.

Now kids I do not condone the behavior that I'm about to describe, but you have to realize, that this was some 35 years ago, and the UK was a hugely different place back then. As far as my Mum and Dad knew the lads had got me a ticket for gig in London on the 1st August, and as it was a birthday treat we had decided to make a weekend of it, and have a sleep over from Friday evening through to Sunday afternoon, taking in the gig on the Saturday.

You may well see where this is going............. To this day, Paul's parents thought we were all sleeping over at mine, my parents thought we were all sleeping at Pauls' and I can't remember where my other mates parents thought we were meant to be?

Friday 31st July arrived, and that evening saw us all meet up at the local train station, each with a sleeping bag tucked under one arm and a gig ticket in the back pocket of our jeans. We purchased train tickets and boarded the train to London, followed by a short trip on the tube over to Victoria where we found a fish and chip shop just over the road from the station to eat at and wait. So far so good, but it was the next bit of the plan that needed to be executed with impeccable timing. You see we had to just miss the last National Express Coach out of Victoria Coach station that was bound for Stoke, which meant we would then be able to purchase tickets for the first coach to leave on the Saturday Morning at 06:00-06:30, and this coach was due into Stoke at around 11:00am, an hour before the gates were due to be opened for the gig. This was achieved and we bedded down on the benches inside the coach station to await our early start, not much sleep was had if any, with three 15 year old lads on an adventure and all excited about the gig, couple that with the fact that we were not the only ones to come up with this sort of a plan, as there seemed to be about 15-20 others there that night, and as it turned out, all with tickets for the same gig.

At about 05:00 on the Saturday the coach station started to spring into life and we were all asked to clear up and move on to wait for our coach, I can't remember much of the coach journey, apart from that it was all very quiet, having had a distinct lack of sleep, and being sat in a nice warm coach, along with its motion, it is highly likely that we all spent the entire journey asleep.

The coach arrived in Stoke at bang on 11 o'clock and dropped us outside the railway station, I remember seeing hundreds of Denim and leather clad people, they appeared to be everywhere, piling out of the station, stepping off an endless stream of coaches, and all making there way to the bus stops and taxi ranks to make the short journey to Burslem, there were Motörhead and Ozzy t-shirts as far as the eye could see.

By the time we got to the ground the gates were already open, the sun was shining and it turned out to be a scorcher of a day, our tickets were checked and we went on in. If my memory serves me right it was a dry gig, no alcohol just soft drinks and drinking water taps, so our quest to get pissed didn't really work out.

"I am sitting here wishing I could have been at Hammersmith, where I should have been tonight.
The first time I saw Motörhead was as a 17 year old Punk Rocker in 1978 at Tiffany's in Bristol. I don't actually remember an awful lot about the gig except that I loved them, and they would stay my favourite band for the next nearly 40 years.
I saw all of the tours with the original lineup, mostly several dates on each tour. I can remember being particularly deaf for nearly a month after one gig at the Bristol Colston Hall where I made the mistake of sitting under the balcony, where the sound reverberated.
I also went to the 'Summernight Festival' in Darmstadt, Germany, while I was on a university course near Frankfurt, and saw them in Vienna, during a year I spent there as part of my degree in 1982-'83. I think the 'Darmstadt Festival' was the one Lemmy referred to in 'White Line Fever', when he mentioned being on the same bill with Blue Oyster Cult.
The gig in Vienna was a really funny night. Lemmy got incensed by the Austrian crowd who sat and clapped politely. He let out the longest string of swearwords I have ever heard and stormed off the stage. Their music had kept me going during a horrible year away from my friends, and he just about summed up what I thought about it all too. Cheered me up for a week!
I had first met the band at a Motörheadbangers party in Manchester in 1982. It was the day they finished recording 'Iron Fist'. I had had a terrible crush on Fast Eddie Clarke for several years, and I managed to get a backstage pass by mentioning the name of a mutual friend. I spent the evening with Eddie and was offered a lift back so far with the band in their minibus. There was only the three of them, me and (I think!) their manager in the bus.
Lemmy was very friendly but I remember Phil Taylor being really cranky. As far as I remember, he was not allowed to speak to any of the girls cos he had just got engaged.
We stopped at the services near Birmingham and all went in and played on the pinball machines and drank coffee. Then they went off back to London, and I got into my friends' car to go back to Exeter, where I was at University.
I went to several gigs on the 'Iron Fist' Tour, and by the end of it reckoned I had seen Motörhead over 40 times.
I rode down to Cornwall Coliseum on my A65 Lightning Clubman. Because it was "local" I went early, and Lemmy saw me outside and recognised me and invited me backstage. He came out to the car park to see my bike and had a little ride round. We had a long

chat about bikes and music and he took me backstage and got me a drink. It's funny 'cos I could have sworn they all drank vodka in those days!

I watched the gig from backstage and stayed for the party afterwards, Lemmy arranged for one of the roadies to deliver me and my bike back to Exeter afterwards, in one of the huge articulated lorries holding the set and equipment. He was such a kind man. I only had eyes for Eddie, who obviously was not interested, but Lemmy looked after me anyway!

Years went by. I settled down and did not go to gigs anymore, and then in 1992 emigrated to Australia. A couple of years after that, I split up from the other half and started going to lots of gigs and festivals again.

As far as I am aware, Motörhead only toured three times down under while I was there, but I saw each of these and was blown away by what I'd missed. They blew Motley Crew off the stage, the first time I saw them. We only stayed for half the Motley Crew set after Motörhead. I saw them again with Rose Tattoo as support in Brisbane, and the last time at the Gold Coast Convention Centre.

It never failed to amaze me how many fans they had in Australia when they toured there so little (of course I may have missed some tours in the early years). I returned to the UK at the end of 2013 and was able to see them one last time at the Eden Project last year. I was so looking forward to the Hammersmith gig - I was looking forward to Girlschool and Saxon as well, both of whom supported Motörhead in the early '80's.

I have spent the last month since he went buying newer albums that I have never heard in full before, and tonight listening to the early albums that kept me going in difficult times. The more I hear about Lemmy in later years, the closer he is to the man I knew briefly in 1981. I am glad for him that he died without ever having to give up doing what he loved, but I miss him terribly tonight."

Alison Beddoes (Bristol)

Eden Sessions

Eden Project, St Austell
27th June 2015

We Are Motörhead
Damage Case
Stay Clean
Metropolis
Over the Top
The Chase is Better Than the Catch
Rock It
Lost Woman Blues
Doctor Rock
Orgasmatron
Going to Brazil
Ace of Spades
Overkill

"Lemmy spoke to me once at a gig in Cardiff Uni. He threw his cigarette in the crowd and I caught it.
He only said "great catch, bet it burnt", but he spoke to ME!!!"
Gary Pardoe (Pontypridd, Wales)

"I met Lemmy numerous times after seeing them for the first time in 1980 on the 'Ace of Spades' tour.
Some memorable ones: At the Port Vale "Heavy Metal Holocaust" in 1981, I waited backstage and got lucky meeting Lemmy, he was a true gentleman and even gave me his vodka and orange!
At a festival at Wrexham football ground in 1982, my friend and I had taken vodka to take in but it wasn't allowed so we had to drink it all before entering, needless to say it was interesting for a while!
Motörhead had to come off stage early due to the noise at a nearby hospital, he came back on stage at the end and told everyone to rip the ground to pieces, there was turf flying everywhere!
We met Lemmy backstage and he gave me his almost empty pack of Winston cigarettes, I cherished that for years!!
One other memorable meeting was backstage at Donington "Monsters of Rock" in 1986, I worked for a radio station given the

go ahead to record Motörhead. I was standing in the doorway of our trailer unit backstage when Lemmy walked up to me with a very attractive young lady in a very short skirt, he asked if I had any black "gaffer" tape as she had split her skirt and he was going to repair it for her! Of course I obliged.
I miss Lemmy so much, there will never be another like him.
A true gentleman.
Simon Davies (Newcastle Under Lyme)

D. & N. PROMOTIONS present
Motörhead *PLUS SUPPORT*
WREXHAM ROCK FESTIVAL 1982   Nº 5911
Wrexham A.F.C. Racecourse Ground
on Saturday, 24th July, 1982
Gates open 11.30 a.m.   Show ends 10 pm prompt
Ticket: £6.50 (inc. VAT)
NO RE-ADMISSIONS   For conditions see reverse
This portion to be retained and produced on demand

"I never met Lemmy, but I wish I had. After 30+ years of seeing Motörhead live, it felt like he/they would always be around.
The first time I remember hearing Motörhead was when my brother bought the 'On Parole' album when it was first released. I would have been about 11 then, and just getting into rock music for the first time.
I first saw them live in 1983 at Hammersmith, on the 'Another Perfect Day' tour. As a huge Lizzy fan, seeing Robbo and Motörhead together was an amazing experience. The 'APD' album and tour got some mixed reviews, but I thought they were great that night, and I loved the album. Years later, I spent a long and wonderful night in a pub with Robbo and my girlfriend Joe. Robbo spoke highly of Lemmy and his time in Motörhead.
From '83 onwards, Motörhead gigs were a regular event most times they played in the UK (plus a fantastic evening in Islington when we were lucky enough to see Head Cat). We had tickets for the Saturday and Sunday at Hammersmith on the 'Bad Magic' tour, and although Lemmy had been ill for a while, we all had high hopes that his problems were behind him
One of my best memories is the time we travelled over to see them in Berlin in 2012. Motörhead played amazingly that night and the

atmosphere at the front of the crowd was incredible (despite Lemmy walking offstage before they'd played a single song due to someone throwing a glass at him).

After the gig, we went to a club called 'White Trash' and had the pleasure of meeting Mikkey Dee briefly..... alhough our attempts at persuading the bar staff that Mikkey was picking up our bar tab fell on deaf ears! :-)

When I heard the news that Lemmy had died, it hit me far harder than I ever thought it would, and a month later (as I write this) it still feels incredibly sad.

Lemmy said himself that when Motörhead are gone, there will never be another band like them; and it's so true.

Matt Scott MHB 3220 (UK)

"Good evening, we are Motörhead and we play rock and roll".

Those immortal words send goosebumps down my spine the same now as they did the first time I saw Motörhead perform at Wembley arena. I remember the gig being terrific but the half full venue felt wrong somehow.

The following year I saw them at the Hammersmith Apollo and this was much better. A smaller, more intimate venue, that this time was fit to burst with fans meant everything felt right.

Another storming set, the buying of a Motörhead England t-shirt and the evening was complete. I was hooked.

I bought all the studio albums that had been released at that time and got a few of the live albums to boot. I've always enjoyed music from all genres but this was the first time that I avidly bought all the CDs of one particular band and regularly went to see them live.

Their music meant something to me, which is not something I've ever really experienced before and it was never more profound than after learning of Lemmy's passing. Since that sad day I've found myself welling up with tears when listening to albums or watching live DVDs and it's because that music mattered to me as it did to a lot of other fans out there.

The tears have subsided a little now but every time I put on an album or listen to my favourite songs ('Born to Raise Hell' and 'Killers' are my personal favourites, followed by 'Overkill' and 'Orgasmatron') I can definitely feel something stirring in my emotions and that is a good thing. Shows the music still matters.

RIP Motorhead.

RIP Lemmy.

Born to Lose. Lived to Win."

Paul Hussey (UK)

"I've been a Motörhead fan since 1982, when my older sister got me listening to the 'Ace of Spades' album on a cassette. I wanted to go see Motörhead on the 'Iron Fist' tour, but my dad deemed me too young to go. So, on 18th June 1983 I was allowed to go with my friend to my first ever Motörhead concert at the Glasgow Apollo featuring fellow Scotsman Brian 'Robbo' Robertson. Nothing out of the ordinary there there, except that I must be one of the very few Motörhead fans in the world to have been onstage with them before ever seeing actually seeing them live in concert.

Having turned up early afternoon and just milling about, we both heard the start of the mid-afternoon soundcheck, and went racing towards the noise of drums at one of the open doors. Not able to see anything much, we were craning our necks around the door entrance when a roadie spotted us and beckoned us inside. Twenty seconds later I was stood staring at Philthy Animal hammering the drums. He glanced over at us and before we could even wave to him, there was an almighty movement of air and Robbo wandered on riffing the intro to "Marching Off to War" from the new "Another Perfect Day" album.

Philthy immediately stopped what he was doing and joined Robbo in the song, playing together and presumably checking levels, when from the other side of the stage on strode Lemmy and immediately drowned them both out in a thunderous rumble of noise. With a slightly startled nod to us when he clocked two 14 year old boys, Lemmy turned around, gestured to the roadie and in the next five seconds we found ourselves steered out to the back door. By way of explanation, the roadie laughed and said "Lemmy doesn't like anyone inside for the soundcheck. Sorry boys".

I'll never forget the intensity of the sound onstage with all three playing together and sometimes in the middle of a Motörheadache gig with everything at full tilt and sounding powerful, I remember that feeling. That's why I think I ended up settiing up my Motörhead tribute band. Listening to them in the crowd or even at the side of the stage never matched the full roar of Motörhead onstage. So I've been chasing that rush ever since with Motörheadache and I sometimes I get a shudder and I'm that little boy gazing up at those monsters of noise.

Plus, I always wanted to be Lemmy. Not being able to grow a moustache until I was 27 held me back a bit but I played a succession of Rickenbacker 4001 basses throughout my twenties trying to learn the Lemmy bass style. There was no internet, or learn to play Lemmy bass books or dvds. I had to look at his fingers and try to work out what he was playing. Double stops, the E string as a drone, but mainly root and fifth inversions.

Lemmy is very under-rated for his percussive and rhythmic style of bass playing and the sound he achieved with the original Rickenbackers and the hot rodded Marshall Super Bass gave Motörhead a fuller mid range sound than other bands That's what made it seem louder and it was. There was no bass in the mix to soften the tone. Fast Eddie told me that they tried to sneak a DI from Lemmy's bass rig and he heard the difference and shouted "Who's been fucking with my sound?"

After the gig that night, we joined the long queue of fans waiting to get signatures from all three sat at a table. I didn't say anything to Phil and was just about to say "Remember us from the soundcheck today" to Lemmy when he glanced up and said "Alright?" and that made me freeze, speechless. By the time I'd got to third in line, Brian Robertson, I'd recovered enough to say to him that my name was Robbo (on account of Robert being my first name and not Robertson as my last name. Robbo smiled and signed my tour programme 'From Robbo to Robbo. Yodel'.

That tour programme got utterly destroyed when my garage got flooded. Along with my signed copy of the 'Stone Dead Forever' 5 CD set and the signed 'White Line Fever' biography. I'm much more careful these days. My Lemmy signed Rickenbacker 4001 says "To Rob, Lemmy". Or it did until it rubbed off completely because I was still using it at all my gigs. Explaining this to Lemmy merited that glare and he signed it again on the next tour.

Lemmy was also capable of quiet acts of kindness too. I had a copy of Bassist magazine for him to sign because he was on the front cover and there was a feature article. I handed it to him to sign and he started reading it and said "I've never seen this". I just said to him to keep it for himself and he shook me by the hand. On the way out of the dressing room at the Manchester Apollo, Lemmy muttered something to his assistant and as was walking up the stairs he said "Lem says you can have some things from the merch stall".

We got there and again a mutter from the assistant to the merchandise man with something about Lem's account and I picked a few hoodies and t-shirts. At which point merchandise man said "Lem said you can have one of everything". I walked out with handfuls of gear and managed to give some of it away to some friends who were left wondering why I had bought so many things until I explained that it was a gift from Lemmy.

I miss Lem a lot and he's been a tremendous influence on my life.

Rob Campbell of Motörheadache 2003 to date (London)

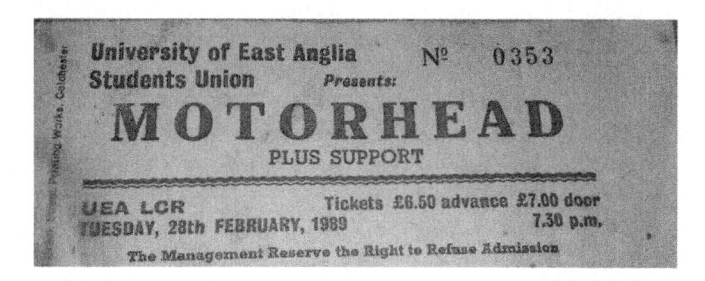

> University of East Anglia   Nº 0353
> Students Union   *Presents:*
> # MOTORHEAD
> PLUS SUPPORT
> UEA LCR   Tickets £6.50 advance £7.00 door
> TUESDAY, 28th FEBRUARY, 1989   7.30 p.m.
> The Management Reserve the Right to Refuse Admission

"*Seeing Motörhead in November 2014, Lemmy had replaced his traditional alcohol on his mic stand with mineral water. He took a sip, turned to the crowd and said "fuckin mineral water, who needs it eh? Me, apparently" before launching into his signature gravelly chuckle.*
It felt genuinely unreal to be looking at Lemmy with my own two eyes and being in the same room as him.
Seeing Lemmy in person made me feel as if there was nothing left in life to accomplish, and I managed to be lucky enough to have that exact same feeling on each of the three times I got to see the great man.
And Lemmy is also the guy who everyone channels whenever they do anything they shouldn't.*"*
Tomos Vincent Powell (Walsall)

"*It was round about the third day, I remember it so clear...August 1977 in fact and I, an impressionable 16 year old, had just been blown away by a five star review by Phil Sutcliffe in Sounds magazine of the first album by a band called Motörhead. Apparently it was very loud indeed. Even louder than a war if they had thrown the whole thing together and held it in a telephone box. The review was accompanied by a photo of three scruffy, longhaired denim-clad guys called Lemmy, Philthy Animal and Fast Eddie. Lemmy had a sledgehammer over his shoulder and was grinning at the camera with an unlit cigar between his teeth. I got the message: they were loud, they were dangerous - and I was hooked.*
I bought the album as soon as it came out. It was everything Phil Sutcliffe had promised - and more: filthy, dirty, extremely loud, ramshackle, hard rock'n'roll. I wanted more - but all things come to he who waits (the waiting never ends).
Fast forward four months and Motörhead announced that they

were coming to a metropolis near me, to play Shrewsbury Tiffany's to be precise, a tiny nightclub for over 18s only. My three friends and I - all 16 at the time- didn't consider that a problem.

On Sunday 22 January 1978 (iMotorhead.com gigography incorrectly lists it as 1977) the four of us blagged our way past the bouncers and up a flight of stairs into a small dimly - lit room. There was a bar in one corner and a stage in the centre which seemed tiny -probably because it was crammed with Marshall stacks and a massive drum kit. I was struck by how few people there were but, through the gloom about six feet away, leaning against the bar, were those three scruffy, longhaired, denim - clad figures; Lemmy in his maroon and silver striped shirt and bullet belt, Eddie in his FUs black cord shirt and Phil in his trademark blue and white striped Tshirt.

These demi - gods beckoned us over, bought us drinks, signed our posters, invited us to their dressing room to eat their food, and answered all our questions like it was the first time they had ever heard them. No other fans got a look in all evening. Lemmy was genial, friendly, patient, funny - but not at all patronising to us teenagers. At one point I said that I thought Abba were crap. Lemmy disagreed, saying that he wished that he could write songs like that which everyone wanted to listen to. Such humility. He didn't think he was a star, he just wanted his music to be heard and he maintained that attitude 'Til The End'. He treated everyone as his equals.

We spent an hour or so with band that night before they played the loudest gig I have ever been to even to this day. In truth, if I hadn't known every note of every song I wouldn't have had a clue what they were playing. But that didn't matter. There weren't more than 30 people at the gig but the band played like there were 3000 by giving it everything they had.

My friends and I, who are now in our mid - fifties, have never forgotten that night. I went on to see Motörhead a further 13 times. I met Lemmy again backstage after the Heavy Metal Barn dance at Stafford Bingley Hall in 1980 and once more, out of the blue, in a deserted Dingwalls in London in December 1983 when he wandered in on his own. We spent an hour talking about why Brian Robertson had been so wrong for Motoörhead and where the band might go next. That was Lemmy, he had time for anyone, stranger or friend, he'd always give you a chance.

And now we all have to come to terms with no longer having Lemmy and Motörhead as the soundtrack of our lives."

Alistair McIntösh (York)

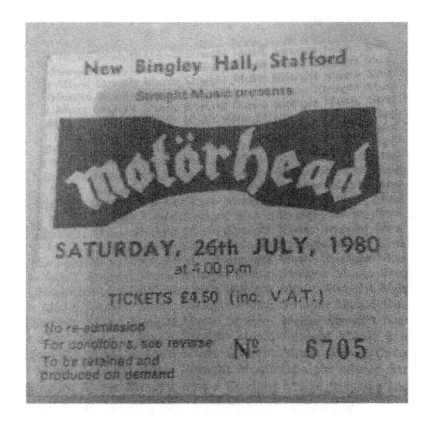

"I remember the first time I heard Motörhead, I was about 8 or 9 years old, I was sat in the back of my Dad's car and he had a "Best of the 80's" CD on. '99 Red Balloons' had just finished playing and then all of a sudden the first note of 'Ace of Spades' kicked in and it blew me away instantly.
I asked "Dad, what's making that noise?"
"That's a bass guitar" and my obsession with music came to life. I'd sit and play bass riffs on my old acoustic guitar with the strings tuned an octave lower just to feel a bit as cool as Lemmy.
After watching interviews and live videos when I got older I realised that not only did Lem make great music, but he was just as great a human. His tenacity and "Stop for nothing" attitude helped me battle some of the toughest times in my life to date and to this day and still continues to.
I remember the first time I saw them live, (Manchester 2010) it was the most eye opening experience for me ever, sure I loved music, but that show made me want to create and play it. And he did all that without even knowing who I am simply by being himself.
I can't think of anyone who's influenced me more musically and as a person who will give up anything to chase his dream.
The world will never ever see another man as determined, honourable, gentlemanly, wild or as unique.
Lemmy was simply THE man."
Harry Woods (Chester)

O2 Apollo, Manchester

16th November 2010

We Are Motörhead
Stay Clean
Be My Baby
Get Back In Line
Rock Out
Metropolis
Over the Top
One Night Stand
The Thousand Names of God
I Got Mine
I Know How to Die
The Chase is Better Than the Catch
In the Name of Tragedy
Just 'Cos You Got the Power
Going to Brazil
Killed by Death
Ace of Spades
Born to Raise Hell
Overkill

"I first saw Motörhead in Wolverhampton in 1994, it was captivating. I was so impressed with Phil Campbell's guitar playing have seen them on every tour since I would always do two dates Birmingham and Bristol, or Wolverhampton and Bristol.
They were a special help to me in 2010 when I had one of my daughters in ICU with a life threatening illness those two gigs that year in Wolverhampton and Bristol gave me the release I needed to get through what was a difficult period. My daughter Becki survived she was in ICU Coventry for 4 months and rehabilitation 5 months, she had 'Gullain-Barré' syndrome (Google it in and it explains it).
I have seen Phil Campbell's All Starr Band three times in Coventry, where I live, Poole and Cardiff last August. I was lucky enough to

meet him in Poole after the gig. He is a top man really down to earth. He is going out with the All Starr band later in the year if you get the chance go to one it's Phil and his sons."
Eamonn Bolger (Coventry)

"I'll never forget my first festival in which Motörhead performed during my first mosh pit experience (and last). Lemmy was kind enough to give me a wave as I sat above the crowd on my brothers shoulders. I felt like my life had been blessed and I'll cherish that memory forever.
Lemmy's music and character helped me overcome heartbreak, self esteem issues and left a mark on the world that will never be forgotten.
I remember first watching the 'Lemmy' movie and being awestruck: I'd never seen anyone like him.
He set the grand example of being confident in your own skin without giving a toss about what others think. And yet he was still a friendly, generous, loving individual. Inspiring millions of people all over the world, he can never be replaced or forgotten."
Iona Woods (UK)

"Motörhead is truly the best of all time.
Lemmy will always be immortal in his music.
The 30th of Jan 2016 would of been my first Motörhead concert at the Hammersmith Apollo but unfortunately that can't happen so instead I'll be getting the record player out and playing Motörhead as LOUD as possible!"
Amelia Maycock (UK)

"My dad first introduced me to Motörhead when I was about 10 years old with 'Bomber'.
Shortly after I watched his film and from that moment on I knew he was my inspiration! Since then I have set about knowing all about him, his lifestyle and his music.
I'm not old enough yet but I am already planning my tattoos about Lemmy and Motörhead.
Everything I do I got my inspiration from the legend himself.
As a bass player myself he influenced me and I'm sure he influenced many many others.
Sadly I've only seen them live once but wow, what a night! The best night of my life... Front row, him standing right there in front of me, and to top it all I got his signed pic!!
So this is to the legend himself... Mr Lemmy Ian Fraser Kilmister...

*Thank you!!
And here's to enjoying his music for many many more years!"*
Jack T. Watkins (Cannock, Staffordshire)

*"It was the early '90's; I was 17 and spending weekends at the local rock club, and some week nights out with my father in Gloucester - watching local bands and chatting to Wurzel, who was mad as a box of frogs and safe as houses - everybody loved him.
After a Saturday night of classic rock at the local rock club, or an evening of live music, my Dad and I would invariably wind up at the Outlaw's Clubhouse for some more music and beer.
My friend Rose - more often than not - would already be ensconsed in the big armchair that everybody else wanted to sit in, swaddled in her big black rain coat, and so Dad and I would end up on the sofa of dubious origin that probably doubled as a bed for various people now and again.
There would always be Motörhead, without fail. 'Ace Of Spades', 'Killed By Death', 'Orgasmatron'... even that fabulous 'Please Don't Touch' track when Lemmy teamed up with Girlschool.
My home town of Cheltenham isn't a good place to be living in poverty, and spending those hours at the Clubhouse listening to Motörhead made all of that go away for a while. They were good times that I still look back on fondly and with a smile. My friend Rose and I are even still in touch, despite moving to different cities. Motörhead and our memories of the Outlaws kept us united."*
Gemma Wright (Chelmsford)

*"Met Lemmy a number of times whilst following the band 'Tank' when they first formed in the early 1980's.
I was one of the original 'Filth Hounds' (then known as 'Flash') to which Algy Ward & Tank named their first & finest album after, called 'The Filth Hounds of Hades' ('There gunna be there Shane,Mick & Flash out there somewhere').
Lemmy always had time for people even when they were drunk as would often be the case, Lemmy gave many bands like Tank the opportunity to support Motörhead thus giving them better recognition & publicity, I also followed Girlschool in 1980/81 & Lemmy gave them their 'break' by letting them support Motörhead."*
Simon Hayward (Tamworth)

"I still remember the first time I saw them. It was the 'Iron Fist' tour at Newcastle City Hall.
The auditorium lights went out, and a massive cheer erupted. Motörhead started to play, but the stage was in darkness, we were thinking what's going on, when a chink of light appeared at the top of the stage. The boys were being lowered from the roof. Absolutely fantastic.
They didn't disappoint at all. Fantastic gig, and I was deaf for nearly a week, which was not ideal, as at the time I was in an office job, but had to fetch and carry for people. So I was getting bits of paper thrown at me with messages on as I couldn't hear. Happy days."
Richard Mattison (UK)

"Motörhead were my life! I got to see them a lot!
Sad to say my other half 'Gini' only got to see them twice!
Next weekend would have been her 3rd! Such a shame it's not to be! Or will ever be again!
R.I.P. Lemmy!"
Mick Watford 'Spike' (Waltham Abbey)

"I like all Motorhead music. My memory of Lemmy is his voice and his kind smile."
Sarah Harris (UK)

"I went out with the roadie for the infamous 'Another Perfect Day' tour for three months, Paul Copeland Watts.
He told me even though he got the sack, Lemmy invited him to a party. Anyway, when CW told me that, I got too excited. Paul changed his mind. Been a fan since 'Ace of Spades'. That would have been in April 83/May."
Maggie Bevan (High Wycombe, Buckinghamshire)

"The weekend of 28th and 29th of January will stay with me forever we should have been seeing the mighty Motörhead at Hammersmith. Over 100 of us turned up to pay our respects to the great man, Lemmy.
We cried, laughed and shared memories and drank lots of beer's and Lemmy's.
Fan's from all over the world turned up and I met some really great people.
I know Lemmy would have been proud we all miss and love you Motörhead Forever."

Ian Hornsey (Kingston Upon Hull)

"Motörhead from the '80's, I've seen the band over 30 times and met them loads of times due to being friends with Graham Oliver from Saxon."
Mark 'Biff' Griffiths (Port Talbot)

*"The first time I met Lemmy was in London.
I flew over from Ireland to see Motörhead play at Wembley Arena.
Hawkwind also played that night, it was an absolute pleasure seeing Lemmy coming out to sing 'Silver Machine' with them before the Motörhead show!
Seen Motörhead many times but that night was special. Had the added bonus of seeing the 'Bomber' lighting rig for the first time that same evening.
Brilliant memories!"*
Colin Murdy (UK)

*"All I can really think of is the power that Motörhead had in bringing people from different 'tribes' together.
My first gig was the Stranglers in 1978. I was 15 and after the show we got chased by some 'rockers' and my mate got a bit of a kicking.
When Motörhead were being played it gave common ground to punks and rockers and I don't know how direct their influence was, but trouble between punks and rockers faded away around that time and we became solely focussed on the music.
The music and beating up Mods."*
Peter Clifford (Gateshead)

*"Well Lemmy, what can I say. A gent, a man with a great sense of humour and a very intelligent conversationalist. I got to meet him when I joined Girlschool and at every festival, gig or tour we've done or been to where I've had the privilege of talking to him, I've always come away smiling.
The first tour we did with them I remember me and Den going to his dressing room every day to chat with him whilst he was playing his fruit machine as we only had beer on our dressing room rider and we both wanted JD. We drank pretty much all his every day until 1 day he grabbed his walkie talkie, called Dan his runner and said
"get these girls some JD as they're drinking mine every day.""*

Since then every gig we've done with them there's been JD on our rider, as it should be.

When we were recording the Legacy album I sent Lem a text from the studio in Wales, being a different time zone I didn't want to wake him. I asked him if he'd do something on the new album, his reply was

"Jax what do you want, bass, vocals, harmonica or triangle?"

Well of course I replied "triangle please." So we sent him the track of music with no words or anything then in the early hours one night me and Kim were up drinking and called him to see how he was getting on. He said so what are the words and melody...so we sang down the phone at him "Don't talk to me...and then lah lah lah lah lah lah lah lah dont talk to me" as we hadn't written anything else but the title.

So when he got to the studio in LA he said to our friend who'd driven him, "I can't make out a word Jax and Kim sang they were so drunk, it sounds like lah lah lah lah lah lah lah lah don't talk to me so I'm gonna have to write some words myself." Oops sorry Lem...we hadn't written anything but that title and the music. Anyway the next day we came into the studio and there was his bass track, his vocal track which sounded amazing and right at the very and of the song, there was the triangle in all it's glory! Yay what a pro!

The last tour we did, and Lemmy's final tour 2015 in Europe, I was chatting to Lemmy at sound check and we were chatting about Monty Python, me being from Yorkshire he started to recite the 4 Yorkshire men sketch and he pretty much knew it word for word, nothing wrong with his mind that was for sure. He had a great sense of humour and his Yorkshire accent made me smile. I get the feeling he'd done that sketch a few times as Mikkey Dee came and joined in too with that conversation."

Jackie 'Jax' Chambers (Girlschool – Guitar/Vocals)

"Saw Lemmy hit his head on the 'Bomber' rig at Hammersmith in the 80's, I think it was 1982."
Rowan Ashley (Hemel Hempstead)

"Lemmy is the rock and roll god. Nobody will ever take his spot."
Richie Matthew Scott (Crook, UK)

"Been a Fan since 1977 'ish.
One of my most memorable Gigs was in Bristol 02, then named the Studio. It was smaller then.

It was the return of Philthy Phil in the warm up gig for the '1916' Tour, back when Motörhead still toured with there own sound system, and it went from the floor of the place to the roof and when the band came on it waved about.

It was defining ,came away with the set list and some of Phil's sticks. Saw them 3 times in one week on that tour.

Fab times. I feel I'm a part of Motörhead, as do all fans and with Lem passing a bit of all of us went with him.

I'm the son of a Teddy Boy and brought up on Rock 'n' Roll, but Motörhead gave me a whole new way and it will stay with me to the grave. Cradle to the Grave.

I was at the 25th Anniversary show in Brixton that was the 'Boneshaker' DVD and to my surprise you see my feet going over the front of the crowd during 'Killed By Death', lol.

Or the time we travelled down to Hammersmith, and my mate 'RAH RAH' Rigs wanted a piss saw an exit door open and went for it. The door then closed behind him, and he missed the whole show. Hysterical lol."

James Outlaw MHB 4052 (Malmesbury, Wiltshire)

"I've been posting songs for the month of January in memory of Lemmy on Motörhead Europe.

Day 31

I've left this till the end as the band did. It is a personnel favourite (I play the drums) and one of my happiest memories. Indulge me please.

I remember a gig at the Hammersmith Apollo. I was down the front, knackered, bruised and still slightly pissed (all the sweating and dancing had sobered me up a bit). The band came back on and Lemmy walked up to the mike and says, "Here it is!"

Wallop 'Ace Of Spades'! Followed by 'Killed By Death' then this song 'Overkill'. Well my feet never touched the ground through all three songs. At the end, I remember laughing so hard my soul was having an orgasm, and other people were laughing.

I walked from the front with some people arm in arm, happy, still laughing and singing. Everything was right with the world. I still smile when I remember this; you see this is why I always went.

The daily grind that we have to put up with is 'Spiritual Death' (a Lemmy quote). I would be able to cope with this daily grind, safe in the knowledge that I would be going to see the band and have my soul kicked in again by the sound! It was a deep and soul nurturing experience seeing and listening to the band.

I never had the pleasure of meeting any of them.

Where will I get this feeling again? It was like a drug an addiction, I feel I grew up with them in my life, somewhere I belonged, where will I go from here, where will I find this again, sadly never I think. I am heartbroken.

I hope you enjoyed the songs I picked this month in my #rememberlemmy

Take it easy people, peace to you all. #motorheadforlife and always #turnitupto11

BORN TO LOSE! LIVE TO WIN!!"

Barry Scott (Romford, Essex)

"My first introduction to Motörhead was in early September 1977, as I entered my local Record shop the guy behind the counter was just placing the stylus down on to an album on the stores record deck, propped up beside the deck was the black album cover, with the large white 'Snaggletooth' front and centre and curved above it also in white was just one word 'Motörhead.

God knows how loud he had that thing turned up? But the speakers in the store almost vibrated themselves free from the brackets holding them to the wall, when Lemmy's bass sprang into life, with Phil on the high hat, followed by the rumbling floor tom, that heralded the entrance of Eddie on guitar, and then Lemmy's vocals.......

Holy Fuck, I thought, what was this? It was as if someone had turned the light on in my head, I was well and truly hooked and just had to have it!!

I'd gone in there to get something for my brother for his birthday........ and I have to admit I was tempted to buy it for him, just so I could, well borrow it, I didn't and so he didn't get anything from the shop for his birthday.

Oh why is that Dave I hear you ask? I'll tell you why, I spent all the money that I had gone in there with, because I brought the album for myself and went home and played the fuck out of it!!!
And the rest as they say, is history \m/\m/ "
David Gamlin aka 'Gambo' (Waterlooville, Portsmouth)

"I remember turning up at Norwich UEA to see Motörhead with my late brother and another friend, we didn't pre-buy tickets, but we're paying on the door.
My brother and friend managed to get the last ones before the venue was at capacity and 50 or so of us stood outside in the cold and rain. Within 40 mins I was the only one left outside, and still not allowed into the gig!
As I stood outside smokin' and listening, a guy came up to me and asked what I was doing? I told him the story and with that he said "you're fuckin kiddin"! and took me past the door men (saying what he thought of leaving one guy outside) and straight to side of stage!
He was one of the roadcrew.... I think his name was mark? Cheers mark!!"
Karl Facey (UK)

"A man passed away today 28/12/2015 his name was Ian Frazer Kilmister he was a living legend, he was Mr Motörhead and they kicked ass as the loudest band in the world for some 40 years.
He had some fantastic fellow band members, Fast Eddie Clark, Phil Taylor, Wurzel, Pete Gill, Mikkey Dee and Phil Campbell and not just in Motörhead, but Headcat, Hawkwind, and a few more.
I was never lucky enough to meet him, but did manage to see him play live with his band many times in England.
I have played his music for over 34 years and can relate it to many, many things that have happened in my life, each and every song he wrote or co-wrote I can relate to some part of it, one line in a song. I can relate it to something at some points in time in my life, if that makes any sense, how fucking awesome is that, that is what made him so special and a great man, my hero.
He was always there on the tapes, vinyl's, CD's, DVD's, by all accounts he was a funny man with a great sense of humour, an honorable man, a fair man, a decent human being, a legend in my life time.
I thank you for all you have given me, you have lived your life as you wanted, he brought and gave so much to so many, for so long, I will miss him very much, because for some 34 odd years he has

helped me through so much and will do for the remaining years of my life.
Thank you Mr Kilmimster, Lemmy you have given so much, to so many, and will do for many, many more years to come. You may be gone, but you will live on in my head and heart and your music will live on forever.
R. I. P. Lemmy.
We are Motörhead - And We Play Rock 'N' Roll."
Brian Linford (Brackley)

"Lemmy is the reason I play bass guitar and the most badass rock 'n' roller ever!"
Tom Whitby (London)

"He was a light in my darkest times."
Lewis Lee (Risca, Wales)

"Lemmy's one of the main reasons I play a Rickenbacker bass!"
Lee Cotterell (Bristol)

"Lemmy, the original, the best, the king, long live Lemmy."
Lofty Hadyer Maw (York)

"One word - Gutted"
Billy Gaylor (Newcastle Upon Tyne)

"Ace of Spades' LP, changed our generation.
R.I.P Lemmy. Rock God."
Kevin Dixon (Eyemouth, Berwickshire)

"Lemmy was a musician I looked up to. He fucking kicked ass and made incredible music. Nobody could take over from him.
We have lost a brother of rock. Keep on rockin."
Jay Black (Winchester)

"I first saw Motörhead in late 70's. Met Lemmy, what a gent, having a ciggy outside Heathrow took a photo with him, enough said!
I told him he made me deaf for a while. We talked about my daughter's luv off Sid Vicious, Lem said.
"I taught him everything he knew, which was fuck all ha ha."
Lem was exactly same off stage as on.

He was due in my local gig in Newcastle not long before he died...I was devastated.
RIP Lem."
Ron Horseman (Peterlee, Co Durham)

"I saw Motörhead in Bristol, UK and Lemmy said it wasn't loud enough so he turned the amps up!!! NEVER SEEN A BAND SO LOUD!!"
Adam Laasna (Cwmbran)

"Ok here we go...
I fucking loved Lemmy!
He was everything awesome and rock 'n' roll with this world.
No one will ever be able to replace him. We shared birthdays; Christmas Eve and he gave me my love of Jack and Cokes.
New Year's Eve 2015 I dressed as my hero for our rock star theme at Project Orange, London.
Love you Lemmy xxx "
Gemma Greenwood (York)

"Saw Motörhead around 25 times since '87.
Never met him, don't need to, his music speaks for itself.
We Are Motörhead & We Play Rock & Roll."
Simon Mottram (Stafford)

"My son Callum is autistic. He is 10.
He was having quite serious behavioural issues prior to seeing Motörhead at the Eden Project. The week we went in June 2015 his teacher at the special school suggested he attends a residential school for a few months as he was getting way out of hand and becoming very aggressive. Well, he came back from Cornwall a changed boy.
He is a total Motörhead fan and self regulates his emotions by playing his music. He don't talk much but he sings all the words to many of the songs. He don't understand that Lemmy is gone. I told him that Lemmy went to play for god as god was bored. He just don't get it.
We have seen a few bands since and there is a lot of interest from other parents locally to get out and take their kids to see bands too. We are having a fund raising event on a Saturday night to watch bands together.
Life really did change for us that day in June.
Cal waited for two hours at the gate and a further hour to see King

Creature, boogied to the Stranglers, then Motörhead came on.
Oops no ear defenders so Cal couldn't cope with the noise so security lifted him over the railings. He sat and cried in the vunerable area as he wasn't near Lemmy.
All the Motörhead fans around us helped us stay at the railings at the front but really it's not there job to protect my boy from the crush. It's all about the music, music that gives you a buzz and makes you feel strong.
Who would have thought I'd be able to go out on a Saturday night. Take my wee laddie with me.
Thanks Lemmy, things were getting really bad and sad.
Now, I get to keep my boy and party with him.
Patricia O'Callaghan (Northampton)

"Today's the day I learnt that Lemmy had died,
Oh my god, yes my god Lemmy had gone on his eternal ride,

No more shall I see that great giant of a man,
Playing 'We are Motörhead we play rock and roll,
He will always be remembered in my heart and my soul?

From On parole to bad magic and every track in between,
Not forgetting my childhood favourite Silver Machine,
For I will listen and remember with great joy,

Today is a sad day, a day to mourn,
But do it how the great man would want,
Play his music good and loud smile and laugh as if he was re born,
Have a drink to his life, and share your thoughts to,
Because after all one day this will be you."

RIP Lemmy

Glyn Taylor-Ball (Eynsham, nr Oxford)

"I first saw them in 1978 at Digbeth Civic Hall supported by The Damned. I do remember the balcony bounced up n down that night - POGO MADNESS
I then first met the periodical son the following year at HMV New Street Birmingham just up the way from The Odeon for a what we now would class as a meet 'n' greet!
Utter madness place was rammed but Phil, Eddie and Lemmy took

the time to have a quick chat with anyone who asked a question while people with anything wanted a siggy thrust anything under their noses

The concert itself was spent with me sitting amongst The Hell's Angel's that was hell of a night support band that night was Girlschool. Tried meeting up with them all after the gig, but Lemmy I was told was unavailable for reasons we won't go into !!

I didn't even see the Girls!!

I then saw every night of every tour when they played the Odeon Birmingham up until 'Another Perfect Day' tour with Robbo..........so 2 nights for 'Bomber', 2 more nights, throw in Stafford Bingley Hall and Port Vale somewhere along the way then 'Ace of Spades' what made this worse was I did 4 LOUD gigs in 6 days....

F*** M* my hearing was screwed!!!

Met Lemmy again at BBC 'Top of the Pops' when doing TOTP miming 'Ace of Spades' up in bar while playing the bandit.

Too many stories to cover in such a short night 3 nights 'Iron Fist', as well as seeing them at the legendary Hammersmith Odeon.

THOSE HEADY DAYS and nights

Then the last time I met the guys was for a VIP for my 50th at Leicester De Montford Hall when I spoke with Mikkey Dee about Ice Hockey and a good friend presented him with a coloured drawing he'd done as an album cover, was knocked out by the pic had a great night with them all.

The last time I saw them live was at NIA Birmingham with The Boss Hoss opening. What a start followed by going full circle with The Damned up next then finally THE HOMECOMING of Fast Eddie and Phil Taylor ...and we are back where we started with the original 3 together (yes I know we had Larry and Lucas) back in Brum 2014, we know the rest from here

As an anecdote I will add I have taken both my wives to a Motörhead gig and ONE FELL ASLEEP! How the f*** did she or could she LOL and the other twisted her ankle. Footnote to self go on your own boys night out much more fun

Regards "We are Motorhead and we play Rock n Roll " be loud be proud

Mike Taylor-Lane (Arley nr Nuneaton)

"First and second Motörhead gigs, I remember my brother had seen them at Bolton Tech on the previous tour and took me and my best mate Graeme Halsall to watch them.

I think Johnny Moped should have been the support but didn't

show up!! They let us in but we couldn't go in to the stalls or circle, remember them doing a sound check played 'Motörhead', opened the show with it and closed with it.
Was deaf for about a week!!!"
David Robinson (Leigh, Wigan)

"Remember the first time I saw Motörhead, it was Stafford Bingley Hall in July 1980, what a baptism of Sent before I had finished. It was a baptism of fire and the rest is history.
Been into Motörhead since '77, they are my fav band and always will be."
Anthony Croft (Chester)

"Lemmy and Motörhead have been the soundtrack of my life from age 11 when I first saw them in 1982 until the final UK concert last year at the Eden project.
Even my first date with my wife was to go and see them at Newport in1991.
Everybody needs to play some Motörhead every day to not forget how great he truly was."
Mike (Dartmoor, Devon)

"Back in the '80's a group of us went on a coach trip to the Hammersmith Palais to see a punk band. Anyway, they weren't up to much so we went upstairs to the bar.
Being country folk we hadn't come across a video jukebox and the only metal song on it was 'Killed By Death' by Motörhead.
That jukebox took some money off us that night!
RIP Lem and Phil and Wurzel."
Tony Parks (Ninfield, East Sussex)

"My earliest memory of Lemmy was seeing Motörhead playing 'Ace Of Spades' on TV. It was the British music show 'Top Of The Pops' circa 1980. Being only eight at that time and having no taste in music I thought that's loud and thought nothing more of it. Little did I know back then.
In 1987 I was given a heavy metal tape to listen to by a friend, consisting of the bands of that era. I was hooked on the sounds I heard, popular music on TV and radio was all the usual manufactured bullshit the record companies plied and I found it all fake.
On that tape a couple of songs stood out for me, the vocals in particular, I checked out the name of the band whose songs they

were. It was Motörhead and I asked my friend if he had any more of their music. He did indeed and my love for Motörhead had begun.

Over time I sought out more of Lemmy's music, blown away each time I heard something new from past albums to the new records released. Nothing else has or will compare to this band.

As I found more of the music so began my knowledge of Motörhead's history and they became a big part of my life. Each line up and everyone who played in the ranks, all heroes to me. All the times I saw them live, awesome, those gigs treasured memories.

I never met Lemmy personally but regarded him as someone who you could put your trust in, always there when someone needed him.

His passing saddened me and tears are shed now and again, but the man and his music will live on.

Till we meet in Rock & Roll Valhalla..."
Jonathan Hanton (Sheffield)

"I've been a fan of Motörhead and loved Lemmy for nearly 30 years.

His music, humour, his intelligence and philosophy and an all round nice guy, a true gentleman and that is the reason I've followed them and loved him for all those years xxx."
Loz Nana Atkinson (London)

"The first time I seen Motörhead was at the Glasgow Armadillo on October 14th 2002 support was Skew Siskin and Anthrax, anyway it's also where I met the love of my life who would put up with me long enough to become my wife and because of this Lemmy and Co saved me from a downward spiral of self destruction.

I always thought I would never meet anyone nevermind have a family and because of that I am eternally grateful to Motörhead.

Up until last year I had seen Motörhead 9 times since that fateful day 14 years ago, I was trying for 10 but it wasn't to be and even to this day I still thank Motörhead for saving my life"
Jim 'Glowstick Nips' Wilson (Bonnybridge, Scotland)

"Remember smoking during 'Ace of Spades' and gettin "stoned deaf" for the end of the week...missed class few days after and didn't give a damn."
Idriss Richards (Cardiff)

"My memory of Motörhead and Lemmy is one I'm sure many have but its this: Brixton Academy London, Lemmy says the following
"Can you hear us out there?"
We all scream
"I said, can you hear us?!"
We scream louder.
"Then you haven't been to fucking see us enough then!" then the bass begins!
Loudest show I ever saw without a doubt!"
Matt Ayton (London)

"Motörhead played for two consecutive nights at De Montfort Hall, Leicester.
The first night I met Lemmy he was playing the fruit machine in the bar. He invited me to meet the rest of the band back stage which I did. During the set he dedicated 'Love Me Like a Reptile' to me. I was only 17, and I spent the whole of the next day at college in a daze.
The next night he spotted me amongst the crowd and signaled for me to come over. Once again we went backstage.
He was so kind and totally understood why I couldn't come out with him after the show (my dad was picking me up!).
I'll never forget those two nights.
He was a real gentleman!"
Suzanne Dutton (Market Harborough)

"I've been a fan from day one and they helped me through the bullshit in life. Lemmy was such a wonderful amazing guy Motörhead for ever till my last breath."
Michael Lawton (Penrith, Cumbria)

"NO!!!!
BORN TO LOSE, LIVED TO WIN, KILLED BY DEATH, REMEMBER HIM, HE'S GONE L.A.M.F
ALGY=TANK=ALGY= STRATEGIC BASS DETERRENT X"
Algy Ward (Tank - Vocals/Bass)

"The first time I ever saw Motörhead was on the 'Rock 'n' Roll' tour at the Edinburgh Playhouse.
It was only my third ever gig, so I was really excited, particularly as I was lucky enough to be in the front row. Anyway, come showtime, the band appeared onstage and Lemmy took one last draw from his cigarette before passing it down to me. I was

completely awestruck to say the least!
I have followed Motörhead slavishly ever since then and they will always be my favourite band."
George Nisbet (Edinburgh)

"I first got in to the band in late 1979 when I was about 14 years old and I first heard 'Overkill' & 'Bomber' don't think that they had been out that long
I didn't get to see the band live until I was 17 years old on the 'Iron Fist' tour in 1982 were I saw them at the Deeside Leisure Centre in North Wales U.K., as I live on The Isle of Anglesey, not too far from where LEMMY lived as a child / early teens about 3 miles from the village of Benllech.
Have seen the band countless times over the years and met them too. But the best time I ever met Lemmy was in 2010 when they played in Llandudno, Wales and I got to meet him after the show. I got to go in to his dressing room and had a long chat with him about the time he lived on Anglesey and he confirmed to me all of the story's I heard of him when he lived on the island.
The last time I saw the band live was at Wembley Arena in 2014.
Was also meant to see 3 more shows in January, the Hammersmith weekend the other week was a fantastic tribute to Lemmy!"
Billy Coxon (Pentraeth, North Wales)

"They say that you should never meet your idols... Well that couldn't be more wrong.
I can't remember if it was '81 or '82, but I went to Dingwalls in London, I think Lee Aaron was playing.
I was 15/16 and was an out and out headbanger complete with denim cutoff and of course the Motörhead England patch. Walked in the door and there having a heated debate with a fruit machine was the guy I idolized. I knew I had to speak to my hero...
"Awright Lem" I said as if we were old friends. (I wish).
"Can I buy ya a drink"... Lemmy looked at me and just said...
"na ya alright mate" ....Just as my heart began to sink he said
"I'll get em, what's yours?"
We probably only chatted for about 2 minutes but it felt like 2 hours.... just had time to get the patch signed when a head popped in the door... "Cabs here Lem" (I thought bollocks).
"Good to meet ya mate," he said as he shook my hand and off he went.
The most down to earth rock star that ever lived... Miss ya. X."

Geoff Wlodarczky (London)

*"Never saw Lemmy or Motörhead, but they were possibly the greatest band I've ever heard.
Lemmy inspired me to pick up a bass guitar and start playing.
Never forget him and will always have their music blasting out of every stereo it comes out of. R.I.P Lemmy."*
Dagen McHugh (Great Yarmouth)

"Always tried to see Motörhead whenever they performed in Manchester & on the odd occasion when they played Liverpool."
Stephen Berry (Liverpool)

"Watching Motörhead on YouTube, my 10 year old son just said " if only Lemmy could ride out of his grave in real life, like in 'Killed by Death.' Made me feel gutted that another generation won't get to see the band live again. I guess the music lives on."
Andy Eyles (UK)

*"Going to see Motörhead at Newcastle City Hall on the 'Iron Fist' tour. Got on the train at Sunderland with my mates three long haired fellas walk past us on the train and sit down it's only Lemmy, Philthy and Fast Eddie!
I get up walk over and say "hello."
Lemmy says "where you going"
I say "to see you", dry as sticks.
He says "well you've seen us now hahaha."
They all gave me their autographs and the gig was fantastic, one of my great memories of Motörhead.*
Gary Taylor (Sunderland)

*"I saw Motörhead once when I was about 11 and was going to see them last month - now being 17 - it was such a loss when Lemmy past away, a star that shall never be forgotten.
RIP"*
Rebecca Godfrey (UK)

*"Lemmy – well what can I say? Motörhead was one of the first heavy metal groups that I ever listened to, and looking back, I certainly have no regrets!
When I first listened to 'Ace of Spades' in Art in late 2013, I thought "Damn! They're really good! I have to check out their entire catalogue!" I was totally hooked from that moment on. I had to*

have anything they had brought out, whether it was CD's, tapes of old radio recordings, t-shirts etc.
The first thing Motörhead I bought was 'Ace of Spades' on CD and boy, I didn't half play it to death. I needed another copy after a couple of months.
But I didn't stop there, I went on to get EVERYTHING, even a 'Snaggletooth' pass case for my student cards. The only one regret I have is being born in the wrong generation. Being born at the end of the 1990's meant that I never got to see any of my idols live, including Motörhead themselves. Thank god for YouTube! Lemmy became the highlight of all my conversations at school and at home, I drove my parents mad! I was completely and utterly obsessed! It went so far that even my pals used to call it me, but my theory is because of my obsession, nothing else.
I hoarded all magazines that even just mentioned his name in the hope I could make a killing off of them some day. He was even the subject of my art exam!
I knew he hadn't been well for a long time, but no one expected him to die suddenly. That morning when my dad told me to log on to Facebook as there was some shocking news. I was assuming it was a family member announcing their engagement or pregnancy, but it was Lemmy! Emotions? Speechless.
At first I thought it was a hoax, like those that are flying round the Internet but when it came up as 'breaking news' on BBC 1, my heart sank.
Although I wasn't related to this amazing, artistic, talented guy, I'd been listening to his music for just under two years and it became a part of my daily life. When he died, part of me died too.
I bet I wasn't the only person who cried watching the live stream of his funeral that night…"
Megan Taylor Ure (Barnsley)

"Met him once backstage at Hellfest.
Told him I was in a band that did 'Iron Fist, he says
"so was I…" - sarcastic bastard :)
Paul Puggy Pugh (Huntly, Aberdeenshire)

"I first saw Motörhead on December 21st in the year 2000 at the Apollo in Manchester. The show was billed as 'Lemmy's 55th Birthday Party'.
I was fairly new to the scene, I'd only discovered heavy metal and hard rock a few years previous and I'd never been to a gig before. I wasn't that well up on Motörhead either so I had no idea what to

expect.
I'd heard 'Ace of Spades' and 'Bomber' and 'Overkill', but that was about all I knew about the band. It was my friend who was the big fan of theirs and he dragged me along.
We got there early out of excitement and ended up right at the front of the crowd. I can't remember who the first support band was, but Skew Siskin came on second. They were pretty good. I was having a good time stood there with the crowd calmly nodding away to the music.
Then Motörhead came on. We were right under Lemmy. He stood there looking up into the mic with a cig dangling from his lips and his shirt unbuttoned with this awesome bass guitar in his hands. The only way to describe him was cool as fuck. He hadn't even started yet and he already reeked of cool and I thought to myself I hope I'm that cool when I'm his age.
"Good evening," he barked. "We are Motörhead and we play rock 'n' roll." Then they kicked off with 'We Are Motörhead' and everyone went apeshit. The crowd surged forwards, crushing me and my friend into the barrier. The sound was deafening, people were crowd surfing over me and kicking me in the head. It was amazing.
It being my first gig, I didn't know what to do. I looked to my left and saw a sea of leather clad, hairy biker looking bastards banging their heads and pumping their fists. I looked to my right and saw the same. So I joined in, banging my head and pumping my fists to the music. The band hadn't even been playing for 10 seconds and my friend couldn't handle it and had to get one of the security to pull him out. But for me, I was in Heaven.
With each couple of songs, Lemmy would get the sound turned even higher. At one point he flashed his nipple. He joked with the crowd and his banter with Phil Campbell was hilarious. He told us we were being filmed for a TV show called 'Roadies'. I recorded it when it finally aired and you could see me a few times in the crowd and a couple of times in the same shot as Lemmy. That's my claim to fame.
Anyway, even though I didn't know most of the songs, I was still really getting into it. It was even better when they played songs that I knew. When they played 'Bomber', a big fuck off airplane appeared over the stage, it was spectacular. Then they played 'Ace of Spades' and everyone went full blown crazy. It was brutal. I was black and blue.
Finally they ended with 'Overkill'. The sound of it was like nothing I'd ever heard. It was so loud. It felt like it was inside me, rattling

my bones and ripping my eardrums out. It sounded like Hell. How did Lemmy, Phil and Mikkey still have hearing? I had ringing in my ears for about two days and shortly after I had to get my ears syringed. I've tried recreating the sound by blasting it in my car on full volume, but it doesn't come close.
When it was over, Lemmy started to shoot everyone with his bass and then he held it up and started punching it before he leaned it up against the speakers causing them to make that chirping sound. They gave a bow and that was the end of the show, but the beginning of something new for me.
It wasn't long before I owned the entire Motörhead back catalogue. They became my favourite band and I went on to see them more times than I've seen any other band. Lots of times in Manchester, in Liverpool, Derby, even in Germany.
I last saw them in November 2014. There was no secret about ill Lemmy's health. You could tell he was struggling and it was heart breaking to see, but even then, he still blew everyone else off the stage. He was still Motörhead giving it everything he had and nobody was left disappointed.
I learned from Lemmy that you've got to do what you love. Life is too short not to. He did what he loved right until the end and he deserves nothing but respect for it. It's really sad that we'll never experience the deafening sound of Motörhead live again, but I feel privileged that I got to see and hear it. The memories will live on and I'll continue to blast Motörhead as loud as I can until I'm stone deaf forever!"
Gareth Alan Houghtön (Newton Le Willows)

"Motörhead were alright I guess."
Nathan Carroll (Glider - Bass/Vocals)

"I grew up listening to my big brother playing Motörhead on vinyl.
I have seen them live many times over the years with my brother Darren Crofts and took my son Richard Clayton to see them for the first time for his 14th birthday!
We all continued to support Motörhead for many years at various venues and festivals right to the end and will continue to play Motörhead loud for life!
RIP Lemmy Xx"
Sarah Crofts (Thorney, Cambs)

"The first time I saw Motörhead was back in 2014 with my mum! I was just getting into metal at this point, and it's safe to say that

Motörhead had a huge impact in my life at the time as I was finding myself.
Was lucky enough to see Motörhead a second time that year!
I loved Lemmy's laid back attitude to life and I wish that I had been able to meet him, but I feel so blessed to have been able to see Motörhead live twice!"
Steph Carys Williams (Woking, Sussex)

"First of all, my beautiful dog is named after the man, the legend, Lemmy.
He was born on the 22nd of September 2000 and was a miracle pup (his mum was a full bred Staffy and dad was a Japanese Aquita cross so vets recommended she have the abortion drug as she wouldn't be able to have the pup as she was so small so she had 2 lots of the drug, but Lem still popped out) and due to him having warts on his face, he was named Lemmy.
Lemmy is 16 this year and I never ever thought that he would out live his name sake!
I was lucky enough to meet the absolute LEGEND that was Ian Fraser LEMMY Kilmister back in 2010. Myself and my partner Stephen went to see Motörhead at the Manchester Apollo. Stephen had been a Motörhead fan since the beginning and he'd never met them so I made it my mission to get him to meet them. After waiting for what seemed like forever, we managed to get backstage to meet Lemmy.
I remember hearing him whilst we stood at the bottom of some stairs and I will never forget just how humble he was. My partner brought his card from his Lemmy figurine to sign and Lemmy knew what it was from He didn't rush us or anything and we had a really nice chat with him. I told him how much Stephen loved Motörhead, how our dog was named after him and just how much of an influence he'd had on us.
I'm so happy that I was lucky enough to meet him."
Helen Löuise Butterfield & Stephen Föź Foster (Huddersfield)

"Motörhead have been a constant support throughout my life, honest true rock 'n' roll.
Nothing has ever touched this true legacy. I still can't believe he is gone and their will be no more gigs or albums, this legacy will live on through MHB throughout the world.
A true gent in rock so polite and respectful. When I met him the 3 times I did he was so polite and spent time to talk and appreciate his fans and sign albums.

His legacy will live forever in MHBangers, hearts love you Lem."
Matthew Botterill MHB1294 (Felixstowe, Suffolk)

"I have been a fan of Motörhead for years and used to work for a band bus company as a mechanic that Motörhead used when they were on tour in Europe and UK.
One day the boss told me he was short of drivers and needed a second driver to take the band and crew from Wolverhampton to Cologne; as you can imagine I didn't to be asked twice.
I met up with them at Wolverhampton and took advantage of my AAA pass I was given as a driver.
After the show we set off for Germany.
I was on the crew bus so I didn't see Lemmy till we were on the ferry where he stood and fed a fruit machine an obscene amount of money for the entire crossing.
By the time we dropped them all off at a hotel in Cologne, parked up at the gig and by the time we got there we were shitfaced just from the fumes in the bus
I just remember stuffing my face with Pringles crisps and anything else we could find and giggling uncontrollably for no reason at all.
Rock on where ever you are Lemmy L&R."
Jon Clark (Bristol)

"I first went to the City Hall to see Motörhead in 2007 with my teenage son Adam Kadmon Bradley.
I bought tshirt at every concert from then until 2012.
I've seen them at Newcastle Arena and O2 Academy but the only place that cud cope with Motörhead was the City Hall.
My Son is now married and living in Canada and is still mad on Motörhead.
I had a ticket for Jan 23rd this year, I cashed it in but I bought their last t'shirt of 'Bad Magic' and their last album of 'Bad Magic'. It's brilliant.
I've never met Lemmy personally but I've never been disappointed at their concerts."
Kim Bradley (Newcastle Upon Tyne)

"I used to drink in the Carlton Bridge on G.W.R near 'Bronze' offices where Motörhead, Girlschool, Algy from Tank used to use in the 80's. One day I was talking with Lemmy then 'Silver Machine' came on the juke box I said "this is a good song" not knowing he sang it.
He said "that's me" & I said "that ain't you" then he proved me

wrong be by singing some of it. Couldn't believe it, in his company and singing to me!!!
I look at my autographs, passes, only had a few photos & I think how very privileged I was to be in that company.
Thank you Lemmy safe journey."
Bert Roberts (London)

"I can't remember when I first heard Motörhead, but it was in the early 1980's, thanks to Tommy Vance's 'Friday Rock Show'. They were on 'Top of the Pops' at some point then too, when Fast Eddie was still on the band.
My first time seeing them play live was actually my first live gig, in 1983 on the 'Another Perfect Day' a Tour, in Aberdeen Capitol Theatre, supported by Anvil!
My favourite album, and one of the first few I owned, is 'Ace Of Spades', I love everything about it.
I've seen them several times since, never enough though, but can't remember how many.
I had a ticket for the sadly cancelled 2016 tour with Saxon and Girlschool, which was the perfect billing for them.
Lemmy was, and will forever be, a LEGEND! RIP."
Stuart Blackhall (Inverness)

"I saw Motörhead five times in my life with my little brother, twice at Bradford St George's Hall and three times in Leeds (Town and Country Club and O2 as it later became).
I managed to catch one of Lemmy's bass plectrums and 2 of Phil Campbell's guitar plectrums over the years.
I was 9 years old the 1st time I ever heard Lemmy sing "Silver Machine" on a cassette called "After Dark" and it changed my life.
Thank you Lemmy, you changed my life, you gave me the strength to fight through all the low times, the high times and the times in between....
Love and respect."
Stuart and Frazer Green (Leeds)

"I realise this goes without saying, but I will never forget the first time I met Lemmy.
I had been introduced to Motörhead's music at a very early age by my dad. He'd been a fan since the very early days and I always enjoyed hearing his stories of the times he saw them play while we listened to their albums. So you can imagine the excitement of a 16 year old me, heading to the Leas Cliff Hall in Folkestone (UK) to

see Motörhead live for the first time!
My dad and I arrived at the venue early so we were first in the queue. Motörhead's tour bus was parked only a short distance away so we decided to wander over and see if any of the band or crew were about.
There was no sign of anyone for about half an hour. We had just begun walking back to the venue when we heard the bus door open. We turned around and right there, walking towards us, was the man himself.
The feeling as he approached was surreal. I was in total awe of his presence. The only way I can describe it, may be an odd thing to say, but it was like that iconic moment when Darth Vader first walks on screen in Star Wars.
Grinning from ear to ear, my dad asks
"Hey Lemmy, can my son get a picture with you?"
Lemmy led us just inside the stage door saying
"Yeah of course. Just a quick one but come in here, the light's better." He put his hand on my shoulder as we posed for my dad to take the photo and said
"Thanks for coming. I hope you enjoy the show," before heading inside.
Such a humble man who never let success go to his head and always made sure his fans got the best Motörhead experience.
In music and memories, may Lemmy's spirit live on forever."
Adam Topley (Maidstone, Kent)

"I only saw Motörhead twice, although have listened to their music on and off for nearly 20 years.
Wasn't till I got with my partner Mick Watford that I went to gigs.
They were amazing live and the atmosphere was electric.
Had tickets for their January gig but obviously due to the sad untimely death of Lemmy I couldn't make it a hat trick. Decided to make a present for my other half for Valentine's day and framed the tickets, can't go wrong with this on the bedroom wall :) xx "
Gini Watford (Waltham Abbey, Essex)

"When I was in my first band the question was asked
"What should we play?"
That was simple. There was only one problem though should it be 'Ace of Spades' or 'Motörhead'?
What a choice. We settled on both.
Lemmy was a legend amongst legends.
RIP big man."

Alan Lewis (Braintree, Essex)

"I first met Lemmy at Glastonbury free festival when Hawkwind played in the 70's. I met him several times more over the next few years as I used to free gig a lot and before he got ousted out of the band in '75.
He was a perfect gent and always remembered me by name whenever I went over to see the guys after the gig. We weren't best mates by a long chalk but I guess you could say we were buddies for a while.
I never saw him again after he left the band but I will always remember him as witty very charming and funny.
Motörhead were awesome and gave us a taste of speed thrash metal long before its time.
You are Sorely missed Lemmy R.I.P dude x x "
Kim Smart (Sheffield)

"I met Lemmy once in 1980 at an amusement arcade in the Strand London. This was after a Hawkwind gig at the Lyceum, where he had just guested playing guitar on 'Route 66' with support band 'Inner City Unit', who ironically were fronted by Nik Turner (who had got him fired from Hawkwind)."
Andrew Woodman (Tetbury, Gloucestershire)

"First time I seen Motörhead back 12 years ago in 2004 I just love everything of Lemmy he was one badass motherfucker and when he smoked on stage and told the crew to fuck off, I knew that this guy was my idol.
Never got to meet the guy, however the people that I know that did meet him also said he was a gent, but a jokester all the time.
I have idolised a lot around him, I had even named my dog after Lemmy.
Born to lose. Live to win!"
Jonny Gray (Belfast)

"I was lucky enough to see Lemmy perform with Motörhead in Birmingham in 2014 and it was the loudest concert I've ever experienced, purely one of the best nights of my life.
He inspired me to learn bass guitar and I use his ideology as a way of helping myself through life's difficult times.
A great inspiration and role model - a great man."
Tom Sumner (Telford)

"It was Download Festival 2012, the first one I ever went to.
I'd seen load of bands with these huge stage sets and long rambling speeches about heavy metal and stuff like that.
Motörhead came on and all they had was a couple of amps and a drum kit. In the first thirty seconds of Lem appearing on stage he managed to get the essence of the music he loved to the crowd.
"We are Motörhead and we play rock and roll," he grunted, and then proceeded to knock out one of the best rock and roll performances I'll ever see.
Pure class, no bullshit. What a legend. I'll remember that gig for the rest of my life."
Dan Willis (Durham)

"I've been listening to Motörhead since I was 10....I am now 45.
Totally blown away by the 'Ace of Spades' album both then and still now. Every album was great.
RIP Lemmy. True legend...."
Jez Hutchings (Bristol)

"My band 'Dealer' supported Motörhead in 1983.
Lemmy was really supportive! He and Phil stood at the side of the stage throughout our whole set. The crowd wanted us to do an encore, we didn't think it would be allowed and started to leave the stage area at which point Lemmy insisted we did an encore!
My pleasure! He was a great guy! Bought me a pint at the Marquee one night also. We used to share rehearsal studios in Willesden, got to know him quite well at the time.
He was a genuinely kind and generous man. I have always held him in the highest regard. RIP you are a legend!"
Trevor Short (Dealer - Vocals/Guitar)

"Many years of seeing the fantastic Motörhead in the UK and at festivals abroad.
All loud rock 'n' roll, always the same big happy smile when you left the gig.
We had tickets for Glasgow in January of 2016...sadly it wasn't to be.
RIP Lemmy."
Neil Russell (Ceres,Scotland)

"I never met Lemmy sadly but I've been a fan of Motörhead since around 1980 .
Being a long life fan of punk rock, Motörhead seemed to fit right in

with the UK punk scene at that time.
Needless to say I have seen Motörhead a few times, up until recently when they played Glasgow supported by the Damned and Anti Nowhere League and the UK Subs.
Lemmy and the band gave us fantastic albums over the years in their various line-ups, we salute them all.
Lemmy though had this aura about him which will shine on forever, the man is most certainly a rock god in a lot of peoples eyes, legendary bass player he most certainly is.
He will be missed ."
Jock Hart (Glenrothes, Scotland)

MCP presents
MOTORHEAD
Plus Guests
GLASGOW BARROWLAND
Monday 12th October 1998
Tickets £11.00 Advance
(Subject To Booking Fee)
Doors 7:30pm
00574

"Lemmy, I think is just a pure icon of rock 'n' roll. The way he is and the way he dresses I think is amazing as most people don't do that anymore, which I hate cos I think Lemmy's style is awesome! His Music is just incredible.
As a starting musician myself, I find nothing better then listening to his albums and they inspire me to work on more music.
I think Lemmy will always be missed and I'll certainly remember him and his great music years from now!"
Tyler Sorsby (Treflys, Porthmadog, Wales)

"I was at his 'Eden Sessions' gig last June.
Had been hoping for years he would be doing another gig locally and fantastic news when I saw he would be here at Eden in Cornwall!
What a brilliant night it was too - I got to see him at what I believe was the gig before his last appearance at Glastonbury. Also saw him taking off in his helicopter after the show. I have to say the

best ever gig I have been to and to hear him play 'Ace of Spades' - a legend indeed.
R.I.P. Lemmy ♠ "
Penny Tyler (St Austell, Cornwall)

"I'm only 14 and people call me weird for loving classic rock music, but I don't get it.
How can you go wrong with the all time greats, Lemmy, Coverdale, Mercury and Gillan?"
Ethan Amos (Sheffield)

"I don't want to jump on the band wagon, but I knew Lemmy Ian Frazier Kilmister as a man, he befriended me when he really didn't have the time or energy.
I knew him when I was a young man and he set me free from abuse and later on in life as a bodyguard I really did love him.
He gave me so much caring advice and comforted me when I was on the edge of totally giving up and ending my life and it was my fault we lost contact (long story).
I wouldn't be where I am now, successful and retired at 50.
I really do owe my friend Lemmy because he saved me, kept in touch and he cared.
He really didn't have to, but he did, love ya pops (that's what I called him).
Thank you. God will know all your good deeds I'm sure of that."
Ian Sutton (Kingston Upon Hull)

"In the 90's I went to see Motörhead at the Mayfair in Newcastle UK. Shoe horned into my tightest leather dress I decided it would be a good idea to scale the stage and have my moment of glory with the mighty band!
After gracefully (not!) scrambling up I boldly walked over to Lemmy and started to dance, we had a brief wiggle of bums before security escorted me from the stage, legs swinging with a mahoosive smile on my face! Now I thought I was sure to be evicted at this point, but no, they settled me down at the side of the stage and told me to 'stay' like a naughty dog!
I watched the rest of the show from the wings! Amazing!
After the show again security escorted me to what I thought was the exit but was actually a room filled with beer, buffet and Lemmy with his hair washed and wrapped in towel (how rock n roll), he laughed at my antics, congratulated me on logistically getting on the stage in my completely inappropriate attire for climbing and

had a brief chat!
One of my best memories EVER!
He was an amazing, genuine, down to earth guy who had time for his fans! x "
Emma Sloan (Newcastle)

"Motörhead were the band that got me into Rock 'n' Roll back in the 80's. The first album I bought was 'No Sleep 'Til Hammersmith' and the first gig I ever went to was Motörhead at the Ipswich Gaumont in 1983.
I was mesmerised by Lemmy that night, thought he was fuckin' awesome.
He was the ultimate 'Rock 'n' Roll Machine'.
We will never see his like again.
God Bless You Lemmy."
Anthony Sawyer (Ipswich)

"I saw my first Motorhead gig in '83, at West Runton up in North Norfolk. Back of beyond, support act didn't turn up but Lemmy and the boys did, and they were awesome!
Also great in Southampton in 2011, still as loud and proud as ever. You could always rely on Lemmy to deliver..."
Alex Mitlehner (Wallingford, Oxfordshire)

West Runton Pavilion
West Runton
July 1st 1983

Back at the Funny Farm
Die You Bastard!
Dancing on Your Grave
Shine
Rock It
Marching Off to War
Iron Horse/Born to Lose
Train Kept A-Rollin'

"It didn't take me long once I had discovered Heavy Metal to

discover Motorhead, and Lemmy. Back in the early nineties I went to see them in Hammersmith, or Kentish Town and having gone on my own, getting there a few hours early, decided to put a few away in a local hostelry.

Having got my pint I looked round at the other punters and saw someone who must have also been early, dressed a bit like Lemmy and sat at the fruit machine, so being an inveterate gambler myself I wandered over and asked how the machine was doing 'fucking crap' came the reply.

On closer inspection this geezer even looked like Lemmy, about ten minutes of general talk later the penny finally dropped, I was in the presence of the great man himself! Having worked this out I then asked him if the bits of screwed up tinfoil next to the machine were his, he replied yes, and then gave me a look that suggested there had better be no windup or piss taking about to happen!!

I pulled out the little yellow eggs which were my 'Kinder Eggs' I ate on the way to the gig had contained and said 'Great Minds!' to which I got my first proper Lemmy Grin aimed at me!!

He then started to complain about how many he had been through trying to get a particular painted tortoise, and when I pulled one of it out of my pocket and offered it to him, I got the most grateful appreciation imaginable, nothing fake or contrived.

Lemmy then made me accept a few of his spare ones, rather than just take mine from me!

We talked about family history (we both had the right to wear the Fraser Tartan) and put the world to rights with basic alcohol fuelled common sense! (I'm also sure he found me during the gig and kept looking straight at me, but that might just be my imagination...)

A few years later I bumped into him again, also in London before a gig, and before I had even noticed him, I heard

"Skull, over here mate" from him (cue one seriously impressed ex girlfriend!) Where the conversation carried on as if our last chat had been a fortnight earlier.

I was lucky enough to meet Lemmy a further half a dozen times, he always remembered who I was, brought up old conversations, and was a joy to be in company with.

When I tell people that the Lemmy you saw interviewed was exactly the same Lemmy that I saw when I talked with him they were surprised, but the great man was always himself, a lesson a lot of people could learn!!

I still have my old patched up gig jacket, to which Lemmy once went through my patches –

"played with them, toured with them, toured with them, toured with

them, I think I toured with them (early 70's, if you know what I mean!) toured with them, toured with them." The only group he could not remember sharing a bill with were Led Zeppelin, and he was probably just too zonked at the time to remember!!!)
I will miss him for the rest of my life, but always be grateful for the time I spent with him, and the Fuckin' amazing music he gave the world!"
Paul 'Skull' Gutteridge (King's Lynn, Norfolk)

"Loved 'em since childhood but the live experience somehow evaded me 'til the 'Inferno' tour.
Fuck, they were loud.
Next time I saw Lemmy he was playing 'Back in the USA' with Wayne Kramer at Download. Awesome and then Motörhead.
I know Donington's next to the airport and Concorde used to drown out the noise a little but if Concorde had come down on the tent that day the first we'd have known about it would have been seeing the nose cone. No one will ever be as loud or probably as great.
I was on a trip to London when I found out THE devastating news and promptly ordered a large JD on the first boat of the day on the Thames in his honour.
Rock In Peace Lemmy and thanks for the soundtrack to my life. \m/ "
Dale Nicholson (Skipton, North Yorkshire)

"When I first met Lemmy, I took the opportunity of introducing myself as 'Shaun - drummer for 'My Dying Bride' ....
His immediate response was,
"hello mate' .... ahh yes, you're that bunch of miserable bastards from up north."
We laughed a lot after that statement, from that moment, I took a real shine to Lemmy. We spoke at length about our passion and personal interest in our German Reich memorabilia although, my collection paled significantly compared to his.....
I've always been a huge fan of Motörhead so, I was tempted to ask Lemmy if he would hire me then fire me for Motörhead drumming duties but I never got around to that....hehe..........
I will never forget how kind and generous Lemmy was.
After our first meeting at the 'Grasspop Festival' and at future gigs, even going out of his way to say 'hello' and shake my hand whenever we met.....he always gave me good advice just like a wise older uncle...I said to him ,

"So you mind if I call you Uncle Lemmy?"
His reply was, "not at all son, I've been called worse!"
I miss you very much Lemmy, every day I think about you......
Love you mate eternally,
I will miss you so much Lemmy and I feel so very privileged to have known you....."
Shaun 'Winter' Taylor-Steels (My Dying Bride – Drums)

"Saw Motorhead at Exeter University in 2008. Lemmy was imperious throughout their set, thrashing out hits such as 'Iron Fist' and 'Ace of Spades'.
I didn't understand a bloody word of the new tracks, but they were loud and rocked.
May Lemmy and his mesmeric mole rest in peace."
Gary Martin (Plymouth)

The University Great Hall Exeter, Devon 19th November 2008

Iron Fist
Stay Clean
Metropolis
In the Name of Tragedy
Rosalie
Just 'Cos You Got the Power
Going to Brazil
Killed by Death
Bomber
Whorehouse Blues
Ace of Spades
Overkill

"Only saw the great man once.

'Orgasmatron' live made the hairs on the back of my neck stand up.
RIP Lemmy X"
Graham Orr (Johnstone, Renfrewshire)

"Saw Motörhead in June 1983 at Leicester UK, they were magnificent! Robbo played a blinder.
Beforehand Anvil were playing and Lemmy just walked through the band put his hand up, the place went crazy!!
'Another Perfect Day' is my fave album by them especially the dainty little ballad 'Die You Bastard' is a killer track!"
Ian Eric Muddiman (Loughborough)

"Only every saw Motörhead twice, Sheffield where I got told off for taking too many pics of Lemmy :) still carried on and I have the pics blown up and laminated and then in Newcastle while I was pregnant with my eldest who's now 7. She was going mad in my stomach listening to them."
Michelle Wainwright (Workington, Cumbria)

"I told Lemmy that we, (The Babysitters), play 'Overkill' faster than Motörhead."
He replied,
"I don't give a shit, I get £20 every time your version's played".
Buttz (The Babysitters - Vocals)

"I first got into Motörhead back in the 80's it all started for me when I got a copy of 'Ace of Spades' signed by Fast Eddie Clarke.
The first time I put it on my turntable and dropped the needle I thought WOW!! Who are these guys?
Since then many albums and singles later I'm still as huge fan. The friends and friendships I have made because of Motörhead and their fans is amazing.
I was gutted when the news that Lemmy had died so I sat at home all day and played non-stop Motörhead.
Lemmy left all Motörhead fans a true legacy with his music. The man was a true rock and roll giant, gone but not forgotten.
Thanks for the music and the memories.
R.I.P... IAN LEMMY KILMISTER."
Mick Lamont MHB4210 (Barnsley)

"Best memory of all for me of all the gigs I've been to was the Southampton gig supported by The U.K.SUBS & A.N.L. 15th Nov

*In my drunken stupor on the night I heard he'd died I Tweeted that "He was the best friend that I'd never met", I still believe that.
He, and Motörhead, had been in my life since I was 10 years old. Both are gone, but neither will ever be forgotten. Ever."*
Jason Lavender (Dudley)

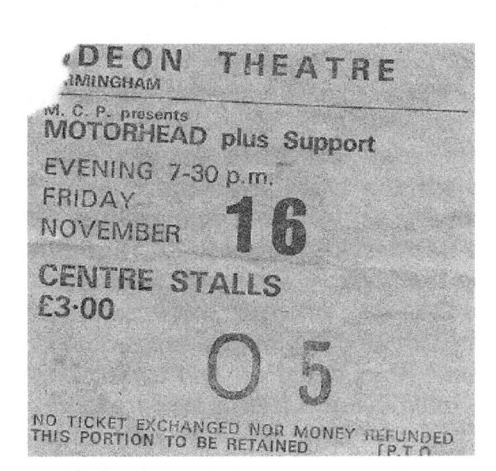

> ODEON THEATRE
> BIRMINGHAM
> M. C. P. presents
> MOTORHEAD plus Support
> EVENING 7-30 p.m.
> FRIDAY
> NOVEMBER 16
> CENTRE STALLS
> £3·00
> O 5
> NO TICKET EXCHANGED NOR MONEY REFUNDED
> THIS PORTION TO BE RETAINED. [P.T.O

"My most memorable Motörhead gig was at Birmingham back in 2000 when they were supported by Anthrax and Vixen. Was a fab evening, not long after John Entwhistle died, something not lost on Lemmy who insisted on a rousing cheer for the Who bassist. His sense of humour too always made us smile.
But my memory is of a Hawkwind gig .
Early December 1972 and Hawkwind were touring the 'Space Ritual'.
I and two school friends went to the Margate, Kent leg of the tour and had great seats; about 10 rows back in the centre. We had heard that they played the ritual then came back to do 'Silver Machine' as an encore. Well, we never had 'Silver Machine' that night as a power cut stopped the show for 20 minutes or so, not long before 'Brainstorm'.
There we were, in the dark, being treated to a drum solo. And it got better and better and better.
We couldn't see a thing, but the quality of this solo was beyond measure. How many sticks did this guy have? Six as it turned out as we got the answer.
After about twenty minutes a small generator gave the stage some light. There was Lemmy and Nik Turner helping out from the front of the kit. No wonder it sounded good. Anyway the light came on

and an alarmed Lemmy turned round looking very much like he had been caught in the act. With wide eyes he look at us in the crowd and shouted
"SHIT! WE'VE BEEN RUMBLED!"
At which point he threw the sticks in the air and ran off the stage, to loads of laughter and applause from us out front.
What a star! Genuine Guy even back then."
Paul Richardson (King's Sutton, South Northamptonshire)

"I can't say I was ever a massive fan but I was lucky enough to see Motörhead support Alice Cooper in November 2007 at Newcastle Arena. Other ageing rockers, Joan Jett & the Blackhearts opened.
No offense to them but unlike Joan Jett and co, Motörhead were not a nostalgia act.
Tearing things up immediately with 'Doctor Rock', along came 'Stay Clean' and 'Killers'. Unfamiliar with most of their newer material or set lists in general, had I not believed that this was just an after effect of bleeding ears, I could have sworn that they even tossed a Bob Seger cover in there... Of course, 'Ace of Spades' and 'Overkill' sent the arena into a frenzy as lager flew in the air, mine without warning that such an event was going to happen, and then it was time to go home. Except it wasn't and Mr Cooper was still to come. Good luck following that.
It's become cliché to say but Lemmy may well have been the last real rock star.
He didn't have a gimmick, he didn't play a character, he definitely wasn't a poser and he never marketed himself as anything other than a regular guy. He was a tough fella in a leather jacket who drank whiskey and yet, despite playing loud music, always came across as very lovable.
It occurs to me that there's not enough likeable rough looking blokes in the world anymore."
Stevie Aaron (Stockton-on-Tees)

"**1979** I was 15 & a total Punk fan. Obsessed with Crass and the like.
On my weekly visit to the mighty Records & Tapes in Falmouth I used my limited funds and purchased, what I had been led to believe (not by the shop I hasten to add), a new Punk single, a certain 'Overkill' 7" by Motörhead.
On getting home and playing it I was slightly bemused and if I'm honest a tad disappointed as it certainly wasn't what I expected (being young and narrow minded). 12 months later I had an

epithany and discovered NWOBHM and rediscovered my "mistaken" purchase. Now all these years later it is one of my all time favourite singles by anyone. Pure Classic

1981 Cornwall Coliseum my first Motörhead gig. Though I'd seen Saxon previously, I was not quite prepared for the aural onslaught that I was about to get from Motoörhead. All I can remember was how great they sounded and my ears rung for about two days.

1986 on my second Donington 'Monsters of Rock', watching an incredible set from Motörhead, a plane flew over (from East Midlands Airport) and for the first time the band drowned out the jet.

Lemmy 1 Jet Plane 0

I was there with my lady, Catherine (many years before we got together), I was shocked to see her wearing an Orgasmatron t-shirt, her being a nice girl and all lol.

Still to this day she reminds me that, perhaps, I was being a bit hypocritical as I was wearing a W.A.S.P. 'F*ck Like A Beast' shirt – ooops!!!

2015 was a spectacular but, in hindsight, a very sad gig at the Eden Project. After a truly magnificent set by the Stranglers we had an immense (but now understandably short one hour set) .It was obviously a bit of a struggle for Lemmy as I don't remember him moving much but to the end he gave every bit of himself. A legend right to the end."

Rick Mathews (Falmouth, Cornwall)

"Met Lemmy many times over the years, never failed to be a gentleman.

Back in the days of the Marquee Club in Soho, London he was often in there, playing the machines, listening to the bands, talking to the punters or signing autographs he never came across as the ' big rock star '.

He earned a lot of undying respect around then..."

Jo Bicheno (London)

"I first saw Motörhead in 1977, at the art college in Maidstone, I was hooked. I brought the first album I could lay my hands on 'Motörhead' followed by 'Overkill'.

In 1983 I got the chance to work for the fan club 'Motörheadbangers'. Philthy's sister was organising a battle of the bands to be staged in Manchester and a few of us from around the country looked for bands to take part by sending demo tapes to her.

We all met one day in Manchester, all of Motörhead were there and I was greeted by Lemmy clutching a bottle of Smirnoff. I was given a pass for all areas, wow!

The day went on with many memorable moments culminating with a few of us chatting with the band in a small room with a table full of food and alcohol. I had done it I had met my idols and the legend that is Lemmy.

Moving on a few years, I have a son who's just as much a fan as I am.

Folkestone 18.11.2005 Adam and I are at the Leas Cliff Hall a few hours before the gig, the tour bus is parked a couple of hundred yards away, not wanting to disturb the band we wait patiently.

The door of the bus opens and a solitary figure appears out of the darkness, easily recognisable as Lemmy. We walked towards him said hello and exchanged pleasantries. I asked if I could have a picture of him with my son. He obliged with a huge smile dragging us into an open door where the light was better. Picture taken we were happy. Whether the photo made a difference I don't know but the show was amazing.

17th November 2012. The O2 academy Brixton, here we are again camped outside the stage door with several other diehard fans. A couple of hours pass with the door opening and closing frequently with the usual road crew coming and going occasionally stopping for a cheeky smoke.

The question is has Lemmy done the sound check? Then close to 5pm a black limo pulls up outside and out gets the man, sharp dressed in his usual gear unique only to him. There is a jostle for position and I manage to speak with Lemmy once again asking if Adam can take a picture of us. Once again the request is greeted with a smile. Adam is a member of a band himself and hands Lemmy an album, he opens it ready to sign it before we say, no, it's for you. Thanks he says placing it in the hands of his female assistant. He then carries on signing and posing for pictures with at least a couple of dozen others before making his way inside.

We saw Motörhead last at Wembley Arena, access to the band impossible but a fantastic evening once again. It was obvious that Lemmy was slowing down as his movement around the stage wasn't as it was in his younger days but the voice and the bass guitar were there in all their glory.

We were due to see Motörhead in January 2016 but Lemmy passed away a month before.

Rest in peace Lemmy."

Steve Topley (Maidstone, Kent)

"I saw them 18 times in total, last time Cambridge 2012. Me and a friend in 2009 saw them in Treptow Arena Berlin. A massive box ticked I'm so glad we saw a German show."
Tim Harvey (UK)

"I maybe an old rocker but it was Lemmy who was responsible for sewing the seeds. Hawkwind and the classic 'Silver Machine' was a catalyst to my interest in music and it was Lemmy who stuck to his rock principles.
Motörhead will be an everlasting legacy to rockers both old and new."
Paul Paskins (Plymouth)

"I am Led Blything, Motörhead fan since 1978.
My name is Led due to me finding a Led Zeppelin '3' LP when I was 13.
We all taped our mates LP's back in the day. A friend wanted to lend my LP. He offered in exchange Motörhead's 'Overkill'. I heard it once and my love of Motörhead started there
I have seen 'em 159 times, even in East Berlin.
I got drunk with Lemmy and Motörhead on so many occasions I feel blessed.
My grandson Raven is learning drums and uses Mikkey Dee drumsticks lol. His favourite song is 'Year of the Wolf' off 'Inferno'. Storm is only 5. Her favourite song is what ever I play lol.
They both love Motörhead cause their friends in school love their t-shirts and everything else I get them.
Lemmy and Motörhead are my life. I know they haven't been all my life but I can't remember them not being there.
My favourite track, well 'Devils' off 'Bastards' but I love 'em all
I am ex-army so obviously I was really close to Wurzel.
Favourite album? Mmm.. all of 'em lol"
Led Blything (Haverfordwest)

"My name is Sam Westrup, I'm 23, and probably not the typical rock fan to look at. Growing up in rural Suffolk, there was defiantly no long hair, no tattoos, no piercings. I was a decent school student and to be honest I never had a need to 'rebel'.
So how did I associate with Motörhead and in particular, Lemmy?
Like so many others, I discovered the rich world of Rock 'n' roll in my early teens, bands like AC/DC, Status Quo, Blue Oyster Cult and Ted Nugent being some of the earliest bands I found in a case

of my Father's old Cassette tapes.
Wow what a box of treasures that was. Every cassette held a new band, and with it a new history to discover. My father noticed my new 'interest' and had soon set up his old PAL record player and unboxed his similarly vast collection of Vinyl, picking out the choice cuts of Zeppelin and Skynyrd, before handing me the record that became 'The One'.
With 'The Bomber' hanging over the stage, heaps of amps and cabinets on stage and the bright stage lights 'No Sleep 'till Hammersmith' just looked right. There was no cheesy Sci-Fi inspired artwork, just a live band playing live.
"Now this is a favourite" my father said, "of course its mainly just noise but...."
'But' indeed.
From the opening tape intro and Lemmy's rattling bass I was hooked. This was the band for me. Loud, Fast, Dirty, Raucous. Everything my life hadn't been. Dressed in jeans and jackets they didn't care, they just loved their music. If it wasn't for you... then move along.
I soon collected as many LP's as I could. The earlier albums being quite easy to find cheaply (shout out to Out Of Time Records Ipswich!) and with my high school friend/deviant Chris Lawrence, we began our consumption of Motör-history.
In 2008 I found the band were playing my local town, Ipswich Regent and me and Chris snapped up tickets at once (paid for in loose change if I remember ha-ha!). Third row on the balcony we sat through openers Danko Jones and then the support band Saxon who we were also in awe of. We had never seen a band play like them before, and we enjoyed every minute (especially Biff's reference to their earlier ban from the venue)
But Motörhead were a cut above.
The 'Motorizer' tour featured a huge light rig, with the twin TV screens on either side of the stage showing shots of the band and album covers.
"Good evening Ipswich!"
"How-are-you-alright?" Lemmy blared at once.
"We are MOTÖRHEAD and we play Rock 'N' Roll."
'Iron Fist', 'Stay Clean', 'Be My Baby', 'Metropolis'...
Wow. You Never forget your first Motörhead gig. The sense of power, volume, intent, the electric, crackling atmosphere, the deafening roar of approval from the crowed as the support bands backdrop came down and Motoörhead's was raised. The feeling of unity. We were all there to see our favourite band. Because at

least for the gig only, Motörhead was EVERYONE'S favourite band.

Lemmy stayed true to his vision of Motörhead in 1975 "A loud rock and roll band. Of the MC5 variety. On stage Bang bang bang, done"

I started seeing every gig I could. I saw the band 10 more times – Cambridge, Norwich, London, Leicester, Donington... The tour shirt collection grew the flyers the tickets the LP's and cd's.

I joined the Motörheadbangers fan club, and got a MHB magazine signed by Lemmy outside the Cambridge Corn Exchange. A brief handshake, a "Did you enjoy it? Loud enough for ya?" "thanks for coming out" and he stomped on to the bus.

The first gigs were cancelled in 2013, rescheduled for February, and cancelled again. Lemmy showed signs of ageing. Christ, he was in his late 60's, but eventfully the 2014 Wembley show came around.

I never really imagined this would be my last show, but I am glad to have seen the band on one last hurrah, playing a packed arena at full throttle. A great set list with some different tracks added, 'Shoot 'Em In the Back', 'No Class' and 'Suicide' before a crushing 'Overkill'.

I had tickets booked for the 'Tour That Never Was', Swindon and both Hammersmith shows, but sadly now just the tickets remain.

Lemmy will never be forgotten.

"Don't forget us; We Are Motörhead, and we play ROCK N' ROLL!"

Sam Westrup MHB 3465 (Suffolk)

The SSE Arena, Wembley, London 8th November 2014

Shoot You in the Back
Damage Case
Stay Clean
Metropolis
Over the Top

The Chase is Better Than the Catch
Rock It
Suicide
No Class
Lost Woman Blues
Doctor Rock
Just 'Cos You Got the Power
Going to Brazil
Killed by Death
Ace of Spades
Overkill

"So it's Newport October 2002 on one of the tours when they were playing 'God Save The Queen' (and R.A.M.O.N.E.S!!!).
Lemmy intros the song by asking,
"Are there any punks in?"
Of course everyone's shouting and Lem's taking the piss out of people-
"You ain't a punk, you've got long hair!"
I'm right down the front with my mate Jez, who's the biggest punk rocker ever. I've got my Ramones gig t-shirt on which I'm holding out displaying the band name and screaming at Lem.
Lemmy looks down, points at me and says,
"Ramon-ez" like it's in Spanish!
Of course, my name is Ramone (I changed it 'cus I kind of like The Ramones) so it was like Lemmy knew me and recognised me in the crowd!
They launch into 'God Save The Queen' and we all go crazy.
So although I never actually met Lemmy we did 'connect' on one of the many times I saw Motörhead over the years. It's something I will never forget.
Thanks Lemmy, for all the music and memories."
Keith Ramone (Hereford)

"Growing up in our house in the late 70's couldn't be described as a musical cornucopia, neither of my parents were musical and thus our exposure consisted of Top of the Pops on Thursday nights and the Chart run down on Sunday evening. In fact, the next door neighbours habit of coming home wrecked from the pub and putting on Terry Jacks at all hours did more for my musical journey *than any of my mother & fathers dismissive rants about the 'state of music today!'*

Around 1980 everyone in my class, suddenly appeared with the names of Rock bands scrawled across their bags, even better; TOTP and the chart show now interspersed rock bands in between dross like the Barron Knights, Showaddywaddy and St Winifred School Choir. I couldn't help but notice the roughest, nastiest looking band of all were Motörhead. After my best mate bought 'Ace of Spades', we spent many happy hours listening to it. I was hooked, I was happy!

A glorious 18 months ensued where Motörhead appeared on every two bob kids show, upset the disco freaks at the BBC and generally made peoples lawns die across the UK. 'No Sleep Til Hammersmith' saw more TV & radio and then . . . . . It all hit a bit of a brick wall; my classmates decided that Duran Duran, Wham! and Boy George offered a more female friendly avenue to pursue. My best mate gave me the copy of 'Ace of Spades', which I still have!! But apart from one kindred spirit, I carried on my love affair with this aural assault alone.

Gigs weren't really an option for 2 reasons, primarily because Cambridge's main venue was in the midst of a 5 or 6 year long refit, but also, travelling alone to London wasn't really an option with parents who saw London as dangerous and Motörhead as a 'bloody row'

Fast forward to September 1986, I'm now at 6th form, the '8 days in June' tour to support 'Orgasmatron', some like minded mates from the new school decided it was time to go to London. One chap persuaded his highly religious father to drive us in his Lada, fine in theory, but obviously 4 blokes in a Lada?! It was always going to break down, it duly did close to Hanger Lane Tube station. We left the auld fella to haggle with the AA, leapt on the Tube and made it to the Hammersmith Odeon only about an hour after curtain up.

The road leading to the Odeon brought into sharp focus all my parents warnings as it did appear to be filled with every sort of crazy looking nutter imaginable. Clearly a lot of chemical and liquid refreshment had been taken.

In we trooped, it was hot dark, reeked of cigarettes of every composition. All around me vast behemoths clad in denim & leather milled around the venue, the hair long, faces weathered.

We moved to our places! Then, a vision appeared, the great man himself through clouds of smoke, the PA burst into life, I was transfixed for the hour and 15 mins of the show, my ears were crushed, I sang every word, stared intently and drank in the experience. Fellow Motörhead fans know the feeling, but for those outside, I have always likened it to going to church if you are a truly religious person. You are inspired, you feel uplifted and you feel renewed.

Suitably renewed, we left the venue, and in the pre mobile phone era, wondered how to get the 55 miles up the road to Cambridge. The God fearing Lada driver was nowhere to be seen, I knew better than to dare to ring my parents. Finally we coaxed a friend into driving down! I got home about 04:30. I couldn't hear, I could barely speak, and I managed to spend at least 3 days in a slightly befuddled state.

Attendance at the 'Church of Motörhead' carried on, I took friends, girlfriends and anyone who enjoyed what to me was heaven on earth. Across London, Cambridge, Leicester, Birmingham, Bristol, Nottingham and Belfast I caught almost every tour in the subsequent 30 years. In 1988 I met the man, it was raining, for some reason he seemed 20 feet high, his scantily dressed girlfriend was infinitely more enticing than talking to me, but he stopped & said Hi. Whilst normally so garrulous I was tongue-tied and mumbling.

Through every stage of my life over 35 years, the band was omnipresent, dealing with every set back, there were lyrics to help, as a sound track to party to, there was always a tune. It didn't matter if your girlfriend has run off with the janitor, it doesn't matter that your fathers ill, lost a job? Wife spent tens of thousands on credit cards? Not to worry, there is some solace, some advice and some reinvigoration courtesy of the man with the white cowboy boots and his friends.

I last saw the boys in 2012, I had to tell a little white lie to my wife just to be there, whilst I stood in the circle looking down as Lemmy played the same beautiful tunes I had first heard all those years before, I looked around and saw that the sea of long hair had gone bald and grey in parts but amongst us there were people with their children and first time teenagers enjoying it just as I had all those years ago.

Lemmy always said that you shouldn't have regrets, my only regret is that my own son will never experience that unadulterated joy that you feel when you see Motörhead walk out on stage and the first notes from the bass spring forth from the PA.

Ian Fuller (UK)

"Great gig (Exeter) - supposed to leave early to catch last train back to Plymouth but took a chance and after nearly killing

ourselves plunging down what seemed like a ravine in the grounds we made it back to the station where, true to form the train was running late so we made it home having seen the whole gig!"
Kirsty Tonks (Plymouth)

> Live Nation present
>
> # motörhead
>
> Plus Special Guests
>
> **In The Great Hall**
> Exeter University
> Wednesday 19th November 2008
> Doors 7:00pm
> Ticket £25.00 Advance (STBF)
> Over 14's only will be admitted
>
> 01417

"I started listening to heavy rock Music when I was around 11 years old, much to the annoyance of my parents, and always followed the code of "everything louder than anything else".
By the age of 13 I wore nothing but denim and my Levi jacket that was of course customised with embroidery and patches of the bands I loved, I still have it now, I also accumulated 7 different stereos to see which had the best sound and volume.
Motörhead were a big part of my youth and helped me through my teenage angst, even if it was just to backlash at the world, and my parents, the power and energy of the music, the anarchic attitude, all helped to shape my world and supported my need to be different and not just one of the crowd, while others girls my age were into Wham! etc I was rocking hard to AC/DC, Gillan, Sabbath etc and the only thing I wanted for my 16th birthday was a ticket to Monsters of Rock! Reluctantly my parents agreed to let me go and I had a great time. My love of heavy rock has never altered and although I am interested in all kinds of music, rock always pulls me back to my roots.
I didn't get to see Motörhead live until Download Festival 2013 and I have to say they were worth the wait.
I almost cried when "Philthy Animal" Phil Taylor joined them on stage; it was such an emotional moment. I was so sad when he passed away and appreciated even more that I had got to see the band live.
I was planning to see Motörhead again this year but of course then came the News of Lemmy's death! Such a shock!

The Godfather of rock had left us!
There was no one quite like Lemmy, he lived his life the way he wanted and was a hero to many. Motörhead's music will always survive through their fans and will be passed to future generations I am sure.
The world has lost an icon!
RIP Lemmy and thanks for helping me become who I am!
Over the last 35 years you have inspired and helped me to survive this world.
I salute you!"

Helen English (Barnsley)

"In the early/mid 80's Tank were under the same management as Motörhead so our paths crossed on a regular basis. Be it on the road, in the office or more likely down the local pub.
Lemmy was a familiar face in several of the London clubs I frequented around that time. The St Moritz on Wardour Street being one of his regular watering holes as it had the all essential fruit machine, a good selection of Euro slags and a plentiful supply of his drug of choice.
He very rarely engaged in conversation while playing the machine and would only take a break to order a Jack and Coke before leaving unnoticed into the night.
He only spoke to you if he wanted to. Sometimes for hours, other times he'd just blank you.
I never saw any evidence of him being the wild man of rock that he was portrayed as, just a nice mild mannered chap who liked a drink and to mind his own business.
He had nothing to prove when he wasn't on stage.
Obviously when he was on stage it was a different story!
As a kid growing up in the 1970's, hearing 'Silver Machine' for the first time immediately turned me into a Hawkwind fan and I started to collect their albums which I mainly bought secondhand from the record stalls of Portobello Road market.
On a Saturday afternoon I would go with friends to the Mountain Grill Cafe on Portobello, because of the Hawkwind connection, and get a plate of greasy chips as we studied the sleeve notes on the latest albums we'd picked up.
We met a hippy biker called 'Speed' in there one afternoon who very kindly informed us that Lemmy could always be found drinking in a pub called the 'Earl of Lonsdale' which was just a little further up the Portobello Road.
Motörhead's limited edition 12 inch EP single 'Motörhead' had just

been released by the Chiswick Label which I'd bought from Rock On records next to Camden Town tube station the previous week.
We walked up the road to the Lonsdale, slightly nervous, not just at the thought of seeing Lemmy but because we were only 15 year old school kids and doubted that we would be allowed into the pub. Fortunately we were tall for our age and the barman looked so whacked out of it he could have actually been in Hawkwind at some point so there was no problem getting served a bottle of Sam Smiths.
Across the bar in the far corner was the unmistakable figure of Lemmy.
He was standing on his own, feeding the fruit machine with attitude. Looked like he didn't care if he'd win or lose. Just playing the game.
We watched him for what seemed like several hours and tried to avoid any eye contact so he wouldn't get pissed off with us.
We returned to the Earl of Lonsdale every Saturday for the rest of 1977 and on the odd occasion he'd take the time to chat to us which made the weekly pilgrimage more than worth while.
He was the first real rock star I'd ever met so having the privilege of touring, working and occasionally drinking with him several years later, in a professional situation, was something I never could have imagined.
RIP Lemmy.
An irreplaceable loss to the spirit of rock and roll."
Cliff Evans (Tank - Guitar)

"Saw the great man at Port Vale in the 80's, went with my young brother it was his first open air festival.
What an awesome day we ended up being interviewed by a local radio station.
Great memories R.I.P Lemmy \m/ \m/ "
Maurice Dicky Denwood (Whitehaven, Cumbria)

"I saw Motörhead twice. Once at Wembley Arena and Sonisphere. At Wembley Arena he sang two or three Thin Lizzy songs as he was mates with Phil Lynott.
He blew my mind as I am disabled, it was even more special for me as I ain't the most mobile or quick person, but well worth it.
R.I.P LEMMY KILMINSTER."
Danny Rana (London)

"I wasn't a huge Motörhead fan, admired from afar really until my

buddy Matt Wilkes messaged me saying he had a spare ticket for December 2014 at Birmingham.
I thought what the hell, might be a good gig so I paid for the ticket and started to listen to the back catalogue.
This is when I went from an occasional listener to a fanatic, the music, the way Lemmy enjoyed his life, almost like a religion.
We were so lucky to witness them that December and when Philthy Taylor and Fast Eddie came on stage for the rendition of 'Ace of Spades' was of dreams.
I might have only seen Motörhead once but they made a mark on my life forever."
Wayne (metalhead) Griffiths (Tywyn, Mid Wales)

"I first saw Motörhead in 1976, got the bug straight off.
I saw gigs at the Marquee, Music Machine, Nashville, Roundhouse, Dingwalls and anywhere in London if it was possible. As a 17yr old being deaf for 3 days afterwards was a right of passage.
One gig that really stands out was in a Pub, in Putney called The White Lion I think. There were 15/20 of us who would turn up most places and be down the front. I really thought I could handle anything noise wise, but not this time.
Being pretty much 5 foot in front of the band, after 20 or so minutes trying desperately to face front ways, I had to turn my head to one side, giving 1 ear a brief respite.
Not sure how I made it thru' to the blissful end.
Happily deaf again!!!!!!!!!"
Rob Martin (Camden, London)

"I was working for a PA company providing a sound rig for a Motörheadbangers battle of the bands competition in mid 1980 at which Lemmy, Eddie & Phil had attended.
It was a long day during which we frequently crossed paths with Lemmy, Eddie, Phil and various other members of their entourage which inclued Phil's sister Helen.
After the gig we were invited up to a room set aside for Motörhead and being a fan of the band I took the opportunity to sit with them in this room listening to the various conversations and jokes that bounced around the room and drank my bottle of vodka & orange that Lemmy had thrusted into my hand.
After some time I found myself chatting with Phil's sister (Helen) about the band amongst other things and she asked if I was going along to watch the band on their latest tour. I told her that I was

planning on going to the gig at Deeside Leisure Centre in North Wales (the nearest to my home at the time).

Helen said to come along anyway as she would be there and I could come backstage before the gig and hang out with the band & crew and that I should just ask at the Leisure Centre for her or the lads and they'd let us in to see them....

November 8th - 1980

So there I was with my mate Joza who was a avid Hawkwind & Motörhead fan making our way to a side door (which was basically a gateway into the back of the building) surrounded by loads of shouting fans who cheered every now and then as they witnessed a passing figure (regardless of who it was) walking across the bottom of the long corridor that ran down from this doorway.

The doorway had some kind of metal security gate on it and was manned by one of the leisure centre's security staff...and this guy was a proper Jobsworth.

People would be told to "move away" and to "keep the area clear..." as the fans gathered for an opportunity to see their heroes. Shocked at the amount of people gathered we made our way towards the gate where this security guard was (stood inside of the gate).

As I managed to get to the front pushing my way forward I'm greeted with a surge of fans pushing towards the doorway cheering as yet another shadowy figure walks passed the end of the corridor (another member of the road crew) they just look out towards the crowds as they walk on by.

"Excuse me!" I say to the Security guard

"I was told to come to this gate to meet someone and that you'd be able to let me in?..."

The guard looks at me with squinting eyes of disbelief like he hadn't heard me correctly (probably because of the noise)...

"What did You say?" he replies ..

"I'm here to meet someone, they're expecting me!" I say to him.

"Really? And who might that be?" he replies.

Confidently I answer back with "Yes Helen Taylor and the guys from the band.... Motörhead? They know I'm coming, they're expecting me?"

He looks at me for a second with a blank look on his face as if he is digesting the statement then his face changes to a smirk as he replies with the words "yeah of course mate! You and all these people behind you son

I look at him, I turn to my friend who's giving me that 'I Knew It' look of disbelief in my story on his face, and I turn back to the

security guard and in frustration reply back to him with
"Honestly I am! Just go and get someone, go and ask for Helen Taylor she knows me."
But it was clearly falling on deaf ears as he just begins to shout out at the fans (me & my friend included) to move away from the doorway.
I'm not sure how long I was standing there for (probably not that long at all) but it seemed an eternity. I'm standing there by the doorway trying to convince my friend that my story was true and that I had been invited backstage - him looking at me then looking at his watch as he says
"we best start thinking about getting round to the entrance to get in if we want a good view otherwise we'll be stuck at the back."
The crowds cheer again as another figure passes the end of the corridor ... Again the crowd give a little shuffle towards the gate as they try to see who it is (it's a member of the support band) he gives a quick wave as he walks away.
At this point I'm beginning to think am wasting my time, no one's gonna let us in and my story of meeting Motörhead a few weeks previous and the promise of getting in to meet them was starting to look like a yarn to my friend Joza.
Suddenly there's a huge roar as the crowd catch a glimpse of a tall longhaired dark shadowy figure walking past the end of the corridor.
"Lemmy!" "Lemmy!" they shout ...
It was indeed the man himself raising his hand to the crowds to signal his gratitude for support from the crowds waiting patiently for a glimpse of their idol. And then just as quickly as he appeared he turns and walks off....
Suddenly the crowd cheers loudly again as Lemmy appear again but this time he's walking towards the gateway... heading towards us all.
To my amazement - he walks right up to the gate and looks directly at me and winks - I'm standing there with fans pushing me and my friend forward as they surge in excitement towards the gateway.
Lemmy looks at me then turns to the security guard and says
"He's with us - let him in!" And turns to walk away...
I shout to Lemmy "Lemmy! I've got my mate with me...."
He looks back at the guard and says
"let him in too!"
My mate is stunned - the face on the security guard was a picture as I give him that 'I f**king told you so' look on my face as he lets

us in through the gate... Lemmy walks off down the corridor and we follow him into the green room where the support band Tank and Phil Taylor are sitting drinking and talking.
"Get yourselves a drink and find a seat" Lemmy says and walks off into another room...
I felt honoured that Lemmy had remembered me from that Motörheadbangers gig and could have quite easily have just walked off considering all the amount of screaming shouting fans standing at that gate... He could have picked anyone, but he didn't, he picked me, because he remembered me.
That was a big turning point in my life that gave me the fortuitous opportunity to get to know and work with the band (albeit for a short time) something I will always treasure.
Lemmy never forgot people, he was a gent.
He never forgot me that day and for that I will always remember him.♠"
Gary 'Chopper' Lee (Liverpool)

"Fond memories of my biker days, many a drunken bike rally spent rocking out to Motörhead.
A legend has gone, but still lives on in many a person memories."
Jane Carden (Plymouth)

"I never met the great man himself but know others who have.
I have over the years always seen Motörhead at the Manchester Apollo, a friend of mine worked security there and told me that one of the best bands in its treatment of people was Motörhead.
He said that Lemmy was a gent, always spoke to the security staff and invited them to after show parties.
Sadly the last few years when Lemmy became poorly, took its toll. The last time they played there was no party and he had difficulties getting up the stairs to the dressing room - you would never have known this from the performance - it saddened me when my mate told me this but you expect them to go on forever, we forget they're mortal.
Will miss my annual ear-bashing and the man himself, but am happy in the fact that I'd seen the band that was louder than the rest."
Jo Casson (Manchester)

"I have known Lemmy personally for 35 years. I will tell you how I met him and a couple of funny stories.
My boyfriend at the time was in a very good metal band and

arrangements had been made for them to support a band called Tank. We went out one Sunday afternoon to a pub/venue in Wandsworth south London to meet Tank and management.

When we got there I saw Lemmy propping the bar up, I had no idea he was managing Tank. He came over to us for a chat. I was wearing this shocking pink cat suit and had pink glitter high heels and peroxide blonde hair; apparently he liked the tarty look in those days. What a sight ha! This was in the year 1981/2 so details are sketchy. Motörhead were famous then but not like they are now. I gave Lemmy my phone number and he put it in his top pocket.

Six weeks later I got a call at home, it was Lemmy. He apologised for not calling sooner and said he'd been away on tour and we arranged to meet for a drink. We arranged to meet in his favourite pub in an obscure location towards north London. I was living in Colliers wood so he had to explain where this pub was over and over.

I got there an hour late and one thing no one knows about Lemmy and I found out to my detriment later he will not tolerate lateness! He was on the fruit machine for ages. I said –

"Hi Lemmy its Sharon."

He refused to speak to me for ages and carried on playing on the machine. Eventually he softened, sat down with me and bought me not one, but about 25 drinks! I just drunk the one vodka and lime but he would buy himself a Jack and Coke every 10 minutes and me as well, a vodka. Also bought me packs of Marlborough Lights.

It was kind of hard to make conversation as I had pissed him off. I remember asking him if he had a house. He said –

"What do I want a house for?"

Then I asked, "Have you got a car?"

He said "What do I want a car for?"

I remember him telling me he lived on a house boat and didn't drive as he was always too drunk.

He always had, at every meeting, a porno magazine and a copy of Kerrang. He would slap them on the table where we were sitting with great delight. I was so embarrassed. No one gave us so much as a sideways glance. I don't think anyone knew who he was.

At the end of the evening he walked me to the tube station and threw me over his shoulder in front of every one. I nearly died as I was wearing a mini skirt and everyone could see my underwear! I was very shy in those days. Me and my friends used to joke and mimic the gruff voice 'Meet me in the pub behind the fruit machine'

That's what he said every time we arranged to meet.

I would write him these love letters on leopard skin print paper covered in lipstick kisses and perfume and would send them to his record company. He loved those and would always call me when he had received one of them.

Another time he asked me where I wanted to meet him. I said "Tavern in the Town' Croydon."

He said "Ok see you there."

When I arrived, late as usual...yikes, he was propping up the doorway at the pub. He really told me off for 1. being late again and secondly he said there were 2 'Tavern in the Towns' in Croydon! I never knew that.

He was furious as he said he'd been waiting for hours in the wrong pub. Who would keep a superstar waiting but me!

I was so dense in those days but Motorhead, Girlschool and our band used to hang out together in south London so I was not star struck in the slightest. As usual he slapped his magazines down on the table. Full centre spread. I went bright red but besides that not a soul took any notice.

I can't remember our conversations but I wished I had asked him more about his music. I remember he had booked an appointment to have his teeth fixed at the dentist in Croydon. He was terribly nervous. I asked him if he wanted me to come with him and he said 'No' ever the brave man.

Another time he took me backstage at Hammersmith and introduced me to these 4 spotty boys who looked about 12. I looked at them pityingly and thought, 'oh dear they'll never make it'. Lemmy was very proud of them and I shook all their hands. They were sitting in a row. I found out later their band name was Metallica.

We went out together on and off for a couple of years and then I got married (to someone else). My husband and I ran a metal club in Wimbledon called Nelsons. A gang of us always used to go to the Hippodrome for metal night on a Wednesday. Lemmy was often there.

We were giving out leaflets one night to promote the club. Bless him, he asked for a handful and gave them out to the punters. My husband asked him to come down the club and offered him a string of bouncers. Lemmy said –

"What do I want bouncers for?" He was so down to earth.

He was the only ex boyfriend my husband was never jealous of. He chatted to my husband more than me in those days.

I always went to Motörhead gigs but never bothered with back stage for some reason as I always got passes anyway through a journalist friend in the business.

Many years later when my scene had disbanded I went to see Motörhead with my husband at Wembley. After the show I decided to go backstage. I knocked on the backstage door and these big bouncers answered who were very unfriendly. I said
"Can I come in and see Lemmy."
They said "Who the F*** are you? F*** off."
I said "Tell Lemmy Sharon is here." That is all I said.
They very doubtfully said "Oh yeah right, we'll ask him huh." They did and they came back and said,
"Lemmy said go and wait for him in the VIP lounge and have a drink."
They were shocked. We went straight in to the party actually and Lemmy was sitting there surrounded by 100's of well known rock stars, Girlschool were there. I was looking for an old friend who had disappeared and asked Kim if she knew where he was. She held my hand and took me right to him. That was a brilliant night.
I spoke to Fast Eddie Clarke and loads of others. I knew most of them anyway as I was linked to the music business myself and went clubbing at the Marquee quite often. I didn't know it but my husband went outside to sit on the steps. Lemmy joined him for a chat and a drink. This really tells you what a truly amazing wonderful genuine unaffected by fame bloke Lemmy was.

Another time me, my husband and my girlfriend went to a metal gig somewhere in London. Cant remember the band, big name. Afterwards my girlfriend literally kicked me up the backside and said –
"Get on that tour bus!"
I was terrified as I had no idea where it was taking me. We were off to an after party miles out of London. We ended up getting into this 'A' lister metal celebrity bash. I can remember Lou Gramm, Iron Maiden and loads of others being there. We had said to my husband.
"Follow that tour bus!"
Hours later Lemmy was beating on the door shouting...
"It's Lemmy let me in!"
The bouncers shouted, "No, you haven't got a pass!"
He was really bashing the door and yelling at them. He shouted
"I AM LEMMY. LET ME IN, I DONT NEED A PASS."
They weren't having it. By now my husband arrived furious we had left him in the lurch and he actually broke the door in he was so angry. I was actually sitting on some blokes lap. In came Lemmy

and my husband! Lemmy got in through Alan bashing the door down. I was in big trouble that night. Couldn't believe they wouldn't let Lemmy in. This was during the early 1990s.

Any gig of Motörhead, I only had to say the name Sharon and doors would open. He never ever forgot me. I just loved that man. He was amazing, unique, sensitive loving, funny wonderful, intelligent. I have met most people in the rock music business over the years and there's not one that comes even vaguely close. Not one. They all have attitudes and wont mix with the 'common' man. What rockstar phones a chick at home???? No one.

It's not amazing in content but demonstrates that fame never changed him one bit. My only regret is that my Dad Lived 30 minutes from the Rainbow and I used to go to LA very year. I always intended to visit Lemmy there but never did due to family problems.

He would have been the same sweet person.
Never forgets a friend."

Sharon Demmon (Hastings, East Sussex)

"I went to boarding school in Malvern from 1976 - 1981.

Bands were always playing at the Malvern Winter Gardens back then. I remember as one of the older girls being allowed to walk up into Malvern village at the weekend.

One such day I did precisely that, in those days all was very quiet and calm. I don't remember exactly what time it was, probably a mid morning and there was absolutely nobody else about as I was making my way up to the village, most likely with my usual aim in sight which would have been to stock up on sweets.

There I was all alone walking up the hilly paths surrounded by greenery and pretty buildings, dressed in my school uniform. I'm guessing I was about 14 or 15. Lo and behold, I see a dark figure appear in the distance at the top of the same path I was on, walking towards me. A cowboy of a figure, tight jeans, and denim jacket.

As the figure got closer I nearly died, the figure walked nearer and nearer to me was Lemmy. It was around 1979, a towering hunk of a rock star, walking right up to me and as the path was quite narrow was literally only a foot away from me as we passed each other.

I have always remembered that moment, it's as if it was frozen in time. Lemmy and me, Lemmy and me, just us, in the middle of hilly Malvern. I was a terribly shy schoolgirl and my heart pounded as he approached me and then walked past. It was a kind of

privileged moment.
I always wonder what may have happened had I had the wherewithal to say something to him.
The first time I saw Motörhead perform was about 30 years later and then I saw them several times. It was poignant to have been so close to him for a moment when he was so young and then to see him perform so magnificently just under a year before he left this earth for Valhalla.
My admiration of him had gone full circle."
Amalia Grassi (UK)

In the 1970's I had a group of friends that went to all rock concerts at the old Liverpool Stadium and later the Empire.
We got older and some moved away got married etc ....then in April '79 myself and the remainder of our gang saw Motörhead!
It was then I realised that of all the bands I'd seen, this was the one with the same attitude, I could identify with them.
Lemmy looking down at us in the front row. Smiling at us then snarling with a frantic rhythmic bass. Deaf Forever.
This was it. I saw them 50 odd times and was never disappointed. Lemmy also helped me through difficult times, so it was truly MOTÖRHEAD FOR LIFE!"
Doug Earle (Liverpool)

"I was on leave (Army) in 1980, I was 18 and my mate Mark Treleaven had two tickets to see Motörhead at Carlyon Bay in Cornwall.
I didn't even know who Motörhead were tbh, went along that night in my trousers, shirt and cardigan, yes a cardigan!
Although feeling a right square, had a great night. Nobody gave a flying fuck what you were wearing!
From that night on I knew who Lemmy and Motörhead were and I still have the tinnitus to prove it."
Mark Trebilcock (Cornwall)

"I'm founder member, singer and songwriter of NWOBHM band Sacrilege.
I was in the Standard London back in 1984, Sacrilege had just played on the David Jensen show for TV and Lemmy was in there.
I remember him telling me to keep the band going as there are so many ups and downs.
In 1986/7 I decided I'd had enough of all the hassles that come with running and playing in a band so I stopped.

In 2012 I was persuaded to start playing live again and got Sacrilege back on the road albeit with new band members and I am now enjoying it more than ever.
I now think back to what Lemmy told me and think what a waste of 25 years, why did I stop?"
Bill Beadle (Sacrilege – Vocals/Guitar)

"It was the late '90s and at the time, I was the landlord of a small country freehouse in Oxfordshire.
A customer of mine, who was also a close friend, invited me to join him to go and see Motörhead at the Wolverhampton Civic Centre. He knew I was a dedicated fan although I had never seen them live; I jumped at the chance.
He was a hardened pro who had seen them several times, met Lemmy on one of those occasions and had his denim cut-off signed by the man himself...lucky bastard!
The days running up to the gig were a blur for me; I couldn't stop going on about it to anyone who was in the bar at the time, interested or not...I didn't care!
Another regular customer, named Paul, who was very much into his music, had obviously been paying close attention to my nightly ramblings. The gig happened, I was no longer a Motörhead virgin, I was as happy as a pig in shit!
The following night, the first punter through the door was Paul.
"Evenin' mate" I said.
He didn't say a word. From behind his back he produced a small wad of A4 paper with words written in black marker pen. He showed me the first one, "Hi". The second one read "How was Motorhead?"
"Fuckin' awesome" I said.
His last sheet of paper?.... "Good, can I have a Murphy's please?"
Somehow he'd figured out how the conversation was going to play out and also had a good guess at me having a slight hearing defect. He wasn't wrong. I was suffering from raging tinnitus for the next two weeks!
It didn't take a great deal of persuasion to get my brother, who has contributed to this book, to come and see Motörhead with me, again, at The Civic Centre, nor my partner Sarah, who accompanied me to their one and only time at The Bulldog Bash in Long Marston, Warwickshire...a good time was had by all!
Lemmy...I went on to see you perform on another six occasions. You were the best, you are a God.
Thank you for being part of my life.

Skip Milo (UK)

*"First heard Motörhead in '79, seen 'Bomber' on TOTP, I was 12/13.
First got to see them in '82 on the 'Iron Fist' tour, seen them most tours over the years.
First time I met Motörhead was in '83 on the 'APD' gigs. I had seen Eddie a few weeks earlier and he signed my jacket, when Lemmy saw that he said he was going to sign over it to piss him off, he didn't though. Also I had had Robbo looking for my pen after I dropped it, quite funny looking at him under the desk and he had a massive glass of something, you could tell he was pissed, Phil was funny, also met Anvil that night.
30th Anny gig in London, I lost my ticket.
Phoned Ticketmaster who didn't help, so I asked my friends in totalrock.com if they could help. They put me on a pass. When I went to get it I found this card, didn't know what it was for.
Anyway my ticket was upstairs and I wanted to be downstairs, so I kept asking one of the event people if I could go downstairs, it took me about 1 hour asking him to let me in, he did after that (think he wanted to get rid of me) only thing though, the bar was outside and I couldn't get to it or I wouldn't get back in.
Anyway, great gig as usual, lost my mate who I was staying with, so after the gig, went outside to see if I could find him, everyone was out and I didn't see him, then I remembered the card, I asked where it would get me too, and they said, the after show!
Well that was me running back in and up to the bar. That's where I found my friend, who was with Krusher (Motörhead friend), few beers and the band came in, so we bought Lemmy a Jack and Coke, had a little chat to them, as well as Biff Byfford, and they signed my card.
Another time, Lemmy was on Krusher's show on Total Rock, I phoned him and he let me talk to Lemmy, we had a good talk and he said he would give me a pass for Manchester gig. I got the pass but didn't meet him that time
I met Wurzel after an Accept gig in London, he was a nice lad, my mate thought he was a friend just because how he was talking to me."*

Dave O'Brien (St Helen's, Merseyside)

*"First time I saw Lemmy he was still fronting Hawkwind at the Round House London in the early 70's.
The next time I saw him was fronting Motörhead in 1991 in*

Newport which was my first date with my husband. We saw them many times together after that, the last time being at the Eden Project last summer.

Always loved the man for his uncompromising attitude - he never sold out and never changed - wish I could always have said the same!

A true legend and a damned good bloke."
Angie Butler (UK)

"My biggest regret was thinking I didn't get to see him.
But then I got to thinking, 1972 a little place called Bickershaw held a 3 day festival in May and guess what? I went and guess what? Hawkwind performed and guess what?
Woohoo, yep you've guessed it - Lemmy was in the band
How could I forget!! (Well it was the 70's!!)"
Brenda Turner (UK)

"I met Lemmy at the O2 Academy, Glasgow, Friday 9th November 2012, with Anthrax supporting. I thought I'd be dedicated enough to wait outside the venue from 11am onwards until 7pm (when the doors were due to open).

I had skipped breakfast, lunch and such. So, I will admit, I did feel kinda 'iffy' and it was cold. Anyway, I waited outside on the right side of the venue where the bands equipment gets loaded in, praying and hoping I would meet any members of the band, especially Lemmy.

It was around 2:00pm at this point. I hadn't seen any members of Motörhead walking around. So I was asked to come over by this girl, who was doing door supervision on the same side of the venue I was on.

She said –

"Who are you mostly here for tonight?"

I said –

"Well if I'm being completely honest, I'm here for both. What about you?"

"I absolutely love Anthrax!" she said.

So, we struck up a conversation, I can't actually remember her name. It's bugging me now because she was so lovely.

It was now 3:30pm. I was still waiting about, then she asked me to come over again. She said –

"Hey I'm not supposed to be telling this at all, but erhm, Lemmy is coming on this side of in a taxi."

"Really? Surely not? I could have imagined Lemmy to be getting out of a limousine," I said.

It then struck 4:20pm. I saw this taxi on the same side of the venue I was on. I saw the door open, then suddenly seen these awesome cowboy/military looking boots step out. All I could think of in my mind was 'Holy fucking shit, I'm actually gonna meet, as well as talk to Lemmy.'

I kept myself calm, then said –

"Hey Lemmy, how you doing? Looking forward to the show tonight."

"Have you seen us before?" he said.

"Well, tonight is actually my first Motörhead concert, so I'm really looking forward to it.

He then says –

"Well kid, I can tell you this right now. You're gonna be stone deaf for 5 days straight. I can assure you!!" 'laughs'.

I was so excited at this at this point and said –

"Lemmy, I hope you don't mind, but can I get my ticket signed as well as a photo with you?"

"Sure, no problem at all" he says and he proceeds to sign my stuff and was happy to oblige to take a photo.

After I met him, I saw these two dudes come towards myself and Lemmy and got interrupted mid-conversation after signing some shit. One of them had an Asda bag with EVERY single Motörhead vinyl to date. One of them said –

"Hey Lemmy can you sign all these?"

He then laughs and says –

"I'm only signing one, so take your pick."

Funnily enough, it was 'Ace of Spades'.

After they had gone, I told Lemmy how much of an influence Motörhead were to me, as I am a guitar player. He then puts one hand in his back pocket, takes out two guitar picks and says –

"Use them well kid, I can tell you're a huge fan! It was a pleasure meeting you."

I can honestly say, I won't forget that story for as long as I live.

RIP Lemmy.

We were Motörhead – we played rock and roll."

Ryan Gormley (Paisley, Renfrewshire)

*"Met Lemmy in 1980 Birmingham Odeon.
Stood in front of the speakers for the whole gig.
Great memories and a true gentleman.
Love you always Lemmy*
Lorraine Draper (Birmingham)

"He gave me tinitus a few times watching him, especially when he leans his bass up against his cabs for feed back at the end of each gig."
Joss Bass (Kingston upon Hull)

*"Lem and I do go back a few years, we first met up in 1982 when we went to see the Damned together.
Lem had a boat moored on the Thames next to John Curd, our manager, so to get to John's boat we always had to go over Lem's boat. He always had a welcoming line of speed or a few 'ladies' hanging around, so of course we all hit it off, he also knew a lot of the London bikers I hung around with.
One night we went out to see the Damned play in the Greyhound, obviously it was a drunken night and of course speed by the handfuls. At the end of the evening Vanian asked Lem and I up on stage to sing 'Silver Machine' with the band, so we fell onstage. I hogged the mic as I thought Lem was looking fragile!!
At the end of our rendition I said to Lem –
"You alright mate? Didn't you know the words or something?"
"Cunt" he said, "I fuckin' wrote 'em".
We fell about laughing, derrr, I had forgotten he was in Hawkwind.
We had a few nights outlike that but lost touch, after he moved out of his boat.
A few years later we met up again in the TV studios to play a couple of songs from our new album 'the Perfect Crime' for a show called 'Meltdown'. Motörhead was also there playing a couple of tracks from their latest album, I think it was 'Orgasmatron'.*

Our band had changed a lot over the past couple of years (for some strange reason), so when I met up with Lem in the corridor of the studio he said to me –
"What the fuck has happened to the Anti Nowhere League? You look like a bunch of ponces and your songs are shit." (say what ya mean eh Lem).
"Well your new albums shit" was my stupid reply...I was hurt.
Lem was with Phil and they bot looked amazing, 'leather and metal', I was dressed like a fucking reject from Duran Duran!
Lem just shook his head and walked off, but I tell you what, it was the most truthful thing anyone had ever said to me, although at the time I didn't realise it. We did look shit and our songs WERE shit! If only I had taken his advice onboard, maybe we would have not split up for the period we did.
I do have the pleasure though of saying Lemmy was a good mate of my past, the only real rocker I have known.
When we toured with Motörhead in 2012 we were back on talking terms seeing as I was now back on track with my band and spent some time together reminiscing of the 'good old days'.
Rock will never be the same, a bit of all of us died with him."
Animal (Anti Nowhere League – Vocals)

Uruguay

Capital City: Montevideo
Population: 3,324,460
Currency: Uruguayan Peso
Bands: Garron, El Cuarteto de Nos, Fixion

"Rest in peace my friend, the very best big hug to all my fucking friends and Motorheadbangers, it's a simple thanks for all Lemmy Kilmister Motörhead, the best front man bass player in rock 'n' roll on the face of the earth.
The best man in the world for all the things he has done, I showed that the last remains old is he heart and then go on dreaming and kick his ass God, good night."
Adriano Silverbullet (Canelones, Uruguay)

USA

Capital City: Washington D.C.
Population: 322,369,319
Currency: United States Dollar
Bands: Metallica, Anthrax, Megadeth, KISS

"It was November 2007, Berlin and the last night of the Motörhead/Overkill tour, the walls are heaving as the place is filled with Motör-headbangers. I was high, I usually am under such circumstances, doing what I love to do best with those I love to do it with and Motörhead would crown that list of contenders.
My close friend and light-man, 'Big-E' grabs me backstage and says; "Lemmy wants a word with you". Well shit, I snap to attention and accommodate the man;
"Bobby I want you to join us for the last number. I think you know it, Overkill".
I am now higher. I knew the tune cold, but was a bit nervous, a killer opportunity, you know? I wrote the first word of each verse on my forearm as to not 'fuck it up'.
When the moment came, I was higher still, and it seemed like a dream, I didn't really need the helpers written on my arm, but glanced down anyway. I was even higher now as the song was ending.
I looked Lemmy in the eye, I was smiling, he laughing, as he yelled over the massive volume: "CHEAT NOTES, HAHAHAHAHA!" I panicked from embarrassment, dove head on into the sea of Rock n' Roll, looking back I could see him standing on the edge of the stage a toothy grin; "CHEAT NOTES, CHEAT NOTES HAHAHA!"
We had a drink and a good laugh after, unforgettable for me.
My Motör-moment."
Bobby 'Blitz' Elsworth (Overkill – Vocals)

"I am a huge Motörhead/Lemmy *fan.*
Have been going to shows for over 30 years and privileged

enough to go on the last 2 Motörboats..
My favorite Lemmy story actually happened at the 42nd Grammy awards in 2000 (ex was nominated for Jennifer Lopez 'Waiting For Tonight'... Blech) I went to the after party at the Biltmore Hotel. This was the first time I ever saw Lemmy not on stage and it was the epitome of everything I wanted a Lemmy sighting to be (as I was to shy to go up to him) there he was at a table with at least 4 women (not a dude in sight. Lol).
He really did look like a rock God (or at least 'Sheikh Lemmy' with his harem) I wish I had a picture of that moment. He really looked like he was enjoying himself.
I still cannot believe I will never see him again as he was such an integral part of my life (his music & seeing him live.
Dawn Hetzel (Huntington, New York)

"There's one song that stuck in my head ACE OF SPADES."
Joanne Campa Hellet (San Antonio, Texas)

"I never got the privilege to meet him:(
It would be a treat to read stories about him though. I haven't met many famous band people.
I'm a fan of bad movies...I was stoked to see him in "Tromeo and Juliet" ....Troma, of course."
Ami McCuaig (Seattle, Washington)

"I was fortunate in 2014 to find there was to be a Motörhead cruise. I had just experienced my first rock cruise ever, 'Monsters of Rock', albeit far from what the lineup would be on MB14, the inaugural sailing. What would come to fruition, would become an historical event.
The anticipation was beyond compare for me. Let alone that, for those few I knew were going. There was no way for me to know how intense, or how far, the many that would arrive. Only to become part of a special family. Something I couldn't anticipate. Something that to me now, seems commonplace.
The love from kooks who enjoy and thrive upon that which is unique to us. That which encompasses more than geological location. It's the spirit of the underdogs that thrive upon the beat and screams, "MORE!
Pursuit of Happiness.
That was found and had, not once, but twice in 2014. Damn right I wasn't missing MB '15. I was now a veteran and survivor of the first MotörBoat. Not only did the music beckon, but the family was

there to reunite with.
Members of the world uniting for the ultimate cause. Music, led by Lemmy & why we were there to begin with. Supporting cast obviously the icing.
Yet, the man, the Legend, The Motörhead for fucks sake! I never met Lemmy.
Saw all the shows on both cruises. Never ran into him on the ship(s). Didn't attend the M&Gs. And for me, that was the way it was to be. He was a Legend to me. I basked in the glow of what was. I was a fan. And I was experiencing what no one else could experience, unless they were there with me. For that, it is mine. Grateful for all in my Motörhead family. RnFnR"
Ben Lagos (New Jersey, USA)

"I was only able to see Motörhead one time, Sept. 23rd 2009 at the Pageant in St. Louis, 'Motorizer' tour.
My wife didn't want me to go. She thought I would drive the 150 miles to St. Louis and get stabbed or something. So there I was before the show in line outside.
Everybody talking about Motörhead and heavy music in general. And here they came, Bikers with Motörhead flags on their bikes. You know the type. Covered with tattoos. Beards and biker boots. The kind of guys that make some people go to the other side of the road if they see them coming.
I thought the college kids next to me were going to crap their pants. Anyway, about half way into the set I see the biker guys in front of me. They were hugging random people and shaking hands. With tears running down their faces pointing to the stage saying "It's Motörhead.... It's fucking Motörhead!"
That's what Lemmy and the boys did. Their music brought people together.
MOTORHEAD FOREVER!"
Harold Cagle (Dexter, Missouri)

"I met Lemmy at Foundations Forum, what a great guy!
He talked to us for a long while and even had some funny comments as only Lemmy will do when the person taking a picture of us had trouble with the camera.
I had the pleasure of talking to Lemmy several more times what a great guy he will be missed but never forgotten RIP Lemmy, Motörhead Forever!
It was Foundations Forum '88 or '89 I was sitting at a table having a beer with Lemmy. King Diamond was sitting with us and all of a

sudden Robert Sweet of Stryper asks if he can sit with us.
It's cool but Lemmy looks at me and we are thinking the same thing you could tell by the looks on our faces we have a Satanist and a Christian at the same table. We are both waiting for it to explode but it never did.
We sat their and listened to Robert and King have a great conversation about religion and never get upset or angry with each other we just enjoyed our drinks and hung out; what a cool day. Everybody joined in the conversation my best memory of Lemmy."
Daryl Banks (Springdale, Arkansas)

"I went to see Motörhead at The Wiltern in L.A. about 10 years ago around 2005 or 2006 anyway, I went with Brian Perera of Cleopatra Records & we were rocking at the Show.
Well, a whole lot of Whiskey & soda & beer was flowing I remember going down in the pit, threw my T-Shirt on stage, & can't remember much else.
After the show we went to the VIP area. I remember I was pretty drunk by then & I thought Motörhead weren't their best that night, at least that is what my 'drunk ass' thought, & I was yelling around how they played terrible tonight, I kept saying it & Philthy Animal Taylor was right there talking to Brian Laughing at my dumb drunk ass.
He said "so you thought they were not Tip Top tonight?"
"No! Bad show" I said.
Then I looked down at his Feet. He had purple shoes on. I always had this thing about purple shoes. I said "purple shoes, oh nooo I hate purple shoes, I will buy you some new shoes Philthy & I will take you to The Robin Hood in the San Fernando Valley & get you a Steak & Mushroom Pie & some Guinness."
"Okay" he said, "it's a deal".
Well it was time to go and I couldn't find Brian P. - my ride - so Philthy pulls up in his Corvette & said "Get in I will take you home before your get arrested."
After all the stupid stuff I said this fine gentleman took my drunk ass home so I wouldn't be stranded down town. I will never forget that. What a great man Philthy Animal Taylor. I still owe you some shoes, a Steak & Mushroom pie & all the Guinness you can drink. Cheers! That was the 1 & only time I didn't enjoy a Motörhead show 100% it was only about 97% that night."
Darius "DokTor Sep" Sepanlou (Hollywood, California)

"I met Lemmy 9/14 2008 in Columbus Ohio at the Newport Music

Hall (Augora).
That day the remnants of hurricane Ike barreled through Ohio at 70 mph knocking power all over the state setting in a dark alley in a typhoon typically would suck except for we wound up finishing the night with the band and crew leaning on a bus drinking and trading story's.
Lemmy was a great person funny polite intelligent great manners and down to earth just like a couple guys hanging out.
The show was rescheduled for the following night and was brutally loud even for them. I'll never forget those two days.
The world is so much quieter with out Lemmy but at least I have a constant ringing in my ear to remind me of you. You where more then a star or a legend... You were our friend.
You gave yourself to us till the very end. One day I hope to see you again.
RIP. Rock n Roll.
Dustin Bowers (Columbus, Ohio)

"Miss you Lemmy - see you on the other side"
Fred Baker (Mohave Valley, Arizona)

"I only listen to his music, never got a chance to meet him or see his shows but the first song I listened to was 'Ace of Spades' by him and that's what got me hooked on Lemmy's music."
Eric Kenyon (Schenectady, New York)

"When I was in high school I had a friend named Peter Vollmer (still friends to this day) He was a Motörhead fanatic.
He had every album the band had released at the time, including any rare imports that he could get his hands on. He lived, breathed and shit Motörhead 24/7...there was no fan more dedicated to Lemmy and Motörhead than Pete.
He began writing to Lemmy while Lemmy was still living in England. Pete would go to every single show that Motörhead played in Los Angeles and the surrounding California area and over time they became friends.
The first time I saw Motörhead was in 1982 when I went with Pete and another friend named Jim. It was at the Hollywood Palladium.
When we arrived, Pete instinctively knew what to do; Find the bus! Which was not hard to do...it was the bus with MURDER ONE written on the front, just over the windshield.
We followed Pete, he was armed with a large bottle of vodka which was a gift he planned on giving to Lemmy and within a few minutes

we were standing outside the bus with the man himself, Lemmy Kilmister.

Pete introduced Jim and myself to Lemmy as he handed him the vodka. Lemmy was very pleased with the gift seeing as he was already drinking a screwdriver!

I was awestruck to say the least. I couldn't believe I was hanging out with Lemmy. We all just stood around chatting and joking with each other, like we'd known each other for years.

I remember a very hot looking blond girl that walked up to him. They spoke to each other for a minute or so then she walked away. As we all watched her, Lemmy turned to us, smiled and said with a wink, "I fucked her last year".

Fortunately Pete never went anywhere without his trusty Polaroid camera. And he took several pictures with us goofing off with Lemmy. He still has all those old Polaroid pictures and he has recently posted them on his Facebook page and a few on my page as well.

Lemmy also had a camera with him that he needed film for. He asked us where he could get some film and we said, "Right across the street, at Thrifty Mart" He said "Let's go" and we proceeded to accompany him to the store.

It was so funny walking across the street through traffic as Motörhead fans were showing up to the Palladium. I could hear people in their cars; "Holy shit! It's Lemmy!"

We made our way into Thrifty Mart and followed Lemmy over to the film isle. He asked a few questions, making sure he was getting the right film. As we stood in the cashier line behind Lemmy, the three of us just grinned from ear to ear, shaking our heads and trying our best not to bust out laughing as people kept turning their heads to stare. We couldn't believe it...we were shopping with Lemmy!

After the show we met up with Lemmy outside the bus. We shook hands and congratulated him on a killer show. Phil Taylor walked off the bus for a minute and we met him as well. We said our goodbyes and we headed for home with a headful of memories, a handful of Polaroid's and a ringing in our ears that lasted for days...we had the time of our lives.

Pete, by the way, remained friends with Lemmy for 35 years. Often visiting his apartment when Lemmy moved to Los Angeles...he remained friends with Lemmy until his death."

Tom Komisar (Brookville, Indiana)

"My Friends call me Sep Or DokTor Sep. Here is one of the first

times I met Lemmy & talked to him.
It was around Early 1990 or '91 I was working at 'The Rock Shop Hollywood'. I was manager of the Record Shop.
I had a Friend named Henry who Played Guitar in a Garage Punk band kind of like The Dead Boys or New York Dolls style band. Henry had a really hot girlfriend. She was of Asian descent with piercings & tattoos. She has a dragon tattoo that starts at her neck & shoulders & runs past her really nice ass.
Well I was working one evening at 'Rock Shop' and she comes in the shop with Lemmy. I was like 'Hey that's the hottie of Henry & The Kilmister'.
I remember Lemmy going through the Vinyl and he came up to me at the counter with a bunch of Records. I said hello and that I am a big fan of Motörhead.
Then I looked at what he was buying; it was all Motörhead and Hawkwind records.
I said "Hey Lemmy, why are you buying your own albums?"
He said with that mumbly scratchy voice,"because we have been on so many different labels over the years, it's just easier this way."
He spent around $150.00+ or more on records which helped our business. I thanked him & said 'what's up' to the tattoo vixen and they left. Then I thought to myself she definitely upgraded her 'Rock Star' boyfriend, because Henry was a 'wanna be Johnny Thunders Heroin Junkie'.
And we all know SpeedFreaks make better Lovers."
Darius SEP Sepanlou (Los Angeles, California)

"I gave Lemmy one of my dolls and he held it through all the pictures he took on the Motörboat.
I got to sit with him and play the slot machines for about an hour but we didn't talk much. It was still a really good memory."
Alicia Smith (New Orleans, Louisiana)

"If it weren't for Lemmy or the 'Motorboat' in 2015 I would have never met the love of my life in the Motörhead cruise.
He was a fellow cruiser and Motörhead fan from the Netherlands. And we are not 20 year old fans we are 20 year fans!!!
We had such a great time on the ship and getting to know each other that we were literally the last passengers off the ship and to our surprise when we were at customs there was Lemmy, with one of his girlfriends/nurses and we had the pleasure to thank him as we walked past him.

My regret is that we did not get a chance to tell him now how our love grew in the past few months. Tom is now looking to move here to the State's to be closer to me and all because of Lemmy and the motorboat.
I will forever be grateful for him and I hope for many more years of rocking together with my new man."
Dulcy Deleche (Fort Lauderdale, Florida)

"I've known and been best of friends with Lemmy, Mikkey etc and the crew since 1985. I've been on serious personal levels along with both of our desire's on collection WWII Everything & a serious collection we both have and shared and traded.
All the 'all access shows' world wide I've been on with Lemmy and crew, party's girls & personal family issues to even have my mother cook him dinner. Just a very long time as friends throughout the years.
He's put my name on a few cool cds, 'Inferno' as an endorsement as a joke, 'Kiss of Death' cd 'Motorizer' ect.
I did Mikkey's one and only tattoo.
I loved Lemmy like a brother and I've learnt so much over 30 years of knowing him.
So much stuff 30 years of stories, gifts memorabilia, world wide tours, picks from every tour, signed guitars, All Access passes from just about every tour, memories and endless photos, Switzerland Pala festivals, USA from Florida to Texas to Cali and back.
I have passes that are older than some of the crew and I've been around Lemmy longer then some actual band members.
I have a 'Snaggletooth' tattoo on the back of my head and I just got it in September or October and when I text Lemmy the photo he said it was brilliant but I'm still a cunt hahaha.
One more thing that small cuff title on my crew jacket came from Lemmy, a gentleman from Germany made him only two & he has the one on his coat and he gave me the only other one, now that's 1 out of hundreds of gifts he's given me that is special and so dear to my heart. It will go to the grave with me for sure."
Thomas 'TattooTommy' Beerman (New York)

"The year was 2000. I was thirteen years old, on the way to the record store to buy my first cd. I knew I wanted something by Motörhead because I'd heard ACE OF SPADES and had never heard--and still haven't since--anything so heavy. I flipped through the rack, looking for anything by Motörhead, but all they had was EVERYTHING LOUDER THAN EVERYONE ELSE. I hated 'live' music, but I bought it, took it home, put it in the player. What blasted from my speakers was not a band. It was the living spirit of Rock and Roll. Not a year later from buying that cd, I'd bought every Motörhead cd I could find, and they've remained the constant band I've listened to all these years.

Lemmy will be missed. But he will never be truly dead, because he lives inside anyone who has ever put their music on, made the sign of the horns, and headbanged, and he will be with us forever."

Bradley Smith (Lexington, Kentucky, USA)

"February 23, 2012
San Jose State University Event Center
San Jose, California

The Bill:
Megadeth
Motörhead
Volbeat
Lacuna Coil

Seeing **Motörhead** was like attending an historic event. The lineup for the night was superb. I'd been a long-time fan of Megadeth and new fan of Volbeat and Lacuna Coil, but having **Motörhead** on the bill just felt like the icing on the cake. I'd heard the hits, I loved the glimpses I'd had into Lemmy's life and personality. The night promised to be the whole package, and it delivered.

Lacuna Coil set the tone for the evening and I was blown away. The combination of vocals, the groove set by the bass player and drummer... It appealed to my inner alternative rock lover and my diehard metal fan equally. Cristina Scabbia is just brilliant and their music, dark and sensual, really inspires me.

Then **Volbeat** came on... Suffice it to say that when you see Volbeat, you surrender your heartbeat to the pounding of their rhythm section. They celebrate all that came before them from rockabilly to hard rock and to metal. Their songs grab you by the spleen and take you over. I was beginning to feel as though I'd found my new favorite live band.

But then **Motörhead** took the stage. I was swept away to a timeless place where rock 'n' roll was balls out, unapologetic, and full of life. 'Ace of Spades' is really an anthem and when the crowd shouted "That's the way I like it, baby, I don't want to live forever," I shouted right along with them, horns proudly in the air. I wished I could have seen them in their heyday and thought how rowdy and exciting their early shows must have been. But I was grateful to be seeing them. It was like taking a final course in my metal education!

Megadeth performed as the headliner and I was enthralled watching the technical prowess of Mustaine and Broderick as their guitars dueled over songs I'd jammed to for years. It was a brilliant set. But my fondest memory of the night was finally seeing Motörhead.
Shortly after the show the Lemmy film aired and I watched with my husband. I felt as though I was watching a documentary of a favorite uncle or a treasured member of the community. That's who Lemmy is to me. Perhaps not my favorite musician ever, but just the nicest guy who lived the life other people could only write about. His career is legendary, his music will entertain us for generations to come, but behind all that was just a guy from Stoke who loved playing music. Long live rock 'n' roll!
R.L.Merrill (San Lorenzo, California)

"When I was a kid about 14, making it like '91 or so, I went on a camping trip with my family. Well there was a flea market next to the camp ground and there was a table with old cassette tapes for a buck or so a pop. My dad gave me ten bucks and said pick out what you would like!
I picked out Ozzy's 'Blizzard of Oz', 'Led Zep IV', KISS 'Alive 1 & 2' and a few others I can't remember, but for my last pick that day I remember seeing the name with a birthday cake on the cover, it was the 'Birthday Party' live album, I was like 'Who is Motörhead?'
I knew nothing of Lemmy or Motörhead, but something about the song titles drew me to buy it, so I did.
It was the first tape I put in the Walkman and I WAS FUCKING BLOWN AWAY!!!!!
That whole 2 week vacation I didn't touch the other tapes till we got back home!! Needless to say Lemmy drained a lot of batts in that 2 weeks.
BORN TO LOSE, LOVE TO WIN!!!!!"
Geo Zaccone (Steele, Missouri)

"I never got to meet the Lemmy, but saw concerts and videos of

him. Everything I saw told me he was a very down to earth man. He had a huge impact on me musically.
I will forever remember him and sadly miss him."
Tim Cline (Grand Marsh, Wisconsin)

"I had the pleasure of interviewing Lemmy Kilmister of Motörhead *in January of 1988 at the Charlotte Coliseum. Grow-ing up, I had seen everyone there: Heart, Black Sabbath, Billy Idol, Judas Priest, Van Halen, Robert Plant, Aerosmith, ZZ Top, and AC/DC. When I was a kid, others my age were going to see Barnum and Bailey; I was going to see KISS.*
Excerpt from the book Kill the Music:

It was a thrill to enter the Charlotte Coliseum through the press gate in an official capacity as a staff member of WUSC-FM (Columbia, SC), with my clipboard and tape recorder. The security guard ushered me to Motörhead's *dressing room. After some pleas-antries meeting the other band members, the representative from Profile Records sat me down in a small room, with a table and some folding chairs. On the table sat a phone with a rotary dial next to an ashtray filled with cigarette butts. I was a little apprehensive, as I waited.*
After a few minutes, Lemmy Kilmister emerged. He was wearing a wifebeater, flared black polyester slacks and white patent leather zip-up ankle boots. He had long brown hair, a mustache and chops, and pronounced moles on his face – he resembled one of the federales in Treasure of the Sierra Madre.

Lemmy, a bit irritated, sat down and rubbed his eyes. He smoked his cigarette, and stared into the ashtray with his palms to his forehead. He spoke with a gravelly British accent:

"All right. Let's get this over with."

Nervously, I set up the tape recorder and microphone, produced the pad and paper, and began the interview.

"So, Lemmy, tell me a little bit about your latest, entitled Rock and Roll. It sounds like the songs are more about women than they are about rock and roll."

Interestingly, Lemmy gave a laugh, as if he had just been called out, "Well, rock and roll is about women, and the songs are about women, so you could probably say that, I suppose."

"You are familiar with the British 'Grebo' movement. This month's Sounds Magazine proclaims that you're the 'Godfa-thers of Grebo.' How do you feel about that?"

Lemmy was indifferent. "We're not the godfathers of any-thing. We play what we play, and that's it."

At first, I could tell that Lemmy didn't want to be there. He figured that I was just another moron with no grasp of how influential his band was to the Brits. Motörhead wasn't that well known in the U.S., like some of the English flavors of the month such as Whitesnake, but among the hipsters in the college radio crowd, bands like Motörhead, Slayer, Anthrax, and Metallica were at the top of the food chain. Today, these same bands have been glorified far more than the others, and they now adorn today's video game soundtracks such as Rock Band and Guitar Hero, exposing a whole new generation of listeners to their music.

Lemmy spoke a little about how Motörhead had missed the first wave of metal and punk, and was in tandem between the two. He said that the band wasn't Led Zeppelin, or the Sex Pistols. He likened Motörhead to The Ramones. They had, in a sense, carved their own niche, because of two reasons: one reason was that the music was heavy, but not easily categorized, and the other because none of the band members, Phil Campbell, Wurzel, or "Philthy Animal" Taylor were poncy or attractive, in the same fashion as the other touring gits in their tight knickers.

"What is Grebo?" I asked.

"I dunno, really," Lemmy responded. "It has something to do with motorbikes. Biker metal or something." *Lemmy dismissed it as a fad.*

"Like maybe The Cult?" I inquired.

"That's more like Bad Company, isn't it?"

I continued. "Zodiac Mindwarp? Gaye Bykers on Acid?"

"Gaye Bykers? A bunch of shit there. Queens aren't they, the lot?"

"Do you dislike homosexuals?"

Lemmy responded matter-of-factly, "I don't mind faggots, as long as they're not swishing, screaming faggots."

(A number of years later, there was an internet rumor that Lemmy was indeed gay, but I knew it wasn't true from his candor in the interview. Later, Out Magazine had to retract it.)

I changed directions a little. "I had read that you believe in reincarnation. What are your thoughts on the subject?" Lemmy examined me for a moment, as if he thought I was clever, and offered me a cigarette. Lemmy placed his hand on the back of my chair, as he responded.

"I believe that I was reincarnated from an SS Officer of the Third Reich."

He leaned back, and took a draw off of his cigarette. The coal brightened, and as Lemmy exhaled; he flicked the smoke into the ashtray and continued.

"It makes the most sense, you know, reincarnation. I think souls are recycled. If you die a good person, you get upper wrung, and if you're bad you get backer wrung."

"I read in the liner notes of No Remorse that **Motörhead** *had a reputation as 'England's loudest band.' That's quite a title to have."*

Lemmy shook his head, and retorted. "No. We were truly England's loudest band at one point. I'm sure that there have been louder bands since that was printed. There was this one time, we were playing in Detroit…"

I quickly followed with, "At a hundred-twenty decibels, and…?"

"Yeah, in this theatre. The plaster started falling from the ceiling. Big chunks of it. We were afraid the building was going to come down on top of us."

After forty-five minutes of interview, I asked my last question. "I read recently, that you had considered having your moles removed. Is that true?"

"No. These are in too deep. I'm getting old. I'm forty-two. I'm no spring chicken. I went to a plastic surgeon, and he told me because of my age, if I had them removed, the scar tissue would be worse than the moles, and that was it. I had all my teeth done. They're not mine. But they don't come out at night or anything. I'll admit, I'm no day at the beach, you know."

We laughed together. We talked back and forth, as if we had known each other for years. I did have one last request. "Before I go, would you be kind enough to give me station identification for our radio station?"

Lemmy grabbed the microphone, and read the call letters from the side of the recorder, and brashly spoke, "Hello, sons of bitches! This is Lemmy from Motörhead and you're tuned to WUSC-FM. Keep listening or I'll come around and saw your face off, all right!"

So there it was. Lemmy was as forthright, honest, and as offensive as I had hoped. When I left the Coliseum that night, I was as jubilant as a horny Catholic school girl.

So let's fast-forward 20 plus years. Motörhead, with openers Reverend Horton Heat, and Nashville Pussy were slated to play September 11, 2009 at the new Fillmore in Charlotte, NC. It was the first time Motörhead had appeared in the Queen City since I interviewed Lemmy back in the day. The band's lineup has changed a bit, and is now back to a three piece (how it was originally), with Phil Campbell on guitar and the legendary Matt Sorum on drums, supporting **Motörhead**'s new release, 'Motorizer'. The Fillmore is a new concert venue incorporated into an entertainment complex known as the North Carolina Music Factory. The Factory is also home to the recently built Uptown Amphitheatre; both projects helmed by Live Nation, centered in Uptown Charlotte.

For old time's sake, I started making some calls to see if I could stir up passes. After first contacting the venue, then the wrong agent, and then the right agent, I was given a resounding "thumbs down" by everyone I spoke to, due to the lateness of the request, or "there are no passes left," etcetera. But, I was determined to get in to see Lemmy, as I had already told everyone that I was going to review the show. When I woke up the day of the show, I was pouring my coffee around 8:15, when a brilliant idea popped into my noggin: I'll email Lonn Friend and see what he could do for me. Lonn Friend is the "Zen Master of Heavy Metal", very much like "The Dude" is the "Zen Master of Bowling." Friend was "The man for his time and place," during the era of California hair music and if there ever was a fabric that weaved itself into every facet of that period, it was him. The ex-RIP Magazine Editor-in-Chief and Author of Life on Planet Rock, also well-thought-of friend to metal's last, best age, and was arguably responsible for breaking most of the more durable bands during his tenure at RIP, including (but not limited to) Guns N' Roses, Metallica, and of course, **Motörhead**. In so many words, Lonn Friend is a legend. And sometimes he has a hard time letting you forget it.

When I was in L.A. to attend the Newport Beach Film Festival to meet with Jasin Cadic and Scott Rosenbaum, Co-writers of Perfect Age of Rock n Roll (produced by Spike Lee still yet to be released theatrically), I had dinner with Lonn and some dingy tart he brought with him (who sent her filet mignon back twice and then left her to-go box in the car), along with my girlfriend and editor, Anne. It was my birthday. And having just written my own book, Kill the Music, I was eager to meet the guru, who I had met only casually on MySpace of all places, and pick his brain a little. We scooped up Lonn and his muse at Friend's loft, and then drove into Hollywood. After stopping by Sirius Studios and catching the last song by a showcasing band, The Operation, we went to grab a bite. Poetically, we ate dinner at Lemmy's favorite jernt, The Rainbow Bar and Grill. And much like Lemmy would, Lonn and I hammered down mucho Jack Daniels shots. Afterward we went back to the

House of Friend, which by this time was consigned to moving boxes scattered across the apartment floor, just prior to his trip to suburbia (and out of the Hollywood Hills). While there, we explored what made Northern California famous and cracked a bottle of Dom, as it was all there was to drink; save some skim milk that had expired. Anne and I barely made it to the Comfort Inn on Sunset around 4 AM.

Anyway, Lonn got back with me promptly, with the email address of **Motörhead's** manager, Todd Singerman. My specific instructions from Lonn were to, "Tell him we're buds." So I sent Todd the logistics, and waited all day to hear something. After 8 hours or so, I heard nothing. Finally, after throwing in the towel on the whole situation, I dozed off on the couch around 5:15, only to be awakened by my cell phone. I looked at the number. It was a 310 area code. I answered. Lo and behold, it was Todd Singerman.

Todd's exact words were, "Any friend of Lonn Friend, is a friend of mine." Cool. We were in. The caveat was, "I can get you the tickets, and 'After Show' passes, but I can't get you an interview this late. Lemmy's been a real asshole about giving interviews, anyway. And I can't guarantee that he'll come out after the show. They might just start drinking and never come out." Fair enough. I wouldn't expect anything less from the maestro of mayhem, judging by my encounter 20 years ago. Luckily, I was prepared for the interview way back when, and that scored me some points. Otherwise the interview would have ended abruptly. I could only speculate how gruff and impatient he is now. I imagine his demeanor something like Captain Quint from Jaws, but instead of a boat, he's driving a 1987 Delta '88 with a peeling Landau roof, on the wrong side of the road, laughing maniacally at the oncoming traffic. Anyway, I had already been there, and done that. I then sent Lonn a text to inform him that he had worked some magic for me, and I was appreciative. He hit me back with, "It's not magic. It's a relationship." I couldn't help but think of Artie Fufkin from Polymer Records. There again, I couldn't get shit done in my own back yard, so I had to outsource it, and Lonn came to my rescue. Luckily, I've met some folks in my travels, and occasionally they'll do me a solid.

That evening, we picked up the tickets from will call and entered the venue around 9:30. Reverend Horton Heat had just taken the stage, which gave me an opportunity to examine the venue a little closer. The Reverend bores the shit out of me. I had promoted a few Social Distortion/Reverend Horton Heat shows in the 90's in

Charleston, South Carolina, and Savannah, Georgia. I didn't care for him much then either, especially after I lost my ass in Savannah.

The room was cavernous with 2,000 plus black t-shirt wearing, biker, metal-head, and post-punk concert attendees. In other words, there were a lot of dudes, all relatively still during Reverend Horton Heat's set (and probably hungry for some more Nashville Pussy, a hard act to follow with that electric tape and all). The stage was easily 70 feet across with huge stacks on each end, and more hanging above with 100 or so par 64 cans on trusses. The venue has a ballroom feel; above the hardwood dance floor; an array of crystal chandeliers. The Fillmore is tiered, very much like the House of Blues in Myrtle Beach, South Carolina, and it has a similar interior arrangement, although the venue feels a little claustrophobic opposite the stage, due to limited head room. The show was standing room only, with the exception of the VIP area, which seemed to be the only spot with chairs and tables. But if there were chairs, there wouldn't be a bad seat in the house; you can see the stage from practically anywhere in the venue.

Motörhead came on around 10:45 opening their set with "Iron Fist" and man, it was loud. Almost deafening. Lemmy's was as energetic as possible on stage, at 63, taking into consideration his diet of Marlboro Reds and Jack Daniels. But his bass thundered with the might of a rhinoceros herd. Ably assisting was Campbell on guitar, who's been with Lemmy off and on for almost thirty years, and "Neil Pert-status" drummer Sorum, helping to bring the heaviest heavy monster sound available. Next up was "Stay Clean", followed by songs such as "Metropolis" and "Another Perfect Day" although I got a little lost during the middle of the set. Lemmy brought me back home, ending the set with "Killed by Death" and "Bomber." Then the band left the stage. After a few minutes the crowd began to chant "Motörhead" over and over; then came time for the anthem. I first heard "Ace of Spades" on the BBC's comedy show The Young Ones sometime in 1984 or 1985. The last time I heard the song performed live by Motörhead (and not the countless times I've heard it covered) was at Atlanta's mythical Metroplex in May of 1988 shortly after I graduated from college. Hearing the song played after a 20 year hiatus was almost subliminal. And to add aural assault to injury, Lemmy finished out the encore with "Overkill". Surprisingly, Motörhead went through the entire set without playing one new song from 'Motorizer'. Don't ask me why. Probably has something to do with unit sales, as

Lemmy continuously complains, "We don't sell any bloody records in the States." Frankly, the experience was almost like a homecoming. But Motörhead could never have had its origins here. They're just too English; that's part of their mystique. But Lemmy's crew has become so entrenched in American pop culture that even AT&T adopted an "Ace of Spades" reference a year or two back. I can't, for the life of me, imagine Rock and Roll without Lemmy Kilmister. And it's funny. In a recent interview, Lemmy was quoted, as if a galley slave chained to a ship's oar, en route to an Australian prison colony: "We don't know how to do nothing else. I'm trapped behind this bass guitar. I really wanted to be a postman, but they wouldn't let me."

Well, we're certainly glad you didn't take that job, Lemmy. But if you had, you'd be the coolest postman who ever lived. **Michael G. Plumides, Jr. (Charlotte, North Carolina)**

"When it comes to recalling the memories of a man like Lemmy Kilmister and a band like Motörhead, it's hard to really pick out where to begin, especially for someone like me. Lemmy and Motörhead have left such an impact on my life, I don't know if words could ever really do it justice, but I'm about to give it a try.

My name is Kevin Lara, and I have lived in Los Angeles California for all twenty-four years of my life. I consider myself to be quite dedicated to Motörhead, and I always will be.

In a distant second place, I would have to put the faux-sport spectacle that is professional wrestling. I don't know exactly what it is about it, but I have remained (and also probably always will be) a dedicated fan of that as well.

I was first exposed to it in late 1999, at the age of seven years old by my cousins. I followed and watched the Monday and Thursday night TV broadcasts of WWF (now known as WWE) religiously, almost never missing an episode. One of the characters on the programming was a wrestler named Triple H. He was one of the most dastardly, mean, and vile people on the show.

When the wrestlers make their way to the ring, their entrances are all accompanied by the sound of music. All of it written specifically for their characters. Not long after I became a fan of this TV show, Triple H began arriving to the ring to the sound of pounding drums, screeching guitar, powerful bass, and the dirtiest, gravelly voice I had ever heard behind a microphone at that point in my life. This was before a point I had come to truly enjoy any kind of music in particular. Nothing I heard on the radio or TV ever caught my *interest. But, this sound that I heard now...there was nothing like it I had ever heard. For quite a long time, this was one of my favorite songs. It was called "The Game," and it was performed by the mighty Motörhead.*

I continued watching the show for a few more years, and by 2004, Triple H began using a secondary entrance theme, again by Motörhead, titled "Line in the Sand." Two of the coolest songs I have ever heard now. I was further intrigued. I had to know and hear more.

That year, I went to a record store (remember those?) to see what else I could find by Lemmy and company. I found a best of collection, and bought the newest album they had released up to that point, 'Inferno' (I eventually got Lemmy to sign my copy. It's probably my most prized possession). I set them both to spin, and by the end of it all, that was it. I was Motörhead fan. I played those CDs to death for months. 'Inferno' is my favorite record by any band or singer, even today. I think I remember Lemmy saying himself, to loosely quote him, 'It's the first things you hear that stick with you forever.' I still haven't heard anything better.

I started looking up videos of the band, exploring and listening to the rest of their discography, and I only became more devoted to them. I couldn't get enough. Motörhead were my gateway to the world of Heavy Metal. I started listening to other bands and fell in love with the sounds Judas Priest, Anthrax, Metallica, and Overkill, among others, but Motörhead was still number one."

Kevin 'Motör' Lara (Los Angeles, California)

"I was first exposed to Motörhead when I was 16. They opened up I think for Blue Oyster Cult in 1980.

When they played I was in awe, I had never heard anything so awesome. I was hooked and little did I know I would be hooked for life.

After they finished and the crew was breaking down the stage Lemmy came out and helped the road crew break down the stage. We were floored having never seen any band member ever help the road crew before!

When most of the equipment was put up he looked over and saw me and my friends hanging out by the stage. Then he did something that had never happened to me before he came over jumped off the stage put his arms on her shoulders and asked what we thought of the band. So we gave him a beer and shared are fine California skunk with him. He spent about 45 minutes telling us the history and

all the trials and tribulations of the band that's how I know why the first album was released later.
That's why I have been a lifetime fan ever since!"
Mac 'Motorhead' MacDonald (Atlanta, Georgia)

"He was my friend for 35 years.
I have many great stories about Lemmy.
I will never forget one day he invited me to the band room in Burbank, California around 1992.
I took my friend Ben, it was 105 that day, and I was wearing short pants.
I walked into the room, loud as fuck, hot as hell.
Lemmy was in short cutoffs and those cheapo rubber flip flop sandals. All of a sudden he stops playing looks at me and says into the microphone "JESUS CHRIST MAN...!!!! LOOK AT THE SIZE OF THEM LEGS."
Yeah I have monster calves lol! Never forget that.
Never let me down, always very kind and giving.
When I told him that no 'Bad Magic' tour shows were planned in the Pacific Northwest, he immediately said, "pick a show Pete and I will make it happen for you."
I said LA of course, my hometown. Boom the next day I get a call from Ian Gainer from London, booking me a flight to LA for the show. Very grateful to have the chance to see Lemmy again for the last time and say goodbye and thank him for everything over the last 35 years in person.
He was a great friend, paid for it himself, awesome guy.
When I was scared shitless and worried about my bout with 'Malignant Melanoma'. Lemmy would say "Don't worry about it mate, you will be ok."
Always made me feel good and made my day to talk to him or text him.
In 1992 I was sitting on the couch with Lemmy at his apartment.
Phone rings, I can hear an insane conversation. Lemmy hangs up after a few minutes and says, "Dear god, Osbourne has gone off! Hope he doesn't show up here smashed." Lol.
I moved to Battle Ground, WA from So. Calif 2003.
My daughters would mention that I knew a lot of bands from back in the day; I didn't think they believed that. So when Motörhead played Portland, Oregon on the 'World Is Yours' tour my daughter and her friends came with me to the show.
We got 'All Access' and got to hang out with him before the show.

Lemmy made sure to give the kids shirts and take pictures with us, good times...
I was just a fan who got lucky in 1980 or 1981. Who got the chance to know him as a friend over the years and hang out with him a lot.
I will never forget everything he gave me and did for me and that's not to mention his music.
He was a great guy, the real deal, at his apt or the shows, he lived for rock and roll, heavy and loud!!!
So glad I got to spend all those times with Lemmy at his apt.
One on one, no distractions like at the gigs.
Grabbing swords and daggers off his wall. Giving him and showing him lots of my dad's Luftwaffe stuff.
Giving him rides to the Rainbow and the band room in my car. Playing my demo tape for him. Giving him a Rickenbacker. Priceless memories live on forever, so will his kind giving spirit. RIP mate, cheers!"
Pete Volmer (Battle Ground, Washington)

"Typing anything to do with Lemmy is difficult right now.
Lemmy was a HELL of a lot more than some Rock star... Motörhead kept me company for twenty-nine years before Lemmy went away.
I'd read in several interviews with him that he stated that Motörhead fans never read the lyrics anyway. Well, that's untrue.

That's just one of many things that I Wanted to let Lemmy, and ALL of them know. We read 'em, or we all just flat-out KNEW 'em. Made a bunch of us Better, inside and out.
Motörhead are, still the most honest notes that anyone will ever hear. I came along late, in 1986. But I never looked back. How could anyone?
Idiots jump for trends, that's how. You'll never see the likes of that man, or that band ever again. They were the .44 magnum revolver that always fired when the .9mm automatic pistols couldn't. Loudly. Made your fucking head lean over when you left a show. Try that one on... I've heard lots of great artists over my forty-four years, but never ANY other form of music that rang so clear..."
Sean Taylor (Lebanon, Ohio)

"I would not know where to begin if asked about Lemmy.
I have never heard anything like him before or since and I know now that I never will either.
The shock and awe of the impact him and his band Motörhead left upon me as a teenager, was something I was never able to comprehend, recover from or get enough of."
Ian Anthony (Brooklyn, New York)

"My only close contact with Motörhead was seeing them open for Dio and Iron Maiden in 2003 in Washington D.C. with my best friend John.
It was a great show that I will always remember.
Years later John was getting married in L.A. My girlfriend Jodi and I made the trip out to California and had to see the Sunset strip and visit the legendary Rainbow Bar and Grill.
I never got to meet Lemmy and tell him what a fan I was, of him and his music. I did however get to spend all night at the Rainbow during the halloween costume party, and sit in his chair at the end of the outdoor bar. I have a picture of me in that seat, drunk on Jack and Coke that I will display forever.
Now that Lemmy is no longer with us I hope they keep his seat open so we can all sit there, and if just for a minute feel a little bit closer to our fallen hero.
I look forward to reading every one else's stories about Lemmy and whatever emotions they stir up. The world has lost an icon. I have lost a hero. So many others have lost a friend and a father. I think this book can help us all deal with what has happened and start to heal a little bit.
Michael Todd Bull (Saint Cloud, Minnesota)

"Never met the man. He had no idea I existed, yet a profound effect on my life and my way of thinking.
His music was the sound track to my life. A song for every experience, good or bad. Motörhead was there for me.
Was able to see them live once and will never forget it. I will always remember being 12 years old and seeing them play 'Hellraiser', it sent a chill down my back. Was hooked ever since.
Having Lemmy and his 'Murder One' tattooed on me will always serve as a reminder to 'live to win'. RIP Lemmy."
Ryan Shanahan (Buffalo, New York)

"My son had a school project, he sent a typed letter to Lemmy. Because Lemmy was one of our heroes.
A month or so goes by and my son gets a letter back from Lemmy. In the letter, which was handwritten, Lemmy thanked me for naming my son after him and thanked Ian for including him in his class project as one of our heroes.
I thought it was extra special that Lemmy hand wrote a return letter to my son for his class project. What an outstanding person.
Motörhead for life!!!"
Glen & Ian Youker (Moscow Mills, Missouri)

"My Favorite is 'The Chase Is Better than the Catch'......lot of truth in it for me, whether it was when I was young chasing girls or now older and married chasing cars. Great Song.
Thank You Lemmy........R.I.P."
Douglas R Starry (New Alexandria, Pennsylvania)

"Was hooked on Motörhead from the first time I listened to 'Ace of Spades' and then trying to find all the press clippings I could on this trio of kick ass band.
But the main thing I loved was how they did it their way and never gave in to the record labels like many of the other artists/bands did during those times.
The songs Lemmy had you covered with whatever your feelings were he had something in his discography to cheer you up if you're sad, pumped up - if working out or needing to blow off steam, to just in the mood for some good 'ole Rock and Roll."
Patrick Connelly (USA)

"Motörhead or go to bed."
Nicky Glaser (Chicago)

"I was working Security at a Metal bar in Long Island NY that Motörhead played at a couple of times.
After the show Lemmy asked me to watch his back while he signed some autographs and I replied, "Come on Lemmy who would fuck with you?" At which Lemmy said, "Oh you would be surprised!"
So my brother who was also working said to Lemmy "don't worry Lemmy my brother is harmless" at which Lemmy looks at my brother then looks at me then turns back to my brother and says "Harmless? He wouldn't be harmless if he was armless!"
He had such a great sense of humor and we proceeded off to the bar to have a few! ♠ "
Joe Brigz (Islip Terrace, New York)

"1983 I had the pleasure of hanging out with Lemmy, for an entire afternoon. We drank Jack Daniels and talked music. I gave him a Rory Gallagher red vinyl LP.
Twenty years later I'm at the Rainbow Bar Hollywood, I have seen Lemmy playing his game. I had seen him there before but I didn't want to bother him or someone else was bothering him. But this one day. He wasn't playing and he looked at me like he knew me, it was weird.
So I walked up to him and said "Hi Lemmy, how's it goin?" He smiled and said "I'm good how have you been?" Like he knew who I was. Anyway we talked (I showed him this pic I keep in my wallet from 1983) he blew my mind, he remembered that day, he remembered the Rory Gallagher red vinyl album ... I was in shock, he's a legend, I'm nobody in particular, but that was unreal, that was the person he was, he didn't act like the legendary person he was, he acted like a regular guy.
That's something that really set him apart from everyone else. Lemmy was a great person, I admired him very much.
When he passed, I felt like I lost a friend, not just because I've been a hard core Motörhead fan since 1979, not because I hung out with him one day. But because he made me feel like a friend. It's still hard for me to listen to Motörhead, without being depressed, that we're not going to have anymore new greatness to listen to.
I know that will pass someday. I'm just fortunate I was able to meet him and know just how cool he was. I will always miss him."
Rych T. Biggs (Orange, California)

"Great tunes, just wish I could have met him. Kinda like the time I met Dime and Peter Steele now they both have passed it's just hard to listen to Pantera or Type O, but I just remember the good times and the great music they gave us."
Steve Solo (Walnut Cove, NC)

"Lemmy was my inspiration playing bass guitar.
I was given the leather bound copy of "No Remörse" by a friend in 1985. That was the beginning of it all.
On my 17th birthday, two years later, I bought my first bass guitar from a local piano shop in Los Angeles. It was a crappy red and white Electra. I then picked up a Fender amp from a local pawnshop. My mom was pissed.
I immediately started covering Motörhead songs in my living room every day after school. Never swayed by trends or the opinions of others, Lemmy was my rock & roll icon. His music and bass playing style was down and dirty... just the way I liked it.
I joined the United States Marine Corps in December of 1987. I was sent to the Philippines in 1988 where I got my first tattoo, 'Snaggletooth', on my back. Later, after being deployed to the Persian Gulf, I found a bootleg copy of '1916' in a local store, that I played in my Sony Walkman (remember those?) Whenever I got the chance.
Motörhead has been a HUGE part of my life... nearly my entire life, and at the ripe old age of 47, I still play Lemmy's music on a daily basis. Although my crappy red and white Electra that started it all for me is long gone, I now proudly play a Rickenbacker modeled after one of his older 'Rickenbastards'.
I may have been born to lose... but I definitely live to win!
Oh... I almost forgot... an interesting side note to this story is: I still have that leather bound copy of "No Remörse", but it has since been signed by Lemmy and is proudly displayed along with my other prized possessions of the last 30-some-odd years of my Motörhead collecting life!"
Michael Petersön (Los Angeles)

"Lemmy was the reason I picked up the bass.
He taught me to always be true to your self and fuck the rest. To realize the difference between those who are there for you and those that are there for themselves. That no matter if you're born to lose you can still live to win, no matter how big that win may be for you.

He gave us all rock 'n' roll until the day he died and lived his life the way he wanted with plenty of women, speed, jack and coke, (officially now the Lemmy) cigarettes, and enough good people, funny jokes, and good music.
He was even around before rock 'n' roll. Think about that for a moment kiddies. He was my idol, my hero as he was too many.
Motörhead was the band that got me really into metal and everything else I'm into now a days and the reason I got my first tattoo of the 'Ace of Spades'.
R.I.P. Lemmy you were so much to me."
David Bueller (Wixom, Michigan)

"Be comfortable in your own skin, do not be ashamed of what is in your heart but embrace it. Think for yourself and don't be a lemming. Stand up for what you believe in. Be compassionate and kind but don't be a push over. Make the most of life, live it hard, live it fast, play it LOUD, enjoy it! Live without regrets and don't take it so damn seriously all the time. Shall I go on? ♤"
Jöe Henry (Manheim, Pennsylvania)

"Motörhead has been a major influence on forging my life since 1981.
I was a junior in high school in Orange, California, and trying to find my identity. Trips to the record store were important. I discovered Kerrang! magazine and discovered the "new wave of British metal", mainly Iron Maiden and Motörhead. I picked up 'No Sleep 'Til Hammersmith' and the first 10 seconds changed my life. How could three guys make that sound? I was hooked.
From 1982 until 2014, I saw Motörhead eleven times in concert, and met Lemmy on three separate occasions. But one story sticks out for me.
April 8, 2002, Motörhead headlined the Rialto Theater in Tucson, Arizona. I got there real early and was first in line for the general admission show. The front of the venue faced a busy main street downtown and traffic was noisy.
Suddenly, someone tapped me on the shoulder. I turned around and there stood Lemmy. In his thick accent, he asked me a question that sounded like "do you happen to know where any porn shops are?" I repeated, two separate times "porn shops?" After the third time he said "No pawn shops p-a-w-n" He had to spell out pawn before I figured it out.
said "sorry no, but I do know where a porn shop is" He chuckled a bit and said "no worries" and walked back around the theater. I felt

like a real idiot, figuring that he thought I was a complete moron. But about 5 minutes later, he appeared again with a cup of Jack & Coke and gave it to me. That's how he was. The only other rock star that came close to caring more for his fans was RJ Dio. I also had a picture of me and Lemmy at a record store appearance in 1983. I gave him a full bottle of Jack as a gift. The picture won an award and appeared at a showing at the Tucson Museum of Art a few years ago.
Randy Walton (Scottsdale, AZ)

Rialto Theater
Tucson, Arizona
8th April 2002

We Are Motörhead
No Class
Bomber
Civil War
Damage Case
God Save the Queen
Brave New World
Metropolis
Stay Out of Jail
The Chase is Better Than the Catch
R.A.M.O.N.E.S.
Born to Raise Hell
Sacrifice
Just 'Cos You Got the Power
Going to Brazil
Killed by Death
Iron Fist
Ace of Spades
Overkill

*"Lucky enough to have seen Lemmy live, Lemmy and Motörhead pure inspiration and great music.
R.I.P. LEMMY the world will miss you.
Thanks for the great music and memories."*
Max Bastastra (Rock Island, Illinois)

*"I'm submitting this for my husband, James Bye.
The first time he heard Lemmy, was his guest spot on 'The Young Ones'. He was watching in Minnesota, USA, btw. They played 'Ace of Spades'.
This was the moment that my husband realised he was a 'Metal Head'. He was also very intrigued by Lemmy having his mic above his head, and having to angle his head, in order to open his larynx and create the desired vocals."*
Heather Bye (Naples, Florida)

*"I was introduced to Lemmy in the early '90s after a Motorhead show at The Masquerade in Atlanta. I was a struggling musician at the time and a big Motörhead fan. Though that initial meeting was brief, Lemmy was very personable and we instantly bonded talking music.
One year later my band was playing The Masquerade when Motörhead returned to Atlanta. I approached Lemmy after their soundcheck in the afternoon. He remembered me from the year before and offered me a drink. For about 8 hours we sat backstage talking music, playing music, switching off between guitar and bass, trading licks, trading jokes and getting drunk. We shared personal aspects of our lives as if we'd known each other a long time. Then they played. After the show Lemmy and I hit the Cheetah strip club and who knows where else. We swapped numbers and stayed in touch.
Over the next few years we'd shoot the shit over the phone when he was home and he'd call when Motörhead came to town. We'd hang at the hotel a while, hit the strip clubs and of course, laugh. He was funny as Hell and always supportive of other bands. In 2000, I was recording a solo album and asked Lemmy if he'd consider singing on a song I wrote as kind of a tribute to Motorhead. He said, "Send it to me." Thanks to Lem's support and the help of Bob Kulick, Lemmy recorded vocals on a song called "Call To Arms". Lemmy's appearance on the recording garnered attention and led to great reviews of the album worldwide. I was an unknown, unsigned musician with Lemmy Kilmister singing with

me on my album because of his altruistic nature and his support of other bands. I don't know of another instance where a star of Lemmy's stature gave so freely to an artist as unknown as myself.

Each time Motörhead came through the South, Lemmy would put me on the list and we'd catch up a bit. We stayed in touch and a few years ago I took him up on his long-standing invite to come see his legendary collection. I'll never forget refilling Lemmy's ice trays as we listened to rough mixes of his solo stuff. I asked, "Man, why don't you get an ice maker?"....sadly I was too messed up to remember what his grizzled response was. He had so much stuff crammed into that apartment you could spend a week and still not see every priceless relic of world history that he owned. Freaking amazing. That's not to mention all the cool Motörhead stuff there. That place should be a shrine. Lemmy turned me onto Dave Edmunds and some other great Rock and Roll that I'd never heard. He was truly in love with Rock and Roll music and that was the only common ground needed to connect with the man. Later Lemmy would have to cut me off at the bar at The Rainbow. Thanks to all the bourbon, some other goodies and Scotty's killer weed, I got a bit out of it. I don't recall much except Lemmy turning to me and saying, "Ernie, time to switch to water." (I think I was drunkenly singing loudly at the bar along to the Motörhead songs that Scotty had loaded in the jukebox. But who knows).

Several times over the years he told me, "I'm getting too old for this shit". But he wasn't. It was just his humble attempt at self deprecation but he was still as energized about music as ever. Album after album and world tour after world tour, Lemmy and Motörhead brought the Rock and Roll to their fans. He was a trooper and a Rock and Roll soldier who NEVER sold out and NEVER compromised. He was everything they say he was and a gentleman at the same time. Everybody who ever met Lemmy has a Lemmy story because he was so down to earth and approachable. Show me another Rock star that's as personable with their fans as Lemmy was. You can't.

Over the last few years Lemmy would tell me about different health issues he was dealing with. During a recuperation period he was only thinking about getting back out on tour. And he did. Again and again, despite some increasing difficulties due to health issues.

I last saw Lemmy in Charlotte 3 months before he passed away. He'd put me and my best friend on the list and we showed up right as Motorhead took the stage. Lemmy sent for us after the show and we went backstage to say hey. His health issues had taken quite a toll in 3 years but he was still all Rock and Roll ALL of the time. Lemmy was not up to the usual meet and greet backstage crowd that night, yet he spent considerable time with us trading jokes, talking music and catching up. When we eventually left the venue my friend and I noticed that nobody else had been allowed backstage. It meant alot that Lemmy made time to hang out despite how he was struggling at the time. We texted the usual back and forth up until his birthday. I usually called on the 24th to say howdy and wish him well. This time, because I knew of his health issues, I decided to text, not wanting to intrude during his time off the road. Four days later I got the news.

Lemmy was born to do what he did and he did it as long as he possibly could. He did it his way and he did it for an undying love of music. He was a true old soul and a true musician. He set a standard by which all Rockers will be measured, in one way or another. Forever.

We ALL Salute You, Lemmy, and By God, we always will.
Ernest Robert Boetz (Helen, Georgia)

"I'm missing him. The world is so boring now!"
Lauren Kosanovich (Scottsdale, Arizona)

"I've listened to Motörhead for a long time.
I had never seen them live until last September in Charlotte, NC at the Fillmore. I took my niece and stepson. Told them they were gonna get to watch a legend.
I remember saying that there was no way in hell I was missing that show because it might be the last chance I would get. Didn't realize how prophetic that was until the news broke of his death.
I sat on my deck and cried for a while. Knowing now how sick he was during those last few months has to be one of the most courageous things I've ever witnessed.
He went out and left it all on stage for all of us every night. Who else would have done that? No one but Lem. He never sold out, never compromised the music, and gave it his all for 40+ years. And he taught me to live as I saw fit. That's what I've tried to teach my kids and niece.
RIP Lemmy and thanks for everything you've done for music."
Jason Elrod (Greenville, South Carolina)

"I was lucky enough to see Motörhead in September 2015! Best part was I took my 2 sons with me they are 17 and 19! And before the concert we met Lemmy, Phil and Mikkey!

I couldn't believe how genuine they were and how they took the time to talk to each of us!!
I looked Lemmy in the eye and told him thank you and that his music has really helped me thru bad times in my life.
What an awesome concert it was and I'm so thankful I got to share it with my sons!!
Thank u Lemmy and Thank u Motörhead!!!"
Curtis Lawton (Davenport, Iowa)

"Lemmy is a great man and he is with all of us anytime we play his music and Motörhead will live on forever though all of us play it all the way up and pass the Jack Daniels around and say hell yeah my brother's and sister's we never die our spirits live forever and always love to all."
Kelly Smock (Lakeland, Florida)

"Was so sad to hear about the passing of Lemmy.
I have been a fan of Motörhead and anything that Lemmy took part in. He will be missed.
He really was a legend so I hope you're Rocking away up there.
RIP Lemmy."
Neal Fickes Sr (Niles, Ohio)

"I saw Motörhead open for Ozzy Osbourne in 1981 at the Palladium in NYC and was totally blown away by them.
The mere presence of Lemmy on that stage was life changing for me. The thunderous wave of energy they created...Lil' Filthy, Fast Eddie and Lemmy.
They kicked my ass severely and I've never recovered from it and thankfully so.
Thanks for being a bad-ass motherfucker and brutal bass player!
Never give in to fads and mediocrity, make your mark and play by your own rules!"
Frank Herbert (Bremerton, Washington)

"Relentless force in rock-n-roll. And my fucking hero!!!'
Jeff Mackert (Dunedin, Florida)

"Lemmy has inspired me to play bass.
Look at life through his outlook and humor.
Rock 'n' Roll is not just music it's a frame if mind and a way of life..
Motorhead is not just a band, but a way of life
Strips away all the bad shit and puts you there."

Doug Buswell (Marysville, California)

"The first time I met the late, great Lemmy, rest his merry soul, was after a show at Cabaret Metro in 1983. He and drummer Philthy Animal Taylor (also RIP) were holding court on Clark Street, cracking wise about everything and everyone. Guitarist Brian "Robbo" Robertson had a rough night with the fans, opting to remain on the bus.
One of many true honors occurred at Chicago's Vic Theatre. During the show, Lemmy said
"I'd like to dedicate this song to Tim Shockley and his wife, Ellen. They've supported us for a very long time and we appreciate it!"
I almost crapped my pants! After the show, I jokingly told him
"It's about f**king time!"
A couple amazing moments occurred on Motörhead's tour bus before two different shows at Otto's in DeKalb, IL. After sound check, Lemmy walked up to my wife and me and asked
"Are you busy?"
Are you kidding? Lead the way, kind sir! He took us to the back of the bus, poured me a (strong!) drink from the bottle of Maker's Mark I had brought him, and talked about releasing a solo album. He then proceeded to play five or six songs on the bus sound system at an excruciatingly LOUD level. It had to be 115 decibels, literally louder than the actual show. It was glorious! And just the three of us experienced it. Speechless…
Also at Otto's, I was interviewing Lemmy when he suddenly took out a yellow note pad for me to read some of his unpublished lyrics! He asked me to turn off my recorder, but it still showed me an unparalleled amount of trust. Greatly appreciated and certainly an honor.
Later, he asked if anyone on the bus had the new album. No one did, including the band and crew! I said
"I have it in our car. Would you like it on vinyl or CD?!"
I noticed the next day he had signed my CD! Sneaky!
I actually had the good fortune to interview Lemmy three times- first, by phone, then, twice, in-person. I'd be lying if I didn't admit I was a tad nervous by the initial conversation. After all, I was going to talk to… THE MAN! Also, I was sober…
I was given Lemmy's personal home phone number. After I introduced myself, a familiar, gruff voice said "I know you from the f**ing magazine!"- referring to the official Motörhead fan club, 'Motörheadbangers', which I contributed to quite regularly. Consider the ice broken!

We talked about everything under the sun. I think it helped that he knew I was a die-hard fan who knew every album, every song, and almost every damn lyric! So, he wouldn't have to endure any time wasting
"Do you write the lyrics or music first?" type drivel on my watch.
With my tape nearly exhausted after almost an hour, I admitted to Lemmy I had run out of questions. He replied
"Well, if you think of any more, feel free to call me back!"
Trust me, that never happens! Half the time, interviewees wanna bail after they've pitched their product. One in a million, folks. One in a million...
I prefer to remember Lemmy with one unforgettable moment that forever will be etched in my mind. It occurred at the Vic Theatre.
The show was over and most of the crowd was long gone. Out the front door onto Sheffield Avenue strolled, nay, strutted, Lemmy, with a bottle of bourbon in one hand, a bottle of vodka in the other, one arm around a blonde, the other around a brunette. All three were whisked away in an awaiting limousine, into the night and lord knows where else. That, my friends, is rock and roll!"
Tim Shöckley (Chicago)

"All I can really say is without Lemmy and Motörhead there may not have ever been a band called Overkill......and that would be sad."
John Shields (Poughquag, New York)

"When it came to music, there was nothing quite like putting on the headphones and listening to a new Motörhead album every couple of years...powerful, honest music...I'll miss that..."
Yancy Boivin (Traverse City, Michigan)

"I love Lemmy Kilmister, him and his music have changed my life.

Lemmy is my hero I look up to him, he was one of the biggest men there ever was."
Brad Mathes (Davenport, Iowa)

"Lemmy was and always will be my hero.
He helped me realize that life is what you make it and you should always push forward no matter what.
He was a living legend, and still is in our hearts.
The world's a much quiet place without him.
RIP, a legend, our hero, our friend, Lemmy."
Austin McCoy (USA)

"Me and a friend Drove 150 Miles to Detroit in 1983 August 4 in a Rent A Wreck that was supposed to be for Local Use Only.
We had a Huge bag of Grass, 1/2 Gram of Killer Crank & 2 Cases of Stroh's Select.
It Was My Girlfriends B-Day & she didn't want Me to go but I went any way! Lol!!
It was 'Another Perfect Road Trip' Indeed!"
Kevin Law (Kalamazoo, Michigan)

"Ah Lemmy Kilmister \m/ !!
As a member of the audience, I saw his band Motörhead many times, an electric fan placed on stage so his hair looked like he was riding a motorcycle.
Later in my life, Dead Kennedys had the honor of being on the same bill with Motörhead at the 'Hellfest Festival' in France.
But my best time with him was hanging out at a party (naturally!) in London back in the mid 80's.
I think, like dog years can be multiplied by 7 to get their people years, Lemmy's age, considering the mischievous life he lived, could be multiplied by at least 2 and he actually lived to be 140 in normal people years. He was one strong character, who could ride his demons and stay on. God bless him."
East Bay Ray (Dead Kennedys – Guitarist/Songwriter - Co-founder)

"Mayhem Fest in Auburn Wa. When Duff McKagan sat in!
Me and my 14 yr old! Loved it!"
Thomas Dinius (Beaverton, Oregon)

"No Remorse" says it all, the best 2 all that appreciated...
.Lemmy and his band "MOTÖRHEAD."

Carl Garrett (Antioch, Illinois)

"He has been such an inspiration to me and all of the guys I've been in bands with!
Amazing how many people he has given that gift to.
Motörhead will always be a GIANT in the music world!!!! RIP LEMMY!!!!"

Michael Thompson (Bloomfield, New Jersey)

"Went to the show in August in Vegas with my brother and spent time with him spent lots of time at the Rainbow as well, an incredible man. I've known lots of band members in my life but have never met anyone like Lemmy, so down to earth and a genuine human RIP."

Johnny Knight (Huntington Beach, California)

"I heard Motörhead for the first time when 'Ace of Spades' was the intro theme song to the 'Tony Hawk's Pro Skater 3' video game. That opening melody, combined with his spot-on roaring tone that just fell into place ultimately amped my childhood, teaching me to not give a single fuck what my Christian school teachers taught me about rock 'n' roll being the 'Devil's music.'
After that, I knew I wasn't meant for Algebra or advanced Physics.
My first time seeing Motörhead in concert was my senior of high school on 'Gigantour'. When he came out, there were few, VERY few things that could get louder than the volume that Lemmy, Mikkey, and Phil were playing at.
After that, I declined my acceptance letter to Northern Arizona in order to move to LA and stop at nothing to enable my rock 'n' roll dream to come true.
I would see Motörhead again on the 'Mayhem' tour 2012 in Dallas, and again on both Motörhead's 'Motörboat' cruises, one of them setting sail the day I turned 21; I don't think that kind of drinking needs much explanation.
I met Lemmy individually at none other than the world-renowned Rainbow Bar and Grill while he was sitting at his iconic video poker on the patio bar. I politely went up to him, saying...
"Not to take up too much of your time, but would you mind if I got one picture with you?"
The bartender jokingly shouted
"NO! Oh sorry, did I say that too loud?"
He ended up taking a picture with me, and could not have been any sweeter.

He respected you, and deemed you his friend whether he knew you or not. Even though I'd sobered up, when I attended his private memorial up in North Hollywood, if they're serving shots of Jack, you drink that shit!
Thank you for everything, Lemmy, and making my childhood and 21st birthday what it was.
Until we meet again."
Will Thompson (Los Angeles)

"Lemmy and Mötorhead are more than just great musician's and inspirations, they're a lifestyle.
I remember being 15 and 16 years old building stages in my backyard for local shows my sister and I put on, working at The Venue in San Bernardino, Ca, and drinking case after case of beer, day after day in my shed with friends. While all at the same time blasting Mötorhead among other favorite artists during that time. Some of my favorite songs were 'The Chase Is Better Than the Catch', 'Please Don't Touch', 'Emergency' both covers from Girlschool, 'Orgasmatron', 'Overkill', 'Ace of Spades', 'Bomber', 'No Class', 'Killed by Death', ahh let me stop.
I love all of Mötorhead.
In one way or another Mötorhead kept the party and Rock 'n' Roll lifestyle alive, and I have and always will live the lifestyle. It's in my blood.
I remember hearing the news of Lemmy being sick back in 2013, I stopped everything immediately and found out when their next show was and bought tickets to see him.
I've seen Mötorhead once, I believe it was at the Key Club in Anaheim that same year. Slash came out and jammed with them, I would've preferred that not to have happened but what can you do.
I celebrated the best way I knew how, with a hotel room, cases of beer, bottles of whiskey, 'White Line Fever' all through the night with friends at a scummy hotel in Hollywood. I'd do it all over again to see him play.
He lives on through people like you and I.
A Legend, a Genius, a God.
Rest in Sin Lemmy and Philthy Animal Phil, remembering you always, C.C.
Cynthia Carter (Baltimore, Maryland)

"I heard Mötorhead for the first time in 1983 when I was 12 years old. Back then I lived in Tuzla in Bosnia and Herzegovina, which was part of Yugoslavia back then.

My older cousin gave me a mixed music cassette tape and one of the bands that I remembered was Motörhead with 'Ace of Spades'. I got intrigued by that type of aggressive music and in next year or two I was able to purchase Motörhead's 2 records 'Iron Fist' and 'Another Perfect Day'. I listened to them all the time. Through my High School and University years I got influenced by other genres of aggressive music such as punk, hard core, thrash metal etc.
One constant band was always there and that was Motörhead.
I am also a bass player and I studied Lemmy's style of playing and always liked it. I think that Lemmy's bass line on 'Stay Clean' from their live record 'No Sleep 'Til Hammersmith' is one of the best bass lines of all time with very cool bass solo. I still love to play that song.
By 1992 I was able to collect all Motörhead records they had released until then but I was not able to see them live not even once back then. Motörhead continued to be part of my life especially during the bloody Yugoslavian civil war of 1990's. Their music kept me sane through those tough times.
In 1995 I escaped from Yugoslavian bloody civil war and I emmigrated to the USA. I have been living in the States since then.
I lost all my Motörhead records, t-shirts etc that I had in Yugoslavia so I had to start my new collection in the States. I was able to purchase all the CD's and I have the entire Motörhead collection now.
I was able to see them 4 times here in the States and first time was in 1999 in St. Louis. It was a great show and I was really excited to see Lemmy and Motörhead live for the first time!
Last time I saw Motorhead was in September 2015 when they played their last US tour before Lemmy passed away. Prior to that show Motörhead had to cancel a few shows on that tour because Lemmy did not feel good.
They came out and gave everything they had. Lemmy looked frail and weak. I was wondering how much longer he would be able to continue playing such physically demanding style of music. The show lasted for an hour and 15 minutes and the crowd was really great and gave the band lots of support and positive energy.
A few months later Lemmy died and really it is a huge loss for me because he is one of my biggest music idols of all time. Since he died I have been listening entire Motörhead album collection and studying songs and thinking about all the great memories I had through the last 30 years of my life with Motörhead!
Lemmy you are gone now but you will not be forgotten!

BORN TO LOSE, LIVE TO WIN!"
Darko Ivanovich (St Louis, Missouri)

"I met Lemmy a few times. Once, while I was living in Phoenix, AZ. Alice Cooper and Motörhead were playing a show. A few days before, I had an accident on my bike and fractured a bone in my wrist. So after the show, was lucky enough to get back stage.
When it was my turn to meet Lemmy, he looked at my cast and said:
"A lefty huh? You know that you can alternate?"
Lemmy had that wicked smile on his face when he said that to me. He had a way to make everything funny.
I will truly miss you Lemmy."
Erick J Dobson (Owingsville, KY)

"I love Lemmy's attitude toward life and his music was a reflection of that. I'm always gonna regret not having seen him perform, or having the pleasure of meeting him."
Devin Boydingo Mollander (Bradford, Pennsylvania)

"Well it was the summer of 1979...
I was 10 yrs old and was on my way out of the KISS era, was listening to VAN HALEN, AC/DC and JUDAS PRIEST.
I remember being out jumping my bike with my best friend at the time. We went next door to his neighbors house who was this big HELL'S ANGEL biker named Den, he was the neighborhood cool guy that we all wanted to be like. We were watching him work on his black Harley, he was converting it to suicide shift.
While we were sitting there watching me and my friend were arguing about the best guitar player, of course I'm saying Eddie VAN HALEN and my friend was saying Angus. Den looks at us both and laughs, mind you Den is in his early 20s, he walks over to his stereo and puts on 'BOMBER'.
Looks at us and says
"This is the real deal here fuck all that other stuff."
We sat there and were blown away by the rawness of the music. It was in your face. Instantly I was hooked, went to work at my dads business for the rest of the summer and bought a 35 dollar record player for my room and rode my bike to the record store and bought my first MOTÖRHEAD record.
Jumping to 1985, I am now driving, got my license and we sneak up to L.A. to the Santa Monica Civic Center where its Wendy 'O' Williams, MOTÖRHEAD...and Megadeth. It was a Saturday night

and it was the loudest show up to that point and probably still is the loudest show I'd ever seen. I remember waking up that following Wednesday and my ears were still ringing.
I continued to see them for the next few years, same venue and always deafening...BEEN MY FAVORITE SINCE 1980...."
Michael Dodson (Miami, Florida)

"Thank you Lemmy, for giving me the best advice in life, when I was only knee high to a grasshopper. It was a life changing experience.
And thanks for pounding out Monster Mash for me on the guitar, sitting on those tall front steps and making me laugh. See you on the other side brother!"
Chad D Gillette (Muscatine, Iowa)

"April 22nd 1981 I went to see Ozzy Osbourne. I had 4th row seats. I never heard of the first band called Motörhead. They walked on stage and blew my mind! This is what I've been looking for!
I went to school the next day and everyone was asking me how Ozzy was. All I could say was "I saw Motörhead!"
That show changed my life!
I went out and bought ever Motörhead record I could get my hands on. Two weeks later I bought a white Rickenbacker bass!
Thank you Lemmy, you're my hero forever!"
Rob Michael (Elkton, Maryland)

"God bless Lemmy."
Elisa Barauskis (Chicago, Illinois)

"I never saw Motörhead or Lemmy live.
But because of a child hood idol of mine 'Psycho Bill Anderson' - RIP Bill - I was hanging out downtown and ran into him and Charlie in 1985.
It was cold and Bill invited me up to party. As soon as I walked in I was handed a beer and what do u know there's Lemmy on 'Headbanger's Ball', I was hooked.
I have listened to Motörhead ever since.
Three decades later I still think you rock Lemmy. I can't help but think everyday when he got up he probably shouted 'It's time to play the game!'
I will miss u Lemmy."
Scott Carr (Putney, Vermont)

"RIP LEMMY!!"
Scotty C. Shredder (Montgomery, New York)

"Lemmy was a true legend long before his death.
The man changed the world in more ways than most can even hope to. He was an incredible friend, a strong vocalist and an amazing songwriter.
As an author with a fascination for rock & roll and guitars it was easy for me to look up to his examples. One of my deepest regrets is that I never got to meet the man who did so much, but I will absolutely never forget him or his work.
The world definitely won't be the same without him."
Damean Mathews (Norton, Virginia)

"He is Lemmy and played Rock 'n' Roll."
Matt Davidson (Portage, Indiana)

"My niece would only fall asleep to 'Ace of Spades', always wanted to meet Lemmy and point him out on TV.
Anything that had to do with Lemmy or Motörhead I have enjoyed the music since my teen years.
Got to see them for the first and only time when they played in Minneapolis and did a meet and greet at 'Hot Topic' even though they weren't allowing pics I always manage to get a couple.
Was an amazing experience for me, a moment I won't ever forget."
Shannon Taylor (Mora, Minnesota)

"Motörhead gave me strength, when I had nothing left."
John P. Tabor (Eastside Detroit)

"Lemmy was one to give music that I can actually listen to every day."
Brandon Underwood (Seminole, Oklahoma)

"Lemmy was my friend, we met in Dallas around 2002 and we just clicked.
I played guitar in a bathroom of a 'strip club'. He thought that was the coolest thing ever.
We hung out every day and night for ten days. Wow that was hard to do I didn't do meth lol.
But he taught me so much about so many things.
We would always visit when he was in town and we spoke quite often on the phone. But what amazed me about Lemmy is

whenever we saw each other he treated me like the rock star.
He would introduce me to people and say:
"This is Spyke he plays guitar in the Fuckin' LOO at a strip club and he kicks ass doin it."
Thanks Lemmy for being my friend and making me feel like the rock star.

(And then the next day….)
I know I posted yesterday. But so much to say like how we went to recording studio and got drunk with Rev Horton Heat.
The Rev got alcohol-poisoning lol, so not a lot of recording got done.
Or how we ended up at the Banshees Motorcycle Club partying till the sun came up. Then heading to my place where we took a recharge break and lemmy crashed on my couch.
Now I know I told you yesterday that I played guitar in a strip club bathroom but this was no ordinary bathroom I've played clubs smaller. That being said I kept a Marshall half stack set up in the bathroom.
I've had the great honor of jamming with some greats in the bathroom. Jon Bon Jovi, Everclear, Elvis Costello, Gene Simmons etc.
But what a thrill it was when Lemmy came in and said
"Gotta extra axe mate?"
And of course I did. He's like what ya know mate. I said
"how about some Beatles or Buddy Holly?"
He gave me that big infectious grin and said
"oh I like you already."
Then we broke into Peggy Sue. Within 10 minutes we were 80 deep in the bathroom and more trying get in. We played some Beatles and Eddie Cochran some Chuck Berry and he jumped in on a couple of my originals. Some yelled out 'Ace of Spades'.
He said "sorry mate this is his gig."
God what a true legend. He was not only in the music sense, but in the fact he was true to his fans and I know that on at least 3 nights people got an impromptu bathroom concert with Lemmy and I. I only hope that he touched those people the way he touched me."
Rick 'Spyke' Workman (Beaumont, Texas)

"My memories of Lemmy: telling him it was my honor to meet him on my birthday last year on Motörboat...
A memory I will always cherish and never forget!!!"
Anita Lismanis (Riverhead, New York)

"Motörhead is considered to be the loudest band in the world. When things get this loud many people can't distinguish any sort of sound variation.
Motörhead could and would fix it no matter what.
Motörhead played up in Ventura in 2002 and had used a few new microphones that were being tested for the drums. The sound engineer did not like what he was hearing so they needed to get the right mics from the Hollywood area up to Ventura.
The task fell on Scott Albanesius, known as 'Nazi Scott' to get them to the gig.
On his way, Scott's motorcycle busted its chain on the 101 around Sherman Oaks and his chain ended up in the middle of the road. I lived just around the corner in Studio City so Scott called me up to see if I could help him.
On the way, I saw his chain and we managed not only to get his bike fixed but Motörhead got the right mics to do the job. Motörhead could have used the new mics, but the fans were more important to them ethically than to just use what was on hand.
Scott was critical in getting these mics up there so the show could go on."
Jon Cyphers (Mesa, AZ)

"Real is the word I always come up with when I'm asked about Lemmy. In rock music many can put on a persona for stage and be very different off of it. Lem was the genuine article for sure. Lemmy was real, the music was real, the band was real. Always doing it on their terms.
I doubt we will see the likes of Lemmy and Motörhead ever again. My first album would have been 'Iron Fist'; I won it in a contest on the boardwalk at the New Jersey shore. As a kid I picked it because I never heard the band before but the album and logo looked cool.
I was pummeled the minute the needle hit the vinyl. And it still rocks as hard today as it did when I first heard it."
Eddie Trunk (US Radio Personality / Talk Show Host)

"I've seen Motörhead three times and they were great everytime. Lemmy loved to turn it up."
Craig Scott (Estacada, Orgeon)

"When pressed to give a story about how cool Lemmy was, I'm torn. Do I talk about singing Elvis songs together backstage with an acoustic guitar? How he invited me onto his bus and made me one of his famous Jack and "Cokes" (change Coke to ice and you're getting closer to a more apt description of the drink) as I was trying not to drink on that tour because my wife was pregnant with our first child and I was trying to show some solidarity there? No, I think the best story begins in Philadelphia...
We were on tour with Motörhead and Nashville Pussy back in the year 2000. We had just played somewhere close to the Canadian border (Buffalo? Not sure) and then we had a day off while Motörhead went up to Canada and did a show in Toronto or something. At that time we were still unwelcome up north due to some prior youthful indiscretions so we got the day off. Next day was Philly and we get to the venue and immediately there is the sense that something ain't right. It looked like Motörhead were packing up their gear and loading OUT of the venue. They said some bullshit about the monitors being a couple of db's too quiet and that it was "unsuitable" for Motörhead's performance. Now, I get it, they're Motörhead, they can do whatever they want, but I smelled something fishy. My theory is (and this is only a theory, I have no actual proof of this, but...) that they had to get rid of their drugs they like to have for a show in order to cross the border and they hadn't been able to procure more yet. This is just me theorizing here, but let's face it, it adds up. So as they were

packing out I went and told the promoter that WE will still play if he wants us to and that I'm pretty sure I can get Nashville Pussy to play as well. Well, the dude was all for it. I figured that even if half of the people stay for the show, that's still a pretty good turnout for us. Maybe we'd sell a t-shirt or two and break even for the night. It turned out that getting Nashville Pussy onboard was a little more of a challenge than I initially thought. I had to call them (luckily they had cell phones then) and tell them to come back. They were already on the road following Motörhead to DC and I had to talk them into coming back. They started to say something about how "we've gotta stick by Motörhead" and I was like, "Why? They certainly weren't thinking about us when they pulled out of the show..." Anyway, they saw the light and came back and we put on a great show for about half of the projected crowd for that night, which was still about 800 people so, for us, pretty good indeed!
Now this is where the story gets good.
Next day is DC and we show up to the venue and after we get loaded in the club someone comes and tells me that Motörhead would like to see me in their dressing room. I'm like, "Motörhead wants to see me? ALL of them?" The guy just said, "That's what I was told to say". Weird. So, anyway, I nervously head backstage, wondering what this is all about and I walk in to the room and there's Mikkey Dee, pacing back and forth and Lemmy sitting down in the corner looking like a bad guy in every good sense of the word. Mikkey sees me and immediately starts in, "Hey, what you did yesterday wasn't cool at all" I'm all "whaa...?" And he starts in with this whole "we need solidarity out here" routine which I found categorically ridiculous. And I proceeded to stand toe to toe with Mikkey Dee and tell him how we're just a 'little' band and we will take any opportunity to rock some asses we can get, etc... I told him my theory about the real reason I think they pulled out of the show and that got a chuckle out of Lemmy and a kind of knowing glance was exchanged between him and Mikkey. We were literally standing there pointing fingers in each other's chests and trying to make the other guy see the light. Finally, after what was probably 5 minutes but felt more like 50, Lemmy stands up, nonchalantly saunters over to us and puts his hands on our shoulders and says, "Are you ladies done now? Can we move on from this Mick?" Thus, kind of giving me the win! When he asked Mick and not me to let it go, I felt so vindicated. Lemmy later told me that Mikkey was wound up about it and that they just wanted to hear my side of it but, if he was in the same position I was in, he would've done the same thing. After that argument, I was treated a

whole new way by the entire Motörhead camp. Everyone seemed to respect me and the band so much more. Lemmy invited me on to his bus to play me the new rockabilly stuff he was working on with Slim Jim Phantom. He would come back stage and play Elvis songs with me on acoustic guitars. He was kind and generous and funny and wise and clever. He was my hero before I knew him. And my friend after I met him. One day he said to me, "If someone doesn't like your band, it's like they don't like rock-n-roll" and THAT is a quote worth repeating.

"If you don't like the Supersuckers, you don't like rock-n-roll"
~Lemmy Kilmister

Man, I miss him. The world was better with him still walking around on it.

Eddie Spaghetti - Rock Guy (Supersuckers – Vocals/Guitar)

"I have always been a rocker and a roller and grew up in Missouri. I started with Black Sabbath and Iron Maiden in the 80's but somehow never got around to listening to Motörhead. I never liked screaming lyrics; I always liked good singers, but never took the time to listen to Lem and the boys. Well, later on in life in 1995, I became a born-again Christian so as the story goes the old rock-n-roll man had to hang on to the Real Rock, so I left music for a while, and of course, that ole devil music is off limits.

Well a funny thing happened to me later on I became surer of my faith and returned to listening to heavy metal once again. As I was studying for seminary in 2013 I was running a Black Sabbath Fan Club and as I was reading where Sabbath's bass player Geezer Butler tweeted Lemmy get well. Shockingly, I did not know who this Lemmy was. I had heard of Motörhead the name, but I thought it was just some German speed metal band, of course everyone has heard of 'Ace of Spades' but with the German military gear that Lemmy had I just assumed he was from Germany with his gruff voice and simple one-liner lyrics.

Well the internet is a great place to find things out, not like the old days. The first thing I watched was the Lemmy movie. It was on YouTube at the time and this man just blew me away. I loved it, his life, his rock-n-roll attitude, the music, the long hair, everything. I got my hands on every song and every concert. I was a Motörhead maniac. I lived, ate, slept, dreamt, and did hours and hours of research. I am a combat veteran and when I saw Jason Everman in the Lemmy movie saying that Motörhead is just good going to war music that got my attention. I immediately joined Alan Burridge's fan club Motörheadbangers and received my membership number MHB/3704. Joined a Facebook page with fellow fans and made up for thirty-one years of lost time. I irritated many of the members and my foolish questions about the band drove everyone insane. Also, people questioned how could a man of the cloth like Motörhead? It is easy. It is great music. It gives you a good feeling; it helps you make it through the day. You feel like you have no barriers in life listening to Lem and the boys, it is pure, in your face rock-n-roll, no fillers, and no fakes.

Well as you know, Lemmy had his share of health problems, so I knew I had to sacrifice everything to get to a Motörhead show before it was too late. The band did an extensive European tour for 'Aftershock', which was my very first new Motörhead record. I was jealous of seeing all my MHB friends going to shows and finally in August of 2015 was my time to see Motörhead on their US tour, supporting their new album 'Bad Magic'. I bought tickets for my 23rd wedding anniversary and we were charged up to see Lemmy and the boys. Lemmy started the US tour very sick however, and my fears of never seeing the band ever live or meeting Lemmy quickly dissolved.

So knowing that Motörhead was coming to Texas I skipped to the Austin show to see the boys before the Houston date. I made it, finally Lemmy's amp Murder One was on stage I met Mikkey D before the show, and there I was. I felt compelled to meet Lemmy and that took all of my efforts, I could not rest, I tried everyway to get backstage. Then I gave up and suddenly I met a Doctor from Austin and his girlfriend, and he had met Lemmy the night before. They could not believe I was a minister at a heavy metal concert. They whipped out two backstage passes for me, due to a bit much of inebriation that night on their part, they had to leave. I wish I could see them again. There I was though with two passes. What to do?

The band took the stage, the thunder and lightning began. All of a sudden the band grinded to a screeching halt, Lemmy said I can't do it and walked off the stage, the lights came up and that was it. No more music. All over. The next show in Houston and Dallas was cancelled. So the next show was in Saint Louis Missouri my original home on September the 8th. I drove the 12-hour drive overnight; borrowing money to go having been flat broke trying to see the other shows. Well Motörhead played the next night and it was really Everything Louder than everything else as expected. Lem was in rare form. I could not even hear halfway through the show. I also got the privilege to get backstage. It was a night to remember; I could finally say I had seen the band. I did not get to *meet Lemmy that night but I was able to give a bible to his Bass Tech. Yes a bible! I had to go because I would miss my ride home. I was 5th in line to meet him too. Oh, well rock-n-roll you take what you get.*

Little did I know or could be prepared for what was going to happen in December though. I was thrilled being able to see the band but questioned my sanity for driving all the way to Saint Louis and being set back financially. It was still Motörhead every day for me. That fateful day came right after Christmas, where we all heard that news that our hero was dead. I was devastated. It was eerie however, just a few days before, I had a thought in my head about what it would be like if Lemmy had died. What kind of funeral would it be? Sure enough now, it had become true. I thought the band would continue. Lemmy was crushed by cancer and did not even want anyone to know, or have sympathy. What a warrior. I am still grieving today along with all my Motörbrothers and sisters. We miss the Chief.

A few days later, I talked to Tim Butcher, Lemmy's tech. He told me that Lem received the camouflage bible I gave him from one warrior to another I signed it and gave my phone number. Tim told me Lem received it with a smile. Thank you! Mission Complete. I learned a lot from Lemmy. His dry sense of humor, his quick wit and mind. He had a great way of just making it through life and I have adopted some of his ways of dealing with the struggles of life. His 'I don't care' attitude taught me to not get too upset at the things that Life throws at you and never give up. We will all miss him.

Long live the king of Rock-n-Roll Ian Lemmy Kilmister.
Dave T. Davis (Brazoria, Texas)

*"I was dating Mark Lewis the sound guy.
I flew to Austin for a show at Stubbs. It's time for sound check and I take a seat on a monitor crate. The crew is warming up the instruments and I happen to look up.
In the rafters over my head is the biggest damn raccoon I've ever seen.
Lemmy steps out from the back and is walking right towards me. He smiles and says "hello".
I say "hello sir take a look up there and what's that thing going to do when your bass rig fires up"?
He laughed and said "fucking bloody dive bomb".
I have my seat all night with that raccoon over my head.
Bet it was glad when that show was over."*
Terri Steele-Potter (Chattanooga, Tennessee)

"I wish I had any, but truth is I never met the dude, I just live life through his quotes."
Kyle Budke (North Platt, Nebraska)

*"I am an American. The only reason that this is relevant is I have never seen the true power of Motörhead until twenty years after I first saw Motörhead.
I was still in junior high school when I first heard Motörhead.
A friend had 'No Sleep 'til Hammersmith' and described it as "Hard core heavy metal". I gave it a spin and it was like nothing I had ever heard before. It had the power and speed of the punk and hardcore I listened to and none of the cliché 'Dungeons and Dragons' crap I despised.
The first time that I was aware of Motörhead playing Boston was when 'Another Perfect Day' came out. I could not go to that as they played a nightclub call The Paradise and you had to be 21 years of age or older to get in. What I do know of the show is Motörhead blew up the clubs P.A. system, Lemmy called the P.A.
"A set of fucking Walkman headphones" in a local music magazine called Boston Rock. I knew I had to see this.
I first saw Motörhead in 1985 at the Channel Club in Boston. I think the show was 18+ but by now I had a fake I.D. that worked. I can honestly say I have never seen anything like it. The Band had full Marshall Stacks from the front of the stage, curving around them from one end to the other, with only a small opening that they squeezed through to get on the stage. The only reason the drummer, Pete Gill, was visible, was they had half Marshall Stacks in front of the drum riser. In the crush of humanity, I ended up*

about 5 people back from the stage, in front of Lemmy, and after the show I couldn't hear for days. After that, there were very few Boston area shows I missed.
Once I got a car, I would go on road trips to see the band. Providence, Rhode Island, Hartford or New Haven, Connecticut, New York City, Worchester, Massachusetts, Montréal, Canada which were anywhere from a one to five hour drive from Boston. The band's popularity would ebb. Some of the shows were in 500 people rock clubs, that didn't matter, if they played, I would go and the band never mailed it in. You got your money's worth every time. The only shows I would pass on were when the band was part of some package tour, playing some outdoor amphitheater, playing third slot out of five, a thirty minute set, in daylight. I am sad to say, in America, Motörhead were always a cult band.
In 2005, twenty years after I saw the band for the first time, I actually saw the band for the first time abroad. I found myself in Dusseldorf, Germany on a vacation and saw Motörhead at Phillips Halle. That was the first time I saw the band with all the production. Lemmy once said that he felt bad for American fans, because they have never seen the whole show. He was correct, it was bigger and better than you see here. That show was released as the 'Stage Fright' DVD, if you look hard, you never see me, but I assure you I was there.
By this time home computers became the norm and everyone had websites. I checked to see if Motörhead still played Hammersmith. They did. I was on my way. I honestly can't describe what it felt like to step foot in the Hammersmith Odeon. I mean, everyone played there from The Beatles, Queen, Bowie to The Clash, but it was Motörhead that made the place famous. To me, it was Mecca, ground zero and the major leagues all rolled together. I read that Lemmy really didn't like playing in there, as he felt other places sounded better. After that show, I made a deal with myself that I would go to Hammersmith until either I die or Lemmy dies, I kept my promise. I remember one year, before the major health issues, the band cancelled a couple of shows before Hammersmith, I had flights booked so I was going anyway. I walked over during the load in and asked the crew if the show was still on and in the thickest Northern accent I ever heard I was told
"He ain't cancelling tonight, this is fucking Hammersmith".
It seems that the band alternated yearly between Hammersmith and Brixton Academy, it didn't matter, I still went. Along the way Berlin and Hamburg, Germany got added in there and a trip to Buenos Aries, Argentina. Seeing the band anywhere else was a

more intense experience than the United States. The Germans looked at Lemmy as a God, the English looked at him as a national treasure and the Argentines were just insane.

Over the years I, as all of us, watched time take its toll on Lemmy. From the first time I saw him, standing center stage of the four man band, moving with agility in the middle of the vortex, to slowing down a bit, moving deeper back on the stage to almost against his amps. The final tour I saw the band in Wallingford, Connecticut and Lem was using a walking stick and needed help getting on and off the stage. While I will admit I have seen the band better, they still brought it. A few nights later I was in Montréal, Canada to see what would be my last show. Funny, I ended up about 5 people back from Lemmy, deep in the crush of humanity, in a two thousand seat room, just like I was 30 years before. Symmetry.

I had tickets for Hamburg and Berlin but both shows were canceled. We all made the best of it going to bars and catching up with people we met at shows before. I couldn't make it back to Berlin for the rescheduled show; that turned out to be the final show. I still have the tickets and they will go in a frame. I had tickets to both nights at Hammersmith, because I kept my promise, even though I thought Lem would out live me.

I understand that the premise of this is to write of story about Lemmy. I have never met the man. I had a feeling I never would. Not that I didn't want to, but I would never bother the man. Hanging out in front of some hotel or bang on a bus door, that just isn't my style. It also dawned on me that I would have no idea what to say to the man, if I did meet him. It isn't like he hasn't heard it all before. A friend once told me to go to the Rainbow and run in to him, but I could not be that intrusive.

I instead write this as an open thank you letter to the man. For every show I saw, song he wrote, time he made me laugh in an interview, every city I visited, good times I had, and persons I met along the way I honestly thank you, Lemmy.

I will see you in Hammersmith again, someday."
Tom Carnali MHB3598 (Boston, MA)

"I think he was cool as Fuck.
I Love his music."
Betty Sullivan (Mobile, Alabama)

"As is the story with so many, my musical life has revolved around Motörhead since at least 1985. It was then that I purchased the

leather 'No Remorse' album and fell in love with it instantly. Being fourteen at the time, I hung it directly over my bed as the centerpiece on the wall where all my albums were displayed by push pins.
Not long after, 'Orgasmatron' was released and I'm almost certain that I listened to it every day for many, many months.
The years and later releases only intensified my total devotion to the music of Motörhead. More to the point, it wasn't until the late 90's or early 2000's that I had my first encounter with Mr. Kilmister. It was poignant and perfect.
I typically went to Motörhead shows alone as my friends didn't quite share my affinity for the rock and metal. I was at Jaxx nightclub in Springfield, Virginia. The place was packed but I had been to that club many times going back to my underage days when it was the Copa. Shhhh! Well, I had only been there for few minutes, Skinlab was playing and I doubt you hear anyone speaking to you even through a megaphone. It was then that I saw Lemmy walk across the club and stand at the end of the bar.
I was shocked that he was out in the crowd and thought he was just getting something from the bar and probably heading backstage. To my surprise, he was hanging out! How could I not acknowledge him?
I wasn't staring the entire time, but for a good portion of fifteen minutes, no one approached him. It was then I decided to walk in his direction.
As I moved toward him, we made eye contact. There were no words exchanged. I smiled with awe and admiration then closed my eyes and nodded to him.
As I opened my eyes, he smiled back, reached for my left hand, kissed it gently as I then curtsied. I know that I had not stopped smiling so I raised my glass, he raised his and I continued on past him to the back part of the club.
Yes, the encounter was brief but certainly one of my most cherished memories!"
Randi Roark (Monrovia, Maryland)

"You will be missed, badass mother fucker...."
Amy Sorel King (Stockton, California)

"I don't know if this counts, but when Hawkwind toured the U.S. in the mid-seventies, my brother's band (Mad John Fever, which became StarCastle) opened for them in Indiana.

I was wandering around backstage and met some of the members, including Lemmy. He was a gent, and really helped open me up to a new type of rock.

This was the tour where their equipment was impounded, I believe, in Canada."

Debbie Stewart (Champaign, IL)

"I hung out with Lemmy in about 2001 after Motörhead played a venue in Northern California.

He was the most brutally honest person you could ever meet and that's another aspect that I believe made him so special to everyone!

It was just a few roadies, the club manager, a bartender and me and Lem.

He had his usual drink and I asked what he was drinking? Putting one hand on my shoulder he answered –

"Jack and Coke, more Jack than Coke."

It's a line I have always used. My girlfriend and I still use it when his name is mentioned."

Jerry Anglin (Paradise, California)

"My first exposure to Motörhead was when I got 'No Sleep 'til Hammersmith' for Christmas '81 and I was hooked.
I didn't get a chance to see them for the first time until '91 on the 'Operation Rock and Roll' tour in Chicago. The next time was also in Chicago on the 'Bastards' tour opening for Black Sabbath. I had after show passes for it so I took my license plate from my van to give to Lemmy.
We never made it back to meet the band but I seen a roadie and asked him if he would give it to Lemmy and he said he would. Had no idea what ever happened to it until I was watching the Lemmy movie and there it was, my Illinois MTRHD 4 license plate hanging above his stove. He still had it after all those years.
I had the pleasure of seeing them 7 more times over the years and in 2010 I finally met Lemmy. It was in Austin TX the day after the world premier of his movie.
The show was at Stubb's and we were early so thought we would eat. I went downstairs and there he was, giving an interview. I went back down a few minutes later and he was playing pool by himself. He was kind enough to take a picture and sign his autograph. My

son was on leave from the Army at the time and it was his first concert and he also got to meet him. That was one awesome day. I had the chance to see them a couple more times after that but wish I could have had one more.
No matter what Don McClean says, December 28th, 2015 is 'the day the music died.'
Long live Lemmy and play Motörhead LOUD!!"
Richard Browning (Terrell, Texas)

World Music Theatre
Tinley Park
20th July 1991

Doctor Rock
I'll Be Your Sister
Traitor
No Voices in the Sky
Metropolis
The One to Sing the Blues
I'm So Bad (Baby I Don't Care)
Going to Brazil
Just 'Cos You Got the Power
Angel City
Love Me Forever
R.A.M.O.N.E.S.
Orgasmatron
Killed by Death
Ace of Spades

"I met Lemmy just a few years ago, when my friend, Joe Siegler, and I were guests of Black Sabbath, so we had virtual free roam of certain areas backstage.
Motörhead performed - oh, yes, we could hear them - and after a while, Lemmy walked towards us in a pair of green tights as he headed for his cab.
I called out to him, asking if I could shake his hand -- shades of a scene from "Lawrence of Arabia" and as he approached his taxi, he turned on his heel and came back towards me.
It was a quick encounter, where I thanked him for his music and for driving my wife, Suzy, crazy and off he went.
That was the last time I saw him, although I have great memories of the first time I saw him onstage:
"Dallas, are you feeling alright?" [crowd goes crazy] "We'll soon change your mind about that."
Steve Quarrella (Argyle, TX)

"Hello ...My name is Freddy Contreras, singer for the Spanish metal band from Los Angeles 'PRO-FE-CIA'. I was born in Jalisco Mexico.
I first heard Motorhead back in late '79, early '80.
One of my older friends had a cassette of the album 'Overkill'. It was really hard in those days to get any metal music in Mexico at all, so hearing Motorhead for the first time just blew me away; too much for an 11 year old kid!!!
Little did I know that Lemmy and Motorhead would be the driving force to make me leave my hometown, move to California, meet Lemmy, form a band and eventually play the 'Hell and Heaven' Festival 2013 with Motorhead in Guadalajara, Mexico, just over an hour away from my hometown, more than 30 years later.
It's almost impossible to count and name all the times and places I ran into Lemmy in the past 28 years, but let me share some of those special moments with you all!!
I met Lemmy for the first time, back in 1988 in Hollywood, I was 20 years old and drinking with a 'fake ID'. I almost went to jail for having an open container and trying to force Lemmy into taking a drink of my Tequila bottle in the middle of Sunset Boulevard!!
I would see Lemmy again backstage and onstage at the 'Rip Magazine Party' 1990 at the Hollywood Palladium, along with members of Metallica, Guns N' Roses and Skid Row...Crazy night!!
Then came 'Operation Rock and Roll' in 1991 with Judas Priest, Alice Cooper, Metal Church and Dangerous Toys.

The following year came the big tour with Metallica, Guns and Body Count etc etc.
In the mid 90's I went to see Motörhead at the House of Blues and after a heavy after party, drinking with the band in the foundation room, I remember saying to goodbye to Lemmy and he said to me in Spanish – "Valla con dios" which means 'go with God' and I almost went to hell when a car almost ran me over crossing Sunset Blvd!!
After all those crazy shows from the early 90's, I became part of the Motorhead family for many year to come, hanging out at the Rainbow Bar & Grill and at many shows.
I was really honored to be part of the few people invited to the funeral and celebration of Lemmy's life and that's something I will be forever grateful to Todd Singerman and the Motorrehead family for, for the rest of my life!!
R.I.P. Lemmy Kilmister."
Freddy Contreras (PRO-FE-CIA)

"It's was '98 or so, Motörhead was playing Axis in Boston and I was working as security.
Being a huge Motörhead fan I arranged to work that show. During the show as I am at the barricade singing along to every song Lemmy noticed it after the show he said have that guy come up to my dressing room.
I was welcomed with a Jack and Coke and sat for many hours drinking talking about music, war history and listening to the knowledge of this great man. At the end of it he handed me a shirt which I still have to this day, it is sacred to me. To me him noticing I was a such a fan and asking for me to be brought to his dressing room to meet me, a fan, showed just how down to earth and real Lemmy was. There was no rock star pretentions no charging a fan for autographs or VIP package crap. He was Lemmy. He was Rock 'N' Roll. He was REAL.
I aspire to live my life as he did by his own rules.
So this is to you Lemmy, you may be gone but you will never be forgotten especially to those whose lives you touched.
I hope you Wurzel and Philthy are blowing out eardrums in heaven and trashing the place !!!!!!!!!"
Larry Bones (USA)

Other Books Available By Ian Carroll

Horror Books

The Lovers Guide To Internet Dating – The dangers and the stalkers

Demon Pirates Vs Vikings – Scandinavian horror

Valentines Day – Gypsy curses

My Name Is Ishmael – Demons are everywhere…

A-Z of Bloody Horror 'A' is for 'Antique Shop'

A-Z of Bloody Horror 'M' is for 'Warning: Water May Contain Mermaids'

A-Z of Bloody Horror 'P' is for 'Pensioner'

Music Books

The Reading Festival: Music, Mud and Mayhem – available in full version or as 1970's, 1980's and 1990's separate editions.

From Donington to Download – available in full version or as 'Monsters of Rock' and 'Download Festival' separate editions.

Welcome to Cornwall Coliseum – covering the iconic South West UK venue that played host to shows by all the big stars of the 70's & 80's – Black Sabbath, Iron Maiden, Rainbow, Paul McCartney, Whitesnake, Saxon, The Clash, KISS, Eric Clapton and hundreds more

King 810 – an introduction to the band

All available on Amazon, on Kindle and in Paperback for bargain prices

Printed in Great Britain
by Amazon